Essays in Honor of Edmond Malinvaud

volume 2: Macroeconomics

Essays in Honor of Edmond Malinvaud

volume 1: Microeconomics (with introduction by J.-C. Milleron)

volume 2: Macroeconomics

volume 3: Empirical Economics (with bibliography)

Essays in Honor of Edmond Malinvaud

volume 2: Macroeconomics

edited by
Paul Champsaur
Michel Deleau
Jean-Michel Grandmont
Roger Guesnerie
Claude Henry
Jean-Jacques Laffont
Guy Laroque
Jacques Mairesse
Alain Monfort
Yves Younès

The MIT Press
Cambridge, Massachusetts
London, England

Published in French as part of a single volume entitled *Mélanges économiques: Essais en l'honneur de Edmond Malinvaud* (Paris: Economica, 1988). Translations provided by the authors.

Set in Palatino by Asco Trade Typesetting Ltd. in Hong Kong. Printed and bound in the United States of America.

Library of Congress Cataloging-in-Publication Data
(Revised for volume 2)

Essays in honor of Edmond Malinvaud.

Includes bibliographical references.
Contents: v. 1. Microeconomics / edited by Paul Champsaur ... [et al.]—
v. 2. Macroeconomics / edited by Paul Champsaur ... [et al.]
1. Malinvaud, Edmond. 2. Economics. I. Malinvaud, Edmond. II. Champsaur, Paul.
HB173.M4213 1990 330 89-48826
ISBN 0-262-03158-2 (v. 1)

volume 1
ISBN 0-262-03158-2

volume 2
ISBN 0-262-03159-0

volume 3
ISBN 0-262-03160-4

3-volume set
ISBN 0-262-03174-4

Contents

I Microeconomic Foundations of Macroeconomics

12 The Dynamics of Mixed Unemployment

A. d'Autume

In the very book which was to make so famous the distinction between Classical and Keynesian unemployment, one could already find E. Malinvaud wary not to oversimplify this distinction and ready to recognize the possibility of "Keynesian unemployment with classical contamination" (Malinvaud 1977, p. 110). A simplistic use of this distinction would not provide an adequate basis to explain contemporary mass unemployment. The introduction of the distinction between classical and Keynesian unemployment undoubtedly represented theoretical progress. The sharp opposition it drew between the channels of transmission of economic policies, operating either through the supply side or through the demand side according to the regime, was, to say the least, highly pedagogical. However, multipliers jumping to zero while passing from one regime to another seem to be absent from macroeconomic reality, which does not know about such jumps. Therefore it seemed more appropriate to think in terms of "mixed unemployment" situations in which several sectors coexist, each facing different disequilibrium constraints, and in which economic policies have more gradual effects. Moreover, the necessity to aggregate different sectors, as was first stressed by Muellbauer (1978) and Malinvaud (1980b), is not the only reason to blur the distinction between classical and Keynesian unemployment. Uncertainty about future demand and therefore about the future regime leads the firm to a complex investment decision, which always depends on the levels of both demand and profitability (see Malinvaud 1980a, 1987). Thus profitability, even in a one-sector model, has a part to play in the static and especially in the dynamic analysis of Keynesian unemployment. Similarly, the role of demand should not be ignored in a classical situation.

Several disequilibrium models based on the aggregation of micromarkets have recently been published (see Lambert 1988, Gouriéroux, Laffont, and Monfort 1984; Gouriéroux and Laroque 1985; Sneessens and

Drèze 1986; Sneessens 1987). To this we might add some earlier references, such as a paper by Green and Laffont (1981), which describes what seems to be the first disequilibrium model in which random terms are systematically introduced and in which regime probabilities can be calculated, and a paper by Hénin (1978) that provides an early analysis of coexisting unsatisfied supplies and demands in a macroeconomic disequilibrium model. Finally, Cette and Taddei (1988) provide an analysis of economic policies in a two-sector model of mixed unemployment.

To build a macroeconomic model based on the rigorous aggregation of micro-markets is a difficult task. The most sensitive point lies in the spill-over effects between micro-markets, and it is usually handled somewhat approximately. Our model will share this last feature as we disaggregate the goods market only and, moreover, we assume that the disturbances faced on this market by individual firms disappear at the aggregate level, according to the law of large numbers. On the other hand, and contrary to most existing models, we focus on the dynamic part of the model and we derive the investment behavior of a firm facing both uncertainty about future demand and adjustment costs. The assumptions of no risk aversion and of intertemporal independence of the disturbances will be crucial to keeping the analysis simple.

We are thus led to a simple but explicitly dynamic macroeconomic model that allows us to analyze the dynamics of accumulation, profitability, and unemployment, and to focus on fluctuations in the proportions between unemployment types. We shall analyze in particular the economy's response to an autonomous demand shock.

1. Demand and Investment

Following Malinvaud (1980a), we consider a producer with a Leontief technology. At any point in time the employment level L is adapted to the production level Y whereas the stock of capital determines a production capacity Y^p:

$$L = aY, \qquad K = bY^p.$$

We assume that the producer faces no constraint on the labor market: there is unemployment, so he may always reach his desired employment level. On the other hand, at the very moment he decides about his capital stock level, the demand he faces is uncertain. The demand is assumed to be equal to $Y^d\tilde{u}$, where $\tilde{u}$ is a disturbance with unit mean and with density $f(u)$ and where Y^d consequently appears as the mean demand.

Ex post, the production and sales level Y will be the minimum of demand and production capacity.

$$
\begin{aligned}
E(Y) &= E\,\mathrm{Min}(Y^d\tilde{u}, Y^p)\\
&= \int_{u=0}^{Y^p/Y^d} Y^d u\, f(u)du + \int_{u=Y^p/Y^d}^{+\infty} Y^p f(u)du\\
&= H(Y^d, Y^p).
\end{aligned}
$$

This defines a function H which is homogeneous of degree one, increasing in each of its arguments, and such that $H(Y^d, Y^p) \leqslant \mathrm{Min}(Y^d, Y^p)$. Its definition as an integral also implies

$$
\begin{aligned}
\frac{\partial H}{\partial Y^p} &= \int_{u=Y^p/Y^d}^{+\infty} f(u)\, du\\
&= \mathrm{Proba}(\tilde{u}Y^d \geqslant Y^p)\\
&= \pi(Y^d/Y^p) = \pi(z). \qquad (1)
\end{aligned}
$$

This partial derivative appears as the probability that demand will be larger than production capacity, or, alternatively, that the firm will be in a classical unemployment situation. The π function just defined is an increasing function, varying from zero to one as the excess demand indicator $z = Y^d/Y^p$ goes from zero to infinity. Finally, the homogeneity of function H allows the definition

$$H(Y^d, Y^p) = Y^p H(Y^d/Y^p, 1) = Y^p\, h(Y^d/Y^p),$$

and we have the following properties:

$$0 \leqslant h(z) \leqslant \mathrm{Min}(z, 1),$$

$$\frac{\partial H}{\partial Y^d} = h'(z), \qquad (2)$$

$$h'(z) \geqslant 0, \qquad h''(z) \leqslant 0, \qquad 0 \leqslant h'(z) \leqslant 1,$$

$$\pi(z) = h(z) - zh'(z), \qquad \pi'(z) \geqslant 0 \qquad 0 \leqslant \pi(z) \leqslant 1. \qquad (3)$$

The function $h(z)$ is pictured in figure 1. The introduction of demand uncertainty suppresses the typical kink of the Min operator and leads to a smooth function, which more closely approximates the "Min" as the demand uncertainty becomes smaller.[1]

Let us now consider a producer anticipating a mean demand $Y^d(t)$ function of time. We assume that fixed capital does not depreciate and that

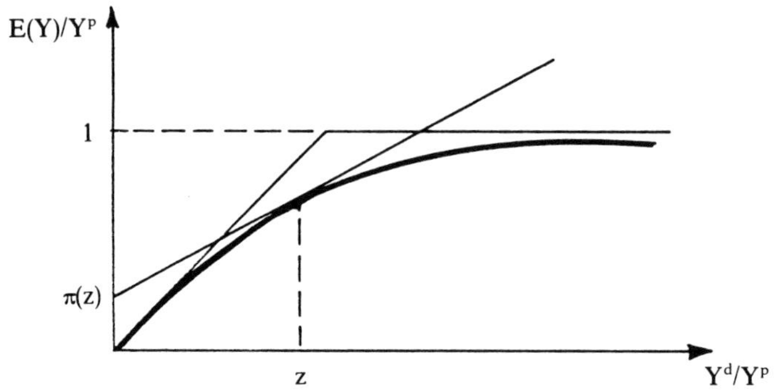

Figure 1.

investment entails adjustment costs. To install (or disinstall) an amount of capital jK, the producer spends (or recovers) an amount $g(j)K$. The adjustment cost function g has the following properties[2]:

$$g(0) = 0, \qquad g'(0) = 1, \qquad g''(j) > 0.$$

Finally, employment will always be adapted to the production level and it is therefore equal to aY. The firm anticipates a real wage $w(t)$ as well as interest rate r, assumed constant.

The model is written in continuous time, and we assume that the disturbances $\tilde{u}$ are mutually independent: demand uncertainty at any point in time is independent of past realizations. In the absence of risk aversion, the producer maximizes the discounted sum of his expected profits, and the following intertemporal optimization problem[3] describes his behavior:

$$\text{Max} \int_0^{+\infty} e^{-rt}[(1 - wa)H(Y^d, K/b) - g(j)K]dt$$

$$\dot{K} = jK,$$

K_0 given.

The optimality conditions are

$$g'(j) = q \tag{4}$$

and

$$\dot{q} = rq - (1 - wa)\,\pi(bY^d/K)/b + g(j) - jq. \tag{5}$$

These conditions are similar to those obtained in standard adjustment-cost models.[4] The first condition is Tobin's pseudo-investment function asserting that the investment rate depends only on the current value of the shadow price of capital q. The second condition says that the user cost of capital $(\underline{r} - \dot{q}/q)q$ must be equal to the gross rate of profit $(1 - wa)/b$, weighted by the probability π and to which one retires the marginal effect of capital on adjustment costs, namely $g(j) - jq$. The innovation with respect to the standard model is the weighting of the gross rate of profit with the probability π of being in a classical unemployment state. This may be easily interpreted: an increase in capacity implies an increase in revenue for the firm only in case of full production capacity utilization and of forthcoming excess demand. Lastly, the solution is completely determined by a transversality condition, which enables the $\dot{q}$ equation to be integrated over the whole future, consequently determining the current value of q and therefore the investment level.

We now have at our disposal a convenient disequilibrium investment behavior model incorporating two key elements: uncertainty about future demand, which is necessary to smooth discontinuities associated with regime changes, and adjustment costs, ensuring that a gradual investment behavior obtains.

2. Perfect-Foresight Dynamics

We now close the model with a demand equation, in order to analyze the dynamics of capital accumulation and unemployment. This will be done in this section under the assumptions of a constant exogenous real wage and of perfect foresight. Both assumptions, of course, are unrealistic, but we find the dynamic analysis they make possible suggestive. It provides insight into the dynamics of an economy characterized by real wage rigidity in which expectations play a crucial role in the accumulation process. The assumption of an infinite horizon is of course not to be taken literally; it is the only simple way to impose terminal conditions in a forward-looking model. To sum up, we claim to render the spontaneous trend of medium-run dynamics. The analysis of this section will usefully be contrasted with the analyses in the following sections, where expectations will be assumed to be myopic and real wage will be endogenized.

We assume that there exist a large number of identical firms, to each of which is associated a specific disturbance $\tilde{u}$, which indicates the proportion of global demand faced by the firm. According to the Law of Large Numbers, we may then identify the mean demand with the mathematical expectation of the individual demands and we may consider that the disturbances disappear at the aggregate level: Y^d, a nonrandom number, now stands for global demand, and $H(Y^d, Y^p)$ for global production. Moreover, the probability $\pi(z)$ of being in a classical unemployment regime is equal to the observed proportion of firms belonging to this regime.[5]

The specification of global demand is very simple. It derives from a constant propensity to consume c, which could easily be made to depend positively on the real wage if one wished to introduce a distribution of income effect between wages and profits, and from the levels of investment and of an autonomous demand G:

$$Y^d = cH(Y^d, K/b) + g(j)K + G. \tag{6}$$

Temporary Equilibrium

At any point in time, for given K and q, the level z of excess demand is determined through the following equation:

$$z = c\,h(z) + bg\,g'^{-1}(q) + bG/K. \tag{7}$$

The levels of production and demand,

$$Y = K\,h(z)/b$$

and

$$Y^d = Kz/b,$$

follow, as well as the proportion $\pi(z)$ of firms in a situation of classical unemployment.

After some calculations we are led to the following multipliers, which sum up the comparative statics properties of the model:

$$\begin{aligned} &\frac{\partial z}{\partial G} = \frac{b}{K(1-ch')} \geqslant 0, && \frac{\partial z}{\partial K} = \frac{-bG}{K^2(1-ch')} \leqslant 0, \\ &\frac{\partial Y}{\partial G} = \frac{h'}{1-ch'} \geqslant 0, && \frac{\partial Y}{\partial K} = \frac{\pi + bh'g}{b(1-ch')} ?, \\ &\frac{\partial Y^d}{\partial G} = \frac{1}{1-ch'} \geqslant 0, && \frac{\partial Y^d}{\partial K} = \frac{c\pi + bg}{b(1-ch')} ?. \end{aligned} \tag{8}$$

The multipliers describing the influence of q have the same signs as the ones describing G's influence, and they are not reported. One should also remember that the proportion of classical unemployment is an increasing function $\pi(z)$.

In order to interpret these multipliers it is useful to examine their limit behavior when the mixed unemployment situation we consider tends toward a pure situation of either classical or Keynesian unemployment.[6,7]

A pure situation of classical unemployment is characterized by $\pi = 1$, $h(z) = 1$, $h'(z) = 0$. The multipliers then take the usual values $\partial Y/\partial G = 0$ and $\partial Y/\partial K = 1/b$. In such a case, production is determined by capacity, that is,

$$Y = Y^p = K/b.$$

A pure situation of Keynesian unemployment is characterized by $\pi = 0$, $h(z) = z$, $h'(z) = 1$. The following multipliers are obtained:

$$\frac{\partial Y}{\partial G} = \frac{\partial Y^d}{\partial G} = \frac{1}{1-c}$$

and

$$\frac{\partial Y}{\partial K} = \frac{\partial Y^d}{\partial K} = \frac{g(j)}{1-c}.$$

Production now is purely demand-determined, so that

$$Y = Y^d = K[g\, g'^{-1}(q) + G]/(1 - c).$$

More generally, it can be checked that the public expenditures multiplier $\partial Y/\partial G$ is a decreasing function of z, or, alternatively, of the proportion π of classical unemployment. It thus decreases continuously from the level $1/(1 - c)$ associated to the pure Keynesian regime to the zero level, which is typical of a pure classical unemployment regime.

One also notes that the capital stock has a twofold influence on production. A high level of capital increases production capacity and therefore production, and, through the multiplier, demand. But the capital stock also exerts a proportional influence on investment, which can be negative if the investment level is so.

Dynamics

The dynamics are determined by the two differential equations that follow, where z is a solution to equation 7.

$$\begin{aligned} \dot{K} &= g'^{-1}(q)K, \\ \dot{q} &= rq - (1 - wa)\pi(z)/b + gg'^{-1}(q) - g'^{-1}(q)q. \end{aligned} \tag{9}$$

A stationary point exists, characterized by $q = 1$ and $z = z^*$, if there exists z^* such that

$$\pi(z^*) = rb/(1 - wa),$$

namely, if and only if $(1 - wa)/rb \geqslant 1$, that is, if and only if factor costs are such that

$$1 - wa - rb \geqslant 0.$$

We shall indicate profitability by the ratio $x = (1 - wa)/rb$. It indicates pure profitability, as determined by factor costs. The capital stock will be stationary if and only if *effective* profitability, namely the product $x\pi$, is equal to unity. For given factor costs this selects a value z^* for excess demand. According to equation 3, this value is determined through the following equation:

$$h(z^*) - z^* h'(z^*) = 1/x. \tag{10}$$

This implies that z^* is a decreasing function of probability x. Indeed, a higher profitability in terms of factor costs enables the firms to be satisfied with a lower demand, that is, with a lower degree of capital utilization.

To complete the characterization of the stationary point we check that to any couple z^*, $q = 1$ we can associate a unique stationary level K^* of the capital stock, which is defined, following equation 7, by

$$z^* = c\, h(z^*) + b\, G/K^*.$$

The stationary point, therefore, is such that

$$K^* = \frac{bG}{z^* - c\, h(z^*)} \quad \text{and} \quad Y^* = \frac{h(z^*)G}{z^* - c\, h(z^*)}. \tag{11}$$

The long-run levels of the capital stock and of production appear as increasing functions of the levels of autonomous expenditures and profitability. One also notes that the long-run multiplier $\partial Y^*/\partial G$ is higher than the short-run multiplier $\partial Y/\partial G$ given in equation 8. Indeed, we have

$$\frac{\partial Y^*}{\partial G} = \frac{\partial Y}{\partial G} + \frac{\partial Y}{\partial K} \cdot \frac{\partial K^*}{\partial G},$$

where the derivative $\partial Y/\partial K$ is calculated at a stationary point where $q = 1$ and therefore is necessarily positive. Thus, the short-run effect is reinforced in the long run by the effect of the increase in the production capacity.

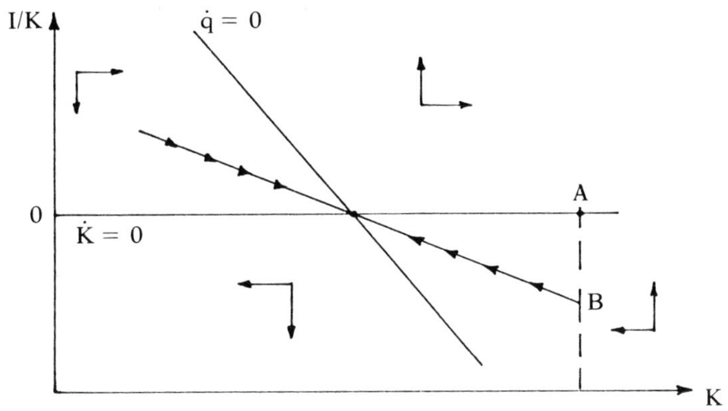

Figure 2.

Finally, we note that a stationary point may be a pure classical unemployment situation, if $x = 1$. It cannot be a pure Keynesian unemployment situation, for $\pi = 0$ necessitates $x = +\infty$, which is impossible as soon as the real interest is not zero; thus profitability is always lower than the value $1/rb$ associated with a zero wage level. This property is easily explained: in a permanent situation of pure Keynesian unemployment, production capacity is underutilized and therefore desired investment is strictly negative.

The path followed by the economy is depicted in figure 2. On the ordinate axis we plot the growth rate of capital I/K rather than the shadow price q as both variables are in a one-to-one relationship. The configuration is the one of a saddlepoint, with the perfect-foresight equilibrium represented by the convergent path. The dynamics are similar to those observed in the pure models of adjustment costs (see, e.g., d'Autume and Michel, 1986). However, gradual modifications in the regime proportions have now taken the place of sudden changes of regime.

This framework can be used to analyze several policy experiments.

Let us first consider the effects of a decrease in autonomous spending. We start from a stationary point labeled A on figure 2. The decrease in G implies a downward shift of the $\dot{q} = 0$ curve and creates the new convergent path that is pictured. The instantaneous effect is a jump from point A to point B. As excess demand z and production Y are increasing functions of G and q, both decrease instantaneously. This Keynesian effect means an increase in the aggregate level of unemployment as well as a relative increase in its Keynesian component. Note that this Keynesian effect is reinforced by the decrease in investment implied by an adverse change in expectations: a permanent decrease in autonomous expenditures implies a decrease in the long-run level of the desired capital stock. The economy then moves toward the stationary point to reach eventually the initial level of z^*, as profitability is unchanged, as well as an even more depressed production level Y^*, since the long-run multiplier, as we have seen, is lower than the short-run one. Thus, unemployment goes on increasing, as production capacity adjusts downward.

Let us now consider the effects of a decrease in profitability. The picture is the same as in the previous experiment. The instantaneous effect is a decrease in the investment level with, paradoxically, Keynesian consequences: unemployment increases and becomes more Keynesian. Only in a second stage does the decrease in the capital stock mean an increase in the classical component of unemployment, so that the economy eventually reaches a stationary point characterized by a larger proportion of classical unemployment than in the initial situation. This episode expresses fairly well the idea that the effects of a shock of truly classical nature may well be initially "contaminated" by Keynesian phenomena.

3. Myopic Dynamics with Constant Real Wage

Let us now revert to the producer's individual behavior, and let us assume that he anticipates a constant demand level Y^d. His optimal leads him to converge toward a stationary point such that $b\,Y^d/K = z^*$ or, equivalently, that $b\,Y/K = h(z^*)$. His behavior in the neighborhood of the stationary point can be approximated by the following relationship:

$$I/K = \lambda[bY/K - h(z^*)]. \tag{12}$$

λ is an adjustment speed which could be linked to the stable eigenvalue of the dynamic system. We shall now use this investment function, which expresses a myopic behavior of the producer, since his behavior at each point in time is based on the current production level, acting as if this level was to remain constant. This function is very similar to the one introduced by Malinvaud (1980a), as they both depend on the two key variables indicating the degree of capacity utilization and the level of profitability.

The model reduces to the following two equations:

$$\begin{aligned} z &= c\,h(z) + \lambda\ b[h(z) - h(z^*)] + b\,G/K, \\ I/K &= \lambda[h(z) - h(z^*)]. \end{aligned} \tag{13}$$

The first of these equations replaces equation 7 as the determination of temporary equilibrium, whereas the second equation describes the dynamics of the system. Taking equation 10 into account, one obtains the following:

If $\Delta = 1 - (c + \lambda b)h'$,

$$\frac{\partial z}{\partial G} = \frac{b}{K\Delta} \geqslant 0, \qquad \frac{\partial z}{\partial K} = \frac{-bG}{K^2\Delta} \leqslant 0, \qquad \frac{\partial z}{\partial x} = \frac{-\lambda bh'}{x^2zh''\Delta} \geqslant 0$$

$$\frac{\partial Y}{\partial G} = \frac{h'}{\Delta} \geqslant 0, \qquad \frac{\partial Y}{\partial K} = \frac{\pi - h'\lambda bh^*}{b\Delta} ?, \qquad \frac{\partial Y}{\partial x} = \frac{-\lambda Kh'^2}{x^2zh''\Delta} \geqslant 0$$

$$\frac{\partial I/K}{\partial G} = \frac{\lambda b^2h'}{K\Delta} \geqslant 0, \qquad \frac{\partial I/K}{\partial K} = \frac{-\lambda b^2Gh'}{K^2\Delta} \leqslant 0, \qquad \frac{\partial I/K}{\partial x} = \frac{-(1 - ch')\lambda bh'}{x^2zh''\Delta} \geqslant 0 \tag{14}$$

These multipliers are similar to those obtained in the case of perfect foresight. To stress this similarity, let us again picture the dynamics in a plane $(K, I/K)$. The economy moves on a curve the equation of which is obtained through the elimination of z between the two equations of the system. From equations 14 the curve is downward-shaping; it shifts upward when autonomous spending G or profitability x increases and there exists on this curve a stable stationary point which is the same as the one in the perfect-foresight model.

Thus, in the present case, the choice between perfect and myopic foresight does not modify the essential features of the dynamics. This similarity would be even more obvious if we reexamined the effects of a decrease in autonomous spending or profitability: they are qualitatively identical to the ones that obtain in the case of percent foresight. The anticipation effects typical of perfect foresight modify only the speeds of adjustment. It is difficult to make these speeds precise, as one should, in the first place, exactly specify the λ parameter of the myopic model. The intuition, however, is that the initial decrease in the investment rate should be,

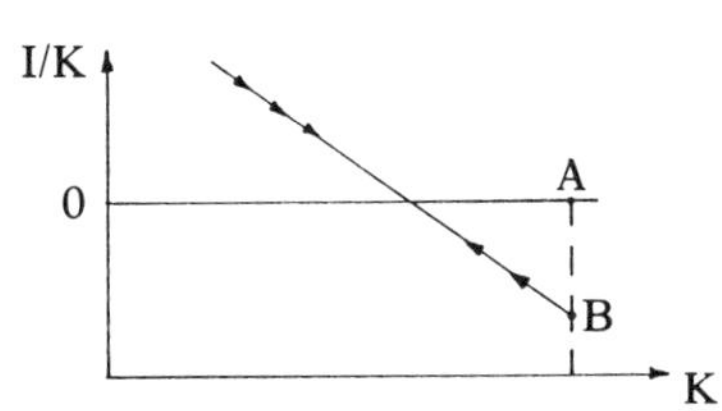

Figure 3.

in these experiments, stronger than in the case of perfect foresight. This would both speed up convergence to the new stationary point and increase the initial amount of Keynesian unemployment.

4. Dynamics with Endogenous Real Wage

Up to now the model has been analyzed under the assumption of an exogenous profitability, and it is desirable to remove it. We assume that the (real) interest rate is controlled by authorities and profitability therefore reflects the evolution of prices and wages. *A priori*, two adjustment processes must be considered.

On the one hand, wages, according to a Phillips effects, react to disequilibrium on the labor market, so that unemployment may contribute to the recovering of profitability, with, no doubt, a fair amount of inertia.

On the other hand, prices react to disequilibrium on the goods market, and this adjustment tends to reduce sale constraints and rationing. However, these constraints do not disappear. They can only be reduced to the normal level compatible with the degree of friction in the market. Formally, one may admit that the normal state of the market, where the price level is at rest, is characterized by the equality of unsatisfied demand and supply, namely, $Y^p - Y = Y^d - Y$ or $z = 1$. To specify this price adjustment we would have to introduce in the model the influence of the price level on demand; that is, in our macroeconomic framework, a real balance effect.

We choose here not to introduce this second adjustment process and to analyze some dynamics where the variations of aggregate demand derive from the behavior of investment and profitability rather than from a real balance effect on consumption.

Unemployment is measured by reference to an exogenous labor supply. As we do not introduce any constraint faced by firms on the labor market, we simply assume that labor supply always adjusts to demand (thanks to overtime work, for instance) even when the latter is higher than the notional labor supply. Lastly, we assume the absence of friction on the labor market and, thus, contrary to the assumption made on the goods market, we exclude the coexistence of unsatisfied supplies and demands on the labor market.

The model is closed by the following equation:

$$\dot{x}/x = \mu[Y^0 - K\,h(z)/b]. \tag{15}$$

For simplification we assume that the adjustment process directly bears on profitability rather than on the real wage which determines it: thus, profitability increases when unemployment is positive. Y^0 is the full-employment production level and μ is a speed of adjustment.

We have to analyze the system made up by equations 13 and 15.

From equations 11 this system has a stationary point, with an adapted profitability, characterized by the levels z^{**} and K^{**} of excess demand of the capital stock, both of which are determined by the following equations:

$$\frac{Y^0}{G} = \frac{h(z^{**})}{[z^{**} - c\,h(z^{**})]}, \tag{16}$$

$$K^{**} = \frac{b\,Y^0}{h(z^{**})}. \tag{17}$$

The associated profitability x^{**} then follows according to equation 10.

The long-run multipliers now are the following:

$$\frac{\partial x^{**}}{\partial Y^0/G} = \frac{-zh''x^2(z - ch)}{\pi} \geqslant 0,$$

$$\frac{\partial K^{**}}{\partial Y^0} = \frac{b(1 - ch')}{\pi} \geqslant 0,$$

$$\frac{\partial K^{**}}{\partial G} = \frac{-bh'}{\pi} \leqslant 0.$$

In the long run, if autonomous spending increases relative to full-employment production, this demand pressure implies a better utilization of production capacities and therefore allows a lower profitability.

We have to remember that the real interest rate determines an upper bound, $1/rb$, for profitability and therefore a lower bound, say $z_{\min}$, for excess demand. The right-hand side of equation 16 is a decreasing function of z which tends to zero as z tends to infinity. The existence and unity of z^{**} and of the stationary point are therefore warranted as soon as

$$\frac{Y^0}{G} \leqslant \frac{h(z_{\min})}{[z_{\min} - c\,h(z_{\min})]}.$$

To sum up: Autonomous demand has to be high enough to ensure that the required long-run profitability is accessible, taking the ceiling imposed by the real interest rate into account. We assume that such is the case.

Let us now consider equations 14 and assume that $\partial Y/\partial K \geqslant 0$. We thus admit that the direct positive effect of production capacity on production dominates the negative effect, which operates through investment and the Keynesian multiplier. The dynamic model then has the following structure, where the sign of the influence of the different variables is indicated:

$$\dot{K}/K = I/K(\underset{-}{K}, \underset{+}{x}, \underset{+}{G}),$$

$$\dot{x}/x = \mu[Y^0 - Y(\underset{+}{K}, \underset{+}{x}, \underset{+}{G})].$$

This system is stable, and assuming away oscillations we obtain figure 4.

Let us again analyze the consequences of a decrease in autonomous spending. We start from a stationary point characterized by the equilibrium proportion not really of classical unemployment, as it is a full-employment situation, but of excess demand on the market for goods. As we have seen, the increase in autonomous spending implies an increase in the stationary levels K^{**} and x^{**}. The loci $\dot{K} = 0$ and $\dot{x} = 0$ shift to the positions seen on the figure and the economy, starting from point A, moves on a path that converges to the new stationary point B. The decrease in demand implies an instantaneous increase in Keynesian unemployment as well as a downward jump of investment, which becomes negative. During the first stage the dominant effects are those which

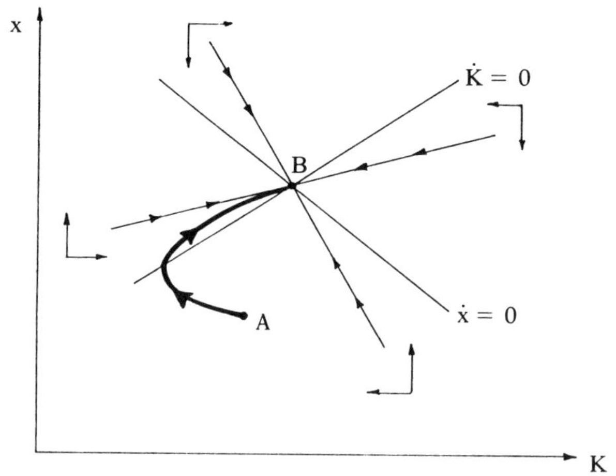

Figure 4.

have been described when profitability was supposed to be constant. The capital stock decreases, unemployment increases and becomes more and more classical. But unemployment implies a decreases in real wages and an increase in profitability, which eventually stimulates investment. Unemployment decreases, as does the proportion of classical employment. The economy eventually returns to full employment with a smaller proportion of excess demand for goods than before the shock. A simple experiment is thus sufficient to give rise to complex enough dynamics of mixed unemployment, characterized in particular by successive reversals of the relative proportions between classical and Keynesian unemployment.

As we have already stressed, the limits to the exercise must be underlined. It rests upon an implicit assumption of prices being more rigid than the real wage. This is clearly not the most usual assumption, but it enabled us to focus on adjustment through changes in production capacity rather than in prices. In this setting the reference to a full equilibrium employment admittedly becomes questionable. It should be understood that it is just a convenient method to analyze some plausible medium-run evolutions, the most interesting result of it being the possibility of a spontaneous reversal of the investment trend, caused by the recovery of profitability.

Conclusion

The simultaneous consideration of uncertainty about future demand and adjustment costs provides some foundations for an aggregate investment function that appears very similar to the one used by Malinvaud in his early analysis of the role of profitability, but which is here cast in a more explicit dynamic framework. This investment function fits naturally in a model of mixed unemployment in which regime proportions vary continuously. It enables a dynamic analysis of mixed unemployment situations and, as an illustration, of the economy's response to a negative demand shock. We first assume that the real wage remains constant and we derive the resulting dynamics of investment and demand. We then introduce a reaction of the real wage to unemployment and therefore also of profitability, in order to analyze what would probably be the medium-run effects of such a shock.

This simplified framework is sufficient to give rise to somewhat complicated dynamics of the different unemployment components. It should, however, be developed with a much more detailed specification of prices and wages adjustment processes. It would, secondly, be desirable to introduce some kind of putty-clay technology. The assumption of fixed technical coefficients, as Malinvaud often stressed, is realistic enough in the short run. It allows a clear definition of unemployed production capacity and postpones to some medium run, probably short enough but not instantaneous, the effects of the real wage on profitable supply. Finally, a more satisfactory model would describe coexisting unemployment and vacancy situations and would therefore extend to the labor market the kind of aggregation process that was introduced here on the goods market only. But in such a model—that is, with two explicit friction parameters—one would have to state precise assumptions about spillover effects, and it is not clear how a simple enough macro model could emerge. This should be the subject of further research.

Notes

1. In a similar framework, with two disturbances, several authors have spelled out necessary conditions for the H function thus obtained to be CES (see, e.g., Gouriéroux, Laffont, and Monfort 1984).

2. See Hayashi 1982 and d'Autume and Michel 1986 for further details.

3. All variables are time dependent. From now on this will not be made explicit.

4. See e.g. d'Autume and Michel 1986.

5. This method is used in particular by Sneessens (1987). More precisely, we assume that firm i faces an individual demand $\tilde{u}_i Y^d$, where Y^d is a nonrandom number common to all firms and where $\tilde{u}_i$ is a firm-specific disturbance with unit expectation. The $\tilde{u}_i$ are assumed to be independent. The Law of Large Numbers then implies that the mean of the individual demands $\tilde{u}_i Y^d$ tends to Y^d with probability one. Y^d therefore represents the empirical mean of individual demands, that is, global demand, up to a multiplicative factor.

6. The same kind of multipliers have been analyzed by Lambert (1988), Sneessens and Drèze (1986), and Sneessens (1987).

7. More rigorously, we may assume that there exists a bounded interval outside of which the H function becomes identical to the Min function. For very low excess demand z, unemployment is purely Keynesian, whereas it is purely classical for very high z. Formally, $h(z) = z$ if $z \leqslant z_1$ and $h(z) = 1$ if $z \geqslant z_2$: the graph of function h then is slighty different from the one on figure 1. If there exists a solution lower than z_1 to the equation

$$z = cz + bg\,g'^{-1}(q) + bG/K,$$

it is a pure Keynesian solution characterized by the production level reported in the text. If there exists a solution higher then z_2 to the equation

$$z = c + bg\,g'^{-1}(q) + bG/K,$$

it is a pure classical solution characterized by the production level $Y = K/b$.

References

d'Autume, A., and Michel, P. 1986. "Déséquilibre général et investissement." *Annales d'Economie et de Statistique* 4: 23–51.

Cette, G., and Taddei, D. 1988. "Chômage mixte et politiques économiques, un modèle de déséquilibre." *Revue Economique* 39: 1119–1141.

Gouriéroux, C., Laffont, J. J., and Monfort, A. 1984. "Econométrie des modèles d'équilibre avec rationnement, une mise à jour." *Annales de l'INSEE* 55–56: 5–38.

Gouriéroux, C., and Laroque, G. 1985. "The Aggregation of Commodities in Quantity Rationing Models." *International Economic Review* 26: 681–700.

Green, J., and Laffont, J. J. 1981. "Disequilibrium Dynamics with Inventories and Anticipatory Price Setting." *European Economic Review* 16: 199–221.

Hayashi, F. 1982. "Tobin's Marginal q and Average q: A Neoclassical Interpretation." *Econometrica* 50(1): 213–224.

Hénin, P. Y. 1978. "Proposition pour unifier la théorie du chômage: un modèle d'équilibre de processus." Mimeo, Université de Paris I.

Lambert, J. P. 1988. *Disequilibrium Macroeconomic Models*. Cambridge University Press.

Malinvaud, E. 1977. *The Theory of Unemployment Reconsidered*. Basil Blackwell.

Malinvaud, E. 1980a. *Profitability and Unemployment*. Cambridge University Press and Maison des Sciences de l'Homme.

Malinvaud, E. 1980b. "Macroeconomic Rationing of Employment." In E. Malinvaud and J. P. Fitoussi, eds., *Unemployment in Western Countries*. Macmillan.

Malinvaud, E. 1987. "Capital productif, incertitude et profitabilité." *Annales d'Economie et de Statistique* 5: 1–36.

Muellbauer, J. 1978. "Macro-Theory vs. Macroeconometrics: The Treatment of Disequilibrium in Macro-Models." Discussion paper, Birckbeck College, London.

Sneessens, H. R., and Drèze, J. H. 1986. "A Discussion of Belgian Unemployment Combining Traditional Concepts and Disequilibrium Econometrics." *Economica* 53 suppl.: S89–S119.

Sneessens, H. R. 1987. "Investment and the Inflation-Unemployment Tradeoff in a Macroeconomic Rationing Model with Monopolistic Competition." *European Economic Review* 31: 781–815.

13 Exchange Policy, Underemployment, and Project Evaluation

D. Bureau

When unemployment prevails, public-policy projects should be assessed on the basis not of market prices—which are appropriate only in neoclassical equilibrium situations—but of shadow prices. These should be calculated by taking account of all the constraints affecting economic policy. Such shadow prices are, however, difficult to define, since they require an understanding of the nature of the obstacles to the restoration of full employment.

It is generally admitted that the chief restriction on the systematic use of Keynesian demand-stimulation measures resides in the accompanying growth of the external deficit. It is therefore logical to regard the external constraint as the first obstacle. Using this approach, Fourgeaud, Lenclud, and Picard (1984) studied a model in which the State regulates demand to guarantee a certain level of external balance as a result of the complementarity of imports with respect to economic activity.

While emphasizing the methodological difficulties involved in factoring macroeconomic stabilization effects, the working Party on project evaluation and disequilibriums reduction of the Commissariat Général du Plan (1984) adopted a largely similar approach. In particular, the group was led to recommend cost-benefit analyses with shadow prices for small-scale policy projects. By way of plausible but only partly verified estimates, the report gave a figure of 1.2–1.3 for the shadow price of the currency and a shadow wage slightly below the real wage.

The model examined here aims to integrate in this type of analysis the flexibility afforded by the exchange policy in managing the external constraint. For this purpose, we posit an economy whose agents are small and competing against one another, but we assume that the country forms an entity large enough to exercise a degree of monopoly power on international trade. To wield this power, the country must improve its terms of trade, for instance, by tolerating a certain level of unemployment.

This leads to a very different interpretation of underemployment at the economic-policy optimum.

Unemployment is no longer the consequence of production complementarities but the result of a trade-off with the terms of trade. It is interesting to study the impact of that trade-off an project evaluation.

The present paper successively examines the two issues of unemployment and project evaluation. At each step, a comparative analysis of the impact of trade restrictions in the same context (Mayer 1981; Dixit 1986) enables us to specify the validity of our findings and to emphasize the role of the choice of alternative instruments at the disposal of the government in defining the rules of project evaluation (Guesnerie 1980; Bureau 1985).

1. Analytical Framework

For the sake of simplicity, the only elements included in the model are those strictly necessary for studying the policy of a country capable of determining its exchange policy at the price of a potential disequilibrium in its labor market. For this purpose, we begin by examining the country in isolation—that is, one country and two goods. We also assume, for practical reasons, that the government determines employment, with the exchange rate adjusting subsequently. But this is obviously equivalent to supposing that the government has at its disposal two instruments—the employment level and the exchange rate—that are forced to comply with the external constraint.

1.1. Model Structure

The first good is produced in quantity Y by the national productive sector, which, for this purpose, uses labor according to a constant return technology ($Y = L$). The second good is imported. On the assumption that redistribution problems are dealt with elsewhere, we consider only a single consumer. We further assume that his preferences are separable between these two goods on the one hand and labor on the other. The only deviation from the pure-competition model is therefore the supply of labor L, posited as directly controlled by the government: the latter has the power to impose any (positive) rationing with respect to the supply expressed by households. Perfect market adjustment follows.

Thus, the price of the national good (p) is equal to the wage (w). Consumer income (R) is therefore wL and its distribution between the two goods is obtained by maximizing the utility function's goods term with respect to the price system (p, p^*) p^*, being the price of imports.

The foreign market meets the matching demand, which here constitutes the only source of imports (M). The foreign market also expresses a demand for exports that is sensitive to competitiveness. The latter is denoted by using the same foreign-price index, namely

$$X = X(p^*/p). \tag{1}$$

The model's adjustment is accordingly summed up by the external-balance equilibrium:

$$p^*M = pX. \tag{2}$$

Because of the homogeneity of the demand functions, the only useful price here is the value of the terms of trade $\pi = p^*/p = p^*/w$, and the entire model can be expressed in terms of the two variables L and π. With national labor therefore taken as the numeraire, the import function is written $M(L, \pi) = M(L, 1, \pi) = M(wL, p, p^*)$. Allowing for equation 1, equation 2 is written

$$\pi M(L, \pi) = X(\pi). \tag{2a}$$

It implicitly provides the value of the terms of trade in equilibrium for a given value of L. We assume that three hypotheses are then satisfied:

- The equilibrium thus defined is unique in the area considered.
- The two goods are normal goods, which notably implies that the marginal import content ($m = \pi \partial M/\partial L$) of consumption is positive.
- Any external deficit can be corrected by a devaluation. Noting the foreign-trade price elasticities as $e_M = -\pi/M \cdot \partial M/\partial \pi$ and $e_X = \pi/X \cdot dX/d\pi$, this requires the fulfillment of the Marshall-Lerner condition ($\Delta = e_M + e_X - 1 > 0$).

1.2. Analysis of the Marginal Transformation of the Walrasian Equilibrium

To examine how such a model works, we may usefully begin by calculating the impact on the terms of trade of a marginal limitation of employment. For this purpose, we need only differentiate equation 2a. Hence,

$$\delta\pi = (m/\Delta M)\ \delta L. \tag{3}$$

Thus, a restriction on employment ($\delta L < 0$) results in an improvement in the terms of trade ($\delta\pi < 0$). In the neighborhood of the Walrasian equilibrium, the result is an increase in consumer welfare. The reason is that the consumption change in real terms is $\delta L - M\delta\pi$, but the first term is entirely offset in the utility function by the effect on labor disutility: in the reference situation, the wage is equal to the marginal disutility of labor, since the government does not restrict the labor supply.

Allowing for equation 3, the welfare change expressed in terms of income thus becomes $-(m/\Delta)\delta L > 0$. This gives us the predicted result, namely, that a return to full employment is not desirable ($m/\Delta > 0$).

In this context, a certain level of unemployment is therefore admissible if offset by the country's exercise of its monopoly power on international trade.

This finding points to the relevance of the notion that employment and external constraint must be linked and that they justify the use of a below-market shadow price for labor. It should be noted, however, that this implies the country's inability to employ other means for exploiting its monopoly power.

1.3. Superiority of Trade Restrictions

Another way to improve the terms of trade is to introduce tariffs or trade restrictions in quota form. It is therefore worth comparing the efficiency of the two methods from this point of view. To do so, we shall examine the government's program when it can simultaneously control employment and introduce tariffs (t). Consumer income becomes $L + t\,\pi M$. As the first term of the utility function is expressed in indirect form, the program is written

$$\max u(R, \pi(1 + t)) - v(L),$$

$$\pi M(R, \pi(1 + t)) = X(\pi), \qquad (4)$$

$$R = L + t\pi M(R, \pi(1 + t)).$$

Its Lagrangian is

$$\mathscr{L} = u(R, \pi(1 + t)) - v(L) - \lambda(\pi M - X) - \mu(R - L - t\pi M).$$

Its derivation with respect to the four control variables (R, π, t, L), after transformation by Roy's identity, leads to

$$\frac{\partial u}{\partial R} - \lambda m - \mu + \mu t m = 0,$$

$$\lambda \Delta + \mu t(1 - e_{M}) = (1 + t)\frac{\partial u}{\partial R},$$

$$\lambda e_{M} + \mu(1 + t - te_{M}) = (1 + t)\frac{\partial u}{\partial R}, \tag{5}$$

$$v'(L) = \mu.$$

After resolving this system, we get

$$\mu = \frac{\partial u}{\partial R}, \qquad \lambda = t\frac{\partial u}{\partial R}, \qquad v'(L) = \frac{\partial u}{\partial R}, \qquad t = 1/(e_{X} - 1).$$

This means, therefore, that the optimum is of a full-employment type provided tariffs are available as an economic-policy instrument.

In this case, the tariffs conform to the standard formula and accordingly appear as a far more efficient means of improving the terms of trade.

Of course, the use of such tariffs is limited by the scope for retaliation by other countries. Nevertheless, it is worth examining the domestic instruments that can be used to reach that objective in keeping with what we have outlined above. In this connection, the role of indirect taxation should also be examined. But this would require a more complex model. Because of the limited number of goods and agents in the model analyzed here, the taxes on goods are equated with tariffs and the tax on labor with labor rationing. Overall, these factors lead us to emphasize the restrictions on economic-policy instruments that are required to envisage the use of a below-market shadow wage in project evaluation.

1.4. External Constraint and Keynesian Unemployment

We can, however, justify the choice of instruments adopted here, spelling out in greater detail the link between this model and conventional macroeconomic analyses. These effectively employ similar terms to discuss the tradeoff between restrictive policy and devaluation in reducing an external disequilibrium, when this cannot be made by capital movements. It is indeed possible to interpret the present model in a disequilibrium context (Malinvaud 1980). For this purpose, we need only consider that we are dealing with a money economy in which the nominal wage is rigid but the exchange rate ensures external equilibrium. If we assume the possession of money by consumers to be governed by the basic Keynesian consumption function (constant propensity c), its equilibrium is Keynesian so long as money creation does not restore full employment. The reason is that the constant returns cause the supply of goods to be constantly in (undetermined) surplus. Accordingly, the main difference with the model studied is the change of variables:

• The monetary variable (m_0) replaces rationing as an economic-policy tool. But the link with employment is immediate, since the Keynesian equilibrium is written $L = (c/1 - c)m_0/p$.

• The adjustment of the terms of trade π to balance the external account requires the adjustment of p^*, as domestic nominal prices are rigid.

Such a presentation thus affords a better understanding of the choice of labor-supply rationing as an economic-policy tool. This rationing should be regarded less as an adjunct to taxation measures (Guesnerie and Roberts 1984) without short-term malleability than as the core of the domestic regulation policy. On the other hand, the hypothesis of a rigid nominal wage is secondary and should not mask the true nature of the analysis carried out here, whose central variable is the wage expressed in terms of currency ($1/\pi$).

2. Optimal Policy and Project Evaluation

We must now focus our analysis on the optimal tradeoff between unemployment and the terms of trade, as well as its consequences for defining the rules of public project evaluation. The latter aspect requires the inclusion in the model of a controlled public sector. We assume this sector produces a public good q, under the constraint of a production function $q \leqslant f(-y^G, -L^G, -M^G)$, with y^G, L^G, M^G its inputs. C is the marginal consent to pay for the good, which we assume to be represented in the utility function by a supplementary additive term (g). L stands now for total employment. Consumer income is then $L - y^G - L^G - \pi M^G$, and the program to be resolved is therefore written

$$\begin{aligned}
&\max u(R, \pi) - v(L) + g(q),\\
&q - f(-y^G, -L^G, -M^G) \leqslant 0,\\
&\pi(M(R, \pi) + M^G) - X(\pi) = 0,\\
&\frac{\partial v}{\partial L} \leqslant \frac{\partial u}{\partial R},
\end{aligned} \tag{6}$$

with $R = L - y^G - L^G - \pi M^G$.

Taking into account the calculation in section 1.2, the constraint $v'(L) \leqslant \partial u/\partial R$ is not saturated (underemployment), and the Lagrangian is therefore reduced to

$$\mathscr{L} = u + g - v - \lambda(\pi(M + M^{G}) - X) - \mu(q - f). \tag{7}$$

We shall successively examine the necessary conditions with respect to L and π, and those with respect to q, y^{G}, L^{G}, M^{G}. The first define macroeconomic policy, the second the public-sector management rules.

2.1. Macroeconomic Policy

The introduction of the public sector somewhat complicates the Marshall-Lerner condition, which becomes

$$\Delta = e_{X} + \frac{M}{M + M^{G}} e_{M} + \frac{M}{M + M^{G}} m - 1.$$

We then have

$$\frac{\partial \mathscr{L}}{\partial L} = 0 \quad \text{or} \quad \frac{\partial u}{\partial R} - \frac{\partial v}{\partial L} = \lambda m$$

$$\frac{\partial \mathscr{L}}{\partial \pi} = 0 \quad \text{or} \quad \frac{\partial u}{\partial R} = \lambda \Delta, \quad \text{taking Roy's identity into account.}$$

Eliminating λ, we end up with

$$\frac{v'(L)}{\partial u/\partial R} = 1 - \frac{m}{\Delta}. \tag{8}$$

This equation therefore specifies the extent to which employment must be set at a level below that of the competitive supply. Indeed, the equation signifies that the relationship of the marginal disutility of labor (expressed in terms of income) to wages (here equal to unity) must be equal to $1 - m/\Delta$. Naturally, in the case of a small country ($\Delta \to \infty$), we find unity—in other words, Walrasian equilibrium.

The explanation is that in this model the government has at its disposal two instruments of macroeconomic policy: employment L and the exchange rate π. These must be implemented simultaneously in order to balance the trade account, a process that links them via equation 3. This results in a marginal rate of feasible transformation between employment and real consumption ($1 - m/\Delta$) that takes the terms-of-trade effect into account. At the optimum, that rate must obviously be equal to the rate of substitution between the two values from the standpoint of consumer preferences, expressed in equation 8.

The analysis of this relation can be illustrated as follows.

Starting from a situation of underemployment, the government could reduce unemployment. All other things being equal, this policy is desirable as it reduces the labor-market disequilibrium. But it adversely affects the external account owing to the imports generated by the additional income (m coefficient). As a result, a devaluation is required to restore the external-account balance (Δ coefficient). Equation 8 consequently expresses the fact that, at the optimum, the resulting deterioration in the terms of trade strictly offsets the first effect in terms of welfare.

2.2. Project Evaluation

Let us now consider the necessary optimality conditions associated with the public firm's production plan:

$$\frac{\partial \mathscr{L}}{\partial q} = 0 \quad \text{or} \quad C = \mu \Big/ \frac{\partial u}{\partial R},$$

$$\frac{\partial \mathscr{L}}{\partial y^{G}} = 0 \quad \text{or} \quad \left(1 - \frac{m}{\Delta}\right)\frac{\partial u}{\partial R} = -\mu \frac{\partial f}{\partial - y^{G}},$$

$$\frac{\partial \mathscr{L}}{\partial L^{G}} = 0 \quad \text{or} \quad \left(1 - \frac{m}{\Delta}\right)\frac{\partial u}{\partial R} = -\mu \frac{\partial f}{\partial - L^{G}},$$

$$\frac{\partial \mathscr{L}}{\partial M^{G}} = 0 \quad \text{or} \quad \pi\left(1 + \frac{1-m}{\Delta}\right)\frac{\partial u}{\partial R} = -\mu \frac{\partial f}{\partial - M^{G}}.$$

This set of conditions can be summed up by

$$C = \frac{1 - \dfrac{m}{\Delta}}{-\dfrac{\partial f}{\partial - y^{G}}} = \frac{1 - \dfrac{m}{\Delta}}{-\dfrac{\partial f}{\partial - L^{G}}} = \frac{\left(1 + \dfrac{1-m}{\Delta}\right)\pi}{-\dfrac{\partial f}{\partial - M^{G}}}. \tag{9}$$

As regards the production factors, this means in particular that the marginal rate of transformation between L^{G} and national good y^{G} must equal unity as in the private sector: any shadow-price bias must be reflected according to the characteristics of the production system. More generally, the public firm must

- minimize its production cost against the price system $1 - m/\Delta$ for labor and the national good, $\pi(1 + [(1 - m)/\Delta])$ for imports

• set its production level so that the marginal consent to pay for the public good equals the marginal production cost assessed with that price system.

Naturally, these "shadow" prices are defined to within one standardization. The one chosen here seems, however, logical a priori in that it does not affect the valuation of the public good. Moreover, if we use this price system to assess a public-policy project with a composition identical to that of marginal consumption, our standardization will not cause our assessment to differ from the customary evaluation based on market prices, for

$$\left(1 + \frac{1-m}{\Delta}\right)\pi\frac{\partial M}{\partial R} + \left(1 - \frac{m}{\Delta}\right)\left(1 - \pi\frac{\partial M}{\partial R}\right) = 1.$$

In these conditions, the distortions to be introduced with respect to the standard evaluation appear only for atypical goods. Lastly, our stardardization corroborates the notion that the public sector should use a shadow price of labor lower than the market wage and should discourage imported products.

2.3. Interpretation in Terms of Taxation

However, this approach does not entitle us to speak here of a "shadow price of the currency," for the import valuation result is better interpreted in terms of import tariffs. From this point of view, the choice of a standardization based on the national good (y^G) seems more appropriate, as the shadow wage ceases to differ from the market wage. With respect to these goods, the price of the imports to be utilized is

$$\pi\frac{1 + (1-m)/\Delta}{1 - m/\Delta}.$$

In other words, the public sector ought to behave as if its imports were liable to a tariff of

$$t = \frac{1}{e_x + \dfrac{M}{M + M^G}(e_M - m) - 1}. \tag{10}$$

In this form, the link with optimal tariffs is quite clear. If the public sector predominates ($M/(M + M^G) \to 0$), we find the rate $1/(e_x - 1)$ again. In general, the rate to be applied is lower, $e_M - m$ being necessarily positive, since we are dealing with a compensated elasticity. Basically, this corrective term expresses the fact that a tax on imports limited to the public sector is an inadequate replacement for uniform taxes. The reason is that the improvement in the terms of trade afforded by the incentive applied to the public sector is partly offset by the resulting substitutions in household consumption.

The use in this context of the notion of "shadow price of the currency" is also ambiguous insofar as, by not tying down the bias to imports, one can give credence to the idea that any currency gain is desirable, for example, on the export side. Now the model examined posits the equivalence between tariffs and export duties. The application of export subsidies is therefore particularly inappropriate here, given the superiority of trade restrictions on domestic policy (section 1.3): a marginal subsidy of t diminishes welfare by

$$\frac{X}{\Delta}\frac{M}{M + M^{G}}(e_{M} - m).$$

3. Implications of Our Analysis

To assess the validity of the project-evaluation rules set out above, we must go back to three main initial hypotheses, as none of these is self-evident. The first hypothesis is that we are dealing with a large country, and therefore with relatively low price elasticities for foreign trade. Such a choice is supported by most econometric estimates, which tend to verify the Marshall-Lerner condition without significant short-term excess. Some caution is required to extend this finding to sectorial public decisions, as these generally have a long application span. Most of the determinants that can explain the low level of price elasticities in the short run are endogenous in the longer run, and this obviously alters the analysis.

The second hypothesis concerns the choice of policy instruments, whose importance has already been emphasized. We mention it here only as a reminder and to point out its connection with the third hypothesis, which relates to the possibility of examining a single country in isolation. Just as the threat of retaliation by other countries provided the main argument against using import tariffs as policy instruments, so the discussion on the tradeoff between exchange policy and domestic policy should raise the question of the coordination between these policies.

We have so far effectively restricted our analysis to a single country, assuming a purely passive behavior on the part of the foreign market. The latter satisfies the country's demand for imports and merely expresses a demand for exports that is conditioned by competitiveness. Such an assumption, which is crucial for defining the optimal policy, implicitly corresponds to a Nash behavior on the part of the government toward the foreign market. To elaborate on this point, it therefore seems useful to enlarge the model to include a fuller description of the foreign market. The simplest way of doing this is to switch to a two-country model in which the two countries are identically described. The values relating to the foreign market carry an asterisk.

The analysis of this type of model is now well known thanks to recent studies on the strategic analysis of trade policies (Dixit 1986) and the coordination of domestic policy (Oudiz and Sachs 1984). We shall therefore confine ourselves to illustrating the model's principles in this particular context. As before, the key variable is the ratio $\pi = P^*/P$. As income is expressed in terms of national good, the import equations are written $M = M(L, 1, \pi)$; $M^* = M^*(L^*, 1, 1/\pi)$. Moreover, we necessarily have $X = M^*$ (and $X^* = M$) and the model's adjustment is summarized as $M^* = \pi M$. This implicitly determines the values of the terms of trade according to the domestic policies (L, L^*). Writing import price elasticities as e_M and $e_M{}^*$, Δ equals $e_M + e_M{}^* - 1$, and the marginal transformation of this equation is

$$M\Delta\delta\pi = \pi(\partial M/\partial L)\,\delta L - (\partial M^*/\partial L^*)\,\delta L^*. \tag{11}$$

Furthermore, we can assess each country's welfare in terms of (L, L^*), knowing that

$$U(L, L^*) = U(L, 1, \pi) - v(L)$$

and (12)

$$U^*(L, L^*) = U^*(L^*, 1, 1/\pi) - v(L^*)$$

with

$$\pi M(L, 1, \pi) = M^*(L^*, 1, 1/\pi).$$

The formal analysis of this model's functioning is analogous to Mayer's analysis of import duties and barriers. Nevertheless, it is rather complicated as several cases are possible (Johnson 1953). Figure 1 illustrates this in the plane (L, L^*) in the case of a "standard" configuration which satisfies the following properties:

- The functions $U(L, L^*)$ present a unique maximum in L at a given L^*.
- The slope of the reaction curves is negative.
- The intersection of the reaction curves is unique.

Hence, we begin by plotting in this plane the network of curves $U(L, L^*) = \text{constant}$, $U^*(L, L^*) = \text{constant}$ (ex. U_e, U_e^*). These curves ex-

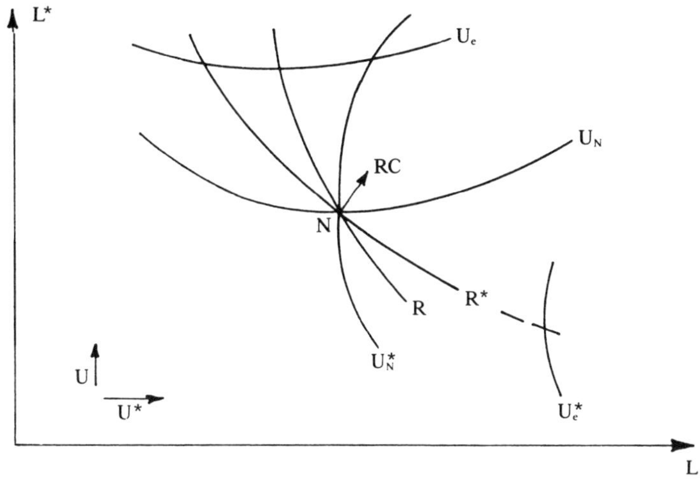

Figure 1.

hibit as characteristic points the minima $\partial U/\partial L = 0$, $\partial U^*/\partial L^* = 0$, which define the countries response functions $L = R(L^*)$, $L^* = R^*(L)$ when each takes the other's behavior for granted. This corresponds to the assumption made in the preceding sections. If both countries behave in this manner, the interaction of their domestic policies will lead to a Nash equilibrium at the intersection of R and R^*. But the latter is inefficient, since an increase in L^* in this point improves U without changing U^* in the first order. More generally, there is a large area of coordinated demand-stimulating policies (RC) that improve the situation of both countries simultaneously. In this context, a coordination of domestic policies would therefore be desirable.

It should, however, be noted that with the exception of the no-intervention equilibrium—which induces an equilibrium of both labor markets—the labor supply does not allow an income redistribution between the two countries except at the price of a loss of efficiency. This loss takes the form of a distortion between productivity and labor disutility where underemployment exists. Overall, the optimal policy defined above must be accompanied by a lack of domestic-policy coordination, which places obvious limits on the validity of equation 8.

Conclusion

In this paper, we have explored the rules of project evaluation to be applied in an economy in which a certain level of unemployment is the tradeoff for an exchange policy aimed at exploiting a monopoly power on foreign trade. Our findings are not categorical. Admittedly, we have substantiated the intuitive assumption that the public sector should use a shadow price of labor lower than the market wage and discourage imports. However, the system of shadow prices to be utilized must primarily be interpreted as tariffs, which is much more restrictive than a "shadow price of the currency." Moreover, these results are obtained in the well-defined context of an isolated country characterized by low price elasticities in its foreign trade and by a limitation of the economic-policy instruments at its disposal for domestic regulation.

Acknowledgments

Thanks are due to Paul Champsaur for helpful discussions on a previous version.

References

Bureau, D. 1985. "Coherence entre choix des projets et politique de régulation macroéconomique." *Annales de l'INSEE* 57.

Commissariat Général du Plan 1984. "Calcul économique et résorption des déséquilibres." Rapport du groupe de travail calcul économique présidé par E. Malinvaud, préparation du IXe Plan. La Documentation Française, Paris.

Dixit, A. 1986. *Strategic aspects of Trade Policy*. Princeton University Press.

Fourgeaud, C., Lenclud, B., and Picard, P. 1984. "Calcul économique, prix fictifs et contrainte extérieure." *Revue Économique* 3: 425–445.

Guesnerie, R. 1980. "Analyse microéconomique normative du modèle keynésien élémentaire: une exploration." Rapport du groupe de travail calcul économique et macroéconomie. CEPREMAP, Paris.

Guesnerie, R., and Roberts, K. 1984. "Effective Policy Tools and Quantity Controls." *Econometrica* 52(1): 59–85.

Johnson, H. 1953. "Optimum tariffs and Retaliation." *Review of Economic Studies* 21(2): 143–153.

Malinvaud, E. 1980. *Réexamen de la théorie du chômage*. Calmann-Lévy.

Mayer, W. 1981. "Theoretical Considerations on Negotiated Tariff Adjustment." *Oxford Economic Papers* 33(1): 135–153.

Oudiz, G., and Sachs, J. 1984. "International Policy Coordination in Dynamic Macroeconomic Models." *Brookings Papers on Economic Activity*.

14 Optimal Banking Contracts

Xavier Freixas and
Jean-Jacques Laffont

1. Introduction

The crucial role of the banking system in the theories of the economic cycle has been recognized by economists since the beginning of the twentieth century. Hawtrey, von Mises, and von Hayek in particular have stressed the instability of the credit system and its influence on the economic cycle. Through the volume of their loans, financial institutions affect the level of investment and the firms' probabilities of bankruptcy, which are major determinants of the level of activity. Recent contributions in this area have focused on the crucial role of investors' expectations and on the dependence of these expectations on the firms' debt levels. Economic fluctuations following the first oil shock are better understood when investors' expectations exhibit this dependence. Professor Malinvaud (1986), when describing the cyclical events of this period, writes: "During the boom economic agents tend to overestimate the productive potential of their society; growth accelerates but disequilibria develop: in particular excessive business indebtedness and a price configuration that cannot be long sustained. Acceleration of inflation solves for a time the problem, but for a time only. When inflation and the growth of demand slow down, profit rates decrease, real interest rate increases, debt liquidation begins, but simultaneously real debts increase, leading to an increase in bankruptcies, to pessimism and loss of confidence."

In traditional rational expectations models,[1] banks provide their loans in view of the future ability of firms to repay them. Then the level of indebtedness cannot play a very different role in recessions or expansions. Malinvaud sets up a model of firm behavior in which the firm's objective function is equal to expected profit minus a penalty if the realized profit does not enable the firm to repay its debt. This objective function is at the center of the macroeconomic model that he uses to formalize the role of indebtedness in cycles.

More generally, macroeconomic modeling of the economic cycle often relies on an hypothesis which seems a priori legitimate: "an increased concern for solvency is likely to lead for some time to a decrease of the demand for labor" (Malinvaud 1986, p. 63). However, a rigorous microeconomic approach of this relation between investors' expectations and the level of activity is more difficult than one might have expected. The first purpose of our work is to study this question and stress the difficulties that arise when the problem is formulated in some generality. It is surprising to find that a greater pessimism of investors implies a decrease in the volume of loans only under quite restrictive assumptions, as soon as there exists an auditing cost to observe the firms' cash flows related to activities financed by these loans. But, such a costly auditing procedure is the only satisfactory rationalization of standard debt contracts. These contracts define a fixed payment if possible, and if the firm cannot repay the loan, bankruptcy occurs and the bank gets the value of all the firm's assets.

Our work also gives some insight in the role of informational asymmetries and auditing costs in credit markets. As such, it extends current research on banking contracts, which pursues two main objectives. The first is to provide a microeconomic foundation for credit rationing, a major phenomenon of the various credit markets. The second is to give a microeconomic foundation to the non-neutrality of money, which gives rise to a reconstruction of monetary economics. Our results are relevant for these two lines of research.

Since Jaffee and Russel's (1976) pioneering paper, a number of authors (Stiglitz and Weiss 1981; Williamson 1986; de Meza and Webb 1987) have presented rationing at the equilibrium with rational agents as an essential consequence of asymmetric information in the bank firm relationship. The basic idea is as follows: the bank faces a set of potential borrowers of unknown quality where quality is, for example, the probability of success in an investment project. It is therefore a classical adverse selection problem. If the project has a fixed size, the optimal mechanism is likely to be a stochastic rule by which a loan is granted with some probability (see Laffont and Maskin 1980). If the bank faces a continuum of borrowers, this mechanism can be interpreted differently by saying that a proportion of borrowers (equal to the above probability) get their loans and the others are rationed.

As soon as investments have a variable size, as here, optimal loan mechanisms use the size of the loan to discriminate between projects of different quality. In general there is no rationing, but each investor would like to borrow more at the marginal unit price he faces. This is simply a consequence of nonlinear pricing.

A weakness of most contributions is to carry out their analysis with standard debt contracts which have no theoretical justification. Incentive theory suggests that reimbursement of loans should be a more complex (nonlinear) function of the cash flow. However, Diamond (1984) and Gale and Hellwig (1985) have shown that the optimal contract is indeed a standard debt contract when the observation of production is costly for the bank and agents are risk neutral. We will borrow their idea of an auditing cost, but we will also add an asymmetry of information on the expected productivity of investment projects, as in Stiglitz and Weiss 1981. The model so obtained is more satisfactory because contracts are optimal instead of being ad hoc. But, this improvement is offset by an increased complexity due to the nonconvexities of the bank's objective function.

To sum up, we will consider a model with investments of variable size (contrary to Stiglitz and Weiss but as in Gale and Hellwig), with an endogenous explanation of the standard debt contract (as in Gale and Hellwig and contrary to Stiglitz and Weiss) and with adverse selection (as in Stiglitz and Weiss and contrary to Gale and Hellwig). In this relatively rich framework, we study the comparative statics properties of optimal contracts and obtain a number of intuitive results if we assume that audit costs are small enough. In particular, we show that the volume of loans decreases with the opportunity cost of banks and with the cost of auditing, and that the introduction of adverse selection leads to a decrease in loans. Finally, we show that an improvement of business expectations increases the volume of loans and that the existence of informational asymmetries increases the sensitivity of the economy to economic fluctuations.

The restrictive nature of the assumptions needed to obtain these intuitive results limits considerably the scope of the recent work, which gives microeconomic foundations to the non-neutrality of money. In this literature the optimal contracts are imbedded in general equilibrium models to study the role of monetary policy (Mankiw 1986; Williamson 1986; Levy-Garboua and Maarek 1985). The results obtained rest in a crucial way on the comparative static properties of the optimal banking contracts.[2] Our work leads to a somewhat negative assessment of this macroeconomic approach. Indeed, as soon as a fairly general model is considered, the qualitative properties of optimal contracts become very difficult to predict. Accordingly, if it is certainly legitimate to think that imperfect information in loan contracting is a major reason for the non-neutrality of money, the way this monetary channel can be used is far from being elucidated.

In a first section, we describe our model in which the bank can observe with some cost the random production level of the borrowing firm. We show that different regimes describe the optimal loan contracts. The second section studies in detail a particular case in which the distribution of the random variable affecting production is uniform. A fairly complete comparative static analysis is provided under a set of strong assumptions. It is shown how the relaxation of these hypotheses leads to ambiguous results. Section 4 shows how the results obtained in section 3 for a single firm can be generalized to a large number of firms. Section 5 introduces an additional asymmetry of information by assuming that firms have private information about their expected productivity: the optimal level of the loan is then obtained by equating the expected marginal productivity of investment to its marginal cost, defined as the sum of the interest rate, the cost of the marginal increase in the probability of bankruptcy, and the marginal cost due to the incentive constraint. Section 6 gathers some concluding comments.

2. Costly Observation of Outputs and Banking Contracts

We consider a bank facing a population of firms. Each firm is characterized by a productivity parameter $\theta \in [\underline{\theta}, \overline{\theta}]$ which enters its production function:

$$\tilde{y} = \tilde{s}\theta f(\ell)$$

with $f'(\ell) > 0; f''(\ell) < 0$ for every ℓ and $\lim_{\ell \to 0} f'(\ell) = \infty; \lim_{\ell \to \infty} f'(\ell) = 0.$

ℓ denotes the investment of the firm, $\tilde{y}$ its output, and $\tilde{s}$ is a random variable which is the same for all firms and which represents the economic environment. The random variable $\tilde{s}$ is characterized by the distribution function $H(s)$ defined on the interval $[\mathbf{s}, \overline{s}]$, with a density function $h(s)$ assumed to be strictly positive.

More generally, $\tilde{y}$ can be interpreted as the cash flow that the firm obtains after an investment ℓ, once production activities have been optimized.

To simplify notations, we assume that firms have no equity and must borrow to invest. In a first step, we assume that the bank can observe the parameter θ *ex ante*, i.e., before the loan decision. *Ex post*, the bank can observe the realized value y of the firm's output only if it incurs an auditing cost of c. The repayment that the bank will obtain for its loan is an amount $\tilde{R}(\ell, \theta, y)$, which depends, potentially, on its observables θ, y, and ℓ.

These exist a clause of limited liability such that the firm's repayment to the bank never exceeds its output (or cash flow). The standard debt contract is defined by

$$\tilde{R}(\ell, \theta, y) = \text{Min}(R(\ell, \theta), y).$$

An amount $R(\ell, \theta)$, independent of y, must be reimbursed following a loan of an amount ℓ. If the firm is unable to reimburse this amount, it is declared bankrupt, all its assets are realized, and its proceeds are given to the bank. In our simplified model the bank gets y net of auditing costs.[3]

When the bank and firms are risk neutral, as we assume in this paper, the existence of an auditing cost c to observe y leads to the optimality of standard debt contracts. This result due to Diamond (1984) and Gale and Hellwig (1985)can be intuitively explained as follows: the nonobservability of production in the absence of audit requires, for obvious incentive reasons, a constant repayment each time auditing does not take place. Moreover, in an optimal contract, auditing costs that are a loss for both partners must be minimized. This is achieved by maximizing the reimbursement each time there is an audit, i.e., by giving to the bank the whole cash flow.

It is important to stress that the Gale-Hellwig result stems from the fact that auditing costs are a loss for both parties. The fact that it is payed by the bank or by the firm does not affect the analysis, if we are willing to assume that the cash flow is always high enough to pay for the auditing costs.

This result enables us to restrict our analysis to standard debt contracts that are not selected in an ad hoc way, but contain necessarily the optimal contracts. A *loan strategy* for the bank is the choice of an *investment function*

$$\ell(\cdot)\colon [\underline{\theta}, \overline{\theta}] \to \mathbb{R}_+$$

and of a *reimbursement function* if the firm is solvent

$$R(\cdot)\colon [\underline{\theta}, \overline{\theta}] \to \mathbb{R}_+.$$

It will often be convenient to use, instead of $R(\theta)$, the variable

$$\psi(\theta) = R(\theta)/\theta f(\ell(\theta)),$$

which can be interpreted as a failure rate. Consequently, a loan policy can be identified with $(\ell(\cdot), \psi(\cdot))$.

We assume that each firm θ has a level of expected profit $\underline{v}(\theta)$ below which it prefers not to borrow from the bank.[4] A firm θ will accept a loan $(\ell(\theta), \psi(\theta))$ only if its expected profit is larger than or equal to $\underline{v}(\theta)$, a constraint that we will refer to as individual rationality ($\mathbb{R}$) constraint.

Let us introduce the notations

$$I^+(\psi) = \int_{\psi}^{\bar{s}} sh(s)\,ds = E(s|s \geqslant \psi)\,P(s \geqslant \psi)$$

and

$$I^-(\psi) = \int_{\text{s}}^{\psi} sh(s)\,ds = E(s|s \leqslant \psi)\,P(s \leqslant \psi),$$

which denote the normalized (i.e., divided by θf) expected production given that the firm is not bankrupt and the expectation of reimbursement given that the firm is bankrupt.

We assume that the bank obtains its funds at a constant interest rate r so that the design of an optimal loan policy is reduced to the problem of an optimal loan policy for a given firm θ. The bank wants to maximize its expected utility under the $\mathbb{R}$ constraint of firm θ; i.e., using our notations,

$$\operatorname*{Max}_{\ell,\psi} \theta f(\ell)[I^-(\psi) + \psi(1 - H(\psi))] - c\, H(\psi) - (1 + r)\ell \tag{2.1}$$

T.Q.

$$\theta f(\ell)[I^+(\psi) - \psi(1 - H(\psi))] - \underline{v}(\theta) \geqslant 0, \tag{2.2}$$

$$\ell \geqslant 0, \tag{2.3}$$

$$\psi \geqslant \underline{s}, \tag{2.4}$$

$$-\psi \geqslant -\bar{s}. \tag{2.5}$$

This way of setting up the problem presumes that the bank realizes non-negative profits. Indeed, constraint 2.2 does not have to be satisfied if the bank chooses not to lend, i.e., $\ell = 0$. Implicitly, and in agreement with most of the literature on banking systems, we assume that the banking sector has an oligopolistic structure. If $\underline{v}(\theta)$ were zero, our modeling would be very restrictive because it would define a sharing of surplus which benefits only the bank. As $\underline{v}(\theta)$ is unconstrained, the good markets considered can also have an oligopolistic structure. When the set of (ℓ, ψ) values that satisfies 2.2–2.5 is nonempty, our assumptions of f and the continuity of $H(\cdot)$ imply that a solution exists. This solution satisfies the two following Kuhn and Tucker conditions (denoting $\mu_1, \mu_2, \mu_3, \mu_4$, the multipliers associated with constraints 2.2, 2.3, 2.4, 2.5, respectively:

$$\theta f'(\ell)[I^-(\psi) + \psi(1 - H(\psi))] - (1 + r)$$
$$+ \mu_1 \theta f'(\ell)[I^+(\psi) - \psi(1 - H(\psi))] + \mu_2 = 0, \tag{2.6}$$

$$\theta f(\ell)[1 - H(\psi)] - c\, h(\psi) - \mu_1 \theta f(\ell)[1 - H(\psi)] + \mu_3 - \mu_4 = 0. \tag{2.7}$$

In the absence of restrictive assumptions, the program 2.1–2.5 is not concave. Let us first describe five possible loan regimes that follow from the Kuhn-Tucker conditions.

Observe first that $\psi = \bar{s}$ implies $H(\psi) = 1$, $I^-(\psi) = E\tilde{s}$, $I^-(\psi) = 0$. Since we then have $\mu_3 = 0$, equation 2.7 can be written

$-c\,h(\bar{s}) - \mu_4 = 0.$

It is a limiting case which is possible, with $\ell \neq 0$, only if $c = 0$ and $\underline{v}(\theta) = 0$. We will neglect this case below.

For a borrower θ, the bank has five different loan regimes:

a. Denial of loan: $\ell = 0$

b. Riskless unconstrained loan: $\ell > 0,\ \psi = \underline{s},\ \mu_1 = 0$

c. Riskless constrained loan: $\ell > 0,\ \psi = \underline{s},\ \mu_1 > 0$

d. Risky unconstrained loan: $\ell > 0,\ \psi > \underline{s},\ \mu_1 = 0$

e. Risky constrained loan: $\ell > 0,\ \psi > \underline{s},\ \mu_1 > 0.$

These different solutions do not appear to us to have the same relevance in modeling the credit market. The most interesting situations correspond to cases where the bank is led to take some risk of nonreimbursement even if these risks are limited. For that reason we assume $\mathbf{s} = 0$, which eliminates cases b and c. Three regimes remain. In the next section we solve for the optimal contracts in the special case where $\tilde{s}$ is uniformly distributed.

3. Optimal Contracts

We assume in this section that the random variable $\tilde{s}$ is distributed uniformly on the interval [0, 1]. The normalization, $\bar{s} = 1$, is unimportant. On the other hand, the choice of the uniform distribution is not innocuous and we will come back to this assumption at the end of the section. In this particular case, expected profits of the bank and of the firm become, respectively,

$$U(\ell, \psi, \theta) = \theta\, f(\ell)\left(\psi - \frac{\psi^2}{2}\right) - c\psi - (1 + r)\,\ell \tag{3.1}$$

and

$$V(\ell, \psi, \theta) = \tfrac{1}{2}\theta\, f(\ell)\,(1 - \psi)^2. \tag{3.2}$$

In the case of the firm, the concavity of f generates an isoprofit that gives us the isoprofit curves described in figure 1.

The equation of the isoprofit curve of level v is $\ell = f^{-1}\,(2v/\theta\,(1 - \psi)^2)$, an increasing and convex function of ψ.

The isoprofit curves of the bank are given in figure 2.

For each value of ψ, the optimal level of loan is defined by the equation

$$\theta\, f'(\ell)\left(\psi - \frac{\psi^2}{2}\right) = 1 + r$$

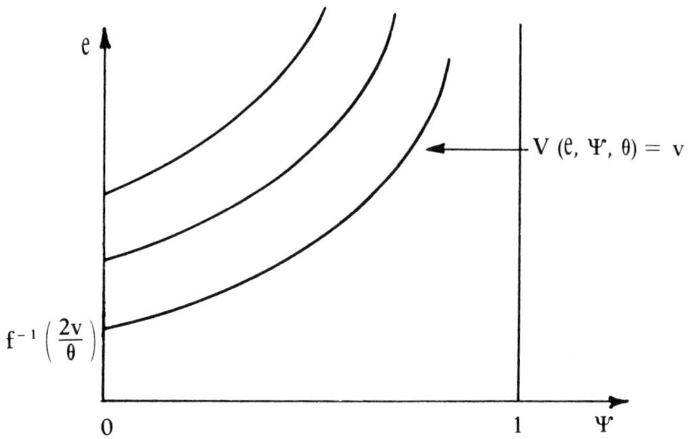

Figure 1.

and is represented in figure 2. The objective function of the bank is not necessarily quasiconcave. We assume that in the absence of asymmetric information about output ($c = 0$) it is concave.[5] Then, we choose c small to remain in the neighborhood of this situation.

When c becomes strictly positive, the objective function of the bank has a saturation point. It is a solution of the following first-order equations:

$$\theta f(\ell)(1 - \psi) - c = 0, \tag{3.3}$$

$$\theta f'(\ell)\left(\psi - \frac{\psi^2}{2}\right) - (1 + r) = 0. \tag{3.4}$$

Because f is strictly concave, equation 3.3 defines a function $\ell_1(\psi)$ that is increasing and convex for any $\psi \in [0, 1[$ and equation 3.4 defines an increasing function $\ell_2(\psi)$ that is not necessarily concave. Let us assume that the values of the parameters are such that the two curves $\ell_1(\psi)$ and $\ell_2(\psi)$ intersect (c is small enough for given values of r and θ). Since $\ell_1(\psi)$ goes to infinity as ψ goes to one, the curves cut an even number of times (generically). Suppose, as in figure 3, that there are two intersection points.[6] The saturation point corresponds to the intersection with the value of ψ, which is the highest (use the necessary second-order condition). For c small, the isoprofit curves remain convex in the north-west region and we obtain the situation described in figure 3.

Gale and Hellwig (1985) maximize the expected profit of the firm under the constraint of a zero expected profit for the bank. Therefore, they identify point E in figure 4.

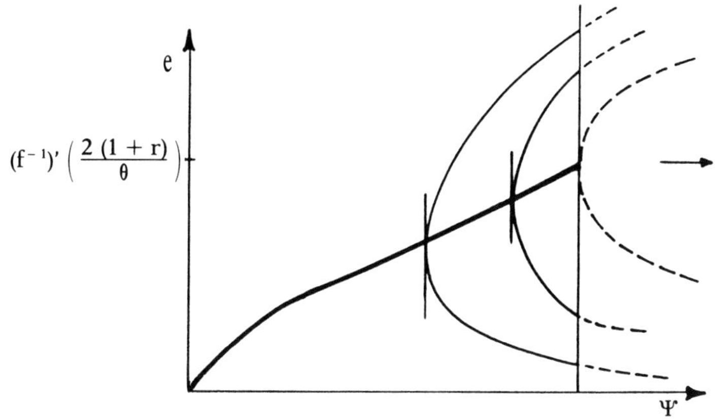

Figure 2.

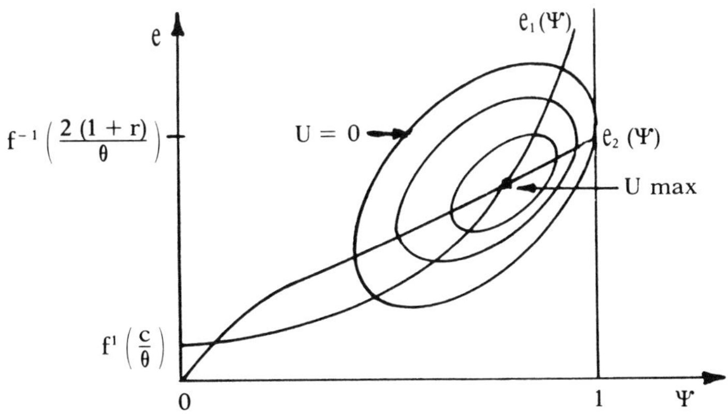

Figure 3.

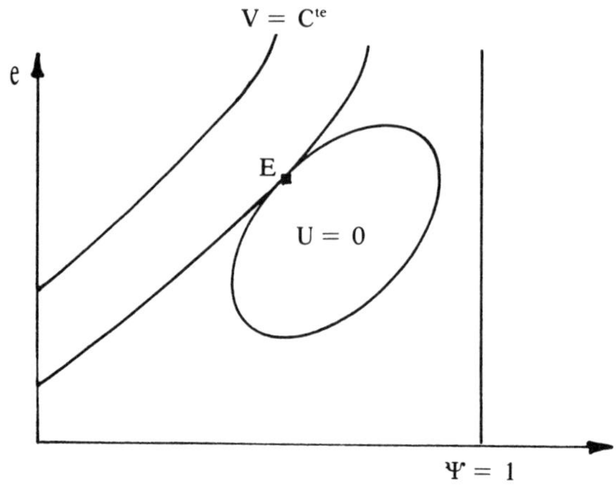

Figure 4.

On the contrary, we maximize the bank's expected profit under the ℝ constraint of the firm $V(\ell, \psi, \theta) \geqslant \underline{v}(\theta)$, and we get three cases[7]:

Case I: Interior Solution

The optimal contract does not saturate the ℝ constraint. This case occurs if $\underline{v}(\theta)$ is small enough (see figure 5).

Case II: Gale-Hellwig Solution

The ℝ constraint of the firm is saturated and the bank has non-negative expected profits (see figure 6).

Case III: No Loan

The ℝ level of the firm is such that the bank prefers not to provide a loan (figure 7).

Let us express the first-order conditions that describe the optimal contract in an intuitive way. In case I, substituting the value of ψ obtained from equation A1.2 in A1.1 and, observing that $E\tilde{s} = \frac{1}{2}$, we obtain

$$\theta f' E\tilde{s} = 1 + r + \frac{\theta f'}{2}(1 - \psi)^2. \tag{3.5}$$

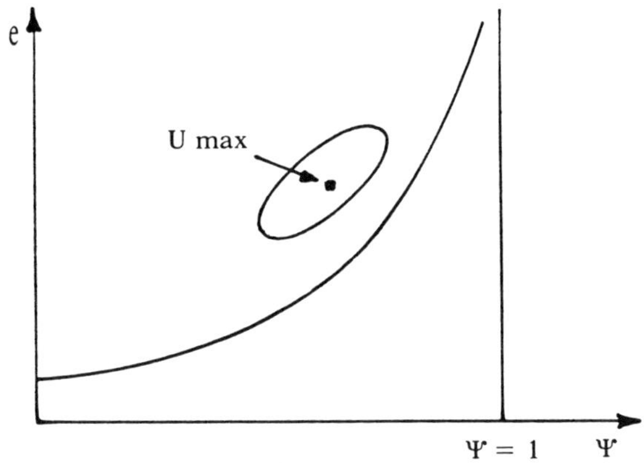

Figure 5.

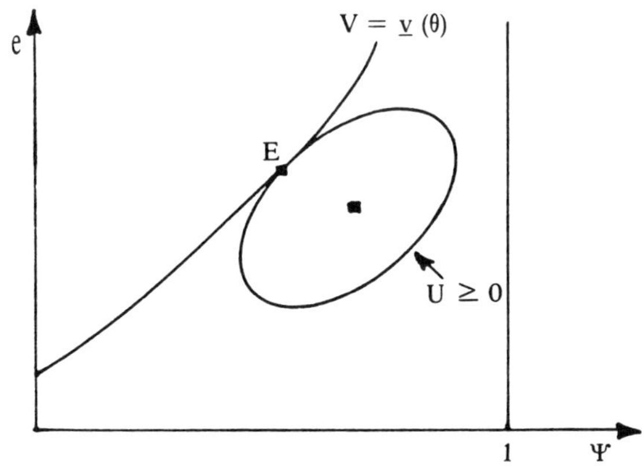

Figure 6.

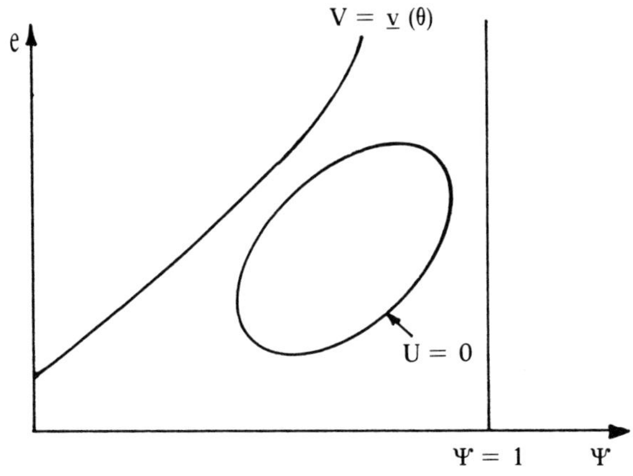

Figure 7.

$d\psi/d\ell = f'(1 - \psi)/f$ represents the marginal increase in the probability of bankruptcy at the optimum due to an exogenous increase of ℓ (when ψ is optimized) in the case of the uniform distribution. Indeed,

$$Pr(\tilde{s} \leqslant \psi) = \int_0^{\psi} dx \; et \; \frac{d}{d\ell}(Pr(\tilde{s} \leqslant \psi)) = \frac{d\psi}{d\ell}.$$

Using this relationship and A 1.1, we get

$$\theta f' E\tilde{s} = (1 + r) + \frac{1}{2} c \frac{d\psi}{d\ell}. \tag{3.6}$$

Similarly in case II, we obtain

$$\theta f' E\tilde{s} = 1 + r + c\frac{d\psi}{d\ell}, \tag{3.7}$$

where

$$\frac{d\psi}{d\ell} = \frac{1}{2}\frac{f'(1 - \psi)}{f}$$

is now the increase in the probability of bankruptcy due to an exogenous increase of ℓ (when the $\mathbb{R}$ constraint of the firm is saturated).

In both cases, the investment is chosen so as to equate its expected marginal productivity to its financial cost $(1 + r)$ augmented by the marginal auditing cost due to the increase in the probability of bankruptcy.[8]

The following propositions summarize our results of comparative statics.

Proposition 1. When the financial cost r increases or the auditing cost increases, the level of loan and probability of bankruptcy decrease in case I and in case II (see appendix for proofs).

In the case of the uniform distribution ψ is, strictly speaking, the probability of bankruptcy (otherwise the probability of bankruptcy increases with ψ). When the auditing cost increases, it is better to observe less often, therefore ψ decreases and as the marginal gain from the loan decreases the size of the loan decreases. When the financial cost increases, the bank decreases its loan (and therefore the probability of bankruptcy decreases).

The analysis of changes in θ is more complex because of its effect on $\underline{v}(\theta)$. Still, we obtain the following results:

Proposition 2. In case, I, the level of loan and the probability of bankruptcy increase with θ. In case II, it is still the case when $\underline{v}(\theta)/\theta$ is non-increasing for small values of c. Otherwise, the results are ambiguous (see appendix 2 for proofs).

It is interesting to interpret θ[9] as a variable that reflects the quality of business conditions. In our model, these conditions are exogenous.

In case I, proposition 2 establishes that the level of loans increases with business conditions. This is due to the fact that, in good conditions, the reimbursement of the firm will always be higher so that the cost associated with bankruptcy can be expected to be lower. This is the fundamental effect of the audit cost. However, in the saturated case (case II), an improvement of business conditions has a positive effect on the outside opportunities of the firm. If this last effect is strong enough, the results become ambiguous. Only a general equilibrium analysis can provide an answer.

The most relevant question for macroeconomics is to ask if the sensitivity to business conditions increases when the banking system is less efficient or the informational asymmetry more severe (c increases). For production functions with a negative third derivative as well as for homogeneous production functions with decreasing returns to scale, ℓ^{α}, $\alpha < 1$, we obtain:

Proposition 3. For c small enough, $\partial^2 \ell / \partial\theta\partial c > 0$ (see appendix 3 for the proof).

In the particular case of this section, uniform distribution with returns to scale that are decreasing enough, the asymmetry of information has the expected effects on the level of loan: the size of the loan is smaller, it decreases with the financial cost r and the audit cost, it increases with business conditions, and it is more sensitive to business conditions than under complete information. Weakening one of these conditions may make the isoprofit curves of the bank (or even the firm) nonconvex. The comparative statics of the model then become inextricable with multiple discontinuities. It is a fact that the marginal rate of substitution between the level of bankruptcy and the level of loan for the bank (and the firm) depends in a complex way on the returns of the firm and the distribution of the random variables describing the uncertainties facing firms. Therefore, nonconvex isoprofit curves must be generally expected. But, if isoprofit curves are not convex, the transition from one regime to another (cases I and II, for example) may create discontinuities in the levels of loans, which invalidate a global analysis even if the desired results are obtained for each regime. For that reason, we must make a strong convexity assumption, which makes possible a local approach in each case. However, even when isoprofit curves are convex, the generality of the results obtained here remains an open question, specially those of Proposition 3, which embody the major result that asymmetries of information aggravate economic fluctuations.

4. Behavior of Total Investment

In section 3 we considered the case of a single firm or a population of identical firms with parameter θ. In this section we generalize the comparative statics results to the case where the bank faces a population of firms, each one characterized by a value θ belonging to an interval $[\underline{\theta}, \overline{\theta}]$. As explained in section 2, the problem of designing an optimal loan policy is the same as before, for each value of θ. We are now interested in the total volume of loans given by the bank and in its dependence upon exogenous variables. Our first objective will be to determine the population of firms which receive a loan. The following lemma shows that, under the assumption that $\underline{v}(\theta)/\theta$ is non-increasing, the bank gives loans to all firms with a θ parameter larger than a critical θ_* value.

Lemma 1. If $\underline{v}(\theta)/\theta$ is non-increasing, there exists θ_* such that

$$\ell(\theta) = 0 \qquad \text{for } \theta \in [\underline{\theta}, \theta_*],$$

$$\ell(\theta) > 0 \qquad \text{for } \theta \in [\theta_*, \overline{\theta}].$$

Proof. Let $G(\theta)$ be the distribution function defined on $[\underline{\theta}, \overline{\theta}]$ which describes the characteristics of the population of firms. The optimization problem of the bank can be written

$$\underset{(\ell,\psi,\Omega)}{\text{Max}} \int_{\Omega} \left[\theta f(\ell) \left[\psi - \frac{\psi^2}{2} \right] - c\psi - (1+r)\ell \right] dG(\theta) \tag{4.1}$$

T.Q.

$$f(\ell)(1-\psi)^2 \geqslant \frac{\underline{v}(\theta)}{\theta}. \tag{4.2}$$

Let $P(\theta, \ell, \psi)$ be the argument inside the integral 4.1 and let

$$P(\theta) = \underset{(\ell,\psi)}{\text{Max}} \left\{ P(\theta,\ell,\psi) \,|\, f(\ell)(1-\psi)^2 \geqslant \frac{\underline{v}(\theta)}{\theta} \right\}.$$

The set $\mathbf{\Omega}^*$ of firms that receive a loan maximizes 4.1 when it is equal to

$$\mathbf{\Omega}^* = \{\theta \in [\underline{\theta}, \bar{\theta}] \,|\, P(\theta) \geqslant 0\}.$$

But $P(\theta)$ is an increasing function. Indeed, $\theta' > \theta$ implies

$$P(\theta', \ell, \psi) \geqslant P(\theta, \ell, \psi),$$

and as $\underline{v}(\theta)/\theta$ is decreasing, the set of pairs (ℓ, ψ) that satisfy 4.2 is increasing. Consequently, $P(\theta') \geqslant P(\theta)$, and $\mathbf{\Omega}^* = [\theta_* \bar{\theta}]$ for θ_* defined as follows:

$$P(\theta_*) = 0 \quad \text{if} \quad P(\underline{\theta}) \leqslant 0 \leqslant P(\bar{\theta}),$$

$$\theta_* = \underline{\theta} \quad \text{if} \quad P(\underline{\theta}) > 0,$$

$$\theta_* = \bar{\theta} \quad \text{if} \quad P(\underline{\theta}) < 0.$$

QED

We now show that θ_* is an increasing function of c and r.

Lemma 2. θ_* increases with c and r.

Proof. The first-order conditions of program 4.1, 4.2 are

$$\theta f'(\psi - (\psi^2/2)) - (1+r)\ell + \lambda f'(1-\psi)^2 = 0 \quad \text{for all } \theta, \tag{4.3}$$

$$\theta f(1-\psi) - c - 2\lambda f(1-\psi) = 0 \quad \text{for all } \theta, \tag{4.4}$$

and

$$\theta_* f(\ell(\theta_*))[\psi(\theta_*) - (\psi^2(\theta_*)/2)] - c\psi(\theta_*) - (1+r)\ell(\theta_*)$$
$$+ \lambda(\theta_*)\{f(\ell(\theta_*))[1-\psi(\theta_*)]^2 - (\underline{v}(\theta_*)/\theta_*)\} = 0. \tag{4.5}$$

Differentiating 4.5, and using 4.3 and 4.4 and the Kuhn-Tucker complementary conditions, we obtain

$$\frac{d\theta^*}{dc} > 0, \qquad \frac{d\theta^*}{dr} > 0. \qquad \text{QED}$$

Let L be total investment, i.e.,

$$L = \int_{\theta^*}^{\bar{\theta}} \ell(\theta)\, dG(\theta).$$

We then obtain proposition 4.

Proposition 4. If $\underline{v}(\theta)/\theta$ is nonincreasing, L decreases with c and r.

Proof. Suppose that there is a single switch of regimes at the point $\tilde{\theta}$ and let us assume without loss of generality that regime I takes place for $\theta \leqslant \tilde{\theta}$, and regime II for $\theta > \tilde{\theta}$. (The extension to several switches of regimes is immediate.)

$$\frac{dL}{dc} = -\ell(\theta_*)g(\theta_*)\frac{d\theta_*}{dc} + \int_{\theta^*}^{\tilde{\theta}} \frac{d\ell_1}{dc}(\theta)\, dG(\theta)$$

$$+ \int_{\tilde{\theta}}^{\bar{\theta}} \frac{d\ell_2}{dc}(\theta)\, dG(\theta) + [\ell_1(\tilde{\theta}) - \ell_2(\tilde{\theta})]\frac{d\tilde{\theta}}{dc}.$$

The first term is negative from lemma 2, the second and the third terms are positive from proposition 1, and the last term is zero. Indeed $\ell_1(\tilde{\theta}) = \ell_2(\tilde{\theta})$, because, under our assumptions, the solution is continuous in $\tilde{\theta}$. A similar proof shows that $dL/dr < 0$. QED

In figure 8, we give the example of an equilibrium with $\underline{v}(\theta) = \delta\theta$. The equation which defines the $\mathbb{R}$ constraint of the firm is then independent of θ.

AB is the locus of saturation points when θ varies between θ_* and $\bar{\theta}$. For $\theta < \theta_*$, the bank does not provide loans. Between θ_* and $\tilde{\theta}$, the bank is constrained by the $\mathbb{R}$ constraint (A′C in figure 8). Between $\tilde{\theta}$ et $\bar{\theta}$, it chooses its nonconstrained optimum (BC).

Finally, with the same method as in proposition 4, it can be shown that a *uniform* improvement of business conditions increases the volume of loans. If we denote

$$L(\lambda) = \int_{\theta^*}^{\bar{\theta}} \ell(\theta + \lambda)\, dF(\theta),$$

we have the following proposition:

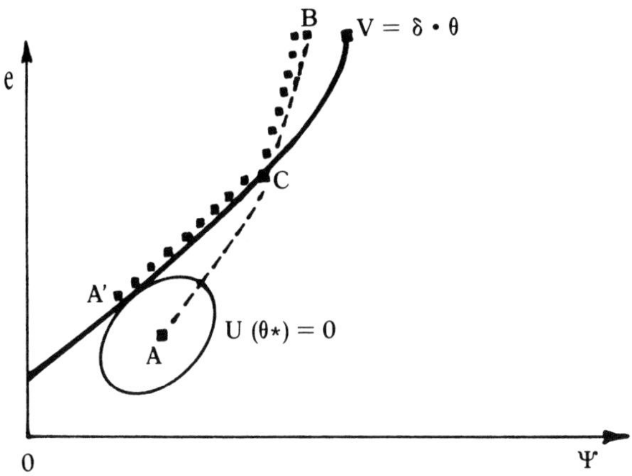

Figure 8.

Proposition 5. If $\underline{v}(\theta)/\theta$ is non-increasing, $L(\lambda)$ is an increasing function of λ.

It is clear from figure 8 that, by choosing appropriate $\underline{v}(\cdot)$ functions, we can generate any partition of regimes that we may wish.

5. Discriminating Contracts

We consider now an additional asymmetry of information, by assuming that the bank does not know the characteristic θ of each firm even though it knows the distribution G.

In this case, the bank chooses a loan policy that associates a level of reimbursement R to each level of loan ℓ, in order to maximize its expected profit. The existence of an audit cost still justifies the use of standard debt contracts. From the revelation principle, we know that it is possible to redefine the problem as the choice of an optimal incentive compatible revelation mechanism

$\ell^*(\cdot), R^*(\cdot)\colon \Theta \to \mathbb{R}^2.$

Let us start by characterizing the incentive compatible mechanisms $\ell(\theta)$, $R(\theta)$. The answer $\tilde{\theta}$ given by a firm θ is truthful if $\tilde{\theta} = \theta$ solves the maximization of the firm's expected utility:

$$\operatorname*{Max}_{\tilde{\theta}} \int_{R(\tilde{\theta})/\theta f(\ell(\tilde{\theta}))}^{1} [s\theta\, f(\ell(\tilde{\theta})) - R(\tilde{\theta})]\, ds. \tag{5.1}$$

The first condition, after integration and division by $1 - R(\theta)/\theta\, f(\ell(\tilde{\theta}))$, is

$$\tfrac{1}{2}\theta\, f'(\ell(\tilde{\theta}))\frac{d\ell(\tilde{\theta})}{d\tilde{\theta}} + \tfrac{1}{2}f'(\ell(\tilde{\theta}))\frac{d\ell}{d\theta}(\tilde{\theta})\frac{R(\tilde{\theta})}{f(\ell(\tilde{\theta}))} - \frac{dR(\tilde{\theta})}{d\tilde{\theta}} = 0. \tag{5.2}$$

The first-order condition of incentive compatibility is that equation 5.2 be true at $\tilde{\theta} = \theta$ for all θ, so that

$$\frac{dR}{d\theta} = \tfrac{1}{2}\theta\, f'(\ell(\theta))\frac{d\ell}{d\theta}(\theta)\left(1 + \frac{R(\theta)}{\theta\, f(\ell(\theta))}\right) \qquad \forall\theta. \tag{5.3}$$

As equation 5.2 is linear in θ, the local necessary condition is here sufficient (see Guesnerie and Laffont 1984) and can be written

$$\frac{d\ell}{d\theta}(\theta) \geqslant 0 \qquad \forall\theta. \tag{5.4}$$

The maximization program can be written as an optimal control program as follows[10]:

$$\text{Max} \int_{\theta^*}^{\bar{\theta}} \left\{ \int_0^{R(\theta)/\theta f(\ell(\theta))} [s\theta\, f(\ell(\theta)) - c]\, ds + R(\theta)\left(1 - \frac{R(\theta)}{\theta\, f(\ell(\theta))}\right) - (1 + r)\,\ell(\theta) \right\} d\theta \tag{5.5}$$

T.Q.

$$\frac{dR}{d\theta} = \tfrac{1}{2}\theta\, f'(\ell(\theta))\frac{d\ell}{d\theta}\left(1 + \frac{R(\theta)}{\theta\, f(\ell(\theta))}\right), \qquad \theta \in [\theta^*, \bar{\theta}] \tag{5.6}$$

$$\frac{d\ell}{d\theta} \geqslant 0, \tag{5.7}$$

$$\theta\, f(\ell(\theta)) \int_{R(\theta)/\theta f(\ell(\theta))}^{\bar{\theta}} s\, ds - R(\theta)\left(1 - \frac{R(\theta)}{\theta\, f(\ell(\theta))}\right) \geqslant \underline{v}^{11} \tag{5.8}$$

for any $\theta \in [\theta^*, \bar{\theta}]$ and $\theta^* \in [\underline{\theta}, \bar{\theta}]$.

The Pontryagin principle enables us to describe the optimal solution $(\ell^*(\cdot), R^*(\cdot))$. In particular we obtain:

Proposition 6. The optimal mechanism $(\ell^*(\cdot), R^*(\cdot))$ is such that

$$\tfrac{1}{2}\theta\, f'(\ell^*(\theta)) = (1 + r) + \tfrac{1}{2}c\frac{f'}{f}\left(1 - \frac{R^*(\theta)}{\theta\, f}\right) + \tfrac{1}{2}\delta_R f'\left(1 + \frac{R^*(\theta)}{\theta\, f}\right) \tag{5.8}$$

with $\delta_R \geqslant 0$. (Proof: see appendix 4.)

Equation 5.8 expresses the equality of the expected marginal productivity of investment with its opportunity cost, which has three elements:

i. $(1 + r)$, the financial cost.

ii. $\frac{1}{2}c(f'/f)(1 - R/\theta f)$, the cost associated with the marginal increase of the probability of bankruptcy, which results from a marginal increase of R.

iii. $\frac{1}{2}\delta_R f'(1 + R/\theta f)$, the opportunity cost due to the asymmetry of information, which is the marginal increase of the rent that the bank must leave to firms for incentive reasons.

We can observe that the two asymmetries of information (nonobservability of production levels and ignorance of θ) are combined additively at the level of first-order conditions because

$$\frac{1}{2}c\frac{f'}{f}\left(1 - \frac{R}{\theta f}\right) = E\,\tilde{s}c\frac{f'}{f}(1 - \psi),$$

which is nothing but the term that we obtained in equation 3.6 in the saturated case. Because of the rent due to the asymmetry of information about θ, all firms except firm θ^* are somehow in the nonsaturated case. This shows the relevance of the study of the nonsaturated case as soon as adverse selection is introduced.

A complete study should then establish the impact of c on the sensitivity of business conditions for the solution of the system of differential equations which describe the first-order conditions. In general, the distortions due to adverse selection depend heavily on the particular specifications of the models and cannot expect general results here.

6. Conclusion

In the presence of auditing costs, the bank has two control variables, the level of loan and the required amount of reimbursement which defines the expected rate of bankruptcy. The marginal rate of substitution between these two variables is a complex object, both for the firm and for the bank, giving rise to multiple nonconvexities.

When these difficulties can be ignored and the quasi-concavity of objective functions holds, the existence of an audit cost, which can be considered as small but not negligible, does not invalidate the intuitions one may have on this problem. Moreover, some confirmation of the idea that asymmetries of information increase the sensitivity of the economy to business conditions can then be obtained. The intuition of this effect is as follows.

When business conditions deteriorate, the level of investment decreases (because the expected marginal productivity decreases). Moreover, the cost of bankruptcies increases because less resources are obtained when bankruptcies occur and this effect increases with c. Surely, the optimization behavior of the bank, by decreasing the number of bankruptcies, creates an opposite effect. But, under concavity assumptions, it does not upset the first effect. In the saturated case, this intuition can be verified easily by differentiating equation 3.7. We obtain

$$\frac{d\ell}{d\theta} = -\frac{f'E\tilde{s} - c\dfrac{d^2\psi}{d\ell\, d\theta}}{\theta\, f''E\tilde{s} - c\dfrac{d^2\psi}{d\ell^2}},$$

with

$$\frac{d^2\psi}{d\ell\, d\theta} < 0 \text{ and } \frac{d^2\psi}{d\ell^2} < 0.$$

To the usual effect $-f'/\theta f''$ is added an effect due to the audit cost. Combined with various macroeconomic multipliers, this phenomenon contributes to the justification of the widespread belief that incomplete information aggravates business fluctuations.

We will note, however, the very restrictive nature of our assumptions and the fact that we have not obtained a similar result in the case of adverse selection. In conclusion, we will stress the need for more research on the design of banking contracts to determine more fully the sensitivity of the economy to the imperfections of capital markets before designing economic policies aimed at mitigating their negative effects.

Appendix 1

Case I

In the nonsaturated case the first-order conditions for problem 2.1 are

$$\theta\, f'(\ell)\left[\psi - \frac{\psi^2}{2}\right] = 1 + r \tag{A1.1}$$

and

$$\theta\, f(\ell)(1 - \psi) = c. \tag{A1.2}$$

At the optimal point, the determinant Δ is positive; hence

$$\frac{d\ell}{dr} = -\frac{\theta f}{\Delta} < 0,$$

$$\frac{d\ell}{dc} = -\frac{\theta f'(1-\psi)}{\Delta} < 0,$$

$$\frac{d\psi}{dr} = -\frac{\theta f'(1-\psi)}{\Delta} < 0,$$

and

$$\frac{d\psi}{dc} = -\frac{\theta f''\left(\psi - \frac{\psi^2}{2}\right)}{\Delta} < 0.$$

Case II

In the saturated case the first-order conditions and the constraint 2.2 imply

$$\tfrac{1}{2}\theta f'(\ell) - (1+r) - \frac{c}{2}(1-\psi)\frac{f'}{f} = 0$$

and

$$\tfrac{1}{2}\theta f(\ell)(1-\psi)^2 = \underline{v}(\theta).$$

We will first show that the determinant Δ of this equation system is positive:

$$\Delta = -\tfrac{1}{2}\theta^2 f'' f(1-\psi) + \frac{c}{2}\theta f(1-\psi)^2\left(\frac{f''}{f} - \frac{f'^2}{f^2}\right) - \frac{c}{4}\theta\frac{f'^2}{f}(1-\psi)^2.$$

The first-order conditions of the maximization are

$$\theta f'\left(\psi - \frac{\psi^2}{2}\right) - (1+r) + \mu_1 \theta f' \cdot \tfrac{1}{2}(1-\psi)^2 = 0, \tag{A1.3}$$

$$\theta f(1-\psi) - c - \mu_1 \theta f(1-\psi) = 0, \tag{A1.4}$$

and

$$\tfrac{1}{2}\theta f(1-\psi)^2 = \underline{v}(\theta). \tag{A1.5}$$

At the optimal point the Lagrangian function is concave in (ℓ, ψ) and therefore the determinant in (ℓ, ψ) of equations A1.3 and A1.4 is positive.

Since A1.4 implies $\mu_1 < 1$, this determinant is proportional to

$$-\theta^2 ff''\left(\psi - \frac{\psi^2}{2}\right) - \mu_1\theta^2 ff''\tfrac{1}{2}(1-\psi)^2 - (1-\mu_1)(\theta f'(1-\psi))^2,$$

which implies, making use of equation A1.4,

$$-\tfrac{1}{2}\theta^2 ff'' + \frac{c}{2}\theta f''(1-\psi) - c\theta\frac{f'^2}{f}(1-\psi) > 0. \qquad \text{(A1.6)}$$

Since we have

$$\Delta = (1-\psi)\left[-\tfrac{1}{2}\theta^2 ff'' + \frac{c}{2}\theta f''(1-\psi) - \tfrac{3}{4}c\theta\frac{f'^2}{f}(1-\psi)\right]$$

and since $1-\psi > 0$, equation A1.6 implies $\Delta > 0$. Therefore,

$$\frac{d\ell}{dr} = -\frac{\theta f(1-\psi)}{\Delta} < 0,$$

$$\frac{d\ell}{dc} = -\frac{\tfrac{1}{2}\theta(1-\psi)^2 f'}{\Delta} < 0,$$

$$\frac{d\psi}{dr} = -\frac{\tfrac{1}{2}\theta f'(1-\psi)^2}{\Delta} < 0,$$

and

$$\frac{d\psi}{dc} = \frac{-\tfrac{1}{4}\theta(1-\psi)^3(f'^2/f)}{\Delta} < 0.$$

Appendix 2

Case I

$$\frac{d\ell}{d\theta} = \frac{1}{\Delta}\left\{\theta ff'\left(1-\psi+\frac{\psi^2}{2}\right)\right\} > 0,$$

$$\frac{d\psi}{d\theta} = \frac{1}{\Delta}\theta(1-H(\psi))[I^-(\psi) + \psi(1-H(\psi))][-ff'' + f'^2] > 0.$$

Case II

$$\Delta\frac{d\ell}{d\theta} = \tfrac{1}{2}\theta ff'(1-\psi) - \frac{c}{2}\frac{f'}{f}\frac{d}{d\theta}\left(\frac{\underline{v}(\theta)}{\theta}\right),$$

$$\Delta \frac{d\psi}{d\theta} = \tfrac{1}{4}\theta\, f'^2(1-\psi)^2 - \frac{d}{d\theta}\frac{\underline{v}(\theta)}{\theta}\left[-\tfrac{1}{2}\theta f'' + \frac{c}{2}(1-\psi)\frac{d}{d\ell}\left(\frac{f'}{f}\right)\right].$$

Therefore, if c is small enough or if

$$\frac{d}{d\theta}\left(\frac{\underline{v}(\theta)}{\theta}\right) < 0,$$

we obtain

$$\frac{d\ell}{d\theta} > 0;$$

if c is small enough and

$$\frac{d}{d\theta}\left(\frac{\underline{v}(\theta)}{\theta}\right) < 0,$$

we have

$$\frac{d\psi}{d\theta} > 0.$$

Appendix 3

Case I

$$\Delta \frac{d\ell}{d\theta} = \theta\, ff'\left[\psi - \frac{\psi^2}{2} + (1-\psi)^2\right],$$

$$\Delta \left.\frac{d^2\ell}{d\theta dc}\right|_{c=0} = \theta\left(\psi - \frac{\psi^2}{2} + (1-\psi)^2\right)\frac{d}{d\ell}(ff')\left.\frac{d\ell}{dc}\right|_{c=0}$$

$$- \theta\, ff'(1-\psi)\left.\frac{d\psi}{dc}\right|_{c=0} - \left.\frac{d\ell}{d\theta}\right|_{c=0}\left.\frac{d\Delta}{dc}\right|_{c=0},$$

$$\Delta = -\theta^2\, ff''(\psi - (\psi^2/2)) - \theta^2\, f'^2(1-\psi)^2,$$

$$\left.\frac{d\Delta}{dc}\right|_{c=0} = -\theta^2\left(\psi - \frac{\psi^2}{2}\right)\frac{d}{d\ell}(ff'')\frac{d\ell}{dc} - \theta^2(1-\psi)\, ff''\frac{d\psi}{dc}$$

$$+ 2\theta^2\, f'^2(1-\psi)\frac{d\psi}{dc} - 2\theta^2\, f'f''(1-\psi)^2\frac{d\ell}{dc},$$

$$\left.\frac{d\ell}{d\theta}\right|_{c=0} = \frac{1}{\Delta}\theta\, ff'\left(\psi - \frac{\psi^2}{2} + (1-\psi)^2\right),$$

$$\Delta\left.\frac{d^2\ell}{d\theta dc}\right|_{c=0} = -\theta\, ff'(1-\psi)\left.\frac{d\psi}{dc}\right|_{c=0}$$
$$+ \left.\frac{d\ell}{d\theta}\right|_{c=0}\left[\theta^2(1-\psi)\, ff''\frac{d\psi}{dc} - 2\theta^2 f'^2(1-\psi)\frac{d\psi}{dc}\right]$$
$$+ \frac{1}{\Delta}\left.\frac{d\ell}{dc}\right|_{c=0}\left[\theta\left(\psi - \frac{\psi^2}{2} + (1-\psi)^2\right)\frac{d}{d\ell}(ff')\right.$$
$$\times\left(-\theta^2\, ff''\left(\psi - \frac{\psi^2}{2}\right) - \theta^2 f'^2(1-\psi)^2\right)$$
$$+ \theta\, ff'\left(\psi - \frac{\psi^2}{2} + (1-\psi)^2\right)$$
$$\left.\times\left(\theta^2\left(\psi - \frac{\psi^2}{2}\right)\frac{d}{d\ell}(ff'') + 2\theta^2 f'f''(1-\psi)^2\right)\right]. \quad \text{(A3.1)}$$

The first two terms are positive. We examine the last one, which has the same sign as

$$\theta^3\left(\psi - \frac{\psi^2}{2} + (1-\psi)^2\right)\left[\left(\psi - \frac{\psi^2}{2}\right)\left[ff''\frac{d}{d\ell}(ff') - ff'\frac{d}{d\ell}(ff'')\right]\right.$$
$$\left. + (1-\psi)^2\left[f'^2\frac{d}{d\ell}(ff') - ff'^2f''\right]\right]$$
$$= \theta^3\left(\psi - \frac{\psi^2}{2} + (1-\psi)^2\right)$$
$$\times\left[\left(\psi - \frac{\psi^2}{2}\right)[f^2f''^2 - f^2f'ff'''] + (1-\psi)^2 f'^4\right].$$

This term is positive if $f''' < 0$. If this is not the case, the second term is positive but the first one is negative. We combine it with the second term of equation A3.1, and obtain a term *proportional* to

$$-f'[f^2f'f''' - f^2f''^2] + ff'[ff''^2 - 2f'^2f'']$$
$$= -f'^2f^2f''' + 2f'f^2f''^2 - 2ff'^3f''$$
$$= \alpha^4(1-\alpha)\,\ell^{5\alpha-5} > 0 \text{ if } f(\ell) = \ell^\alpha, \quad \alpha < 1.$$

Case II

It is possible to rewrite the problem with the individual rationality constraint divided by θ. We obtain

$$\Delta \frac{d\ell}{d\theta} = \tfrac{1}{2}\theta\, ff'(1-\psi) - \frac{c}{2}\frac{f'}{f}\frac{d}{d\theta}\left(\frac{\underline{v}(\theta)}{\theta}\right),$$

$$\Delta \frac{d^2\ell}{d\theta\, dc}\bigg|_{c=0} = -\frac{1}{2}\frac{f'}{f}\frac{d}{d\theta}\left(\frac{\underline{v}(\theta)}{\theta}\right) + \tfrac{1}{2}\theta(1-\psi)\frac{d}{d\ell}(ff')\frac{d\ell}{dc}$$
$$- \tfrac{1}{2}\theta\, ff'\frac{d\psi}{dc} - \frac{d\ell}{d\theta}\bigg|_{c=0}\frac{d\Delta}{dc}\bigg|_{c=0},$$

$$\frac{d\Delta}{dc}\bigg|_{c=0} = \tfrac{1}{2}\theta(1-\psi)^2 f'' - \tfrac{3}{4}\theta\frac{f'^2}{f}(1-\psi)^2 + \tfrac{1}{2}\theta^2\, ff''\frac{d\psi}{dc}$$
$$- \tfrac{1}{2}(1-\psi)\,\theta^2\frac{d\ell}{dc}\frac{d}{d\ell}(ff''),$$

$$\frac{d\ell}{d\theta}\bigg|_{c=0} = \frac{\tfrac{1}{2}\theta\, ff'(1-\psi)}{-\tfrac{1}{2}\theta^2\, ff''(1-\psi)} = -\frac{f'}{\theta f''},$$

$$\Delta \frac{d^2\ell}{d\theta\, dc}\bigg|_{c=0} = -\frac{1}{2}\frac{f'}{f}\frac{d}{d\theta}\left(\frac{\underline{v}(\theta)}{\theta}\right) + \tfrac{1}{2}\theta(1-\psi)\frac{d}{d\ell}(ff')\frac{d\ell}{dc}$$
$$+ f'(1-\psi)^2 - \frac{3}{4}\frac{f'^3}{ff''}(1-\psi)^2$$
$$- \tfrac{1}{2}(1-\psi)\,\theta\frac{d\ell}{dc}\frac{f'}{f''}\frac{d}{d\ell}(ff'')$$
$$= -\frac{1}{2}\frac{f'}{f}\frac{d}{d\theta}\left(\frac{\underline{v}(\theta)}{\theta}\right) + \tfrac{1}{2}(1-\psi)^2\left(\frac{f'^3}{ff''} + f'\right) + \tfrac{1}{2}f'(1-\psi)^2$$
$$- \frac{3}{4}\frac{f'^3}{ff''}(1-\psi)^2 - \tfrac{1}{2}(1-\psi)^2\left[\frac{f'^3}{ff''} + \frac{f'^2 f'''}{f''^2}\right]$$
$$= (1-\psi)^2\left[f' - \tfrac{3}{4}\frac{f'^3}{ff''} - \tfrac{1}{2}\frac{f'^2 f'''}{f''^2}\right] - \frac{1}{2}\frac{f'}{f}\frac{d}{d\theta}\left(\frac{\underline{v}(\theta)}{\theta}\right).$$

Since $\underline{v}(\theta)$ is non-increasing, $f''' < 0$ is sufficient to ensure that this expression is positive.

When the production function is of type ℓ^α, this term is proportional to $-2\alpha/(\alpha - 1)$, and therefore it is also positive.

Appendix 4

The bank's optimization problem may be stated as a control problem with ℓ and R as the state variables and $\Gamma = d\ell/d\theta$ as the control variable.

$$\operatorname{Max} \int_{\theta^*}^{\bar{\theta}} \left\{ \int_0^{R(\theta)/\theta f(\ell(\theta))} [s\theta\, f(\ell(\theta)) - c]\, ds + R(\theta)\left(1 - \frac{R(\theta)}{\theta\, f(\ell(\theta))}\right) - (1 + r)\ell(\theta) \right\} d\theta, \tag{A4.1}$$

$$\frac{dR}{d\theta} = \tfrac{1}{2}\theta\, f'(\ell(\theta))\,\Gamma(\theta)\left(1 + \frac{R(\theta)}{\theta\, f(\ell(\theta))}\right), \tag{A4.2}$$

$$\frac{d\ell}{d\theta} = \Gamma(\theta), \tag{A4.3}$$

$$\tfrac{1}{2}\theta_*\, f(\ell(\theta_*))\left(1 - \frac{R^2(\theta_*)}{\theta_*^2\, f(\ell(\theta_*))}\right) - R(\theta_*)\left(1 - \frac{R(\theta_*)}{\theta_*\, f(\ell(\theta_*))}\right) = \underline{v}, \tag{A4.4}$$

$$\Gamma \geqslant 0. \tag{A4.5}$$

We assume here that $\underline{v}$ is sufficiently large so that θ_* corresponds to the saturated case (with equality in A4.5).

The optimality conditions are given by the Pontryagin equations. In particular, we have

$$-\dot{\boldsymbol{\delta}}_\ell = \tfrac{1}{2}\frac{Rf'}{\theta f^2}(R + 2c) + \tfrac{1}{2}\theta\delta_{\mathbf{R}} f''\left(1 + \frac{R}{\theta f}\right)\Gamma - \tfrac{1}{2}\delta_{\mathbf{R}}\frac{\theta f'^2}{f^2}R\Gamma - (1 + r), \tag{A4.6}$$

$$-\dot{\boldsymbol{\delta}}_{\mathbf{R}} = -\frac{R + c}{\theta f} + 1 + \tfrac{1}{2}\delta_{\mathbf{R}}\frac{f'}{f}\Gamma, \tag{A4.7}$$

$$\Gamma^* = \operatorname*{argmax}_{\Gamma}\left\{-\frac{1}{2}\frac{R^2}{\theta f} - c\frac{R}{\theta f} + R - (1 + r)\ell + \delta_{\mathbf{R}}\tfrac{1}{2}\theta\, f'\left(1 + \frac{R}{\theta f}\right)\Gamma + \delta_\ell\Gamma\right\}. \tag{A4.8}$$

For $\Gamma > 0$, equation A4.5 implies

$$\tfrac{1}{2}\delta_{\mathbf{R}}\theta\, f'\left(1 + \frac{R}{\theta f}\right) + \delta_\ell = 0. \tag{A4.9}$$

Differentiating equation A4.9, we have

$$\tfrac{1}{2}\delta_{\mathbf{R}}\frac{d}{d\theta}\left[\theta f'\left(1+\frac{R}{\theta f}\right)\right]+\tfrac{1}{2}\theta f'\left(1+\frac{R}{\theta f}\right)\dot{\delta}_{\mathbf{R}}+\dot{\delta}_{\ell}=0. \tag{A4.10}$$

Substituting in equation A4.10 the values of $\dot{\delta}_\ell$ and $\dot{\delta}_{\mathbf{R}}$ obtained in A5.6 and A5.7, we obtain

$$\tfrac{1}{2}\theta f'=(1+r)+\tfrac{1}{2}c\frac{f'}{f}\left(1-\frac{R}{\theta f}\right)+\tfrac{1}{2}\delta_{\mathbf{R}}f'\left(1+\frac{R}{\theta f}\right). \tag{A4.11}$$

To show that $\delta_{\mathbf{R}}$ is positive, it suffices to observe that, on the one hand $\delta_{\mathbf{R}}(\overline{\theta})=0$ (as implied by the transversality condition) and, on the other hand, equation A4.7, which we can rewrite as

$$\dot{\delta}_{\mathbf{R}}=-(1-\psi)+\frac{c}{\theta f}-\tfrac{1}{2}\delta_{\mathbf{R}}\frac{f'}{f}\Gamma,$$

implies for c small $\dot{\delta}_{\mathbf{R}}<0$ whenever $\delta_{\mathbf{R}}=0$. Therefore $\delta_{\mathbf{R}}>0$ for $\theta<\overline{\theta}$.

The above argument has assumed $\Gamma>0$ so that the second-order incentive constraint is not binding. If it is binding, $\Gamma=0$, and as before $\dot{\delta}_{\mathbf{R}}<0$ whenever $\Gamma=0$. Since the multiplier $\delta_{\mathbf{R}}$ is continuous in θ, this implies $\delta_{\mathbf{R}}(\theta)>0$ except, perhaps, on an interval $[\theta',\overline{\theta}]$ on which $\delta_{\mathbf{R}}(\theta)=0$.

Notes

1. This is not the macroeconomic model considered by Malinvaud.

2. An example of this type of argument may be found in Greenwald and Stiglitz (1987, p. 15): "A shock such as this increases the degree of asymmetry of information. This in turn... decreases the supply of funds available for investment."

3. Since the analysis is confined to one period the firm's cash flows also represent the market value of its assets.

4. In the analysis of the optimal contracts between the bank and the firms, $\underline{v}(\theta)$ can be interpreted in several ways. It may correspond to the utility reservation level below which the firm prefers to choose an alternative way of financing its projects (for instance by issuing stock). It may also be a way of representing its risk aversion or else its profits if it does not borrow. It is therefore quite natural to make $\underline{v}$ depend on θ. The general equilibrium interpretations that can be derived from the analysis will depend in a crucial way on the particular interpretation that is given to $\underline{v}$ (see section 4).

5. This will happen if $|f''|$ is sufficiently large and ψ has a lower bound strictly positive.

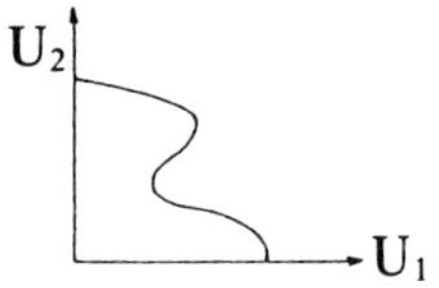

Figure 9.

6. A sufficient condition for $d\ell_1/d\psi/d\ell_2/d\psi$ to be monotonic, and therefore for the existence of, at most, two intersection points, is that

$$\frac{d}{d\ell}\left(-\frac{ff''}{f'^2}\right) \geqslant 0$$

a condition that is satisfied for $f(\ell) = \ell^\alpha$, $\alpha < 1$.

7. Under the convexity assumptions, the maximization of the objective function of one agent at a given (variable) level of the objective function of the other agent characterizes the efficiency frontier, independently of the order in which we take them. When the convexity conditions are not satisfied, on the one hand, we obtain necessary conditions that are not sufficient and, on the other hand, the order of the maximization does not imply the same results as it appears in Figure 9. The maximizaton of U_1 at the given level of U_2 may be simpler than the one of U_2 at a given level of U_1, which implies multiplicity of the solutions.

8. Equations 3.6 and 3.7 are slightly different. It must be noticed that $d\psi/d\ell$ does not exactly have the the same meaning in both cases.

9. We have defined $\tilde{s}$ as the "state of affairs." Nevertheless, since the production function is multiplicative an increase in θ is equivalent to a uniform increase of all the values of the random variable $\tilde{s}$.

10. We assume, in order to simplify the exposition, that the distribution of θ is uniform. Contrary to the assumption of the uniform distribution for the variable $\tilde{s}$, this assumption could be easily generalized to the usual monotonic hazard rate case.

11. We assume here that $\underline{v}$ is independent of θ. This assumption jointly with the incentive compatibility conditions implies that the left-hand side of equation 5.8 is superior everywhere to the right-hand side except for $\theta = \theta^*$. The constraints (5.8) on the state variables can then be replaced by a unique constraint on the border. Any dependence of $\underline{v}$ on θ that does not invalidate this property is compatible with the analysis developed (the assumption is that $\underline{v}(\theta)$ does not increase "too much" with θ).

References

de Meza, D., and D. Webb. 1987. "Too Much Investment: A Problem of Asymmetric Information." *Quarterly Journal of Economics* 102: 281–292.

Diamond, D. 1984. "Financial Intermediation and Delegated Monitoring." *Review of Economic Studies* 51: 393–414.

Gale, D., and M. Hellwig. 1985. "Incentive Compatible Debt Contracts: The One Period Problem." *Review of Economic Studies* 52: 647–664.

Guesnerie, R., and J. J. Laffont. 1984. "A Complete Solution to a Class of Principal Agent Problems with an Application to the Control of a Self-Managed Firm." *Journal of Public Economics* 25: 329–369.

Greenwald, B., and J. Stiglitz. 1987. "Money, Imperfect Information, and Economic Fluctuations." NBER WP 2188.

Jaffee, D., and T. Russel. 1976. "Imperfect Information and Credit Rationing." *Quarterly Journal of Economics* 90: 651–666.

Laffont, J. J., and E. Maskin. 1980. "The Theory of Incentives: An Overview." In W. Hildenbrand (ed.), *Advances in Economic Theory*. Cambridge University Press.

Levy-Garboua, V., and G. Maarek. 1985. *La Dette, Le Boom et la Crise*. Economica.

Malinvaud, E. 1987. "The Legacy of European Stagflation." *European Economic Review* 31: 53–65.

Mankiw, G. 1986. "The Allocation of Credit and Financial Collapse," *Quarterly Journal of Economics*. 101, 455–470.

Stiglitz, J., and A. Weiss. 1981. "Credit Rationing in Markets with Imperfect Competition." *American Economic Review* 71: 393–410.

15

Search and Aggregation in a Fixed-Price Equilibrium Model

C. Gouriéroux and
G. Laroque

1. Introduction

The concept of fixed-price equilibrium is a useful tool for economic analysis. Nevertheless as soon as we are interested in applications, it is not possible to keep at the macrolevel the assumption that the exchanged quantity equals the minimum of demand and supply. As discussed in particular by Muellbauer (1978), Muellbauer and Portes (1978), and Malinvaud (1983, second section), it is better to introduce smooth transitions between the regimes through aggregation.

The first approach to modelize these transitions consists in assuming the existence of a large number of goods and micromarkets. On each micromarket, the exchanged quantity equals the minimum of demand and supply, and, as a consequence, some spillover effects may occur. Since the micromarkets are heterogeneous and the spillover effects only partial, in general the suppliers will be rationed on some markets and the demanders on some other ones. Depending on the proportion of markets in excess supply or in excess demand, we will pass, for instance, continously from a regime of pure unemployment to a regime of full employment. A model with these characteristics has been proposed by Gouriéroux and Laroque (1985) and Martin (1987).

In this paper we try to develop a different approach. There is a single good, which is homogeneous concerning its physical characteristics and its price, but there are multiple localizations and *costs of search*, in the present case the cost of moving from one market to another one. The decision for search depends on the cost of moving and of the probability to be served, assumed to be expected rationally: it is the basis of the spillover effects. In other words, the prices are fixed and the waiting lines play a role to equilibrate the markets. This kind of model is linked to the efforts in the late 1970s to give some foundations to the notion of excess demand (Bohm and Levine 1979; Gale 1979, 1981; Heller and Starr 1979).

The presentation of the paper is as follows. In section 2 we describe the general framework. The decision of search is studied in section 3. The definition of a stationary search equilibrium and an existence theorem are given in section 4. In section 5, we present some elements concerning the resolution of the model and we describe some comparative statics properties, in the case of two markets. The proofs are gathered in the last section.

Several further developments might be considered. First, it should be possible to study a situation in which the price varies with the localization. In such a case, the agents could break an existing contract to move to another market and the analysis would be more complicated. It should also be possible to introduce a continuum of localizations, e.g., the real line. Indeed it would be interesting to determine an analytical expression for the number of occupied jobs, of unemployment, and of vacancies, to be able to perform some exercises of comparative statics, and to propose parametric formulations adapted for econometric purposes.

2. The Framework

We consider an economy with a continuum of buyers and sellers who meet pairwise to exchange a unit of an undifferentiated good. In the sequel it will be convenient to use the terminology associated with the labor market. The economy has a finite number of microeconomic exchange places, i.e., markets, indexed by s belonging to S. We assume that the price of the good evaluated in money is fixed and identical on all the markets. But for both buyers and sellers, it is costly to move from one market to another one.

We use a discrete time formulation: $t = 1, \ldots$. The populations of buyers and sellers are driven by an exogenous process. At each date t, in the city s, some new demanders and new suppliers arrive: their numbers are D_{NS} and O_{NS} respectively, and are strictly positive for any s. Furthermore a proportion of previously existing demanders and suppliers disappear at the beginning of each period. These vanishing agents are assumed to be drawn with the same probability δ, $0 < \delta < 1$, in the whole population.

The economy works in the following way. On each market the exchanged quantity equals the minimum of demand and supply. A random rationing scheme describes who are the participants in the exchange among the ones who are on the long side of the market. We assume that demanders and suppliers, who are participating together at $t - 1$ and survive at period t, remain together. Thus, the rationing may be effective only for the new agents or for the old ones who survive and are without partners;

these latter ones may have been rationed in the previous period or they may have had a partner who disappeared at the beginning of period t. These agents are all treated in a symmetric way vis-à-vis the rationing process. Finally the disequilibria that appear locally may be reduced by the spillover effects: given the costs of moving to and the probability of trading in the neighboring cities, the rationed agents may take the decision to migrate. This search process, the decisions to migrate, and the resulting exchanges are the aim of the present study.

3. The Decision to Migrate

The economy that we consider has a very simple structure.

Assumption 3.1. The buyers [resp. the sellers] are identical. They are risk neutral and get a null utility if they disappear. When a buyer [resp. a seller] exchanges, he earns a surplus $v^* - p$ [resp. $p - v^-$] during the period, where p is the price of the good. If no exchange occurs, the surplus is equal to zero. Finally the price is constrained by

$$v^+ > p > v^-$$

Assumption 3.2. To move from city s to city s', the cost supported by a buyer [resp. a seller] is $c^+(s', s)$ [resp. $c^-(s', s)$]. This cost shall be deduced from his surplus during the migration period. Functions c^+ and c^- are such that

$$c^+(s, s) = c^-(s, s) = 0, \qquad \forall s \in S,$$

$$\left.\begin{matrix} c^+(s', s) > 0 \\ c^-(s', s) > 0 \end{matrix}\right\}, \qquad \forall s, s' \in S, s \neq s'.$$

The price of the good is fixed and is the same on all the markets. To adjust to equilibrium the probabilities of exchange (or the average lengths of the queues) will replace the system of prices and may lead the agents to migrate. We search for a stationary equilibrium with rational expectations, i.e., an equilibrium in which the probabilities of exchange are correctly predicted by the agents. The decision of the rationed buyers [resp. sellers] depends on a vector π^+ [resp. π^-] of $[0, 1]^S$, where π_s^+ [resp. π_s^-] is the probability that on market s a buyer [resp. a seller] without a partner encounters a seller [resp. a buyer] during the period. For a stationary equilibrium these probabilities are time independent.

The analysis of the decision to migrate is similar for buyers and sellers. It is based on a classical problem of dynamic programming. At each date the agent is in one of the $2S$ states depending on the city s and on the fact that he has or does not have a partner. He has to choose an action in S, i.e., to decide the city s in which he wants to be at the next period. Then he will find a partner with the probability π_s, considered as given. For simplicity, let us omit for a moment the index $+$ or $-$: buyers and sellers have to solve the same kind of program. Let φ_s^{u} be the present value of the expected utility of an agent without partner in city s and φ_s^{a} be this value for an agent with a partner in the same city. The classical approach of dynamic programming gives the following system:

$$\varphi_s^{\mathrm{u}} = (1-\delta) \operatorname*{Max}_{s' \text{ in } S} [-c(s',s) + \pi_{s'} \varphi_{s'}^{\mathrm{a}} + (1-\pi_{s'}) \varphi_{s'}^{\mathrm{u}}],$$

$$\varphi_s^{\mathrm{a}} = v + (1-\delta)\{(1-\delta)\varphi_s^{\mathrm{a}} + \delta \operatorname*{Max}_{s' \text{ in } S} [-c(s',s) + \pi_{s'} \varphi_{s'}^{\mathrm{a}} + (1-\pi_{s'}) \varphi_{s'}^{\mathrm{u}}]\}. \tag{3.1}$$

Indeed, an agent without a partner earns nothing today and may choose his preferred city tomorrow by comparing the cost of moving with the expected gain. We obtain φ_s^{u}. Now the expression of φ_s^{a} is obtained by considering an agent with a partner; this agent has an immediate surplus [$v = v^+ - p$ for a buyer, $v = p - v^-$ for a seller] and if it survives at the next period, he remains paired off with probability $(1-\delta)$ and he has to look for another partner with probability δ.

The application of well-known results (see section 6) gives the existence of an optimal stationary plan and allows the description of some properties of this plan. If $\sigma^+(s)$ [resp. $\sigma^-(s)$] denotes the subset of s, giving the preferred displacements of a buyer [resp. a seller] without a partner in city s, this subset is a function of the probability vector π^+ [resp. π^-].

The migrations (or the spillovers) may be described through the transition probabilities $\mu(s',s)$, where $\mu(s',s)$ is the proportion of agents presently in s and deciding to move to s'. The matrix μ has nonnegative elements and is such that

$$\sum_{s' \text{ in } S} \mu(s',s) = 1, \qquad \forall s \in S. \tag{3.2}$$

We assume the existence of a continuum of agents in each city, which implies that the set $\mathscr{M}$ of the transition matrices is constrained only by equation 3.2.

The optimal search is defined through the subset $M^+(\pi^+)$ [resp. $M^-(\pi^-)$] of the matrices μ^+ [resp. μ^-] of $\mathscr{M}$ satisfying

$$\sum_{s' \text{ in } \sigma^+(s)} \mu^+(s', s) = 1, \qquad \forall s \in S$$

$$\left(\text{resp. } \sum_{s' \text{ in } \sigma^-(s)} \mu^-(s', s) = 1, \qquad \forall s \in S\right).$$

The next property, proved in section 6, is important to prove the existence of an equilibrium.

Theorem 3.3. $M^+(\pi^+)$ and $M^-(\pi^-)$ are hemi-upper continuous correspondences with convex values from $[0, 1]^s$ into $\mathcal{M}$.

Moreover since the price is the same on all the markets and since the migration cost is strictly positive, the agent does not move, if he is sure to find a partner in his city.

Theorem 3.4. If $\pi_s^+ = 1$, the demanders stay in s and $\mu^+(s, s) = 1$, for any μ^+ in $M^+(\pi^+)$. Similarly if $\pi_s^- = 1$, the suppliers stay in s and $\mu^-(s, s) = 1$, for any μ^- in $M^-(\pi^-)$.

This property is compatible with the assumption described before and the statement that individuals paired off at $t - 1$ and surviving at t remain paired off.

Finally migration loops cannot exist. If agents move from s_1 to s_2, from s_2 to $s_3, \ldots,$ from s_{k-1} to s_k with $s_i \neq s_j$, they cannot move from s_k to s_1 (this would imply some loss concerning the migration costs).

Theorem 3.5. If s_i, $i = 1, \ldots, k$ are different states of S, then s_{i+1} belongs to $\sigma^+(s_i)$ [resp. $\sigma^-(s_i)$] for $i = 1, \ldots, k - 1$, implies s_1 does not belong to $\sigma^+(s_k)$ [resp. $\sigma^-(s_k)$].

4. A Stationary Search Equilibrium

In order to understand the definition of the stationary equilibrium it is useful to first describe the (nonstationary) dynamics of the economy. Let us introduce the three vectors of $\mathbb{R}_+^s$, denoted E_t, V_t^+, and V_t^-, which measure the level of employment, of unemployment, and of vacancies at time t, on the markets s, s in S. If the migrations described by the matrices μ^+ and μ^- are given, the effective demand and supply, $\tilde{D}_t$ and $\tilde{O}_t$, of the agents who are without a partner at the beginning of period t have three origins: the newborn people (we assume that they cannot migrate during the first period), the surviving agents who were without a partner at $t - 1$, and finally the surviving agents whose partner disappears at the end of period $t-1$. Using Theorem 3.4, the paired agents do not move. With a survival rate equal to $(1-\delta)$, we get

$$\tilde{D}_t = D_N + (1-\delta)\,\mu^+(V_{t-1}^+ + \delta E_{t-1}),$$

$$\tilde{O}_t = O_N + (1-\delta)\,\mu^-(V_{t-1}^- + \delta E_{t-1}).$$

We assume that in each localization the exchanged quantity is equal to the number of agents previously paired plus the minimum of effective demand and supply. If Min(X, Y) [resp. Max] denotes the S-dimensional vector, whose sth component is the minimum [resp. maximum] of the associated components of X and Y, the equilibrium at date t is given by

$$E_t = (1-\delta)^2 E_{t-1} + \mathrm{Min}(\tilde{D}_t, \tilde{O}_t),$$

$$V_t^+ = \mathrm{Max}(O, \tilde{D}_t - \tilde{O}_t),$$

$$V_t^- = \mathrm{Max}(O, \tilde{O}_t - \tilde{D}_t).$$

This analysis explains the following definition of a *situation of stationary exchange*:

Definition 4.1. For given transition matrices μ^+ and μ^- in M, a situation of stationary exchange is a set of vectors (E, V^+, V^-) of $\mathbb{R}_+^s \times \mathbb{R}_+^s \times \mathbb{R}_+^s$, which satisfies the following conditions:

$$E = (1-\delta)^2 E + \mathrm{Min}(\tilde{D}, \tilde{O}),$$

$$V^+ = \mathrm{Max}(O, \tilde{D} - \tilde{O}),$$

$$V^- = \mathrm{Max}(O, \tilde{O} - \tilde{D}),$$

where

$$\tilde{D} = D_N + (1-\delta)\,\mu^+(V^+ + \delta E),$$

$$\tilde{O} = O_N + (1-\delta)\,\mu^-(V^- + \delta E).$$

It is now possible to close the model, i.e., to link the transition matrices to the disequilibria on the markets through the probabilities of finding a partner. Under the assumption that the agents are treated symmetrically concerning the rationing scheme, the probabilities of finding a partner are related to effective demand and supply by

$$\pi_s^+ = \mathrm{Min}\left[1, \frac{\tilde{O}_s}{\tilde{D}_s}\right], \qquad \pi_s^- = \mathrm{Min}\left[1, \frac{\tilde{D}_s}{\tilde{O}_s}\right].$$

The assumption ($O_{NS} > O, D_{NS} > 0$) and the fact that newborn people cannot move during the first period imply that the quantity $\tilde{O}_s/\tilde{D}_s$ is never undetermined, i.e., of the form 0/0. Therefore the probabilities π_s^+, π_s^- are well defined and at least one of these probabilities is equal to 1.

We deduce the natural definition of a *stationary search equilibrium.*

Definition 4.2. Let E, V^+, V^- be some vectors of $\mathbb{R}^s_+$ and π^+, π^- vectors of $[0, 1]^s$. $(E, V^+, V^-, \pi^+, \pi^-)$ is a stationary search equilibrium if there exists μ^+ and μ^- in $\mathcal{M}$, $\tilde{D}$ and $\tilde{O}$ in $\mathbb{R}^s_+$, which satisfy

i. μ^+ belongs to $M^+(\pi^+)$, μ^- belongs to $M^-(\pi^-)$;

ii. (E, V^+, V^-) is a situation of stationary exchange associated with (μ^+, μ^-) with

$$\tilde{D} = D_N + (1 - \delta)\,\mu^+(V^+ + \delta E),$$

$$\tilde{O} = O_N + (1 - \delta)\,\mu^-(V^- + \delta E).$$

iii. For any s in S,

$$\pi_s^+ = \text{Min}\left[1, \frac{\tilde{O}_s}{\tilde{D}_s}\right], \qquad \pi_s^- = \text{Min}\left[1, \frac{\tilde{D}_s}{\tilde{O}_s}\right].$$

Theorem 4.3. There exists a stationary search equilibrium. (Proof: see section 6.)

5. Toward Comparative Statics

In order to obtain formulations adapted for estimation and test purposes, it would be interesting to study the modifications of the equilibrium, when demand and supply vary through prices. The previous model is not easy to work with for this kind of problems (see section 5.1). However, analyses of some simple examples show that the properties may be very different from the ones usually obtained in the literature (see section 5.2).

5.1. How to Find the Equilibrium?

If the proof for the existence of the equilibrium is rather simple, the complete determination of the equilibrium is much more complicated. One method of resolution which gives an idea of the structure of the problem is as follows.

The system is not differentiable as soon as one of the maximum functions has a new determination. Thus, in a first step it is natural to study the problem for *a* given "regime," in an area where the solution is locally continuously differentiable. A regime is characterized by the following states: excess of supply or excess of demand on the markets and the possible moves $\sigma^+(s)$, $\sigma^-(s)$ of the agents, for any s. After a reindexation and without loss of generality we can assume that the m first markets are in excess supply and the $S - m$ remaining ones in excess demand. From Theorem 3.4, we know that $\sigma^+(s) = \{s\}$ for $s = 1, \ldots, m$ and that $\sigma^-(s) = \{s\}$, for $s = m + 1, \ldots, S$ (there are some other coherency conditions between the states of the markets and the migrations at equilibrium, as seen, for instance, in Theorem 3.5; we do not take them into account at this stage). Under these conditions the matrices μ^+ and μ^- can be written as

$$\mu^+ = \begin{bmatrix} I_m & B^+ \\ 0 & C^+ \end{bmatrix}, \qquad \mu^- = \begin{bmatrix} C^- & 0 \\ B^- & I_{S-m} \end{bmatrix}.$$

The elements of column s of matrix μ sum up to one and the element of row s' is nonzero iff s' belongs to $\sigma(s)$. Therefore, for a given regime there are $\# \sigma(s) - 1$ free parameters to determine in each column and therefore $\sum_{s=1}^{S} [\# \sigma^+(s) + \# \sigma^-(s)] - 2S$ unknown parameters in matrices μ^+ and μ^-.

We know that V_s^+ is equal to zero for the first m markets and to $\tilde{D}_s - \tilde{O}_s$ for the $S - m$ last ones, that V_s^- is equal to $\tilde{O}_s - \tilde{D}_s$ for the first m markets and to zero for the $S - m$ last ones. Then some tedious matricial computations give the vectors $\tilde{E}$, $\tilde{D}$, O, V^+, V^- as functions of μ^+ and μ^- from definition 1.1. For instance, let us denote

$$A^+ = (1 - \delta) B^+ (I_{S-m} - (1 - \delta) C^+)^{-1},$$

$$A^- = (1 - \delta) B^- (I_m - (1 - \delta) C^-)^{-1},$$

and the vector E_m of the number of employed people on the first m markets is given by

$$\frac{1}{2 - \delta} (I_m - (1 - \delta)^2 A^+ A^-) E_m = D_m + A^+ D_{S-m} - (1 - \delta) A^+ O_{S-m}$$

$$- (1 - \delta)^2 A^+ A^- O_m,$$

where D_m and O_m are the vectors containing the first m components of D_N and O_N, D_{s-m} and O_{s-m} the last $S - m$ ones. Similar formulas give the other characteristics of the situation of stationary exchange. We deduce the expression of π^+ and π^- as functions of the matrices μ^+ and μ^-. To determine these matrices, we have to use equations 3.1, which characterise the migration for $s = 1, \dots S$, both for demand and supply sides:

$$\varphi_s^{\mathrm{u}} = (1-\delta)[-c(s',s) + \pi_{s'}\varphi_{s'}^{\mathrm{a}} + (1-\pi_{s'})\,\varphi_{s'}^{\mathrm{u}}], \qquad \forall s' \in \sigma(s),$$

$$\varphi_s^{\mathrm{a}} = v + (1-\delta)^2\,\varphi_s^{\mathrm{a}} + \delta\varphi_s^{\mathrm{u}}.$$

This system contains $\sum_{s=1}^{S}[\#\sigma^+(s) + \#\sigma^-(s)] + 2S$ equations for the $4S$ unknown quantities $(\varphi_s^{\mathrm{u}}, \varphi_s^{\mathrm{a}})$ corresponding to the both sides of the markets and the $\sum_{s=1}^{S}[\#\ \sigma^+(s) + \#\ \sigma^-(s)] - 2S$ parameters to determine in μ^+ and μ^- (π^+ and π^- are functions of μ^+ and μ^-). When this system is solved, we have to check the inequalities:

$$\tilde{O}_s - \tilde{D}_s \geqslant 0, \qquad \text{for } s = 1, \dots, m,$$

$$\tilde{D}_s - \tilde{O}_s \geqslant 0, \qquad \text{for } s = m+1, \dots, S,$$

and, for any s

$$\varphi_s^{\mathrm{u}} \geqslant (1-\delta)[-c(s',s) + \pi_{s'}\varphi_{s'}^{\mathrm{a}} + (1-\pi_{s'})\,\varphi_{s'}^{\mathrm{u}}], \quad \text{for } s' \text{ in } S/\sigma(s).$$

Since this structure is rather complicated, we have no general result on the number of equilibria (uniqueness (?)), or on the way the quantities and the regimes the equilibrium depend on the exogenous variables.

Nevertheless, we can easily derive inequalities satisfied by the exchanged quantities. Indeed a direct analysis of condition 4.1 shows that

$$\sum_{s=1}^{S} E_s \leqslant \frac{1}{\delta}\operatorname{Min}\left[\sum_{s=1}^{S} O_s, \sum_{s=1}^{S} D_s\right], \tag{5.1}$$

since the number of occupied jobs cannot be larger than the number of employed people or the number of available jobs. From theorem 3.4, we have either $\pi_s^+ = 1$ and $E_s \geqslant D_s/\delta$ or $\pi_s^- = 1$ and $E_s \geqslant O_s/\delta$. Therefore

$$E_s \geqslant \frac{1}{\delta}\operatorname{Min}(O_s, D_s), \qquad s = 1, \dots, S. \tag{5.2}$$

The lower bound of inequalities 5.2 are attained when the costs of moving are infinite.

To have a more precise idea of the properties of comparative statics of the model we are now considering the particular case of two markets.

5.2. The Nonconcavity of Total Employment

If we assume that supply and demand are, respectively, increasing and decreasing functions of the price, it is interesting to study how the total

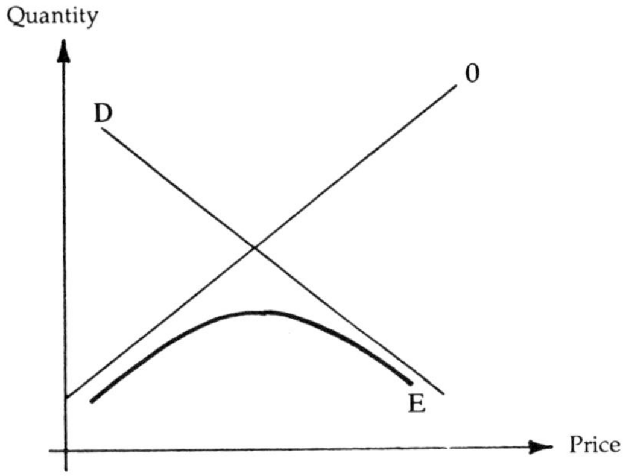

Figure 1.

exchanged quantity depends on the price. In the linear case, the studies existing in the literature typically find a concave curve, located below aggregated demand and supply and asymptotic to these curves for small and large values of p (see figure 1).

What arises for the present model? Let us consider two localizations with, for instance,

$$\frac{O_1}{\delta} = \alpha_1 p, \qquad \frac{O_2}{\delta} = \alpha_2 p,$$

$$\frac{D_1}{\delta} = -\beta_1 p + \gamma_1, \qquad \frac{D_2}{\delta} = -\beta_2 p + \gamma_2,$$

where $\alpha_1, \beta_1, \gamma_1, \alpha_2, \beta_2, \gamma_2 > 0$.

Let $p_1^e = \gamma_1/(\alpha_1 + \beta_1)$ be the equilibrium price on market 1 and $p_2^e = \gamma_2/(\alpha_2 + \beta_2)$ the equilibrium price on market 2 and let us assume $p_1^e < p_2^e$.

If the search costs are very large (infinite), there exists no spillover and total employment is given by

$$E = \begin{cases} \dfrac{O_1 + O_2}{\delta}, & \text{if } p \leqslant p_1^e \\[2ex] \dfrac{D_1 + O_2}{\delta}, & \text{if } p_1^e \leqslant p \leqslant p_2^e \\[2ex] \dfrac{D_1 + D_2}{\delta}, & \text{if } p_2^e \leqslant p \end{cases}$$

and corresponds to the curve $OA_1\ A_2B$ on figure 2.

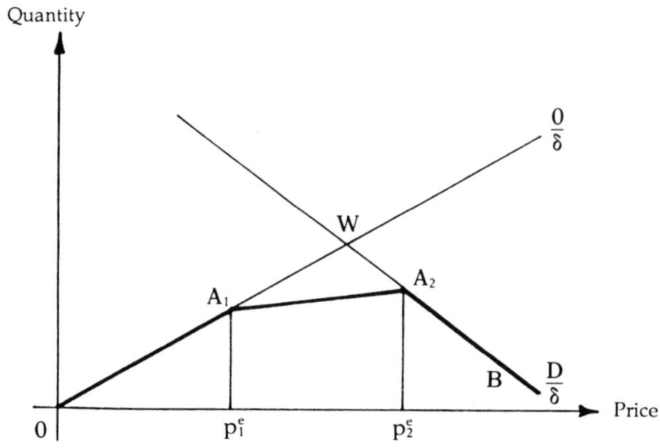

Figure 2.

From this basic situation we can study the modification of the equilibrium, when the cost of moving c from market 1 to market 2 for the suppliers diminishes, all other costs remaining infinite.

From the properties proved at the end of the previous subsection the segments OA_1 and A_2B of figure 2 are unchanged. Furthermore, if p is between p_1^e and p_2^e, market 1 is always in excess supply: $\pi_1^+ = 1$; indeed, if π_1^- was equal to one, the suppliers would not move to market 2 (see Theorem 3.4) and this would imply $\tilde{O}_1 \geqslant O_1/\delta$; moreover the demanders do not migrate since their costs are infinite: $\tilde{D}_1 = D_1/\delta$, but in such a case we would have $\pi_1^- = \tilde{D}_1/\tilde{O}_1 = D_1/O_1 < 1$, i.e., a contradiction.

In summary the exchanged quantity on market 1 is

$$E_1 = \frac{D_1}{\delta},$$

and if F_1/δ is the number of suppliers migrating from 1 to 2, we get

$$\tilde{O}_1 = \frac{O_1 - F_1}{\delta}, \qquad \tilde{O}_2 = \frac{O_2 + F_1}{\delta}, \qquad \tilde{D}_2 = \frac{D_2}{\delta}.$$

From Definition 4.1, we shall have $\tilde{O}_1 > O_1$, or

$$(1 - \delta) O_1 \geqslant F_1 \geqslant 0.$$

Therefore market 1 is always in excess supply for $p_1^e < p < p_2^e$.

We do not know *a priori* if market 2 is in excess demand ($\pi_2^- = 1$) or in excess supply ($\pi_2^+ = 1$). If it is in excess demand with $F_1 = 0$, then $E_2 =$

O_2/δ and, for the associated values of the price, the curve giving the aggregate employment is a piece of segment A_1A_2. If market 2 is in excess supply ($\pi_2^+ = 1$), then $F_2 = D_2/\delta$ and aggregate employment equals total demand: for the associated values of p, the point that is representative of the employment situation is on the segment WA_2.

The new case to consider corresponds to excess demand on market 2 ($\pi_2^- = 1$) with migration of suppliers from market 1 to market 2 ($F_1 > 0$). The study of this intermediate situation will simultaneously give the domains on which the two previously described cases occur.

To describe these other situations, we have first to reconsider the decision of migration (3.2). Since $\pi_2^- = 1$ for the agents of market 2, we get

$$\varphi_2^{\mathrm{a}} = \frac{v}{\delta}.$$

If the suppliers without partners stay on market 1, they obtain

$$\tilde{\varphi}_1^{\mathrm{u}} = \frac{(1-\delta)\,\pi_1^-\,v}{\delta[(2-\delta)\,\delta + (1-\delta)^2\,\pi_1^-]},$$

and it is easily seen that the suppliers stay on market 1 if

$$\tilde{\varphi}_1^{\mathrm{u}} > -(1-\delta)\,c + (1-\delta)\,\varphi_2^{\mathrm{a}} \qquad (F_1 = 0),$$

that they are indifferent between staying and migrating if

$$\tilde{\varphi}_1^{\mathrm{u}} = -(1-\delta)\,c + (1-\delta)\,\varphi_2^{\mathrm{a}} \qquad (0 \leqslant F_1 \leqslant (1-\delta)\,O_1),$$

and that they all migrate if

$$\tilde{\varphi}_1^{\mathrm{u}} < -(1-\delta)\,c + (1-\delta)\,\varphi_2^{\mathrm{a}} \qquad (F_1 = (1-\delta)\,O_1).$$

Let us introduce the ratio

$$\pi_1^* = \frac{\varphi(2-\delta)(v-c\delta)}{v-(v-v\delta)(1-\delta)^2}.$$

π_1^* is an increasing function of c and is equal to 1 if $c = 0$. Then the previous discussion gives the following implications:

$$\pi_1^- > \pi_1^* \Rightarrow F_1 = 0,$$

$$\pi_1^- = \pi_1^* \Rightarrow (1-\delta)\,O_1 \geqslant F_1 \geqslant 0, \tag{5.3}$$

$$\pi_1^- < \pi_1^* \Rightarrow F_1 = (1-\delta)\,O_1.$$

Since by definition

$$\pi_1^- = \frac{D_1}{O_1 - F_1}$$

it is natural to introduce the price p' such that

$$\frac{D_1(p')}{O_1(p')} = \frac{-\beta_1 p' + \gamma_1}{\alpha_1 p'} = \pi_1^*.$$

p' is a strictly decreasing function of c and is equal to p_1^* if $c = 0$ ($\pi_1^* = 0$ for $c = 0$). The interesting case is for c small enough to have p' smaller than p_2^*. The employment on the market is then given by

$$p_1^* \leqslant p \leqslant p': \quad F_1 = 0, \quad E_2 = \frac{O_2}{\delta},$$

$$p' \leqslant p \leqslant p_2^*: \quad E_2 = \frac{1}{\delta}\mathrm{Min}\left[O_2 + O_1 - \frac{D_1}{\pi_1^*}, O_2 + (1-\delta)O_1, D_2\right].$$

(The last equality is derived by noting that if $\pi_2^- = 1$: $F_1 = \mathrm{Min}(O_1 - D_1/\pi_1^*, (1-\delta)O_1)$ and $E_2 = D_2/\delta$ otherwise.) We immediately deduce the total quantity by adding $E_1 = D_1/\delta$ to E_2. Figure 3 describes a typical shape. The aggregate employment is still piecewise linear in this simple case. But immediately before p', E is equal to $[D_1 + O_2 + O_1 - D_1/\pi_1^*]/\delta$, with a slope $[\alpha_1 + \alpha_2 + \beta_1(1/\pi_1^* - 1]/\delta$, which is larger than the slope of the supply curve. Then *the exchanged quantity is not concave in the price.* Of

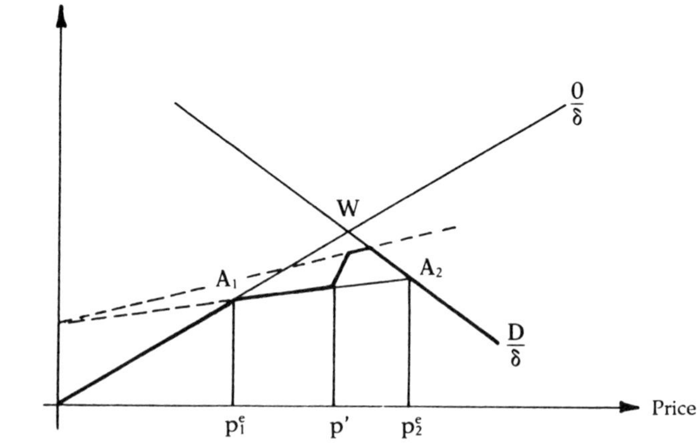

Figure 3.

course this phenomenon is a consequence of the cost of moving. When π_1^- becomes equal to π_1^* at price p', the whole excess supply which appears on market 1 during the price increase will pour out on market 2 and will create some new employments on this market. Moreover, in this particular case the exchanged quantity is a nonincreasing function of the cost of migration. We do not know if this property may be extended to an arbitrary number of markets.

6. Proofs

We first examine the decision of migration of a representative agent using Blackwell's technique (Blackwell 1965, theorem 7b).

Proofs of Theorem 3.3. Let us first note that the mapping F which associates to a vector $(\varphi^{\mathrm{u}}, \varphi^{\mathrm{a}})$ in $\mathbb{R}^s \times \mathbb{R}^s$ the R.H.S. of equation 3.1 is a contracting mapping. Indeed we easily check that

$$\varphi \geqslant \varphi' \text{ implies } F(\varphi) \geqslant F(\varphi'),$$

and

$$F(\varphi + \lambda e) = F(\varphi) + (1 - \delta)\lambda e,$$

where λ is a real number and e is a vector of $\mathbb{R}^s \times \mathbb{R}^s$ whose components are equal to 1.

If we choose

$$\lambda = \sup_s \sup(|\varphi_s^{\mathrm{a}'} - \varphi_s^{\mathrm{a}}|, |\varphi_s^{\mathrm{u}'} - \varphi_s^{\mathrm{u}}|) = \|\varphi' - \varphi\|,$$

the inequality $\varphi + \lambda e > \varphi'$ implies

$$F(\varphi) + (1 - \delta)\|\varphi' - \varphi\| e \geqslant F(\varphi'),$$

or, equivalently,

$$\|F(\varphi) - F(\varphi')\| \leqslant (1 - \delta)\|\varphi' - \varphi\|.$$

F, which is a contracting mapping, has a unique fixed point φ^* and this fixed point gives the expected utility at the optimum. Furthermore φ^* is a continuous function of the parameters appearing in F and in particular of π. Consequently the set of preferred moving of the agent $\sigma(s)$ is a function of π, which is a hemi-upper continuous correspondence from $[0, 1]^s$ into S and the same is true for the $M(\pi)$ function from $[0, 1]^s$ into $\mathcal{M}$.

Proof of Theorem 3.4. The elimination of φ^a from equation 5.1 gives

$$\varphi_s^{\mathrm{u}} = \frac{1-\delta}{2-\delta} \operatorname*{Max}_{s' \text{ in } S} \left\{ -(2-\delta)\, c(s',s) + [(2-\delta) - (1-\delta)\,\pi_{s'}]\, \varphi_{s'}^{\mathrm{u}} + \frac{\pi_{s'} v}{\delta} \right\}.$$

Therefore for any s there exists s' such that

$$\varphi_s^{\mathrm{u}} \leqslant \frac{1-\delta}{2-\delta} \left[(2-\delta-(1-\delta)\,\pi_{s'}]\, \varphi_{s'}^{\mathrm{u}} + \frac{\pi_{s'} v}{\delta} \right].$$

By choosing the city s that gives the maximum of φ_s^{u}, we deduce the existence of s' such that

$$\bar{\varphi} = \operatorname*{Max}_{s} \varphi_s^{\mathrm{u}} \leqslant \frac{(1-\delta)\,\pi_{s'} v}{\delta[(2-\delta)\,\delta + (1-\delta)^2\,\pi_{s'}]}.$$

The R.H.S. of this inequality is an increasing function of $\pi_{s'}$ and equals $(1-\delta)\,v/\delta$ when $\pi_{s'} = 1$. Since $c(s,s) = 0$ when $\pi_s = 1$, a direct look at the formula defining φ_s^{u} gives

$$\varphi_s^{\mathrm{u}} \geqslant \frac{(1-\delta)\,v}{\delta}.$$

Therefore $\bar{\varphi} = (1-\delta)\,v/\delta$, and there is no advantage in moving $[c(s',s) > 0]$ as soon as $\pi_s = 1$. Q.E.D.

Proof of Theorem 3.5. From the first inequality used in the previous proof we deduce when applied to s'

$$\varphi_{s'}^{\mathrm{u}} \leqslant \frac{1-\delta}{2-\delta} \left\{ [(2-\delta) - (1-\delta)\,\pi_{s'}]\, \varphi_{s'}^{\mathrm{u}} + \frac{\pi_{s'} v}{\delta} \right\}.$$

Therefore if s' belongs to $\sigma(s)$, we deduce that

$$\varphi_s^{\mathrm{u}} \leqslant -(1-\delta)\, c(s',s) + \varphi_{s'}^{\mathrm{u}}.$$

This implies

$$\varphi_{s_1}^{\mathrm{u}} \leqslant -(1-\delta) \sum_{i=1}^{k-1} c(s_{i+1}, s_i) + \varphi_{s_k}^{\mathrm{u}}.$$

If s_1 were in $\sigma(s_k)$, we would get

$$\varphi_{s_1}^{\mathrm{u}} \leqslant -(1-\delta) \sum_{i-1}^{k} c(s_{i+1}, s_i) + \varphi_{s_1}^{\mathrm{u}},$$

which is a contradiction. Q.E.D.

Proof of Theorem 4.3. Let us denote by K the convex compact subset of $\mathbb{R}_+^s \times \mathbb{R}_+^s \times \mathbb{R}_+^s$ defined by the values (E, V^+, V^-) satisfying

$$\begin{aligned} \delta\, {}^t e(E + V^+) &= {}^t e D_N, \\ \delta\, {}^t e(E + V^-) &= {}^t e D_N, \end{aligned} \qquad (6.1)$$

where e is the vector of $\mathbb{R}^s$ whose components are equal to 1. We define a correspondence of $K \times \mathcal{M} \times \mathcal{M}$ into $K \times \mathcal{M} \times \mathcal{M}$ in the following way: if $(E, V^+, V^-, \mu^+, \mu^-)$ is in $K \times \mathcal{M} \times \mathcal{M}$, we define

$$\tilde{D} = D_N + (1 - \delta)\, \mu^+ (V^+ + \delta E),$$

$$\tilde{O} = O_N + (1 - \delta)\, \mu^- (V^- + \delta E),$$

$$\bar{E} = (1 - \delta)^2 + \mathrm{Min}(\tilde{D}, \tilde{O}),$$

$$\bar{V}^+ = \mathrm{Max}(O, \tilde{D} - \tilde{O}),$$

$$\bar{V}^- = \mathrm{Max}(O, \tilde{O} - \tilde{D}),$$

$$\bar{\pi}_s^+ = \mathrm{Min}\left[1, \frac{\tilde{O}_s}{\tilde{D}_s}\right],$$

$$\bar{\pi}_s^- = \mathrm{Min}\left[1, \frac{\tilde{D}_s}{\tilde{O}_s}\right].$$

By construction $\bar{E}$, $\bar{V}^+$, $\bar{V}^-$, $\tilde{D}$, and $\tilde{O}$ are nonnegative. Furthermore, since μ^+ and μ^- are in $\mathcal{M}$, we have ${}^t e\mu^+ = {}^t e\mu^- = {}^t e$ and then $(\bar{E}, \bar{V}^+, \bar{V}^-)$ satisfies equation 6.1. Finally $\bar{E}$, $\bar{V}^+$, $\bar{V}^-$, $\bar{\pi}^+$, $\bar{\pi}^-$ are continuous functions of $(E, V^+, V^-, \mu^+, \mu^-)$. From Theorem 3.3 the correspondence which associates the set $[\bar{E}, \bar{V}^+, \bar{V}^-, M^+(\bar{\pi}^+), M^-(\bar{\pi}^-)]$ to $(E, V^+, V^-, \mu^+, \mu^-)$ is hemi-upper- continuous with convex values. From Kakutani's theorem, this correspondence has a fixed point and this fixed point is a stationary search equilibrium. Q.E.D.

References

Blackwell, D. 1965. "Discounted Dynamic Programming." *Annals of Mathematical Statistics* 36: 226–235.

Bohm, V., and P. Levine. 1979. "Temporary Equilibrium with Quantity Rationing." *Review of Economic Studies* 46(2): 361–378.

Gale, D. 1979. "Large Economies with Trading Uncertainty." *Review of Economic Studies* 46(2): 319–338.

Gale, D. 1981. "Large Economies with Trading Uncertainty: A Correction." *Review of Economic Studies*, 48(2): 363–364.

Gouriéroux, C., and G. Laroque. 1985. "The Aggregation of Commodities in a Quantity Rationing Model." *International Economic Review* 26(3): 681–699.

Heller, W. P., and R. M. Starr. 1979. "Unemployment Equilibrium with Myopic Complete Information." *Review of Economic Studies* 46(2): 339–360.

Malinvaud, E. 1983. *Essais sur la Théorie du Chômage*. Calmann-Lévy, Paris.

Martin, C. 1987. Disequilibrium Models with Dispersed Trading. Ph.D. Thesis, Birkbeck College.

Muellbauer, J. 1978. Macrotheory vs. Macroeconometrics: The Treatment of Disequilibrium in Macromodels. Discussion Paper 59, Birkbeck College.

Muellbauer, J., and R. Portes 1978. "Macroeconomic Models with Quantity Rationing." *Economic Journal* 88: 788–821.

16

Market Dynamics with Information Transmission Through Prices

G. Laffond and J. Lesourne

Economists have long noticed that when in an exchange process the information possessed by the various agents on the quality of the commodity exchanged differs, the uninformed agents try to infer the quality from the observed prices. More recently (Radner 1967), they have introduced the concept of a rational expectation equilibrium characterized by a function associating a price to every quality in such a way that, when the agents use their private information and the information revealed by the price, they express demand functions which lead to the same price. In other words, the price reveals to the uninformed agents the quality of the commodity supplied on the market. The existence of such equilibria has been studied among others by Lucas (1972), Green (1973, 1977), Radner (1979), Grossman (1981), and Milgrom and Stokey (1982), and a survey of the literature has been proposed by Jordan and Radner (1982). Laffont (1985) summarizes as follows the results obtained: "let m be the number of random variables and n the number of relative prices. If $m < n$, there exist generically fully revealing equilibria. If $m = n$, there exist robust counterexamples of inexistence. If $m > n$ there exist equilibria with noise when very discontinuous price functions are accepted."

The whole of this research concerns the study of equilibria. On the other hand, the dynamics of information transmission through prices on a market out of equilibrium and the convergence of such a market toward a fully revealing equilibrium have not been much explored. This is the topic of this paper. It is based on a research program on market dynamics developed at the laboratoire d'Econométrie of CNAM (Lesourne and Laffond 1979; Lesourne 1985; Laffond and Lesourne 1985). Therefore, it is useful to facilitate the understanding of the text by summarizing in a few sentences the key ideas embedded in this research.

In the model proposed in 1979, the quality of the commodity exchanged on the market is known and constant through time. The numbers of buyers and sellers are given, each seller having in any period a unit to sell and each buyer demanding a unit per period. Each buyer (each seller) is characterized by a maximum (minimum) price he is willing to accept for a transaction, but at the beginning of a given period, each buyer generally selects a lower ceiling price and each seller a higher bottom price. During a period, all the buyers become active on the market, one after another in a random order. When active, a buyer draws a random sample of sellers whom he visits, and shops, if possible, at a seller who still possesses a unit of good, to propose a bottom price lower than those of the other sellers visited and to propose a bottom price lower than the buyer's ceiling. The last seller from whom the buyer has bought is always among the sellers visited and this seller is ready to offer the same price as last time if he has not yet sold when the buyer is on the market. At the end of a period, buyers and sellers adapt their requirements for the next period, the buyers having not bought tending to increase their ceiling price and the sellers having not sold tending to decrease their bottom price. On such a market, three dynamic processes are at work: a search process, a negotiation process, and a requirements adjustment process. Under rather general assumptions, it may be shown that the market dynamics leads in a finite random time to a stable state, which is thereafter reproduced indefinitely. In this state, all the transactions are made at the same price and they occur between the sellers having a minimum price lower than or equal to this price and the buyers having a maximum price higher than or equal to this price, the number of these buyers and sellers being equal. Two assumptions are essential for the result: any seller has a nonzero probability of being visited during any period by any given buyer and buyers do not bear information costs.

Though slightly different, the model presented in this paper is based on similar ideas. Depending on the period, the exchanges concern one or the other of two qualities of the same commodity, the sellers and a subset of the buyers knowing the quality sold while the remaining buyers do not know about it but try to discover it from observations of the market evolution. Our goal is to examine whether the market state converges toward a stable state and whether the information on the quality is fully revealed in a stable state.

At the present stage of their development, dynamic models imply for their description numerous assumptions. Therefore, we shall have to study a set of related models which may exhibit different convergence properties.

The paper is divided into four parts: the first describes the models informally and sketches the main results obtained, the second develops the market dynamics when all the agents know the commodity quality and present the features of these dynamics, the third deals with the same questions when a subset of the buyers does not know initially the commodity quality, and the fourth considers the meaning of this first analysis of the dynamics of information transmission and discusses the future possible developments.

The mathematical proofs, which are lengthy, are not reproduced in the paper. They may be obtained on request.[1]

Models and Results: An Informal Presentation

We study the market dynamics for a commodity that may through successive periods correspond to two qualities, the quality being constant in a given period, but being liable to change from one period to the next. Sellers and a subset of buyers know the quality from the beginning of the period while the other buyers do not know it. Quality becomes common knowledge at the end of the period.

The two following situations may serve to illustrate the model:

- Sellers produce wine but in any period quality depends on climatic conditions. Sellers and informed buyers are able to infer the future quality of the product at the time of the harvest, while the uninformed buyers discover this quality only much later.
- Sellers distribute in a city a product coming from a developing country, the quality of which differs according to arrivals. Sellers and informed buyers are able to estimate through tests the quality of the batches, while the noninformed buyers discover the quality through use.

The sets of buyers and sellers are invariant from one period to the next, each seller wanting to sell and each buyer to buy a unit per period. All the buyers prefer the same quality.

During a period, all the buyers become successively active once and only once on the market, but the rank is a problem for the noninformed buyers since they have to observe transaction prices to infer the product quality. Therefore we have studied two extreme assumptions:

- The noninformed buyers start arriving on the market as soon as the first transaction has taken place and therefore mingle with the informed buyers (assumption P_1).
- The noninformed buyers arrive only after the informed buyers and therefore constitute a second wave of buyers (assumption P_2).

The noninformed buyer who arrives on the market tries simultaneously to make an assumption on the quality sold and to buy a unit:

• Hence, it is assumed first that he draws at random a sample of transaction prices and compares the observed average to two price indices associated to the qualities. He postulates that the quality sold is the one associated with the index, which is closer to the average.

• It is also assumed that he draws at random a sample of sellers, visits them in a random order one after another, proposes a price to them, and stops searching as soon as a seller accepts the proposal. This proposal may be different (and slightly more favorable for the buyer's privileged seller, if he exists, i.e., for the seller from whom the buyer has bought during the preceding period). Two assumptions are conceivable at this stage:

• the price proposal is made only to sellers still having one unit to sell (scenario V_1), or

• the price proposal is made to any seller (scenario V_2).

Symmetrically, each seller has chosen at the beginning of a period a bottom price above which he accepts the buyers' proposals. This bottom price may be different (and slightly lower) for the seller's privileged buyer if he exists, i.e., for the buyer to whom the seller has sold his unit during the preceding period.

When passing from one period to the next, the buyers have to adapt their price indices and their price proposal and the sellers have to adjust their bottom price.

• At the end of a period, every noninformed buyer learns which quality has been sold and consequently brings the corresponding price index closer to the average of observed transaction prices, while constraining the price index never to be lower for the better quality.

Simultaneously, every buyer adjusts his price proposal for the quality just sold increasing it—but not beyond a ceiling—if he has not been able to buy and decreasing it—except for the privileged seller—if he has bought a unit of the commodity.

But a question has to be raised: does the buyer also modify his price proposal for the other quality, knowing indeed that one of the qualities is uniformally preferred by all the buyers? We have explored the two assumptions: the assumption of a coupling between the markets by the buyers (C) and the assumption of no coupling (NC).

• As for the sellers, they take into account the price proposals they have received—in particular the maximum proposal—and the fact that they have or have not sold their unit.

When the bottom price is reduced, it is never beyond a minimum and when it is increased, it is so for all the buyers except for the privileged one.

The assumption of the existence for all the agents of a privileged buyer or seller is not gratuitous: since buyers and sellers do not know one another, a stable state can be reached only on the basis of stable relations between couples of a buyer and a seller but, for such relations to be maintained, more favorable price conditions have to be sought from agents other than the privileged one.

All the values are supposed to be integers and the adjustments to be equal to unit steps. Therefore a step represents simultaneously the price difference accepted by an agent to change his privileged partner and the variation of reservation prices from one period to the next (this assumption prevents, on the one hand, an increase in the number of equilibria and, on the other hand, the existence of fluctuations; it has the advantage of making sufficient for stability simple adaptive behaviors.[2]

We shall present the results under the hypothesis that the information on qualities is first complete and then reserved to given agents.

The Results with Complete Information

The introduction, when information is incomplete of assumptions P_1 and P_2 about the buyers' arrival, compels us to examine two basic models when information is complete:

• In the first one, all the buyers arrive in a single wave, all the orders of arrival having, in any period, a nonzero probability.

• In the second one, the buyers arrive in two waves, the orders of arrival being random inside each wave.

In the *first model*, the market converges in a finite time toward a stable state, which corresponds for each quality to the traditional equilibrium of elementary theory, the "demand curve" being obtained through a classification of buyers by decreasing order of their ceiling price and the "supply curve" through a classification of sellers by increasing order of their bottom price. The various stable states are equivalent since they correspond only to different allocations of actual sellers to actual buyers for each quality. E_0 will denote the set of those stable states.

In the *second model*, the market also converges towards a state of E_0 when the buyers make their proposals to any seller (scenario V_2). The reason is that in that case, the sellers take into account, when elaborating their requirements, the proposals of the second wave buyers, which prevents the breakdown of the market into two separate markets, one for the first wave and the other for the second.

On the contrary, in scenario V_1, the set of stable states contains states that are not equivalent, since actual sellers and buyers do differ, prices are not identical, and first wave buyers obtain for each quality a more favorable price than second wave buyers. *The stable state that is reached is determined by the random history of the market.* E_1 denotes the set of stable states when buyers do not couple the markets (assumption NC) and E_2 the set when the buyers do make the coupling (assumption C). In addition, it is useful to introduce the set E_3 of the stable states in which the first wave buyers buy from the sellers with minimum price requirements. The states in E_3 differ only through the allocation of sellers to buyers.

It may be shown that

$$E_3 \subset E_2 \subset E_1$$

and that

$$E_0 \subset E_2 \text{ but } E_0 \cap E_3 = \varnothing.$$

Figure 1 illustrates the results. Figure 1a corresponds to a unique wave of buyers. On this figure are reproduced the supply and demand curves of

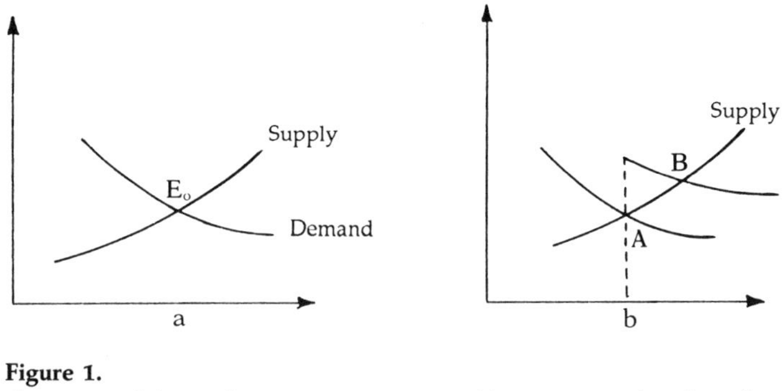

Figure 1.
Illustration of the results. (a) A unique wave of buyers. Reproduced are the supply and demand curves of all the agents, the set E_0 being represented by the intersection of the two curves; (b) two waves of buyers, the first wave being supposed to have discovered the sellers with minimum requirements: the set E_3 is represented by the two intersection points A and B.

all the agents, the set E_0 being represented by the intersection of the two curves; figure 1b corresponds to two waves of buyers, the first wave being supposed to have discovered the sellers with minimum requirements: the set E_3 is represented by the two intersection points A and B.

The Results with Incomplete Information

In the model with incomplete information, a market state is a couple constituted by a market state with complete information and by a set of price indices associated with the two qualities by noninformed buyers. In a stable state, the parameters do not depend on time, except the price indices, which may differ from one period to the next.

Thus, to the set E_0 corresponds a set F_0 of stable states which is obviously quality revealing since it corresponds to the traditional equilibria of elementary theory.

It may be shown that the market converges in probability in a finite time toward those traditional equilibria:

i. when noninformed buyers arrive on the market immediately after the first transaction (P_1), and

ii. when noninformed buyers constitute a second wave (P_2) and sellers have access to the whole set of price proposals (V_2).

In the second case, the knowledge of all the proposals by the sellers prevents the informed agents from gaining an advantage from arriving first and enables the noninformed buyers to infer the quality sold from the observed prices.

More complex is the situation in the case P_2V_1. It is then necessary to introduce the subset E_1' of the states in E_1 that are quality revealing and to consider separately the two following cases: $E_3 \subset E_1'$ and $E_3 \cap E_1' = \emptyset$ (the case in which the intersection of E_3 and E_1' is a nonempty set distinct from E_3 occurs only because the values are integers and may be neglected). Contrary to what happens for the model with complete information the result does not depend on the coupling assumption (C or NC):

i. If $E_3 \subset E_1'$, quality is revealed to noninformed buyers even when informed buyers capture all the sellers with minimum requirements. The market then converges in probability in a finite time toward a stable state in F_1' (extension of E_1' through addition of price indices). The state reached by the market will depend on its history and even if noninformed buyers discover quality, they have to accept prices less favorable than those obtained by informed buyers.

ii. If $E_3 \cap E'_1 = \varnothing$, quality is not revealed to noninformed buyers in the states of E_3. Then, the market does not always converge toward a stable state and does not necessarily reveal quality. Indeed, it may be shown that, as time passes, the market may either reach a stable state in F'_1 or enter irreversibly a subset A of unstable states, the noninformed buyers failing to infer quality from the transactions observed. This case results from the conjunction of three assumptions: noninformed buyers are handicapped by their late arrival, sellers do not know the transaction prices that occur after their sale, and the equilibrium state in which the informed buyers capture the sellers with minimum requirements does not reveal quality.

Thus, the model illustrates the diversity of the market dynamic evolutions depending on the assumptions made.

The analysis will now be resumed in a formal way.

Market Dynamics with Complete Information

The market passes through successive periods ($t \in \mathbb{N}$) and concerns two qualities of a given commodity, the quality being constant during a period. We denote $\alpha_t \in \{1, 2\}$ the quality in period t.

We assume there exists $T \in \mathbb{N}$ such that, for any group of T consecutive periods, the two qualities are observed during those periods.

The agents on the market do not change from one period to the next:

- *Sellers* belong to a finite set M, every seller $k \in M$ proposing during period t a unit which is obtained at a cost $\underline{w}(k)$ independent from t and α_t (the independence of $\underline{w}(k)$ with respect to α_t results from the assumption that the conditions of availability of the product are not related to its quality);
- *buyers* belong to a finite set N, every buyer $i \in N$ being willing to buy during period t a unit at a maximum price $\overline{v}(i, \alpha)$ depending on quality, but not on time; all buyers are supposed to prefer quality 1 to quality 2:

$$\overline{v}(i, 1) \geqslant \overline{v}(i, 2) \qquad \forall i \in N. \tag{1}$$

In this second part of the paper, α_t is known by all the agents since the beginning of any period t.

We shall analyze successively *the operation of the market during a period, the transition from a period to the next, the market states and their stability,* and finally *the consequences of the assumptions on the characteristics of stable states.*

The Operation of the Market during a Period

As already mentioned, buyers during a period arrive on the market in a random order one after another. They draw a sample of sellers and make a price proposal. Sellers accept or refuse.

At the beginning of a period t, *buyer* i is supposed to know

• his privileged seller for quality α, $k_t(i, \alpha)$ if he exists (the definition of a privileged seller will be given later),

• the price he has decided to propose, if it has a meaning, to the privileged seller $y_t(i, \alpha)$, and

• the price he has decided to propose to the other sellers $v_t(i, \alpha)$.

Similarly, *seller* k is supposed to know

• his privileged buyer for quality α, $i_t(k, \alpha)$ if he exists (the definition of a privileged buyer will be given later),

• the minimum price he has decided to accept if the proposal is made by the privileged buyer $x_t(k, \alpha)$, and

• the minimum price he has decided to accept if the proposal is made by another buyer $w_t(k, \alpha)$.

Then, let i_τ be the τth buyer to arrive on the market and MM_τ the subset of sellers having already sold their unit before the arrival of i_τ. Buyer i_τ draws a sample $K_t(i_\tau)$ of sellers not containing the privileged seller and any other seller having a nonzero probability to be drawn. He proposes $v_t(i_\tau, \alpha_t)$ to the sellers in $K_t(i_\tau)$ and if they refuse offers $y_t(i_\tau, \alpha_t)$ to the privileged seller (if he exists and has not yet sold). The contract with the sellers in $K_t(i_\tau)$ may occur in two ways:

V_1: *The buyer makes his proposal only to the sellers k still having a unit to sell;*

V_2: *The buyer makes his proposal to any seller k.*

But those proposals may be made in two different ways: the buyer may contact all the sellers simultaneously or visit them in a random order one after another stopping as soon as a seller has accepted his proposal. The choice has no influence on the dynamics of the model. We shall choose the ideas of the second possibility.

Let us consider now the *sellers'* behavior.

For the *nonprivileged sellers,* two situations have to be considered:

a. *All the sellers in* $K_t(i_\tau)$ *reject the proposal* $v_t(i_\tau, \alpha_t)$ because their requirements are higher.

b. *At least one seller in* $K_t(i_\tau)$ *accepts* $v_t(i_\tau, \alpha_t)$. Let k_0 be the first of those sellers.

For the *privileged seller* $k_t(i_\tau, \alpha_t)$ (who we shall, for simplicity, denote k_1), two situations are also possible:

- *He refuses offer* $y_t(i_\tau, \alpha_t)$. This case corresponds to several possibilities: there does not exist a privileged seller; the privileged seller has already sold; the privileged seller has a unit to sell but his requirements are higher.
- *He accepts offer* $y_t(i_\tau, \alpha_t)$.

Hence, the contact between the sellers and the buyer may generate four different outcomes:

aα. Buyer i_τ does not buy during period t; he has no privileged seller any more for quality α_t and $MM_{\tau+1} = MM_\tau$.

aβ. Buyer i_τ buys one unit from privileged seller k_1 who remains his privileged seller for quality α_t and $MM_{\tau+1} = MM_\tau \cup \{k_1\}$.

bα. Buyer i_τ buys one unit from seller k_0 who becomes his new privileged seller for quality α_t and $MM_{\tau+1} = MM_\tau \cup \{k_0\}$.

bβ. The privileged seller and at least another seller accept i_τ's offer. The latter selects seller k_0 who has accepted a lower proposal (see below); k_0 becomes the privileged seller and $MM_{\tau+1} = MM_\tau \cup \{k_0\}$.

The Transition from a Period to the Next

At the end of period t, agents revise their behavioral plans for period $(t + 1)$ on the basis of what has happened in period t. These plans have to be elaborated for two cases since the quality sold may be the same as in period t or different. In other words, the coupling between the markets of the two qualities has to be considered. We shall examine successively sellers' and buyers' behavior for quality α_t and then the coupling between the markets.

Sellers

When revising his requirements at the end of period t, each seller k takes into account the price proposals he has received and the fact he has or has not sold. We denote $p = p_{\max}$ the maximum price he has been offered during period t. Several situations are possible:

• *k has sold during period t at price p to buyer* i_0. The latter becomes his privileged buyer in period $(t + 1)$ for quality α_t: the minimum price the seller will accept from him will be p and from another buyer $(p + 1)$. Having less strong requirements with respect to his privileged buyer, the seller increases his probability of selling while exploring higher prices as far as the other buyers are concerned. Under such conditions,

$$i_{t+1}(k, \alpha_t) = i_0, \qquad x_{t+1}(k, \alpha_t) = p, \qquad w_{t+1}(k, \alpha_t) = p + 1 \tag{2}$$

• *k has accepted price p (or would have accepted it if he still had a unit to sell) but has not sold at price p*; the seller has no privileged buyer anymore and in the next period demands p from all the buyers.

• *k has refused all the price proposals*; he has no privileged buyer anymore and he decreases his bottom price when possible:

$$\begin{aligned} &i_{t+1}(k, \alpha_t) = 0,^{3} \qquad x_{t+1}(k, \alpha_t) = w_{t+1}(k, \alpha_t) \\ &w_{t+1}(k, \alpha_t) = \max\{\underline{w}(k), w_t(k, \alpha_t) - 1\}. \end{aligned} \tag{3}$$

Buyers

When revising his requirements at the end of period t, every buyer takes into account the fact that he has or has not bought a unit.

• *If i has bought in period t*, let k_0 be his seller and p the transaction price:

$$\begin{aligned} &k_{t+1}(i, \alpha_t) = k_0 \\ &y_{t+1}(i, \alpha_t) = p, \qquad v_{t+1}(i, \alpha_t) = p - 1 \end{aligned} \tag{4}$$

In other words, the new seller becomes the privileged seller and the buyer tends to reduce his price proposal except for his privileged seller.

• *If i has not bought in period t*:

$$\begin{aligned} &k_{t+1}(i, \alpha_t) = 0 \\ &v_{t+1}(i, \alpha_t) = \min\{v_t(i, \alpha_t) + 1, \overline{v}(i, \alpha_t)\} \end{aligned} \tag{5}$$

The buyer has no privileged seller anymore and he improves his price proposal.

The reader will notice that the buyer does not modify his order of arrival since this order is determined at random. However, it is obvious that a late arrival—and not only the level of the proposal—may explain the failure to buy.

The Coupling between Markets

We have just seen how agents adapt their requirements for quality α_t sold in period t. But agents have also to determine their requirements in case the other quality β_t is sold in period $(t + 1)$. Two types of behaviors are conceivable for buyers as well as for sellers: they may not "couple the markets," i.e., revise their requirements independently for the two qualities; they may on the contrary "couple the markets," i.e., control their price proposal or their bottom price so that it is higher for the better quality than for the worse.

A coupling behavior looks reasonable on the part of buyers since they prefer the first quality to the second. On the contrary, such a coupling is less obvious on the part of sellers since these sellers would like to sell at the highest possible price. Therefore, to reduce the number of assumptions, we always assume that sellers do not couple markets.

CS: Sellers do not couple markets. In that case, the adjustment rules for the transition from one period to the next are obvious:

$$w_{t+1}(k, \beta_t) = w_t(k, \beta_t)$$

$$x_{t+1}(k, \beta_t) = x_t(k, \beta_t) \tag{6}$$

$$i_{t+1}(k, \beta_t) = i_t(k, \beta_t)$$

On the contrary, we shall keep the assumptions of coupling and non-coupling for the sellers.

C: Buyers couple the markets. They adjust $v_{t+1}(i, \beta_t)$, $y_{t+1}(i, \beta_t)$ in such a way that $v_{t+1}(i, 1) \geqslant v_{t+1}(i, 2)$.

• *If i has bought from seller k_0 in period t,* the following rules will be introduced:

$$\beta_t = 1 v_{t+1}(i, 1) = v_t(i, 1),$$

$$y_{t+1}(i, 1) = y_t(i, 1), \tag{7}$$

$$k_{t+1}(i, 1) = k_t(i, 1);$$

$$\beta_t = 2 v_{t+1}(i, 2) = \min\{v_t(i, 2), v_{t+1}(i, 1); \tag{8}$$

$$y_{t+1}(i, 2) = v_{t+1}(i, 2) - 1; \tag{9}$$

$$k_{t+1}(i, 2) = \begin{cases} k_t(i, 2) & \text{if } v_{t+1}(i, 2) = v_t(i, 2) \\ k_0 & \text{if } v_{t+1}(i, 2) < v_t(i, 2). \end{cases} \tag{10}$$

• *If i has not bought in period t,* the following rules will be introduced:

$$\beta_t = 1 v_{t+1}(i,1) = \max\{v_t(i,1), v_{t+1}(i,2)\},$$
$$y_{t+1}(i,1) = v_{t+1}(i,1) - 1, \tag{11}$$
$$k_{t+1}(i,1) = k_t(i,1);$$

$$\beta_t = 2 v_{t+1}(i,2) = v_t(i,2),$$
$$y_{t+1}(i,2) = y_t(i,2), \tag{12}$$
$$k_{t+1}(i,2) = k_t(i,2).$$

NC: Buyers do not couple the markets. In such a case, the rules are obvious.

$$v_{t+1}(i,\beta_t) = v_t(i,\beta_t),$$
$$y_{t+1}(i,\beta_t) = y_t(i,\beta_t), \tag{13}$$
$$k_{t+1}(i,\beta_t) = k_t(i,\beta_t).$$

After this description of the transition from one period to the next, we shall now consider the market states and their stability.

The Market States and Their Stability

In this model, a *market state* at the beginning of period t is defined by the set of behavioral parameters relative to sellers (i_t, x_t, w_t) and to buyers (k_t, y_t, v_t). Such a state is *possible* if $x_t(k,\alpha)$, $w_t(k,\alpha)$, $y_t(i,\alpha)$, $v_t(i,\alpha)$ belong to $\mathbb{N}$ for any k belonging to M, and i belonging to N, any α belonging to $\{1,2\}$, and if

$$
\begin{aligned}
&y_t(i,\alpha) = v_t(i,\alpha) + 1 \qquad \text{if } k_t(i,\alpha) \neq 0,\\
&x_t(k,\alpha) = w_t(k,\alpha) - 1 \qquad \text{if } i_t(k,\alpha) \neq 0,\\
&w_t(k,\alpha) \geqslant \underline{w}(k),\\
&x_t(k,\alpha) \geqslant \underline{w}(k),\\
&y_t(i,\alpha) \leqslant \overline{v}(i,\alpha),\\
&v_t(i,\alpha) \leqslant \overline{v}(i,\alpha).
\end{aligned} \tag{14}
$$

Finally, *a market state e_t is stable if it is possible and if e_{t+1} coincides with e_t whatever the events having occurred during period t,* in particular the buyers' order of arrival, the samples of sellers drawn by the buyers, and the quality sold.

To simplify the study of stable states, we shall introduce the two following convenient assumptions:

1. *All the sellers (and all the buyers) have different characteristics, and buyers strictly prefer quality 1.* In other words:

$k \in M,\ k' \in M$ implies $\underline{w}(k) \neq \underline{w}(k')$

$i \in N,\ i' \in N$ implies $\overline{v}(i,\alpha) \neq \overline{v}(i',\alpha)\ \alpha \in \{1,2\}$ and $\overline{v}(i,1) > \overline{v}(i,2)$.

2. *The equilibrium (as introduced by elementary supply and demand theory) is defined for the two markets.* In other words, there exists for $\alpha \in \{1,2\}$ a seller $k_\alpha \in M$ and a buyer $i_\alpha \in N$ such that

$\#\{k \in M/\underline{w}(k) \leqslant \underline{w}(k_\alpha)\} = \#\{i \in N/\overline{v}(i,\alpha) \geqslant \overline{v}(i_\alpha,\alpha)\}$

- $\underline{w}(k_\alpha) = \overline{v}(i_\alpha,\alpha)$ (and we denote p_α as this common value)
- $p_1 - 1 > p_2 + 1$.

The prices, being integers throughout the evolution, the last condition ensures that the prices on the two markets remain different though defined with a margin of one unit. We denote

$$M_\alpha = \{k \in M/\underline{w}(k) \leqslant p_\alpha\} \qquad N_\alpha = \{i \in N/\overline{v}(i,\alpha) \geqslant p_\alpha\}. \tag{15}$$

For reasons that will appear clearly later, the analysis of stable states has to be developed in two situations:

1. *All the buyers' arrival orders have, in any period, a nonzero probability.* Then, let us consider the set E_0 of market states such that $e_t \in E_0$ implies that e_t has the following properties:

- e_t is possible.
- The only sellers having a privileged buyer are those accepting price p_α.
- The only buyers having a privileged seller are those able to propose price p_α.
- e_t is consistent with respect to privileged agents (if $i_t(k_0,\alpha) = i_0$ then $k_t(i_0,\alpha) = k_0$).
- The agents having no privileged partner propose their extreme possibilities.

• The price proposed by buyer i_0 to his privileged seller k_0 is the one that k_0 is ready to accept from i_0 (if $i_0 = i_t(k_0, \alpha)$ then $x_t(k_0, \alpha) = y_t(i_0, \alpha)$).

• There exist at most two prices per quality, those prices differing at most by one unit ($\{x_t(k_0, \alpha)/k_0 \in M_\alpha\}$ coincides with one of the three sets $\{p_\alpha\}$, $\{p_\alpha, p_\alpha - 1\}, p_\alpha, p_\alpha + 1\}$, price p_α being always actual[4]).

It is then possible to prove the following theorem:

Theorem 1.

a. Whatever the assumptions made (V_1 or V_2; C or NC), the states in E_0 are stable.

b. If in addition all the buyers' arrival orders have, in any period, a nonzero probability, all the stable states belong to E_0.

c. The market converges in probability in a finite time toward a stable state.

It is obvious that in this first situation the stable states correspond to the traditional equilibria of elementary theory, supply being equal to demand on the market of each quality and prices differing from equilibrium prices by at most one unit. Actual buyers and sellers are unambiguously determined for each quality. In other words, the states in E_0 may be considered as equivalent since they differ only through the allocation of buyers to sellers.

Therefore, in this case of complete information and of a unique wave of buyers, the market with two qualities behaves as the elementary market studied in Lesourne and Laffond (1979): it converges in probability in a finite time toward the traditional equilibrium.

2. *The buyers are divided into two disconnected groups N_a and N_b and the buyers in N_a always arrive on the market before the buyers in N_b. On the contrary, inside N_a or N_b, all the arrival orders have a nonzero probability.* We shall then introduce assumption (R), which expresses that supply and demand curves cross when the set of buyers is restricted to N_a and that this property is also true for the residual market. (figure 1b).

R: *For every $\alpha \in \{1, 2\}$, there exist*

• $k_\alpha \in M$, $i_\alpha \in N_a$ such that

$$\#\{k \in M/\underline{w}(k) \leqslant \underline{w}(k_\alpha)\} = \#\{i \in N_a/\overline{v}(i, \alpha) \geqslant \overline{v}(i_\alpha, \alpha)\}$$

$\overline{v}(i_\alpha, \alpha) = \underline{w}(k_\alpha)$ (we denote p_α^a this common value)

- $k'_\alpha \in M$, $i'_\alpha \in N_b$ such that

$$\#\{k \in M/p^a_\alpha < \underline{w}(k) \leqslant \underline{w}(k'_\alpha)\} = \#\{i \in N_b/\overline{v}(i,\alpha) \geqslant \overline{v}(i'_\alpha,\alpha)\}$$

$\overline{v}(i'_\alpha, \alpha) = \underline{w}(k'_\alpha)$ (we denote p^b_α as this common value).

In other words, p^a_α is the market price of elementary theory when all the sellers and the first wave of buyers operate, while p^b_α is the market price when the second wave of buyers and the sellers who have not sold to the first wave operate.

Let us consider then the set E_1 of market states such that $e_t \in E_1$ implies that e_t has the following properties:

- e_t is possible.
- The agents without a privileged partner propose their extreme possibilities.
- e_t is consistent with respect to privileged agents.
- The price proposed by buyer i_0 to his privileged seller k_0 is the one that k_0 is ready to accept from i_0.
- The agents' requirements satisfy the following inequalities:

$[i_0 \in N_a, k_0 \in M]$ implies $w_t(k_0, \alpha) > v_t(i_0, \alpha)$

$[i_0 \in N_b, k_0 \in M - M^\alpha_{at}]$ implies $w_t(k_0, \alpha) > v_t(i_0, \alpha)$

denoting M^α_{at} the set of sellers related in state e_t to a buyer in N_a:

$$M^\alpha_{at} = \{k \in M^\alpha / i_t(k, \alpha) \in N_a\} \tag{16}$$

(we shall introduce later in a similar way $M^\alpha_{bt}, N^\alpha_{at}, N^\alpha_{bt}$).

It is then possible to prove the following theorem:

Theorem 2. In the model with two waves, if, in any period and for each wave, all the buyers' arrival orders have a nonzero probability, the market converges in probability in a finite time to a stable state and the set E of stable states verifies the condition

$$E_0 \subset E \subset E_1.$$

Therefore it is important to try to better characterize E_1 and to study the set E for the various combinations of assumptions (V_1, V_2; C, NC).

The two following theorems describe the properties of the states in E_1.

Theorem 3. If e_t belongs to E_1:

1. There exist for each wave of buyers and each quality at most two prices differing at most by one unit:

$$p_t(a,\alpha) \leqslant p'_t(a,\alpha); \qquad p_t(b,\alpha) \leqslant p'_t(b,\alpha); \qquad p'_t - p_t \leqslant 1. \tag{17}$$

2. For the same quality, first wave buyers always obtain a price lower than those paid by second wave buyers:

$$p'_t(a,\alpha) \leqslant p_t(b,\alpha) + 1.$$

3. Price p_α belongs to the set of actual prices:

$$\max\{p'_t(a,\alpha), p'_t(b,\alpha)\} \geqslant p_\alpha \geqslant \min\{p_t(a,\alpha), p_t(b,\alpha)\}. \tag{18}$$

If price differences of one unit are neglected, the important result of this theorem is that in any state in E_1, there exist for each quality two prices (one for each wave) and that those prices may differ significantly.

Contrary to the states in E_0, which are equivalent with respect to agents effectively selling and buying, the states in E_1 are not equivalent and the following inclusions relations may be proved:

Theorem 4. In a state of E_1, the set of effective sellers and buyers verifies the inclusion relations:

$$M^\alpha_{at} \cup M^\alpha_{bt} \supset M_\alpha, \qquad M^\alpha_{at} \subset M_\alpha$$

$$N^\alpha_{at} \supset N_a \cap N_\alpha, \qquad N^\alpha_{bt} \subset N_b \cap N_\alpha.$$

Let us examine now the set E of stable states associated with the various combinations of assumptions.

It is possible to prove Theorem 5.

Theorem 5.

i. Under assumption V_2, the set of stable states for the market with two waves of buyers is E_0.

ii. Under assumptions V_1 and NC, the set of stable states for the market with two waves of buyers is E_1.

Therefore, if the sellers go on receiving proposals after having sold, the existence of two waves does not prevent the market from converging toward the traditional equilibrium.

On the contrary if the sellers no longer receive proposals after the sale of their product and if the buyers do not couple markets, the set of stable states is the greatest possible and coincides with E_1. Hence, the stable state reached by the market depends on the random evolution of this market.

Depending on the individual arrival orders within waves, on the drawings of sellers by buyers, on the contact orders between sellers and buyers, prices paid differ as well as agents selling or buying effectively. For the first time we come across, in this analysis, a phenomenon that is very general in models of this type.

There remains to be considered the intermediate case (V_1 C).

Theorem 6. Under assumptions V_1 and C, the set E of stable state is the set E_2 of states in E_1 satisfying the necessary and sufficient condition:

$$y_t(i, 1) \geqslant y_t(i, 2) \quad \text{for} \quad \forall i \in N.$$

With this combination of assumptions, the set of stable states is more restricted since any buyer proposes to his privileged seller a price for quality 1 at least equal to the price for quality 2.

At this stage, it is interesting to consider another subset of E_1, subset E_3. To do so, we introduce the market surplus S_t for the first wave of buyers[5]:

$$S_t^\alpha = \sum_{i \in N_{at}^\alpha} \overline{v}(i, \alpha) - \sum_{k \in M_{at}^\alpha} \underline{w}(k). \tag{19}$$

By definition, a state e_t belongs to E_3 if it belongs to E_1 and if $S_t^\alpha \leqslant S_{t'}^\alpha$, for any other possible state $e_{t'}$.

In other words, in a state of E_3, the market corresponding to the first wave of buyers is in a situation of extraction of the maximum surplus.

The following theorem may then be proved:

Theorem 7. A state $e_t \in E_1$ is a state of E_3 iff:

1. The sellers selling to the first wave buyers constitute a consistent set ($k_0 \in M_{at}^\alpha$ and $\underline{w}(k_1) < \underline{w}(k_0)$ implies $k_1 \in M_{at}^\alpha$).

2. The extreme requirements of agents having not made transactions on the first wave market are uncompatible ($i \in N_a - N_{at}$ and $k \in M - M_{at}^\alpha$ implies $\overline{v}(i, \alpha) < \overline{w}(k)$).

Theorem 7 implies that *all the states in* E_3 *are equivalent*. They differ only through the allocation of actual sellers to actual buyers. The set E_3 satisfies the following properties:

$$E_3 \subset E_2 \subset E_1,$$

$$E_0 \subset E_2 \text{ but } E_0 \cap E_3 = \varnothing.$$

This analysis of the dynamic operation of the market with complete information will facilitate the study of this operation when agents' information on quality is incomplete.

Market Dynamics with Incomplete Information

From now on, we assume that *at the beginning of any period t*

- all the sellers know the quality,
- some buyers know this quality,
- other buyers do not know it,

and we suppose that at *the end of the period,* quality is revealed to all buyers.

From one period to the next, informed buyers are identical and constitute a set N_a while noninformed buyers constitute the complementary set N_b.

We shall study successively the *information of noninformed buyers, the arrival on the market of noninformed buyers, the stable states,* and the *possible convergence of the market toward fully revealing stable states.*

In this third part, all the assumptions of the second part remain valid except when the contrary is explicitly mentioned. Therefore the market will operate in the same way but the noninformed individuals will have during any period to estimate the quality put on sale.

The Information of Noninformed Buyers

The order of occurrence of qualities may be periodic or random. What is essential is that individuals do not try to discover the law of alternation of qualities.

The noninformed buyers estimate quality from the transaction prices they may observe. Therefore, we assume that on his arrival on the market during period t, the noninformed individual i_τ may observe a sample of transactions drawn at random independently from the set of all transactions. Two cases are possible:

- *No transaction has taken place before the arrival of i_τ*: the individual decides to adopt a prudent strategy and assumes that the quality sold is the worse: $\hat{\alpha}_t(i_\tau) = 2$.
- *Transactions have taken place before i_τ's arrival*: then, let us assume that i_τ has been able to build two indices $p^t_\alpha(i_\tau)$ representing the prices associated to the two qualities $\alpha \in \{1, 2\}$ at date t.

Then let $\overline{p}_t(i_\tau)$ be the average of transaction prices observed by i_τ. We suppose the individual adopts the following inference rule which looks natural:

if $\overline{p}_t(i_\tau) > 1/2[p_1^t(i_\tau) + p_2^t(i_\tau)]$, i_τ decides that $\hat{\alpha}_t(i_\tau) = 1$

if $\overline{p}_t(i_\tau) \leqslant 1/2[p_1^t(i_\tau) + p_2^t(i_\tau)]$, i_τ decides that $\hat{\alpha}_t(i_\tau) = 2$.

At this stage, it is reasonable to ask whether there exists a link between the prices observed by the individual and the prices proposed by him. To simplify, we have supposed it is not so. This hypothesis may look excessive, but one has to take into account that the prices observed contain those of the first transactions while the individual determines his price proposals knowing he arrives on the market later.

We shall also assume that the price associated with the better quality by a noninformed buyer is always higher than the price associated with the worse quality. Such an assumption is reasonable since the buyer knows that the better quality is preferred by all buyers:

$$p_1^t(i) > p_2^t(i). \tag{20}$$

At *the end of period t*, quality is revealed and the noninformed buyer may experience three situations:

• *He has not observed transactions during period t and has not learned anything*:

$$p_\alpha^{t+1}(i) = p_\alpha^t(i), \qquad \alpha \in \{1, 2\}. \tag{21}$$

• *He has observed transactions and knows that* $\alpha_t = 1$. Then he adjusts his index $p_1^t(i)$ in the direction indicated by $\overline{p}_t(i)$:

$$\begin{aligned} p_1^{t+1}(i) &= p_1^t(i) + 1, && \text{if } \overline{p}_t(i) \geqslant p_1^t(i) + 1 \\ p_1^{t+1}(i) &= p_1^t(i) - 1, && \text{if } \overline{p}_t(i) \leqslant p_1^t(i) - 1 \\ p_1^{t+1}(i) &= p_1^t(i), && \text{if } p_1^t(i) + 1 > \overline{p}_t(i) > p_1^t(i) - 1. \end{aligned} \tag{22}$$

He adjusts also $p_2^t(i)$ to maintain the price hierarchy between the two qualities[6]:

$$p_2^{t+1}(i) = \min\{p_2^t(i), p_1^{t+1}(i) - 1\}. \tag{23}$$

• *He has observed transactions and knows that* $\alpha_t = 2$. The behavioral rule is similar:

$$\begin{aligned} p_2^{t+1}(i) &= p_2^t(i) + 1, && \text{if } \overline{p}_t(i) \geqslant p_2^t(i) + 1 \\ p_2^{t+1}(i) &= p_2^t(i) - 1, && \text{if } \overline{p}_t(i) \leqslant p_2^t(i) - 1 \end{aligned} \tag{24}$$

$$p_2^{t+1}(i) = p_2^t(i), \qquad \text{if } p_2^t(i) + 1 > \bar{p}_t(i) > p_2^t(i) - 1$$

$$p_1^{t+1}(i) = \max\{p_1^t(i), p_2^{t+1}(i) + 1\}. \tag{25}$$

The Arrival of Noninformed Buyers on the Market

Before arriving on the market, the noninformed buyers have to wait for a few transactions to take place. Normally, the choice of their order of arrival should be part of their strategy. We shall not explore this possibility, but we shall consider two extreme assumptions:

P_1: *Noninformed buyers start arriving on the market as soon as the first transaction has taken place.*

P_2: *Noninformed buyers arrive on the market after the last informed buyer.*

Of course in P_1, noninformed buyers arrive after all the informed ones if none of the informed buyers has bought the product.

Stable States and Convergence

In the model with incomplete information a *market state* f_t is a couple:

$$f_t = (e_t, p_t) \tag{26}$$

where e_t is a state of the market with complete information and $p_t = \{p_\alpha^t(i), i \in N_b, \alpha \in \{1, 2\}\}$ is the set of the price indices associated with the two qualities by noninformed buyers.

A *market state* f_t *is possible* if e_t is possible and if $p_1^t(i) > p_2^t(i)$ for every $i \in N_b$.

The set E_0 of the model with complete information may be extended in a natural way into a set F_0 of the model with incomplete information:

$$f_t \in F_0 \text{ iff } e_t \in E_0 \quad \text{and} \quad p_\alpha^t(i) \in \{x_t(i, \alpha)/i \in N_\alpha\} \qquad \forall i \in N_b.$$

It must be noticed that, for the problem to be interesting, informed individuals have to buy or sell effectively in the market traditional equilibrium. Therefore, we assume

$$N_a \cap N_\alpha \neq \varnothing \quad \text{for} \quad \alpha \in \{1, 2\}. \tag{27}$$

A market state f_t will be said stable if it is possible and if, for any sequence $\{\alpha_{t+\theta}, \theta \in \mathrm{N}\}$ of qualities, for any buyer's order of arrival, any drawing of sellers by buyers, the state $f_{t+\theta} = (e_{t+\theta}, p_{t+\theta})$ is such that $e_{t+\theta} = e_t$.

As will be noticed, in this definition, the indices associated with qualities may vary from one period to the next, which is understandable, since in a stable state with incomplete information, several prices may exist for each quality. On the contrary, all the other parameters are, in a stable state, independent of time.

We now have to study the characteristics of stable states and the convergence toward these stable states in the six cases resulting from the coupling of assumptions P_1 and P_2 with assumptions V_2, V_1 NC, V_1 C. But the problem can be simplified as a result of the following theorem:

Theorem 8. Under assumption P_1 or under the combination of assumptions P_2 V_2, a state is stable if it belongs to F_0 and the market converges in probability in a finite time toward a state of F_0.

Thus, the states in F_0 are fully revealing, the operation of the market enables the noninformed buyers to discover with certainty beyond a sufficiently distant date, the quality sold in any period.

To have this result, it is sufficient that the noninformed buyers start arriving as soon as the first transaction has taken place or if they arrive on the market after the last informed buyer that the sellers take into account the proposals received and not only the effective price.

Two cases have still to be studied: P_2 V_1 NC, P_2 V_1 C.

Let us examine first the case P_2 V_1 C, in which buyers couple markets. When information is complete, the set of stable states is $E_2 \subset E_1$, but E_2 does not play any role when information is incomplete and the analysis requires the introduction of the set E_1' of states in E_1 revealing quality.

A state e_t in E_1' may be said quality revealing if for two numbers p_1 and p_2 such that[7]

$$\min\{y_t(i,1), i \in N_t^1\} \leqslant p_1 \leqslant \max\{y_t(i,1), i \in N_t^1\}, \tag{28}$$

$$\min\{y_t(i,2), i \in N_t^2\} \leqslant p_2 \leqslant \max\{y_t(i,2), i \in N_t^2\}, \tag{29}$$

$$p_1 > p_2 \tag{30}$$

any buyer using price indices p_1 and p_2 recognizes *quality 1*:

$$y_t(i,1) > \tfrac{1}{2}(p_1 + p_2) \quad \text{for every } i \in N_t^1$$

and *quality 2*:

$$y_t(i,2) \leqslant \tfrac{1}{2}(p_1 + p_2) \quad \text{for every } i \in N_t^2.$$

In other words, $e_t \in E_1'$ is quality revealing when the two relations (31) constituting condition (Q) are satisfied.

$$(\mathrm{Q})\ \begin{cases} \min\{y_t(i,1), i \in N_t^1\} > \frac{1}{2}[\max\{y_t(i,1), i \in N_t^1\} + \max\{y_t(i,2), i \in N_t^2\}], \\ \min\{y_t(i,2), i \in N_t^2\} \leqslant \frac{1}{2}[\min\{y_t(i,1), i \in N_t^1\} + \min\{y_t(i,2), i \in N_t^2\}]. \end{cases} \tag{31}$$

E_1' may be extended into a set F_1' of stable states of the model with incomplete information. The set E_1' satisfies the following conditions in the case under study:

$E_0 \subset E_1' \subset E_2 \subset E_1$.

On the contrary, the relations between E_3 and E_1' depend on the assumptions. Two subcases have to be considered:

• *All the states in* E_3 *are quality revealing*: $E_3 \subset E_1'$. This is so when condition (H) is satisfied:

$$(\mathrm{H})\ \begin{cases} p_a^1 - 1 > \frac{1}{2}[p_b^1 + p_b^2 + 2] \\ p_b^2 + 2 \leqslant \frac{1}{2}[p_a^1 + p_a^2 - 2] \end{cases} \tag{32}$$

and the following theorem may then be proved:

Theorem 9. Under assumptions P_2, V_1 C and assumption H, a state is stable if it belongs to F_1' and the market converges in probability in a finite time toward a state in F_1'.

In other words, assumption (H), which implies that the states of maximum surplus are quality revealing, ensures the convergence of the market toward a stable state in which the noninformed buyers are able to infer with certainty the quality sold.

• *No state in* E_3 *is quality revealing*: $E_3 \cap E_1' = \emptyset$. This is so when condition (H′) is satisfied:

$$(\mathrm{H}')\quad p_a^1 + 1 \leqslant \tfrac{1}{2}[p_b^1 + p_b^2 - 2] \text{ or } p_b^2 - 1 > \tfrac{1}{2}[p_a^1 + p_a^2 + 2] \tag{33}$$

and the following theorem may be proved:

Theorem 10. Under assumptions P_2 V_1 C and assumption H′, a state is stable if it belongs to F_1', but the market does not always converge toward a stable state and does not necessary reveal quality.

More precisely, let us denote by A the set of states f_t of the process in which the k_α first sellers sell to the i_α first buyers at price p_a^α (possibly

($p_a^\alpha - 1$) or ($p_a^\alpha + 1$) but not the two simultaneously). The following properties may be shown:

i. $F_1' \cap A = \emptyset$.

ii. For every $\varepsilon \geqslant 0$, there exists a time T such that for any $t \geqslant T$, the probability for f_t to be in F_1' or A be higher than $(1 - \varepsilon)$.

iii. The states in F_1' are stable. If $f_t = (e_t, p_t)$ enters F_1', the state f_{t+1} is also in F_1' and $e_{t+1} = e_t$.

iv. The set A constitutes a trap: if $f_t \in A$, then $f_{t+1} \in A$.

v. The states in A are not stable: if $f_t \in A$, whatever the series $\{\alpha_{t+n}, n \in \mathbb{N}\}$ of qualities observed after f_t, there exists a date θ and a development of the process between t and $t + \theta$ such that $f_{t+\theta} = (e_{t+\theta}, p_{t+\theta})$ with $e_{t+\theta} = e_t$.

The subcase which has just been considered is highly interesting since the market may be trapped in an evolution during which the noninformed buyers are unable to infer quality from their price observations.

It will be easily verified that there is no reason to examine situations in which neither H nor H′ is satisfied since such situations correspond to limit cases resulting from the use of integers.

The last combination of assumptions to consider is P_2 P_1 NC in which sellers take into account only transactions prices and buyers do not couple markets. When information is complete, the set of stable states is E_1 and differs from the one corresponding to P_2 V_1 C. But this is not so when information is incomplete. With slightly different proofs, it may be shown that Theorems 9 and 10 remain valid under combination P_2 V_1 NC. Everything happens as if the assumption about markets coupling by buyers was not important with incomplete information.

Table 1 presents a synthesis of the results obtained.

Assumptions H and H′ are illustrated in figure 2, with the unit margins resulting from the use of integers neglected.

Prices $(p_a^1, p_a^2, p_b^1, p_b^2)$ are those that the two waves of buyers would observe for the two qualities in a state of E_3 with complete information. The figure assumes p_a^2 and p_b^1 as given while p_a^1 and p_b^2 are taken as variables. Obviously, in addition to relations 30 and 31, it is necessary to take into account the inequalities

$$p_a^1 > p_a^2, \qquad p_b^1 > p_b^2$$

and

$$p_a^1 < p_b^1, \qquad p_a^2 < p_b^2.$$

Table 1

Order of arrival	Buyers' proposals		Convergence	Prices
P_1 noninformed, buyers start, arriving immediately after the first transaction	V_1 or V_2		Towards a quality-revealing stable state	A unique price (with a margin of one unit) independent from the market history for each quality
P_2 noninformed, buyers arrive after informed buyers	V_2: the proposals are made to any seller			
	V_1: the proposals are only made to sellers still having a unit to sell	H	Toward a quality-revealing stable state	A unique price (with a margin of one unit) for each quality and each category of buyers, but depending on market history
		H′	The market does not always converge to a stable state and does not necessarily reveal quality	Market may be trapped in a succession of states where prices are numerous and nonrevealing and fluctuate constantly

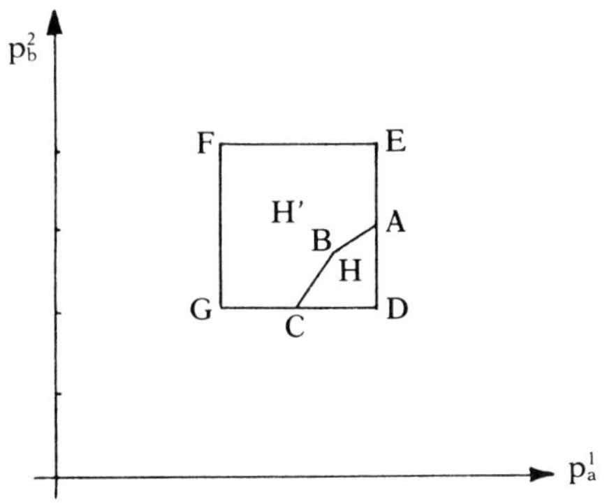

Figure 2.
$p_a = 6$, $p_b^1 = 12$.

Under such conditions, area H is the quadrilateral ABCD and area H′ hexagon AEFGCB.

It is possible to suspect why the market may indefinitely fluctuate under assumption H′: if for the buyers of the first wave the market converges toward price p_a, the noninformed buyers of the second wave may believe that the quality sold is the worse since

$$p_a^1 \leqslant \tfrac{1}{2}[p_b^1 + p_b^2].$$

In the same way, those buyers may interpret p_b as a price for the better quality since

$$p_b^2 > \tfrac{1}{2}[p_a^1 + p_a^2].$$

To conclude, we shall present a few remarks on the analysis made and on possible developments.

Conclusion

The preceding analysis illustrates the problems raised by the study of market dynamics in the present state of economic theory.

i. The number of assumptions to be introduced to define completely a model is extremely high and it is not always easy to separate rigorously the crucial assumptions from those playing a secondary part.

However, practical experience with those models enables us to start distinguishing the hypotheses that are only technically convenient from those that play an essential role. For instance, in the model of this paper, the crucial hypotheses are probably the following, in addition to those mentioned in table 1: any seller has a nonzero probability of being drawn by a buyer; buyers and sellers reinforce or weaken their requirements depending on whether they have or not bought or sold during the preceding period; noninformed buyers use their past experience to build a cut-off price enabling them to decide whether the quality sold is the better or the worse.

The hope of obtaining general theorems therefore does not seem unrealistic.

ii. Meaningful results may be obtained even with unsophisticated individual behaviors. Thus, in the models proposed, individuals content themselves with adapting without trying to anticipate or to adopt optimization strategies. A strategic behavior could be, for instance, for the buyers to choose their order of arrival and for the sellers to adjust their bottom price as time passes inside a period.

Many economists may consider this absence of sophisticated behaviors as a weakness of the models. On the contrary, we consider it important to notice that economic institutions may operate with agents "à la Simon" using simple decision rules.

iii. To simulate realistically the market complexity, it seems presently necessary to resort to models where values are integers. Such a representation generates two types of difficulties: the occurrence of marginal phenomena due to discretization and the need for long and heavy proofs.

In spite of these problems, research work in the last years—among which are those described in this paper—shows that the study of dynamics not only confirms the results of static analysis but also brings an additional knowledge showing that, when some simple assumptions are not satisfied, the market may be unable to converge toward a stable state or converges according to its history toward stable states that may be different from those of traditional equilibrium.

Thus, the market may be conceived as a self-organizing process, but a process that may not converge or lead to various organizational structures. In the case of information transmission through prices, self-organization concerns simultaneously the indirect revelation of quality and the separation of buyers and sellers into two categories: those who play an effective role in the stable states and the others. The static equilibrium corresponds generally to the case in which self-organization goes to completion but there are strong reasons to believe that the other stable states (when they exist) also play an essential part in the actual economy, since they constitute starting points for new dynamic evolutions.

Therefore, we hope to see a development of the systematic study of the dynamics of economic organizations out of static equilibria situations.

Notes

1. Laboratoire d'Econométrie, Conservatoire National des Arts et Métiers, 2 rue Conté, 75003 Paris, France. Proofs concerning a market dynamics with information transmission through prices, May 1988.

2. It would be possible to get rid of it, but with the introduction of more sophisticated behavioral rules, which would imply an adjustment of the steps during the market evolution.

3. By convention, this writing means that the corresponding individual does not exist.

4. The possible existence of two prices differing by one unit for the same quality is a consequence of the assumption that values are integers; such a situation occurs in all the models of this type.

5. For the meaning of the surplus in dynamic models, see Lesourne 1985.

6. Other rules are conceivable. For instance,

$p_2^{t+1}(i) = p_2^t(i)$ if $\overline{p}_t(i) > p_2^t(i) - 1$

and

$p_2^{t+1}(i) = p_2^t(i) - 1$ if $\overline{p}_t(i) < \overline{p}_2^t(i) - 1$.

7. N_t^α represents here the set of buyers having a privileged seller for quality α.

References

Green, J. 1973. Information, Efficiency and Equilibrium. Discussion Paper No. 284, Harvard Institute of Economic Research.

Green, J. 1977. "The Non-existence of Informational Equilibria." *Review of Economic Studies* 44: 451–467.

Grossman, S. J. 1981. "An Introduction to the Theory of Rational Expectations under Asymmetric Information." *Review of Economic Studies* 54: 541–559.

Jordan, J. and Radner, R. 1982. "Rational Expectations in Microeconomic Models: An Overview." *Journal of Economic Theory* 26: 201–223.

Laffond, G. and J. Lesourne. 1985. "Market Dynamics with Search Processes and Information Costs." *Economie Appliquée* 37 (3–4): 739–765.

Laffont, J. J. 1985. "Cours de théorie microéconomique, Vol. II: Economie de l'incertain et de l'information." *Economica.*

Lesourne, J. 1985. "Le marché et l'auto-organisation." *Economie Appliquée* 37 (3–4): 663–701.

Lesourne, J. 1986. "L'auto-organisation et le marché dans Marchés, capital et incertitude, essais en l'honneur de Maurice Allais." *Economica.*

Lesourne, J. 1987. "Un système autopoïétique: le marché." *Revue Internationale de systémique* 1(2): 141–158.

Lesourne J., and G. Laffond. 1979. Market Dynamics and Search Processes. Congrès Européen de la Société d'Econométrie, Athens.

Lucas, R. E. 1972. "Expectations and the Neutrality of Money." *Journal of Economic Theory* 4: 103–124.

Milgrom, P., and N. Stokey. 1982. "Information, Trade and Common Knowledge." *Journal of Economic Theory* 26: 17–27.

Radner, R. 1967. "Equilibres des marchés à terme et au comptant en cas d'incertitude." *Cahiers du Séminaire d'Econométrie* 35–52.

Radner, R. 1979. "Rational Expectations Equilibrium: Generic Existence and the Information Revealed by Prices." *Econometrica* 47: 655–678.

17

Games in Incomplete Market Structures and Difficulties of Coordination through the Market

Yves Younès

The theory of incomplete markets models (I.M.M.) cannot be reduced to the analysis of the canonical model with spot markets and securities and has something general to say about the way exchanges are made and how this phenomenon entails difficulties of coordination through the market.

The approach of trying to picture—in terms of equilibrium concepts—a weakening of interdependence among markets without destroying it totally (i.e., without partial equilibrium analysis, concealed or not) gives some substance to the notion of market. A strong version of the idea that two agents can meet on one market at most (acyclicity) entails at least a partial *absence of double coincidence of wants* and justifies the two basic principles that follow:

Principle 1. Coordination across markets is difficult and surely more difficult than coordination inside each market. That indicates that an equilibrium is not necessarily Pareto optimal.

Principle 2. The relative bargaining power among agents participating in some market must be settled (among them) only on this market because by assumption they do not meet on another market. Thus, although the relative bargaining power among agents attending the same market depends on their rational expectations about outcomes of bargaining on other markets, there cannot be compensation from one market to another one for settling it. This principle justifies the fact that there are many budgetary constraints in the I.M.M. (Radner 1972) and the fact that in market structures for which each market is defined by the exchange of some good for money, a nonzero feasible trade which does not imply an exchange of money ("barter")[1] cannot be an equilibrium and liquidity constraints can arise.

The idea of explaining pecuniary externalities by embedding a given model in a larger one is not new. It is at the basis of the fix-price approach, and it is intensively used, as a paradigm, in the so-called New Macroeconomics. A vicious circle of the Keynesian type is pictured in the following way. One wants to make precise the following idea: The level of activity is low because the typical firm cannot employ the whole labor force, owing to the low expected demand, and the expected demand is low because employment is low. Start with a model with one firm (II), one worker (I), and two markets: market 1 for consumption good and market 2 for labor. Embed this model in a larger one defined in such a way that with each agent one associates two agents of the same type and with each market one associates two markets of the same type. The pattern of meetings is such that two agents can meet on one market at most. The pattern of meetings is plotted in figure 1. A node is a market and an edge is an agent.

The Keynesian vicious circle becomes understandable. Firm IIa cannot provide a full-time job for worker Ia because the demand for consumption good by worker Ib is low, etc. This graph is not acyclic, and it is convenient to have an acyclic graph. A way to make it acyclic is to assume that there is an infinite number of identical agents and an infinite number of markets. This situation is depicted in figure 2.

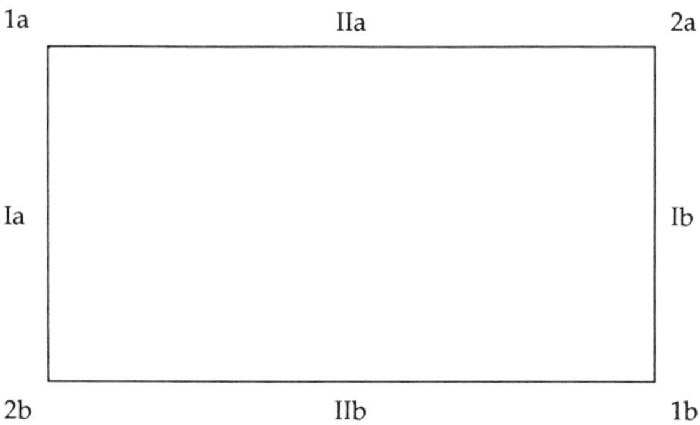

Figure 1.

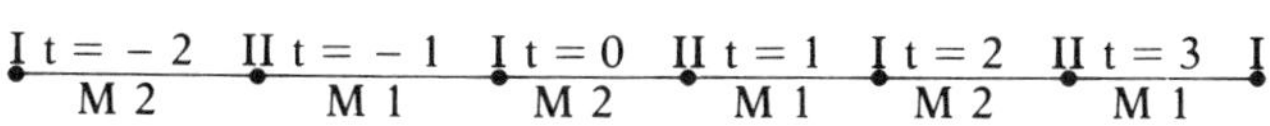

Figure 2.

It is obvious that this is the pattern of meetings of an Overlapping Generation Model (O.G.M.) with one agent per generation, each generation leaving for two periods. To check this assertion, identify a worker (agent I) with an agent born at an odd period, a firm (agent II) with an agent born at an even period, a market 1 with a market that is open at an odd period, and a market 2 with a market that is open at an even period.

For this set-up, one indicates that some Pareto improvements are difficult to implement, i.e., the trade considered is stable with respect to Pareto improvements if the set of Pareto improvements has some property (weaker than that of being empty).

Actually, there are two related ways of looking at this difficulty of implementing coordinated moves.

(i) On the one hand, because of the way agents meet, one can say that binding contracts can be made on each market separately but that agents make rational expectations about the trades they can make on other markets they attend.

(ii) Costs of "transactions" can be very large on a very large set of markets, and coordination for changes of trades is possible only on a subset of markets that is not too large.

It is now understandable why the fine construction of Malinvaud 1953 is relevant for our purpose. In the field of the theory of capital, he has proposed the notion of efficient programs on every finite horizon (finite optimality), has characterized them with supporting prices (called Malinvaud prices because they do not always allow a present value to be defined), and has shown that if an efficient program is stationary it can be supported by a stationary price system (the Malinvaud lemma).

Thus, one embeds every original model in a larger one called the extensive form, exactly as we did above for the model with two agents and two markets; the original model thus becomes a reduced form. The graph of the extensive form is acyclic, and we thus generalize the particular O.G.M. Although finite optimality reduces to optimality in the theory of capital in which there is basically one agent, Balasko and Shell (1980) have shown that it is no more the case in the O.G.M.

Obviously, this implicit way of dealing with difficulties of coordination can be used for many game-theoretic equilibrium concepts. Here we shall use mainly the mechanism of the Core, because (inter alia) it embodies in a simple way the two principles we have defined. Concerning the first principle, as a trade is finitely optimal if the grand coalition cannot block by modifying trades on only a finite number of markets, one takes any coalition (finite or infinite) for blocking with the above restriction, for defining the Core*. One then defines the Core* directly on the reduced form by arguing in terms of a coherent system of a rationally expected set of offers (Hurwicz 1959) such that no coalition can form on any market.

This construction rests (inter alia) on the idea that two agents can meet directly *and indirectly* on at most one market (acyclicity if one does not take into account cycles of agents attending the same market) and on the idea that, when they bargain on some market, economic agents take into account rationally expected offers on other markets. It constitutes an improvement with respect to the formulation which originated in the field of fix-price models (Younès 1975). In this last perspective, agents take as given their trades on other markets when they bargain on some market and no rationalization is provided about the feasibility in the original model (the reduced form) of eliminating some agents from some coalition on some market while continuing to trade with them (at the same level or not) on other markets.

Moreover, these rationally expected sets of offers must, themselves, make incredible the implementation of a blocking coalition which would imply changes of trades on an infinite number of markets. Thus the Core is gotten from the Core* by requiring that the sets of offers satisfy a condition of stability with respect to blocking trades which are different from the reference trade on an infinite number of markets.

The scheme of this paper is as follows. The first part is devoted to models without money. Assumptions of differentiability and interiority entail that the generalization of the Malinvaud lemma is obtained trivially. The first section analyzes the general O.G.M. It is conceived as a comparison point because the pattern of meetings is not acyclic in terms of agents, but only in terms of generations. Contrary to received wisdom, in a double-ended O.G.M. one must require for preserving agents' rational behavior that the value of each generation's total net trades is equal to 0 (Principle 2). One uses the concept of *Core (compare Hendricks, Judd, and Kovenock 1980; Esteban 1986; Chae 1987).

The second section, which is devoted to the I.M.M., shows the equivalence of the finite Core and the Core* defined in terms of a coherent set of expected offers. In the last section, it is quickly shown that the same framework encompasses the Fix Price Model (F.P.M.).

The second part analyzes models with money. The point of the analysis is that the acyclicity of the pattern of meetings formulates a strong version of the "absence of double coincidence of wants" if there is only one desired good on each market. "Barter" is feasible, but it cannot be an equilibrium because it is not rational to give a desired good for nothing to a consumer whom one will not meet again. Based on a simple example, it is shown that equivalence cannot be gotten with the Core*. It is the assumption that two agents can meet on at most one market which is the drive of the result (in the framework of an O.G.M., this phenomenon is not obtained), and this example is due to D. Gale (1986), who argues in terms of pairwise random patterns of meetings and in terms of Perfect Equilibrium, with the same conclusion. On the contrary, there is equivalence when the notion of Core is used. Then, directing by time the pattern of meetings, one generates liquidity constraints. This provides a foundation for the analysis (Grandmont and Younès 1972, 1973) in which liquidity constraints involving monetary prices are prescribed a priori to agents. This approach is not unrelated to those of Cass and Yaari (1966) and Townsend (1980). Finally, one can argue that the analysis of market coordination failures in terms of monopolistic competition can be rationalized if one assumes that the market structure is incomplete with money playing the role of the means of exchange. In this connection, see e.g. Heller 1985, Blanchard and Kiyotaki 1987, and Roberts 1987. Because of lack of space, we shall not deal with this problem.

I

As indicated in the introduction, the O.G.M., the I.M.M., and the F.P.M. shall be studied successively. Let us emphasize that none of these models contains any explicit reference to coordination costs or information imperfections.

A

We shall assume that each generation lives for two periods. There is no loss of generality because by suitably relabeling periods and goods, one can always formulate the problem in this framework (see Balasko, Cass, and Shell 1980). To simplify notations, there are r ($\geqslant 2$) goods h at each period t and ℓ ($\geqslant 1$) agents j for each generation. Thus, $k = (t, j)$ will be an agent born at t. Let $u_{jt}(x^t, x^{t+1})$ be agent k's utility function. $w_{tj} = [w_{tj}^t, w_{tj}^{t+1}]$ is the initial endowment for agent $k = (t, j)$ and $\mathbb{R}^{2r}_{++}$ is his consumption set. As there is no money one shall assume:

A1: For each k, u_k is smooth, strictly quasiconcave, and strictly increasing. The closures of indifference hypersurfaces belong to $\mathbb{R}^{2r}_{++}$. $w_k \in \mathbb{R}^{2r}_{++}$.

Usually, one assumes that time starts at $t = 0$ and thus everything begins with an "old" generation born at $t = -1$ and a "young" generation born at $t = 0$. Here, one shall consider double-ended sequences, i.e., $t \in N$ (the set of integers), but the argument is the same with $t \in N_+$.

An allocation $(x_k)_k$ is feasible if (i) it is possible, i.e., $x_k \in \mathbb{R}^{2r}_{++}$ $\forall k$, and (ii) it is balanced, i.e.,

$$\sum_{k \in G(t) \cup G(t-1)} x_k^t = \sum_{k \in G(t) \cup G(t-1)} w_k^t \qquad \forall t,$$

where $G(t)$ is the set of agents born at t.

In order to write down budgetary constraints, let us take the classical point of view for which time begins at $t = 0$. Then denoting net trades by $\overline{y}_k^t \equiv x_k^t - w_k^t$, one gets

$$\pi^t \overline{y}_{tj}^t + \pi^{t+1} \overline{y}_{tj}^{t+1} = 0 \qquad \forall (t, j), t \geqslant 0$$

and $\pi^0 \overline{y}_{-1j}^0 = 0 \qquad \forall (0, j)$ (π^t being the r-price vector of period t). Because of balance at $t = 0$, $\sum_j \overline{y}_{-1j}^0 = -\sum_j \overline{y}_{0j}^0$ and thus

$$0 = \pi^0 \sum_j \overline{y}_{-1j}^0 = -\pi^0 \sum_j \overline{y}_{0j}^0 = \pi^1 \sum_j \overline{y}_{0j}^1.$$

By induction $\sum_j \pi^t \overline{y}_{tj}^t = 0$ and $\sum_j \pi^{t+1} \overline{y}_{tj}^{t+1} = 0$ $\forall t \geqslant 0$. That entails, when $j > 1$, that the two budgetary constraints are satisfied for each generation, not for each agent as there is more than one agent per generation (this is different from the I.M.M.). More importantly, that means that, at competitive prices, there cannot be gifts in value at a Walrasian equilibrium (Principle 2). Alternatively, for agents meeting only at one time period, i.e., agents of different generations—there cannot be any "lending" or "borrowing."

How do you write this property down when $t \in N$ and $j > 1$? Obviously by discriminating between trades among agents of the same generation and trades among agents of different generations, i.e., by using a framework similar to that of the extensive form but with the proviso that agents of generation t will meet on many markets. Thus, define market Z^t as the market on which agents of generations $t - 1$ and t meet. This market is isomorphic to $\mathbb{R}^r$ (a subspace of $\mathbb{R}^{2r}$). Market Y^t is the market on which agents of generations t met and it is isomorphic to $\mathbb{R}^{2r}$. $K(Z^t)$ is the set of agents that meets on market Z^t and it is equal to $G(t) \cup G(t - 1)$. One can also denote $K(Y^t) = G(t)$.

Let

$$z^t \in Z^t \sim \mathbb{R}^r \subset \mathbb{R}^{2r} \qquad \text{and} \qquad y = (y^t, y^{t+1}) \in Y^t \sim \mathbb{R}^{2r}.$$

Notice that Z^t is conceived as a vector subspace of $\mathbb{R}^{2r}$. Given a feasible $(\overline{y}_k)_{k \in N^\ell}$, one can associate with it a whole equivalence class of $(y_k, z_k)_{k \in N^\ell}$, where $z_k = [z_k^t, z_k^{t+1}]$ for $k \in G(t)$, by

$$\overline{y}_k^t = y_k^t + z_k^t \qquad \text{and} \qquad \overline{y}_k^{t+1} = y_k^{t+1} + z_k^{t+1} \qquad \forall k = (t, j).$$

One shall use only a convenient representative of this equivalence class called an N-normalized trade. For an (N)-normalized trade one assumes

$$z_k^t = z_{k'}^t \qquad \text{and} \qquad z_k^{t+1} = z_{k'}^{t+1}, \qquad \forall (k, k') \in G(t) \times G(t).$$

It is computed according to the following formulas:

$$z_{tj}^t = \frac{1}{\ell} \sum_j \overline{y}_{tj}^t,$$

$$z_{tj}^{t+1} = \frac{1}{\ell} \sum_j \overline{y}_{tj}^{t+1}.$$

It follows that

$$y_{tj}^t = \overline{y}_{tj}^t - z_{tj}^t \qquad \text{and} \qquad y_{tj}^{t+1} = \overline{y}_{tj}^{t+1} - z_{tj}^{t+1}.$$

Thus, one shall assume that all balanced trades $(y_k, z_k)_{k \in N}$ one considers are N-normalized. This ensures a one-to-one correspondence between a balanced $(\overline{y}_k)_{k \in N^\ell}$ and a balanced $(y_k, z_k)_{k \in N\ell}$. Thus, for each generation t, z_{tj}^t represents the contribution made by (t, j) to the total trade between generation t and generation $(t - 1)$. It is the same for all $k \in G(t)$ for a normalized trade. From now on, the reference to N is deleted. In this language a net trade $(z_k, y_k)_k$ is feasible if (i) it is possible, i.e.,

$$\forall (t, j){:}\ w_{tj} + z_{tj} + y_{tj} \in \mathbb{R}_{++}^{2r}$$

and

$$z_{tj} \in Z^t, \qquad y_{tj} \in Y^t$$

and (ii) it is normalized and balanced, i.e.,

$$\sum_{(t,j) \in K(Y^t)} y_{tj}^t = 0 \qquad \text{and} \qquad \sum_{(t',j) \in K(Z^t)} z_{t'j}^t = 0 \qquad \forall t.$$

Let π^t be the price vector on market z^t and $[\pi^t, \pi^{t+1}]$ the price vector on market Y^t.

Definition 1. A competitive equilibrium for the O.G.M. is a pair $[(\pi^{*t})_t, (y_{tj}^*, z_{tj}^*)_{tj}]$ such that

(i) $(y_{tj}^*, z_{tj}^*)_{t,j}$ is feasible (where $z_{tj}^* = [z_{tj}^{*t}, z_{tj}^{*t+1}]$)

(ii) $\forall k = (t, j)$: (y_k^*, z_k^*) maximizes $u_k(w_k + y_k + z_k^t + z_k^{t+1})$ subject to $w_k + y_k + z_k^t + z_k^{t+1} \in \mathbb{R}_{++}^{2r}$ and $\pi^{*t} y_k^t + \pi^{*t+1} y_k^{t+1} = 0$, $\pi^{*t+1} z_k^{t+1} = 0$.

Remark. When $\ell = 1$, this formulation gives $\pi^{*t} \overline{y}_t^{*t} = 0$ because $y_t^* = 0$ $\forall t$. One shall show that this formulation is warranted by an argument based on the core of a large economy, whatever is ℓ. Moreover, notice that this definition corresponds to the usual one $[(\pi^{*t})_t, (\overline{y}_k^*)_k]$ either when there is a first period or, more generally, if $\sum_{k \in G(t)} \pi^{*t} \overline{y}_k^{*t} = 0$ $\forall t$. Obviously a C.E. $[(\pi^{*t})_t, (y_k^*, z_k^*)_k]$ according to Definition 1 *is* a usual C.E. for $\overline{y}_k^* = y_k^* + z_k^*$. Conversely a usual C.E. $[(\pi^{*t})_t, (\overline{y}_k^*)_k]$ with $\sum_{k \in G(t)} \pi^{*t} \overline{y}_k^{*t} = 0$ is a C.E. according to Definition 1 (when one chooses the normalized version for $(y_k^*, z_k^*)_k$. Finally, if for $k = (t, j), (y_k, z_k)$ is better than (y_k^*, z_k^*), then $\pi^{*t}[y_k^t + z_k^t] + \pi^{*t+1}[y_k^{*+1} + z_k^{t+1}] \geqslant 0$ with strict inequality if (y_k, z_k) is strictly better than (y_k^*, z_k^*).

Lemma 1. Under A1, there exists a C.E. (according to Definition 1).

Proof. Elementary.

In this language. a feasible $(y_k, z_k)_k$ is finitely optimal if for every finite interval $[t_0, t_1] \in N$ there is not a feasible $({}^1y_k, {}^1z_k)_k$ with

(i) $u_k(w_k + {}^1y_k + {}^1z_k) \geqslant u_k(w_k + y_k + z_k) \quad \forall k$

and strict inequality for at least one k and

(ii) $y_k = {}^1y_k$ and $z_k = {}^1z_k$ $\forall k = (t, j)$ with $t \notin [t_0, t_1]$.

One casts finite optimality in another language. Instead of requiring that trades can be modified for only a finite number of generations, one requires that the deviations have to belong to a well-defined set of trade offers. There are many ways of achieving this goal but they all amount to the same thing. Members of generation t can exchange among themselves without any restriction. However, when members of generation t make offers to members of generation $t + 1$(resp. $t - 1$) they keep their trades with members of generation $t - 1$(resp. $t + 1$) fixed.[3]

Definition 2. Under A1, a feasible $(y_k, z_k)_k$ is collectively *rational if there is a sequence of sets of trade offers $(\tilde{Y}_k, \tilde{Z}_k)_k$ such that

(1) $\forall k \in G(t)$ and $\forall t$:

$$\tilde{Y}_k = \{{}^1y_t \in Y^t | ({}^1y_k, z_k) \text{ is possible for } k \text{ with}$$
$$u_k(w_k + {}^1y_k, z_k) \geqslant u_k(w_k + y_k + z_k)\}$$
$$\tilde{Z}_k^t = \{{}^1z_k^t \in Z^t | (y_k, {}^1z_k^t, z_k^{t+1}) \text{ is possible for } k \text{ with}$$
$$u_k(w_k + y_k + {}^1z_k^{t+1} + z_k^{t+1}) \geqslant u_k(w_k + y_k + z_k)\}$$
$$\tilde{Z}_k^{t+1} = \{{}^1z_k^{t+1} \in Z^{t+1} | (y_k, z_k^t, {}^1z_k^{t+1}) \text{ is possible for } k \text{ with}$$
$$u_k(w_k + y_k + z_k^t + {}^1z_k^{t+1}) \geqslant u_k(w_k + y_k + z_k)\}.$$

(2) There does not exist a feasible (normalized) trade $({}^2y_k, {}^2z_k)$ with the following properties:

(i) There is $({}^1y_k, {}^1z_k)_k$ that is possible and balanced with $\forall_k$: ${}^1y_k \in \tilde{Y}_k$, ${}^1z_k^t \in \tilde{Z}_k^t$ and ${}^1z_k^{t+1} \in \tilde{Z}_k^{t+1}$, and ${}^2y_k + {}^2z_k = {}^1\overline{y}_k = {}^1y_k + {}^1z_k$.

(ii) $\forall k$: $u_k(w_k + y_k + z_k) \geqslant u_k(w_k + y_k + z_k)$ with strict inequality for at least one k.

Remark. For defining Pareto optimality, one has only to delete any reference to sets $(\tilde{Y}_k, \tilde{Z}_k)_k$. On the other hand, the sets $(\tilde{Y}_k, \tilde{Z}_k)_k$ are the same for each equivalence class of possible and balanced $(y_k, z_k)_k$, because they are defined in terms of the N-normalized representative.

Proposition 1. Under A1, a feasible $(y_k, z_k)_k$ is collectively *rational iff it is a C.E. (with transfers).

Proof. See Appendix.

For defining the Core, one uses, intuitively, the following notion of blocking. All coalitions are possible—recall that the grand coalition can block for defining finite optimality—but although intragenerational trades can be modified without restrictions, intergenerational trades (per head) can be modified only with restrictions. In the language using a set of offers, that gives:

Definition 3. Given a feasible trade $(y_k, z_k)_k$ and thus sets of offers that are associated with it, i.e., $(\tilde{Y}_k, \tilde{Z}_k)_k$, one shall say that it is blocked by a coalition (finite or infinite) $S \in N^\ell$ if there is (an S-normalized version of) $({}^1y_k, {}^1z_k)_{k \in S}$ such that

(i) $({}^1y_k, {}^1z_k)$ is possible for each k and for each t:

$$\sum_{k \in S \cap K(Z^t)} {}^1z_k^t = 0, \qquad \sum_{k \in S \cap K(Y^t)} {}^1y_k = 0.$$

(ii) $\forall k = (t, j) \in S$: ${}^1y_k \in \tilde{Y}_k$, ${}^1z_k^t \in \tilde{Z}_k^t$, and ${}^1z_k^{t+1} \in \tilde{Z}_k^{t+1}$.

(iii) $\forall k \in S$, $u_k(w_k + {}^1y_k + {}^1z_k) \geqslant u_k(w_k + y_k + z_k)$ with a strict inequality for at least one k.

Definition 4. A (normalized) feasible trade $(y_k, z_k)_k$ belongs to the *Core if it is not blocked by any coalition $S \subset N^\ell$.

Replicating means that each k is no longer conceived as an agent but as types of agents. Replicating consists in associating with each k many agents τ of the same type, i.e., having the same characteristics (and thus born at the same period). Let υ be the number of these agents, for each type (t, j). One refers to the economy E^υ when each type is replicated υ times.

Proposition 2. Given A1, a feasible trade $(y_{k\tau}, z_{k\tau})_{k\tau}$ belongs to the *Core of E^υ only if all agents of the same type k get the same utility level. Moreover because of strict quasiconcavity one has, $\forall k = (t, j)$,

$$\overline{y}_{k\tau} = \overline{y}_{k\tau'}, \qquad \forall \text{ pair } (\tau, \tau'),$$

and thus $y_{k\tau} = y_{k\tau'}$ $\forall$ pair (τ, τ') because of normalization.

Proof. See Appendix.

As all agents of the same type k have the same $(y_{k\tau}, z_{k\tau})$, whatever υ is, one can compare directly a trade in the Core with a competitive trade.

Proposition 3. For each υ, a competitive equilibrium for E^υ belongs to the core of $E^\upsilon(*C(E^\upsilon))$. When υ tends to infinity $*C(E^\upsilon)$ converges toward the set of competitive equilibria.

Proof. See Appendix.

Remark. It can be interesting to interpret blocking in terms of rationally expected sets of trade offers and an infinite "coalition" does not require the "physical" presence at the same time of all agents involved in the "coalition."

B

Consider an economy with r goods h and ℓ consumers i. We maintain assumption A1. A market α can be defined equivalently as a "place" where $q(\alpha)$ bundles of goods—which are vectors of $\mathbb{R}^r$—are exchanged, one for another one, or as the vector subspace Z^α of $\mathbb{R}^r$ (Gale 1982), which is generated by these bundles $\lambda_1^\alpha, \ldots, \lambda_{q(\alpha)}^\alpha$.

Thus, a market structure can be defined by

$$M = [Z^1, \ldots, Z^\alpha, \ldots, Z^n]$$

where each Z^α is a vector subspace of $\mathbb{R}^r$ of dimension $q(\alpha) \geqslant 2$. Given M, a trade $\tilde{z} = [\tilde{z}_1, \ldots, \tilde{z}_\ell]$ where $\tilde{z}_i = [z_i^1, \ldots, z_i^\alpha, \ldots, z_i^n]$ is feasible if

(i) $\forall i$, it is possible, i.e., $w_i + \sum_\alpha z_i^\alpha \in \mathbb{R}_+^r$ and $\forall \alpha$:

$$z_i^\alpha \in Z^\alpha$$

(ii) it is balanced, i.e., $\forall \alpha$: $\sum_i z_i^\alpha = 0$.

Alternatively, for each α choose a basis

$$\Lambda^\alpha = [\lambda_1^\alpha, \ldots, \lambda_j^\alpha, \ldots, \lambda_{q(\alpha)}^\alpha]$$

containing $q(\alpha)$ bundles of goods. Let a_{ij}^α be the net trade by some agent i in bundle j and define

$$a_i^\alpha = [a_{i1}^\alpha, \ldots, a_{ij}^\alpha, \ldots, a_{iq(\alpha)}^\alpha] \in \mathbb{R}^{q(\alpha)}.$$

Thus

$$z^\alpha \in Z^\alpha \Leftrightarrow \exists a^\alpha \in \mathbb{R}^{q(\alpha)} \text{ with } z^\alpha = \Lambda^\alpha a^\alpha.$$

For simplicity's sake, one assumes

A2: For each α, there exists for Z^α a basis Λ^α containing only nonnegative vectors.

One can define $a_i = [a_i^1, \ldots, a_i^n] \in \mathbb{R}^q$ where $q = \sum_\alpha q^\alpha$
and

$$U_i\left(a_i\right) \equiv u_i\left(w_i + \sum_\alpha \Lambda^\alpha a_i^\alpha\right)$$

$$P_i = \left\{a_i \in \mathbb{R}^q | w_i + \sum_\alpha \Lambda^\alpha a_i^\alpha \in \mathbb{R}_+^r\right\}.$$

Thus $a = [a_1, \ldots, a_i, \ldots, a_\ell]$ is feasible if

(i) $\forall i\colon a_i \in P_i$

(ii) $\forall \alpha\colon \sum_i a_i^\alpha = 0.$

Notice that as the set of feasible a w.r.t. M is defined without recourse to prices, the definition of Pareto optimality is straightforward. Let π_j^α be the price of bundle j on market α, $\pi^\alpha = [\pi_1^\alpha, \ldots, \pi_{q(\alpha)}^\alpha]$ and $\pi = [\pi^1, \ldots, \pi^\alpha, \ldots, \pi^n]$.

Definition 5. Given $M = [Z^1, \ldots, Z^n]$ and A2, (a^*, π^*) is a competitive equilibrium (C.E.) if

(i) a^* is feasible and $\forall \alpha\colon \pi^{*\alpha} \in \mathbb{R}_+^{q(\alpha)} \setminus \{0\}$.

(ii) $\forall i\colon a_i^*$ maximizes $U_i(a_i)$ over the set

$\{a_i \in P_i | \pi^{*\alpha} a_i^\alpha \leqslant 0 \ \forall \alpha\}$.

As there is no arbitrage at a C.E., one can associate with π^* a price vector p^* of $\mathbb{R}^r \setminus \{0\}$ (one price per good) such that

$$\pi^{*\alpha} = p^{*\prime} \Lambda^\alpha \qquad \forall \alpha.$$

One would like to say that two markets structures ${}^1M$ and ${}^2M$ are different if there is an economy for which the set of equilibria w.r.t. ${}^1M$ is different from the set of equilibria w.r.t. ${}^2M$. This idea leads to a market structure $M = [Z^1, \ldots, Z^n]$ in $\mathbb{R}^r$ that is incomplete iff

$$\bigcup_\alpha Z^\alpha \subset\subset \mathbb{R}^r$$

Given an economy and a market structure, one can associate with this pair an extensive form with an infinite set of agents $k = (i, \gamma)$ for each category of agents i and an infinite set of markets $v = (\alpha, \beta)$ for each type of market α. The pattern of visits of markets satisfies the following requirements.

(i) Each $k = (i, \gamma)$ visits exactly one market $v = (\alpha, \beta)$ of each type α. $V(k)$ is the set of markets visited by k. On each $v \in V$ (the set of markets), the set of agents that attends it is noted by $K(v)$ and it contains exactly one agent of each category.

(ii) Two agents k and k' can meet on at most one market v. More precisely, the pattern of meetings is acyclic in the following sense. The pattern of meetings is represented by a graph the nodes of which are agents k. One joins, by an edge, nodes representing agents who visit the same market.

Then, there is no cycle

$$\{k_1, k_2, \ldots, k_\tau, \ldots, k_\upsilon, k_1\}$$

where all k_τ for $\tau \neq 1$ are different, k_τ and $k_{\tau+1}$ meet on market v_τ, and market v_τ is different from market $v_{\tau+1}$.

Figure 3a pictures the case where $\ell = 2$ and $n = 3$ and figure 3b represents the case where $\ell = 3$ and $n = 2$. The category of an agent is represented by Roman numerals and the type of a market by Arabic ones.

For instance, when $n \geqslant \ell$, one can choose a set $\bar{N}$ of indexes β which is similar with N^{n-1}. One defines

$$\beta = [\beta_1, \ldots, \beta_\alpha, \ldots, \beta_n] \in N^n \qquad \text{with} \qquad \sum_\alpha \beta_\alpha = 0$$

and

$$\gamma = [\gamma_1, \ldots, \gamma_\alpha, \ldots, \gamma_n] \in N^n.$$

Then

$$\bar{N} = \left\{\beta \in N^n \,\middle|\, \sum_\alpha \beta_\alpha = 0\right\} \sim N^{n-1}.$$

$\forall\gamma$, agent (i, γ) visits, for each α, the market (α, β), index β of which is defined by

$$\beta_\alpha = \gamma_\alpha + i - 1 \qquad \text{and} \qquad \beta_{\alpha'} = \gamma_{\alpha'} \qquad \forall\alpha' \neq \alpha.$$

When $n < \ell$, one permutates the roles of γ and β in the above formulas.

Thus, a pattern of meetings is a triple $[V, K, \tilde{K}]$ where V is the set of markets, K the set of agents, and $\tilde{K}$: $V \to P(K)$ associates with each market v the set of agents that visits it. Moreover, one defines $\tilde{V}$: $K \to P(V)$, which associates with each agent k the set of markets he visits. After choosing the same basis Λ^α for all $v = (\alpha, \beta)$ of the same type α, one defines that $(a_k)_k$ is feasible if

$$\text{(i) } \forall k\text{: } a_k \in P_k = \left\{a_k \in \mathbb{R}^q | w_k + \sum_{v \in \tilde{V}(k)} \Lambda^v a_k^v \in \mathbb{R}^r_+\right\}.$$

$$\text{(ii) } \forall v\text{: } \sum_{k \in \tilde{K}(v)} a_k^v = 0.$$

$(a_k)_k$ is symmetric if

$$a_k^v = a_{k'}^{v'}$$

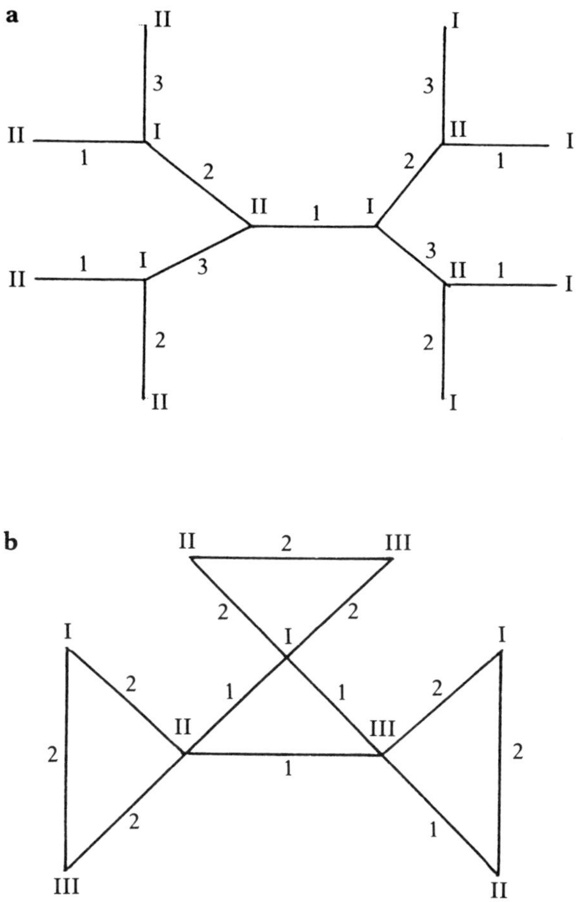
a
II
3
I
II
1
2
II
1
I
2
3
II
1
I
I
1
II
1
I
3
3
II
1
I
2
2
II
I
b
II
2
III
2
2
I
I
I
2
1
1
2
II
III
2
2
1
2
1
III
II

Figure 3.

if $k = (i, \gamma)$ and $k' = (i, \gamma')$ for some i and if $v = (\alpha, \beta')$ and $v' = (\alpha, \beta')$ for some α.

Obviously, there is a bijection ψ between the set of symmetric and feasible $(a_k)_k$ in the extensive form and the set of feasible a in the reduced form.

Definition 6. Given $[V, K, \tilde{K}]$, $[(\pi^{*v})_v, (a_k^*)_k]$ is a C.E. in the extensive form if

(i) $(a_k^*)_k$ is feasible and $\forall v$: $\pi^{*v} > 0$.

(ii) $\forall k$: a_k^* maximizes $U_k(a_k)$ over the set

$$\{a_k \in P_i | \pi^{*v} a_k^v \leqslant 0 \qquad \forall v \in V(k)\}.$$

A C.E. $[(\pi^{*v})_v, (a_k^*)_k]$ is *weakly symmetric* if (a_k^*) is symmetric. It is *symmetric* if $(a_k^*)_k$ is symmetric and if $(\pi^{*v})_v$ is also symmetric in the following sense:

$$\pi^{*v} = \pi^{*v'} \quad \text{if} \quad v = (\alpha, \beta) \quad \text{and} \quad v' = (\alpha, \beta') \quad \text{for some } \alpha.$$

It is trivial to check that because of A1, the generalization of the Malinvaud lemma obtains that a weakly symmetric C.E. $[(\pi^{*v})_v, (a_k^*)_k]$ is automatically symmetric.

Another consequence of A1 is that given a (symmetric) C.E. $[(\pi^{*v})_v, (a_k^*)_k]$, one can associate with it a set of "discounted" prices $(\bar{\pi}^{*v})_v$ at which each consumer k maximizes utility subject to *one* budgetary constraint, i.e., over the set $\{a_k \in P_k | \sum_{v \in V(k)} \bar{\pi}^{*v} a_k^v \leqslant 0\}$. In order to check this statement, start with the system $(\pi^{*v})_v$. Consider some v_0 and the set $K(v_0)$. Choose $\bar{\pi}^{v_0} = \pi^{v_0}$. Consider some $\bar{k} \in K(v_0)$ and $V(\bar{k})$. From A1, one can choose $(\bar{\pi}^v)_{v \in V(\bar{k})}$ as colinear with $U'_{\bar{k}}$ (the gradient of $U_{\bar{k}}$ at $a_{\bar{k}}^*$) in such a way that $\bar{\pi}^{v^0} = \pi^{v^0}$. One can do that for each $k \in K(v_0)$ because of acyclicity. This construction can be continued ad infinitum, again because of acyclicity. If A1 is not made, this is not always the case because some implicit rates of discount may happen to be equal to either 0 or infinity. That will happen in Part II where money is taken into account.

Even when A1 is made, A2 is not strong enough to entail that a C.E. exists for M. One shall adopt, for simplicity sake, an unnecessarily strong assumption which gives the desired result.[4]

Define

$$\Pi = \{\pi \in \mathbb{R}^q_{++} | \exists p \in \mathbb{R}^r_{++} \text{ such that } p' \Lambda^\alpha = \pi^\alpha \ \forall^\alpha\}$$

and for each $\pi \in \Pi$.

$$Y(\pi) = \left\{ y \in \mathbb{R}^r \mid \exists a = [a^1, \ldots, a^n] \text{ such that } y = \sum_\alpha \Lambda^\alpha a^\alpha \text{ and } \pi^\alpha a^\alpha = 0 \; \forall^\alpha \right\}.$$

H3: M is regular in the sense that for each $\pi \in \Pi$, $Y(\pi)$ always has the same dimension.

This assumption also entails that one can argue only in a compact set of feasible and individually rational trades $a = [a_1, \ldots, a_m]$. Let F be a compact set (in $\mathbb{R}^{q\ell}$) of this kind. Define also

$$F_i = \{a_i \in \mathbb{R}^q \mid \exists a = [a_1, \ldots, a_i, \ldots, a_\ell] \in F\}.$$

The finite Core is based on the idea that agents can communicate outside the pattern of meetings and that agents attending a finite set of markets can sign contracts among them. On the contrary, with the Core* there can be commitments only among agents attending the same market, given that they make rational expectations about the trades they can implement on other markets. Because of the structure of the pattern of meetings, I shall refer to "inward induction." I shall show that the two approaches lead to the same result. Then, if in the first approach a coalition contemplates the possibility of modifying trades on an infinite number of markets, its stability must be tested in terms of arguments borrowed from the Bargaining Set or from the "Coalition Proof" theory. Alternatively, the stability of offer sets must be tested against "outward induction." I shall analyze the second approach, which seems more natural.

In the extensive form, the notions of collective rationality* and finite Core are obviously defined. In order to translate them in the reduced form, let us start with the following definition.

Definition 7′. Given $[K, V, \tilde{K}]$, a feasible trade $(\bar{a}_k)_k$ belongs to the Core* if there are sets of trade offers $(\tilde{A}_k^v)_{k,v}$ such that

(i) $\forall (k, v)$, $\tilde{A}_k^v$ is the projection on $\mathbb{R}^{q(v)}$ (market v) of

$$^v\tilde{A}_k = \left\{ a \in \mathbb{R}^q \mid U_k(a) \geqslant U_k(\bar{a}_k) \text{ and } \forall v' \in V(k)\backslash\{v\}, \exists S^{v'} \subset K(v')\backslash\{k\} \text{ with } a^{v'} \in -\sum_{k' \in S^{v'}} \tilde{A}_{k'}^{v'} \right\}$$

where, by convention,

$$\sum_{k' \in S^{v'}} \tilde{A}_{k'}^{v'} = \{0\} \quad \text{if } S^{v'} = \phi.$$

(ii) There is not a market v, a coalition $S^v \subset K(v)$ and $(a_k)_{k \in S^v}$ with

(a) $U_k(a_k) \geqslant U_k(\overline{a}_k)$ $\forall k \in S^v$ with strict inequality for at least one k.

(b) $\sum_{k \in S^v} a_k^v = 0$.

(c) $\forall k \in S^v$: $a_k^v \in \tilde{A}_k^v$.

In Definition 7′, each k is making offers on $v \in V(k)$ because he knows that he can match offers made by other agents k' on other markets $v' \in V(k)$, in turn these other agents k' are making offers on markets $v' \in V(k)$ because they can match offers by other agents k'' .... Thus, these sets of offers are coherent. They can be conceived as sets of offers that are rationally expected. Notice that in (ii) of Definition 7′, it is no longer required that trades be modified on only a finite number of markets, but instead it is required that they belong to this set of trade offers.

Notice also that if $(\overline{a}_k)_k$ is symmetric, it is not a priori required that the sets $(\tilde{A}_k^v)_{k,v}$ are symmetric in the sense that $\tilde{A}_k^v = \tilde{A}_{k'}^{v'}$ if $v = (\alpha, \beta)$ and $v' = (\alpha, \beta')$ for some α and $k = (i, \gamma)$ and $k' = (i, \gamma')$ for some i.

However, it is better to conceive that agents can have only symmetric expectations and we shall show that if $(\overline{a}_k)_k$ is symmetric, one can choose a symmetric system $(\tilde{A}_k^v)_{k,v}$. It follows that when $(\overline{a}_k)_k$ is symmetric and thus when $\overline{a} = \psi((\overline{a}_k)_k)$ is defined directly on the reduced form, one can define the Core* directly on the reduced form, as the set $(\tilde{A}_k^v)_{k,v}$, being symmetric, can be written $(\tilde{A}_i^\alpha)_{i,\alpha}$. The language of Definition 7′ can be kept, choosing everything symmetric. Alternatively, it is possible to introduce a slight change (in the spirit of L. Hurwicz).

Definition 7″. A feasible trade $\overline{a}$ belongs to the Core* if it can be supported by sets of trade offers $({}^\alpha\tilde{A}_i)_{i,\alpha}$ such that

(i) $\forall (i, \alpha)$:

$$
\begin{aligned}
{}^\alpha\tilde{A}_i = \Big\{ & a \in P_i \,|\, U_i(a) \geqslant U_i(\overline{\overline{a}}),\ \forall \overline{\overline{a}} = [\overline{\overline{a}}^1, \dots, \overline{\overline{a}}^n] \in P_i \text{ with} \\
& \forall \alpha' \neq \alpha\colon \overline{\overline{a}}^{\alpha'} \in -\sum_{i' \in S^{\alpha'}} \tilde{A}_{i'}^{\alpha'}, \\
& \text{for some } S^{\alpha'} \text{ with } i \notin S^{\alpha'} \text{ and } \forall^{\alpha''} \neq \alpha\colon \\
& a_i^{\alpha''} \in -\sum_{i' \in S^{\alpha'}} \tilde{A}_{i'}^{\alpha''} \text{ for some } S^{\alpha''} \text{ with } i \notin S^{\alpha''} \Big\}
\end{aligned}
$$

where $\tilde{A}_i^\alpha$ is the projection on α of ${}^\alpha\tilde{A}_i$.

(ii) $\forall \alpha$: There is not a coalition S^α and $(a_i)_{i \in S^\alpha}$ with

(a) $U_i(a_i) \geqslant U_i(\overline{a}_i) \qquad \forall i \in S^\alpha$ with strict inequality for some $i \in S^\alpha$.

(b) $\sum_{i \in S^\alpha} a_i^\alpha = 0$.

(c) $\forall i \in S^\alpha$: $a_i \in {}^\alpha\tilde{A}_i$ and thus $a_i^\alpha \in \tilde{A}_i^\alpha$.

Thus, the difference between the symmetric version of Definition 7′ and Definition 7″ is that in the latter it is possible that some agent does not want to make an offer on market α, that he would make according to the first one: a stricter notion of rationality is embodied in Definition 7″, but it turns out that the two definitions are equivalent. Somehow, Definition 7″ takes into account a higher degree of credibility. By an error in notation, the same notation is used: $\tilde{A}_i^\alpha$.

Assume $(\overline{a}_k)_k$ symmetric and let us show the equivalence of the finite Core and the Core* (Definition 7′). In figure 3a, consider a connected and finite set of markets V^0. Let us say that an agent k_0 is a terminal node if it participates in only one market $v \in V^0$ (when $\ell = 2$, a terminal node in this sense is a terminal node in the usual sense of graph theory). We say that the finite and connected set V^0 of markets on which trades can be modified is balanced if the set of agents k that attends some market $v \in V^0$ can be partitioned into two sets.

- A set of terminal agents that can then modify trades on only one market $v \in V^0$.
- A set of agents k that can then modify trades on all markets attended because $V(k) \subset V^0$.

We can consider only balanced sets V^0 without loss of generality. Thus, with the notion of finite Core, if a terminal agent k_0 belongs to some coalition S, his trades are kept fixed on $(n - 1)$ markets, those markets v with $v \in V(k_0)$ and $v \notin V^0$. Thus, a terminal agent k_0 keeps his trades fixed on these $(n - 1)$ markets when he makes an offer on market $v_0 \in V^0$. Thus, when one takes an increasing net $\{V^t\}$ of balanced sets of markets with $V^t \supset\supset V^{(t-1)}$, one can argue as follows:

1. Consider $(\overline{a}_k)_k$ (which is stationary) and which belongs to the finite core. Define $\overline{a} = \psi(\overline{a}_k)_k)$ and $\forall (i, \alpha)$:

$$
{}^\alpha\tilde{A}_i(1) = \left\{ a_i \in P_i \cap F_i \,|\, U_i(a_i) \geqslant U_i(\overline{a}_i) \text{ and } \forall \alpha' \neq \alpha, \exists S^{\alpha'} \right.
$$

$$
\left. \text{with } i \notin S^{\alpha'} \text{ such that } a_i^{\alpha'} \in -\sum_{i' \in S^{\alpha'}} \{\overline{a}_{i'}^{\alpha'}\} \right\}
$$

and for $t \geqslant 1$:

$$^{\alpha}\tilde{A}_i(t) = \left\{a_i \in P_i \cap F_i \,|\, U_i(a_i) \geqslant U_i(\bar{a}_i) \text{ and } \forall\alpha' \neq \alpha, \exists S^{\alpha'} \text{ with } i \notin S^{\alpha'} \text{ such that } a_i^{\alpha'} \in -\sum_{i' \in S^{\alpha'}} \tilde{A}_{i'}^{\alpha'}(t-1)\right\}.$$

From A1 and A3, one has bounded uniformly the offer sets without loss of generality. As $\forall(i, \alpha)$:

$$^{\alpha}\tilde{A}_i(t) \supset {}^{\alpha}\tilde{A}_i(t-1)$$

(i) of Definition 7′ is satisfied by going to the limit. One can then check that (ii) of Definition 7′ is fulfilled because no coalition can block finitely in the extensive form. Because of its construction, such a system $(\tilde{A}_i^{\alpha})_{i,\alpha}$ will be called *minimal*.

2. Conversely, assume that $\bar{a}$ is supported by a system $(^{\alpha}\tilde{A}_i)_{i,\alpha}$ as in Definition 7′. Define $(\bar{a}_k)_k = \psi^{-1}(\bar{a})$. Ad absurdum, assume that there exists a coalition S which blocks through $(a_k)_{k \in S}$. Consider $k_0 \in S$ with $U_{k_0}(a_{k_0}) > U_{k_0}(\bar{a}_{k_0})$ and a market $v_0 \in V(k_0)$ of type α_0. Define $S^{\alpha_0} = S \cap K(v_0)$, in the reduced form. As a_k^v is different from $\bar{a}_k^v$ for at most a finite number of $v \in \bigcup_{k \in S} V(k)$, there is on the graph of the extensive form, a maximal distance t_0 from v_0, for which $a^v = \bar{a}^v$ if v is at a distance larger than t_0 from v_0. As $\forall(i, \alpha)$:

$$^{\alpha}\tilde{A}_i(t_0) \subset {}^{\alpha}\tilde{A}_i$$

the coalition S^{α_0} will block.

One can say that an element of the finite Core is stable with respect to *inward induction.*

One can then say that the system $(A_i^{\alpha})_{i,\alpha}$ of Definition 7″ (or an element of the finite Core) is stable with respect to inward induction. Thus, now, we are back to the idea that binding changes of trades can be made only on one market, but that each agent is taking into account rationally expected offers he can match on other markets. Notice that $(\tilde{A}_i^{\alpha})_{i,\alpha}$ which supports $\bar{a}$ in Definition 7″ is generated by "response" functions $(\Gamma_i^{\alpha})_{i,\alpha}$ that associate sets with sets

$$\Gamma_i^{\alpha}\colon (A_{-i}^{\alpha'})_{\alpha' \neq \alpha} \to A_i^{\alpha}$$

where Γ_i^{α} is the projection on market α of

$$^{\alpha}\Gamma_i = \left\{ a\ P_i | U_i(a) \geqslant U_i(a) \geqslant U_i(\overline{\overline{a}}), \forall \overline{\overline{a}} = [\overline{\overline{a}}^1, \ldots, \overline{\overline{a}}^n] \in P_i \right.$$

$$\text{with } \forall \alpha' \neq \alpha \text{: } \overline{\overline{a}}^{\alpha'} \in - \sum_{i' \in S^{\alpha'}} A_{i'}^{\alpha'} \text{ for some } S^{\alpha'} \text{ with } i \notin S^{\alpha'} \text{ and}$$

$$\left. \forall \alpha'' \neq \alpha \text{: } a^{\alpha''} \in - \sum_{i' \in S^{\alpha''}} A_{i'}^{\alpha''} \text{ for some } S^{\alpha''} \text{ with } i \notin S^{\alpha''} \right\}.$$

Thus, $(\tilde{A}_i^{\alpha})_{i,\alpha}$ is defined as a solution of

$$\tilde{A}_i^{\alpha} = \Gamma_i^{\alpha}((\tilde{A}_{-i}^{\alpha'})_{\alpha' \neq \alpha})$$

and many systems $(\tilde{A}_i^{\alpha})_{i,\alpha}$ can support a given $\overline{a}$ according to Definition 7″. From the point of view of agent i on market α, it is rational to expect offers $(A_{-i}^{\alpha'})$ given the (conservative) behavior of all agents as it is defined through $(\Gamma_i^{\alpha})_{i,\alpha}$. Finally, one can define the "one step" $\Gamma_i^{\alpha}(1)$ as the projection on α of

$$^{\alpha}\Gamma_i(1) = \left\{ a \in P_i | U_i(a) \geqslant U_i(\overline{\overline{a}}), \forall \overline{\overline{a}} \in P_i \text{ with } \forall \alpha' \neq \alpha \text{:} \right.$$

$$\overline{\overline{a}}^{\alpha'} \in - \sum_{i' \in S'} \{\overline{a}_{i'}^{\alpha'}\} \text{ for some } S^{\alpha'} \text{ with } i \notin S^{\alpha'} \text{ and } \forall \alpha'' \neq \alpha \text{:}$$

$$\left. a^{\alpha''} \in - \sum_{i' \in S^{\alpha''}} \{a_{i'}^{\alpha''}\} \text{ for some } S^{\alpha''} \text{ with } i \in S^{\alpha''} \right\}.$$

Note the difference between $^{\alpha}\Gamma_i(1)$ and $^{\alpha}\tilde{A}_i(1)$.

In order to show that the Core* is equal to the set of C.E.s when each agent is small in each market he attends, we shall replicate. In the reduced form, there will be $\upsilon\ell$ agents $\theta = (i, \tau)$ on each market of the economy E^{υ}. In the extensive form, for each agent of category (i, τ), there will be an infinite number of agents $k = (i, \tau, \gamma)$: the set of agents will be K^{υ} in E^{υ}.

Thus, for each υ, one has an economy E^{υ} in the reduced form. As one does not use equal treatment, consider a sequence $\{u^{\upsilon}\}$ of uniform measures with finite and increasing (w.r.t. inclusion) supports (Supp μ^{υ}) in $[0, 1]$, which converges weakly toward Lebesgue measure λ on $[0, 1]$. In the economy E^{υ}, there are thus $\upsilon = |\text{Supp } \mu^{\upsilon}|$ agents of category i (where $|\text{Supp } \mu^{\upsilon}|$ is the cardinal of Supp μ^{υ}). In this language, a net trade $\tilde{a}$ in E^{υ} is an m-uple of random variables $\tilde{a}_i$: Supp $\mu^{\upsilon} \to \mathbb{R}^q$.
$\tilde{a} = [\tilde{a}_i, \ldots, \tilde{a}_m]$ is balanced if

$$\sum_i \int \tilde{a}_i \, d\mu^{\upsilon} = 0.$$

The concepts of Core* and competitive equilibrium are reformulated, in an obvious way, in this language.

Proposition 4. Given A1 and M satisfying A2–A3, the core is not empty because it contains the set of C.E.s. When υ converges toward infinity, the core tends toward the set of C.E.s, in the usual way.

Proof. See Appendix.

The system of offers $(\tilde{A}_i^\alpha)_{i,\alpha}$ that supports $\overline{a} = \psi((\overline{a}_k)_k)$ also has the following meaning:

C1: When

$$a^\alpha \in \sum_{\substack{i' \in S^\alpha \\ i' \neq i}} \tilde{A}_{i'}^\alpha,$$

for some S^α, agent i thinks that he can match a^α on market α.

C2: When

$$a^\alpha \in \tilde{A}_i^\alpha,$$

and

$$a^\alpha \notin - \sum_{\substack{i' \in S^\alpha \\ i' \neq i}} \tilde{A}_{i'}^\alpha,$$

for every S^α, agent i thinks that his offer is not accepted on market α.

But what happens if some agent i is interested for some reason in making an offer a^α on market α with

$$a^\alpha \notin \tilde{A}_i^\alpha$$

and

$$a^\alpha \notin - \sum_{\substack{i' \in S^\alpha \\ i' \neq i}}$$

for every coalition S^α?

Given two different markets, $\overline{v}$ and v', let us say that v is between $\overline{v}$ and v', with $v \neq v'$, if there is a finite ordered sequence of markets which are all different,

$$v_1, \ldots, v_j, \ldots, v_n, v_1', \ldots, v_j', \ldots, v_n',$$

and a finite ordered sequence of agents who are all different,

$$k_1, \ldots, k_n, k_1', \ldots, k_n',$$

such that

$$k_1 \in K(\bar{v}) \cap K(v_1), \ldots, k_1' \in K(v_n) \cap K(v_1'), \ldots, k_n' \in K(v_n') \cap K(v').$$

Consider $\bar{a} = \psi((\bar{a}_k)_k)$ which belongs to the Core*, being supported by the system of offers $(\tilde{A}_i^\alpha)_{i,\alpha}$. $(\bar{a}_k)_k$ is stable with respect to inward induction because on each market $v = (\alpha, \beta)$, $k = (i, \gamma) \in K(v)$ makes offers taking into account contracts he is sure to be able to implement on other markets $v' \in V(k)$, $v' \neq v$. Let S be a coalition which blocks potentially through $(a_k)_{k \in S}$. Let v be a market for which there are two agents, k and $k' \in S^v \equiv S \cap K(v)$, with

$$a_k^v \neq \bar{a}_k^v \quad \left(a_k^v \notin -\sum_{S^v \setminus \{k\}} \tilde{A}_{k''}^v\right)$$

and

$$a_{k'}^v \neq \bar{a}_{k'}^v.$$

Assume that

$$a_k^v \in \tilde{A}_k^v$$

and

$$a_{k'}^{v'} \in \tilde{A}_{k'}^{v'}$$

for some

$$v' \in V(k') \quad \left(a_{k'}^{v'} \notin -\sum_{S^{v'} \setminus \{k'\}} \tilde{A}_{k''}^{v'}\right).$$

Whatever is $\bar{v}$ for which $S^{\bar{v}} = S \cap K(\bar{v})$ is not empty, agents in S^v can conceive $(\bar{a}_k)_{k \in S}$ and know that they can commit on $\bar{v}$ only if, starting at $\bar{v}$ (outward induction), the wave of new trades will be accepted on all other markets on which agents of S trade effectively. Assume that this wave attains first v, v being between $\bar{v}$ and v'. As v is attained first, agent k' would refuse to accept $a_{k'}^v$, arguing as follows with k: "I already know that you are interested that I accept a_k^v, because $a_k^v \in \tilde{A}_k^v$ and according to C2 you should have expected that a_k^v is not accepted. It would be very risky to accept $a_{k'}^v$, because as $a_{k'}^{v'} \in \tilde{A}_{k'}^{v'}$, according to C2, I expect that $a_{k'}^{v'}$ will not be accepted by other agents in $S^{v'}$." Thus:

OI1: The pair $[\bar{a}, (\tilde{A}_i^\alpha)_{i,\alpha}]$ is stable with respect to outward induction if for every $(a_k)_{k \in S}$ which blocks potentially: Whatever is the starting point $\bar{v}$, at which new nonzero trades $(a_k)_{k \in S}$ $\bar{v}$ are made, there are two markets v and v', with v between $\bar{v}$ and v', two agents $k \in S^v$ and $k' \in S^v \cap S^{v'}$ with

$$a_k^v \in \tilde{A}_k^v \quad \text{and} \quad a_k^v \neq \bar{a}_k^v, \quad a_k^v \notin - \sum_{S^v \setminus \{k\}} \tilde{A}_{k''}^v$$

$$a_{k'}^{v'} \in \tilde{A}_{k'}^{v'} \quad \text{and} \quad a_{k'}^{v'} \neq \bar{a}_{k'}^{v'}, \quad a_{k'}^{v'} \notin - \sum_{S^{v'} \setminus \{k'\}} \tilde{A}_{k''}^{v'}.$$

Remark: Obviously, it is possible to supplement OI1 by writing down that the sets of offers $(\tilde{A}_i^\alpha)_{i,\alpha}$ make noncredible the implementation of some blocking $(a_k)_{k \in S}$ if some agent $k \in S$ increases more his utility by taking advantage of some

$$\bar{\bar{a}}_k^v \in - \sum_{k' \in \bar{\bar{S}}^v} \tilde{A}_{k'}^v,$$

on some market $v \in V(k)$, with $\bar{\bar{a}}_k^v \neq a_k^v$.

Definition 7. A feasible and symmetric $(\bar{a}_k)_k = \psi^{-1}(\bar{a})$ belongs to the Core if the system of expected offers $(\tilde{A}_i^\alpha)_{i,\alpha}$ that satisfies conditions (i) and (ii) of Definitions 7′ or 7″ is large enough to be stable in the sense of O.I.1.

Remark. In general, one must add supplementary sets in order to make stable the system of sets of offers (see Younès 1985).

C

The objective of this section is not only to show that the F.P.M. can be cast in our framework (in order to emphasize that what is important in this model is not so much the fact that prices are not totally flexible as that the market structure is assumed to be incomplete: see, e.g., Younès 1975) but also to have the first opportunity to picture in what sense the notion of blocking while keeping trades fixed outside a finite number of markets is not strong enough. Here, one shall deal only with collective rationality in order to consider only no trade allocations.

First, substitute for A2. A2′: The market structure $M = [Z^1, \ldots, Z^n]$ is such that for each α: Z^α has dimension 1.

For each α, let $\lambda^\alpha \in \mathbb{R}^r \setminus \{0\}$ be the normed (norm 1) basis of Z^α. It is easy to show that A2′ captures the idea that "prices are fixed." Start with a market structure

$$^2M = [^2Z^1, \ldots, ^2Z^n]$$

which satisfies A2. Assume that $\forall\alpha$: $^2Z^\alpha$ has dimension 2. Let $^2\pi^\alpha$ be the price vector on $^2Z^\alpha$. Fix $^2\pi^\alpha = \bar{\pi}^\alpha \in \mathbb{R}^2_{++}$.
Then, for each α:

$$Z^\alpha = \{z^\alpha \in {}^2Z^\alpha | \bar{\pi}^\alpha z^\alpha = 0\}$$

has dimension 1.

Thus, one can use the same formalism as when A2 is made. Formally, let π^α be the "price" of the bundle of market α. As λ^α contains, in general, negative elements, $\pi^\alpha \in \mathbb{R}$. An equilibrium can be defined in the reduced form:

Definition 8. $0 = [0, \ldots, 0]$ is a Dreze Generalized Equilibrium (D.G.E.) if there is $\pi = [\pi^1, \ldots, \pi^n] \neq 0$ such that $\forall i$: 0 maximizes $U_i(a)$ subject to

$$a \in P_i \quad \text{and} \quad \pi^\alpha a^\alpha \leqslant 0 \quad \forall\alpha.$$

Obviously as for each α, $\pi^\alpha \in \mathbb{R}$, π^α can be chosen to be -1, 0, or $+1$. Thus, by convention:

If $\pi^\alpha = 0$, neither supply nor demand is rationed.

If $\pi^\alpha > 0$, then demand is rationed.

If $\pi^\alpha < 0$, then supply is rationed.

Basically, 0 (or by translation any feasible $a = [a^1, \ldots, a^n]$) is a D.G.E. if there is a *quadrant* Q in $\mathbb{R}^n$ such that $\forall i$:

$$Q \cap \bar{A}_i = \phi$$

where $\forall i$:

$$\bar{A}_i = \{a \in P_i | U_i(a) > U_i(0)\}.$$

Thus, if each Z^α has a dimension larger than one, one can say that 0 is a C.E. w.r.t. M if there is a "generalized" quadrant Q in $\mathbb{R}^q$ such that $\forall i$:

$$Q \cap \bar{A}_i = \phi.$$

As the definition of the extensive form does not depend on the dimension of the subspaces, one can use it for the F.P.M. More particularly, one defines collective rationality and symmetric and weakly symmetric D.G.E. As soon as A1 is not made and there are more than two agents and/or more than two markets, a weakly symmetric D.G.E. is not necessarily symmetric. It follows that if 0 is collectively rational, it is (under only the usual convexity assumptions) a weakly symmetric D.G.E. in the extensive form, but not necessarily a D.G.E. in the reduced form.

Example 1. $\ell = 4$, $r = 3$, and $n = 2$.

The last good 3 is a means of exchange on markets 1 and 2 and the fixed price vector of goods is [1, 1, 1]. Thus,

$\lambda^1 = [1, 0, -1]$ and $\lambda^2 = [0, 1, -1]$.

Consumer 1: $X_1 = \mathbb{R}^3_+$, $w_1 = [0, 0, 1]$, $u_1 = 4\,\text{Min}\{x_1, x_2\} + x_3$
Consumer 2: $X_2 = \mathbb{R}^3_+$, $w_2 = [1, 1, 0]$, $u_2 = 5/4\,\text{Min}\{x_1, x_2\} + x_3$
Consumer 3: $X_3 = \mathbb{R}^3_+$, $w_3 = [0, 1, 0]$, $u_3 = 2x_1 + x_2$
Consumer 4: $X_4 = \mathbb{R}^3_+$, $w_4 = [1, 0, 0]$, $u_4 = x_1 + 2x_2$.

Consider the trade $a = [a_1, a_2, a_3, a_4] = 0$. On figure 4, one pictures the set of strictly preferred trades.

It is obvious that 0 is not a D.G.E. because there is no quadrant Q of $\mathbb{R}^2$ such that

$Q \cap \bar{A}_i = \phi \qquad$ for $i = 1, 2, 3$, and 4.

However 0 is collectively rational. Choose $\forall (i, \alpha)$:

$\tilde{A}_i^\alpha = \{0\}$.

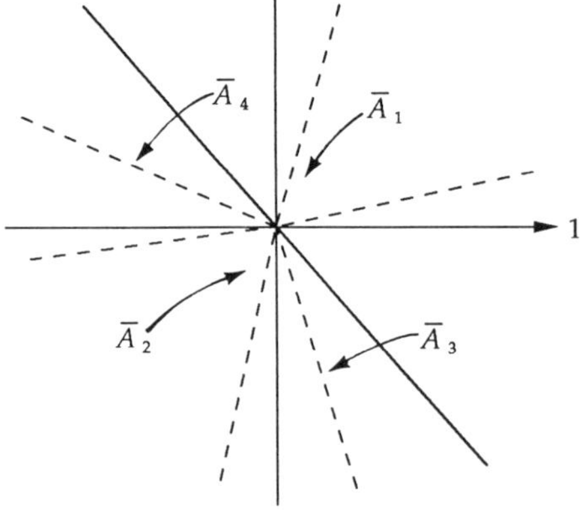

Figure 4.

This is obvious because agent 1 gains strictly only if he can buy on both markets, agent 2 only if he can sell on both markets, agent 3 only if he can buy on market 1 and thus sell on market 2, and agent 4 only if he can buy on market 2 and thus sell on market 1.

Finally, let us check that, in the extensive form, $\psi(0)$ is a weakly symmetric D.G.E. Consider a market $\bar{v} = (1, \beta)$. Choose $\pi^{\bar{v}} > 0$ and thus demand is rationed on this market of type 1. Consider agent $(1, \gamma)$ who attends $\bar{v}$. On the market $v = [2, \beta(1)]$ he attends, one chooses $\pi^v < 0$. On the market $v = [2, \beta(2)]$ attended by agent $(2, \gamma)$ who attends $\bar{v}$, one chooses $\pi^v > 0$. On the contrary, on the market $v = [2, \beta(4)]$ attended by agent $(4, \gamma)$ who attends $\bar{v}$, one must choose $\pi^v < 0$. Because of acyclicity, one can generate a nonsymmetric $(\pi^v)_v$ without encountering an impossibility.

Obviously, such a phenomenon can happen only if 0 is not Pareto-optimal. Because, in this case, it would be possible to use a separation theorem in $\mathbb{R}^n$ to get $\pi = [\pi^1, \ldots, \pi^\alpha, \ldots, \pi^n] \neq 0$, if at least one $\bar{A}_i$ is not empty. If not, one chooses any $\pi \neq 0$. Notice that the construction of sets $\tilde{A}_i^\alpha = \{0\}$ rests on what can be called inward induction on balanced sets of markets larger and larger on which trades can be modified.[5]

When one considers a feasible trade $a \neq 0$, equivalence requires the use of a game theoric concept. In Grandmont, Laroque, and Younès 1978 the bargaining set is used. As the bargaining set is easily defined in the present framework, a general equilibrium analysis can be made, at least under A1.

II

The *absence of double coincidence of wants* must be an important component of a model with money, and this feature can constitute an element of explanation of market coordination failures.

As money has no direct utility in consumption or in production, its value on some market (for some type of transactions) depends on its use on other markets (for other types of transactions). The whole problem is to establish a fruitful dialectics between these general ideas and precise formulations which are general enough. The so-called (double-ended) Overlapping Generations Model (O.G.M.) with money, one physical good, one agent per generation, and each agent living for two periods constitutes a beginning of formulation if we drop the interpretation in terms of a succession of human generations and if we are careful about consequences of agents' rational behavior (Principle 2).

i. The physical good of period t is not available before period t and its costs of storage are infinite. On the contrary, the cost of storage of money is 0.

ii. The absence of double coincidence of wants is formulated through the fact that the pattern of meetings is acyclic.

iii. The consequence of the assumption that there is one desired good on each market and that the pattern of meetings is acyclic is that "barter" cannot be an equilibrium, whatever the reasonable (in this setup and given (ii)) game-theoretic concept of equilibrium that is used. How can we think that some agent would agree to give some quantity of some desired good for nothing to an agent he will never meet again? We have shown that we cannot write, without care, that in an O.G.M., agents are maximizing utility under one budgetary constraint.

iv. Thus, in this particular O.G.M., "barter" and monetary exchange are equally feasible, but "barter" cannot be an equilibrium. This statement is valid even when the pattern of meetings is not directed by time. Assume, on the contrary, that time directs the pattern of meetings. Liquidity constraints arise then very simply: as "barter" cannot be an equilibrium, every agent must sell before buying.

Thus, in this particular O.G.M., money plays a role in transactions at least in the sense that "barter" cannot be an equilibrium. But this conclusion does not hold anymore if there is more than one physical good per period or if there are two different agents for each generation or if a generation lives for more than two periods. The reason is then that there is more than one good on each market and/or the pattern of meetings is no more acyclic (two agents of the same generation meet when they are young and when they are old).[6]

The scheme of section II is as follows. In the first subsection, the structure for which each physical good is exchanged separately against money is analyzed, arguing in terms of an equivalence between the Core* and the set of C.E.s. In the second subsection, the graph of the pattern of meetings is directed in order to formulate the idea of liquidity constraints. The argument is mainly made in terms of C.E., but we consider also the possibility that each agent visits an infinite number of markets, retaining the assumption of acyclicity. This is a way to emphasize that Friedmanian inefficiencies are of a Keynesian type and to give foundations to analysis in which liquidity constraints are formulated through relations involving prices. The last subsection is devoted to the role of money in models of monopolistic competition.

A

Let us introduce inside money in the I.M.M. In the extensive form, one could consider that it is outside money if one abstracts from the idea of time. Consider the economy with r goods and assume that A1 is satisfied. Add inside money which will be commodity 0. The argument will be made in $\mathbb{R}^{r+1}$. Inside money is a commodity the initial allocations of which are 0, and the final allocations of which cannot be negative because nobody can end up as a debtor and which does not enter in utility functions. Thus, A1′ is substituted for A1.

A1′: $\forall i$: The consumption set is $\mathbb{R}_+^{r+1}$, $w_{10} = 0$, and $w_{ih} > 0$ $\forall h \neq 0$. u_i: $\mathbb{R}_+^{r+1} \to \mathbb{R}$ is smooth, strictly quasiconcave, and strictly increasing in the last r goods, does not depend on commodity 0, and the closure of indifference hypersurfaces belongs to $\mathbb{R}_{++}^r$.

The market structure ${}^1M$ formulates the idea that each good can be exchanged separately against money. There are thus r markets $\alpha = h \neq 0$. More precisely:

$${}^1M = [Z^1, \ldots, Z^h, \ldots, Z^r]$$

where

$$Z^h = \{z \in \mathbb{R}^{r+1} | z_{h'} = 0 \ \forall h' \text{ different from 0 and } h\}.$$

We emphasize that ${}^1M$ is incomplete because

$$\bigcup_h Z^h \subset\subset \mathbb{R}^{r+1}.$$

For each Z^h, we choose the canonical basis Λ^h and we can thus confuse a^h and z^h because

$$z^h = \Lambda^h a^h$$

implies then that

$$a_1^h = z_0^h \text{ and } a_2^h = z_h^h.$$

It is well known that the set of C.E.s w.r.t. ${}^1M$ contains two distinct subsets. The first subset corresponds to the set of C.E.s w.r.t. the complete market structure, ${}^0M$. With each C.E. w.r.t. ${}^0M$, one can associate a C.E. w.r.t. ${}^1M$ by choosing the price of commodity 0 to be 1. The second subset contains only the initial allocation. In order to check that the initial allocation is always a C.E. w.r.t. ${}^0M$, choose $\pi_0^h = 0\ \forall h$. Then, for each i, w_i maximizes $u_i(w_i + \sum_h z_i^h)$ subject to $w_i + \sum_h z_i^h \geqslant 0$, $z_i^h \in Z^h$, and $\pi_h^h z_{ih}^h \leqslant 0\ \forall h$.

Notice that every allocation $x = [x_1, \ldots, x_m]$, which is feasible w.r.t. ${}^0M$, can also be achieved in ${}^1M$.

Definition 9. An allocation x is attained through "barter" in ${}^1M$ if

(i) There is z with $z_i^h \in Z^h\ \forall (i, h)$,

$$x_i = w_i + \sum_h z_i^h \forall i, \qquad \sum_i z_i^h = 0\ \forall h$$

and for at least one i: $x_i \neq w_i$.

(ii) $\forall i$ and $\forall h$: $z_{i0}^h = 0$.

Proposition 5. Given ${}^1M$, "barter" cannot belong to the Core*, whatever the level of replication υ. Moreover, every feasible trade is collectively rational.

Proof. Elementary.

Thus, "barter" [7] and monetary exchanges are both feasible, but "barter" cannot belong to the Core*, i.e., "barter" is not rational given ${}^1M$. Moreover, the economy is very amorphous from the point of view of Pareto improvements (credit and institutional and technological innovations are not considered).

The following example, due to D. Gale (1986), shows that if we take into account only the conservative behavior implied by the Core*, then one cannot get equivalence. Actually Gale argues in a Rubinstein model where agents are meeting pairwise in a random way and uses the notion of perfect equilibrium. He shows that in a large economy there is not equivalence and the Core*, in this example, is equal to the set of perfect equilibria with the same "stationary" strategies off the equilibrium path as on the equilibrium path.

Example 2. Assume $r = \ell = 2$ and v as large as one wants. The two types of agents are symmetric in the sense that $u_1(x_1, x_2) = u_2(x_2, x_1)\ \forall (x_1, x_2) \in \mathbb{R}_+^2$ and $w_{12} = w_{21}$, $w_{11} = w_{22}$.

Assume that, under A1, there are two C.E. for ${}^1M$: the zero trade and a C.E. a^* with $a^* \neq 0$ and $\pi_1^{*1} = \pi_2^{*2} = 1$ (because of symmetry), the price of money being one on each market.

Consider a trade $\bar{a}$ for which all agents of the same type are treated equally, all exchanges are made at the same monetary price for each good $h \neq 0 (\bar{\pi}_1^1 = \bar{\pi}_2^2 = 1)$, the price of money being one, and, more precisely,

$$\frac{u'_{11}}{u'_{12}} > \frac{\bar{\pi}_1^1}{\bar{\pi}_2^2} > \frac{u'_{21}}{u'_{22}}$$

with $\bar{a}_{11}^1 = -\bar{a}_{12}^2 = \bar{a}_{22}^2 = -a_{21}^1 = \bar{a} > 0$.

This nontrivial monetary trade is not Pareto-optimal and not a C.E.

Assume now that for every trade a which is better for agents of type 1 and for which $-a_0 + \pi_1^1 a_1^1 = 0$ $(a_0 \geqslant 0)$, $a_0 + \pi_2^2 a_2^2 = 0$ with $\pi_1^1 \geqslant \bar{\pi}_1^1$ and $\bar{\pi}_2^2 \geqslant \pi_2^2$, one has

$$|a_0| < 2|\bar{a}| \qquad \text{and} \qquad |a_2^2| < 2|\bar{a}|.$$

The symmetric relation is obtained for agent 2. In the extensive form, consider some market 1 and agents attending it. Take as V^0 the set of $2\nu + 1$ markets containing the market 1 and 2ν markets of type 2 which are directly connected with it through some agent. Consider an agent of type 1. He would like to buy more (at $\bar{\pi}_1^1$) on market 1 and for that he agrees to sell more (at $\bar{\pi}_2^2$) on market 2. Thus, he can gather a coalition S^1 on market 1 containing agents of type 1 who also buy more at $\bar{\pi}_1^1$ and a smaller number of agents of type 2 who keep their trader fixed. But to buy more, each of these agents of type 1 must sell more on the market of type 2 he attends and recall that acyclicity implies that each of these agents $(1, \gamma)$ attends a different market $(2, \beta)$. As trades are fixed outside V^0, each agent attending a market of type 2 and not belonging to S^1 wants a trade in $\mathbb{R}_+^2 + \bar{a}$. However, what an agent of type 1 belonging to S^1 can do on the market $(2, \beta)$ he attends is at best to eliminate in some coalition another agent of type 1.

Thus, it is impossible to block keeping trades fixed outside V^0. But taking sets (on which trades can be modified) larger and larger does not solve the problem and $\bar{a}$ belongs to the Core*.

Taking the point of view of the reduced form, one notes that

$$\tilde{A}_\theta^h(1) = \Big\{ a^h \,|\, \exists a = (a^h, a^{h'}) \in P_\theta \text{ with } U_\theta(a) \geqslant U_\theta(\bar{a}_\theta) \text{ and}$$
$$a^{h'} \in - \sum_{\substack{\theta' \in S^{h'} \\ \theta' \neq \theta}} \{a_{\theta'}^{h'}\} \text{ for some } S^{h'} \Big\}.$$

One shall call $(\tilde{\tilde{A}}_i^\alpha)_{i,\alpha}$ the minimal system of offers.

Thus, the key is that there is not a small offer on market h at an attractive money price because θ can eliminate at best one agent of his type on market h'. This effect is maintained when one takes t larger and larger for $\tilde{A}^h_\theta(t)$.

In order to make the comparison tighter with pairwise (random) patterns of meetings, let us consider the way exchanges are made on each market. One assumes now that agents meet by pairs but in a deterministic way. Thus, each agent is meeting one other agent on each market but visits $((\ell v) - 1)n$ markets, i.e., for each market α he visits $(\ell v - 1)$ markets of this type. Returning to the example, there are many ways of splitting $\bar{a}$ in pairwise trades among agents of different types: $(\tilde{\bar{a}}^{(h,\theta')}_\theta)_{i,(h,\theta')}$ (for θ a pair (h, θ') is a market).

i. If one chooses symmetric splitting $\tilde{\bar{a}}^{(h,\theta')}_\theta = \bar{a}^h/v$. In this case, trades are small on each "market" when v is large and it is straightforward to check that a finite coalition will block.

ii. If one chooses an asymmetric splitting and for instance $\forall h$ and $\theta \tilde{\bar{a}}^{(h,\theta')}_\theta =$ 0 or $\bar{a}^h_\theta$ then it is impossible to block finitely.

Such a problem cannot appear in an O.G.M. with money because people of the same generation meet on two markets, but then money does not play any role in intragenerational trades. Thus, again, when the number of agents and/or of markets is larger than two the kind of infinity one gets in the graph of the extensive form cannot be dealt with, according to the competitive intuition, when only binding agreements on one market can be taken into account and agents are very cautious as in the Core*.

Now let us check that the minimal system of expectations $(\tilde{\bar{A}}^\alpha_i)_{i,\alpha}$ we are using is not stable in terms of O.I.1: $(\tilde{\bar{A}}^\alpha_i)_{i,\alpha}$ does not contain small deviations from $\bar{a}$. Then consider the infinite coalition ${}^1S$ such that for each market v, ${}^1S^v = {}^1S \cap K(v)$ contains a slightly smaller number of agents of type 1 than of agents of type 2. Agents $k = (2, \gamma) \in {}^1S$ keep their trades fixed on both markets and agents $k = (1, \gamma)$ increase their trades by ε. Trades are made at $\bar{\pi}^1_1 = \bar{\pi}^2_2 = 1$. Thus $({}^1a_k)_{k \in {}^1S}$ constructed in this way is a candidate for blocking by S. It can be implemented because for all $k = (i, \gamma)$ and all $v = (h, \beta) \in V(i, \gamma) {}^1a^v_k \notin \tilde{\bar{A}}^\alpha_i$. But, before concluding that $\bar{a}$ is not stable, we must check if it is not possible to associate it with a system $(\tilde{A}^\alpha_i)_{i,\alpha}$ satisfying (i) and (ii) of Definition 7′ or 7 and which is stable according to O.I.1. This is impossible for the following reason. Because the two types of agents are symmetric, there are coalitions ${}^2S$ that block through $({}^2a_k)_{k \in {}^2S}$, agents of type 2 increasing their trades by ε and agents of type 1 keeping their trades fixed. The system $(\tilde{A}^\alpha_i)$, in order to be stable, must satisfy the following condition.

For $k = (1, \gamma)$ and $k' = (2, \gamma')$, either $a_k^1 \in \tilde{A}_1^1$ and $a_{k'}^1 \in \tilde{A}_2^1$ or $a_k^2 \in \tilde{A}_1^2$ and $a_{k'}^2 \in \tilde{A}_2^2$.

It is impossible to build a system of offers that satisfies simultaneously the above condition and conditions (i) and (ii) of Definitions 7′ or 7″. □

The argument of Example 3 can be generalized and if one accepts the idea of stability formulated in O.I.1, one gets the following Proposition:

Proposition 6. Given assumption A1′ and market structure ${}^1M$, the Core contains the set of C.E.s. Moreover, with each (ε, η), one can associate υ^0 such that for each economy E^υ with $\upsilon \geqslant \upsilon_0$: for each element $a(\upsilon)$ in Core (E^υ), there is a price system π such that

(i) $\forall h$, the proportion of agents θ for whom $|\pi^h a_\theta^h| > \varepsilon$ is smaller than η.

(ii) The proportion of agents θ for whom the distance of $a_\theta(\upsilon)$ from the trade which maximizes utility at π is larger than ε is smaller than η.

Proof. See Appendix.

Thus, blocking is made by eliminating other agents on the market on which one sells in order to be able to sell more and using the additional amount of money one gets in order to be able to buy more (by eliminating agents on the market on which one buys). That explains why the no trade point is a C.E.: one cannot get money by eliminating competitors on the market on which one would like to sell. Thus, what is important is that the presence of money—as a commodity without direct utility—makes the economy very amorphous from the point of view of Pareto improvements. The type of competitive process implied by the Core has the effect that blocking, when υ is large, works only through elimination of competitors by undercutting prices. One would like to conclude this section with two observations:

i. A weakly symmetric C.E. $[(a_k^*)_k, (\pi^{*\upsilon})_\upsilon]$ with respect to ${}^1M$ is automatically symmetric given A1′.

ii. We have interpreted inside money in the strictest sense: agents can create it.

B

In order to be able to refer to outside money, it is better to take time into account in the analysis. Thus, one shall direct the graph associated with the pattern of meetings. In this connection, one shall make the restrictive assumption that the order of visits of markets is given, a priori, for each agent. However, one shall discriminate between two formulations. In the first one, each agent's horizon is finite because one considers only one cycle of visits of a finite set of markets. This approach has the defect—the same as that of the particular O.G.M.—that each agent must sell before buying. In the second one, each consumer visits an infinite number of markets and, more precisely, he contemplates an infinite number of cycles of visits. This last formulation is more flexible and provides a simple basis for liquidity constraints which imply inefficiencies due to impatience.

Given ${}^1M$, associate with each consumer i a permutation σ_i on the set of markets $\{1, \ldots, r\}$, which indicates in which order he visits markets h, i.e., a cycle consists in visiting markets 1, ..., h, ..., r in the order $\sigma_i^{-1}(1), \ldots, \sigma_i^{-1}(h), \ldots, \sigma_i^{-1}(r)$. The set P_i of possible trades now takes into account the fact that the quantity of money cannot be negative at each period of the cycle of visits of markets. Thus, in the reduced form, which is not interesting because of time, P_i registers the constraints.

$$\sum_{\sigma^{-1}(h') \leqslant \sigma^{-1}(h)} a_{i0}^{h'} \geqslant 0 \qquad \forall h$$

and money can be interpreted as being inside money of a strange nature. The analysis is modified only to the extent that P_i is modified, $\forall i$. Thus, as in Part I, barter is still feasible, but it cannot be considered as an equilibrium, whatever reasonable concept is chosen. It follows that liquidity constraints can be active as soon as markets are active. In the extensive form, money can be considered as being outside money. One shall assume that it takes one period to visit a market and that at each period, there is—as soon as $\ell \geqslant 3$ or $r \geqslant 3$—an infinite number of markets that is active.

Now, a node is a market and an arrow refers to some agent going from some market to another one. As one wants to represent all markets opening at the same date with the same abscissa, a market is indexed by $v = (h, \beta, t)$ where t is the date at which it opens. Agent k is also indexed by (i, γ, t) where index t indicates the date at which the market that agent k visits first opens. Symmetry now means the stationarity of distributions of trades at periods $t, t+1, \ldots$. In figure 5, one pictures the case where $r = 3$ and $\ell = 2$. An agent of category 1 (resp. 2) visits markets in the order 1, 2, and 3 (resp 3, 2, and 1). Agents of category 1 travels are denoted by an arrow and agents of category 2 travels are denoted by a dotted arrow.

In order to simplify the analysis assume:

A4: Each agent i can sell one good $h(i)$, i.e., P_i is such that $z_{ih(i)}^{h(i)} \leqslant 0$ and $z_{ih}^{h} \geqslant 0 \; \forall h \neq h(i)$.

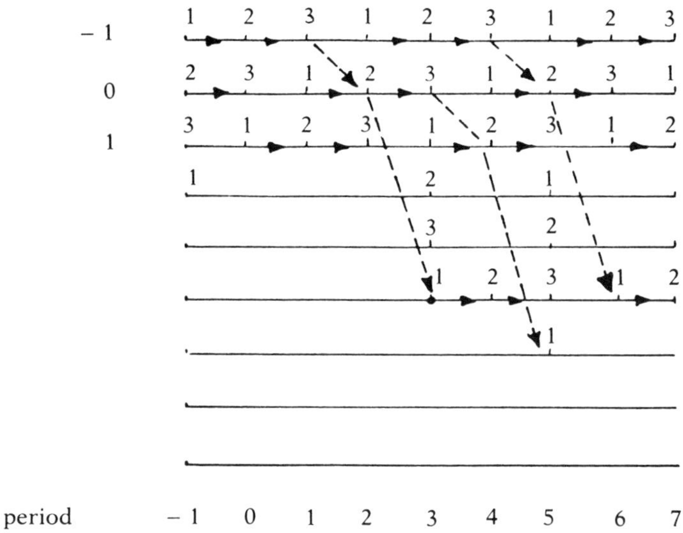

Figure 5.

Moreover, in order that liquidity constraints are not binding at equilibrium, assume that agent i first visits market $h(i)$. Then, in the extensive form with outside money and without short sales of money, the argument is the following. If the quantity of money is 0, only barter is feasible (money is outside money and cannot be created). Then, B.S.1. is enough to show that only the 0-trade can be a candidate for being an equilibrium, because any other allocation will imply for some k $a_{kh}^{(h,\beta)} < 0$ for some $h \neq 0$. This agent has an interest to deviate according to B.S.1. Assume that the quantity of money is $M \neq 0$, but that its price is 0 in the sense that one considers $(\overline{a}_k)_k$ with $\overline{a}_{ik}^{(h,\beta)} = 0$ $\forall k$ and $\forall (h, \beta)$ $(h \neq 0)$, but money circulates among agents without goods being exchanged. $(\overline{a}_k)_k$ satisfies Definition 7 and thus belongs to the Core, whatever is v, if one chooses

$$\tilde{A}_i^h = \{a_i^h | a_{ih}^h \geqslant 0, a_{i0}^h \leqslant M\}.$$

Consider, now, the case in which each agent travels through a large number of cycles of visits. To simplify the analysis, we assume that for each cycle, σ_i is the identity for each i, that ρ is a common rate of discount. One assumes that goods cannot be stored and thus that $w_{i,h(i)}$ is available when market $h(i)$ opens. The cycle of visits of markets is dependent on the consumption cycle that covers r periods in the order 1, 2, ..., r. The consumption cycle $\{1, \ldots, r\}$ allows us to define the undiscounted utility provided by the completion of a consumption cycle. Thus, if one begins the analysis for some agent of type i at his consumption cycle T_0, his total utility is

$$(R) \quad \sum_{T \geqslant T_0} \frac{1}{(1+\rho)^{T-T_0}} u_i(x(T)).$$

There, $\rho \geqslant 0$ is the discount rate and when $\rho = 0$, one uses the "overtaking criterion."

Consider only programs for which the price of money is always positive. Given a (monetary) price vector π^T for cycle T and a net trade in goods z_i^T, agent i needs, at the beginning of the cycle, an amount of money equal to

$$(M') \quad \sum_{h' < h(i)} \pi_{h'}^T z_{ih'}^T + \mathrm{Max}\left\{0, \sum_{h' > h(i)} \pi_{h'}^T z_{ih'}^T + \pi_{h(i)}^T z_{ih(i)}^T\right\}$$

given that $z_{ih'}^T \geqslant 0$ for $h' \neq h(i)$ and $z_{ih(i)}^{T'} \leqslant 0$.

For a stationary program for which the quantity of money owned on each cycle is independent of the cycle, the initial amount of money at the beginning of each cycle is

$$(\mathrm{M}) \quad \sum_{h' < h(i)} \pi_{h'} z_{ih'}.$$

In the reduced form, consider only stationary C.E.s. Agent i, at the beginning of some cycle T_0, faces the stationary sequences of monetary prices.

$[\pi, \ldots, \pi, \ldots]$.

Given his initial amount of money, he maximizes his recursive utility function (R) subject to possibility constraints that include (M'). Marginal conditions for a stationary program, which is optimal for i, are

$$\frac{1}{1+\rho} \frac{u'_{ih'}(w_i + z_i)}{u'_{ih(i)}(w_i + z_i)} = \frac{\pi_{h'}}{\pi_{h(i)}} \qquad \forall h' < h(i)$$

(I)

$$\frac{u'_{ih'}(w_i + z_i)}{u'_{ih(i)}(w_i + z_i)} = \frac{\pi_{h'}}{\pi_{h(i)}} \qquad \forall h' > h(i).$$

It is obvious that for a stationary C.E. different from the no trade one and thus implying a positive price of money, the marginal rates of substitution among goods $1, \ldots, r$ are not the same for all agents i, when $\rho > 0$. Up to now, while considering only the reduced form, we have only proved (I) without having recourse to liquidity constraints defined through prices as in Grandmont and Younès 1972, 1973.

However, it is consideration of the extensive form that explains why agents do not coordinate their trades in order to get a Pareto-optimal allocation and why "barter" cannot be an equilibrium. Assumption of acyclicity and the decision to picture markets that open at the same period on the same abscissa make the graph slightly intricate.

In figure 6a, one draws the graph for $r = \ell = 2$. Agents of type 1 are traveling horizontally and agents of type 2 are zigzaging. Then the two basic principles are still at work, due to the assumption of acyclicity:

i. "Barter" cannot be an equilibrium. It follows that only monetary trades can arise. Given that the quantity of money owned cannot be negative and that it takes one period to visit a market, liquidity constraints appear.

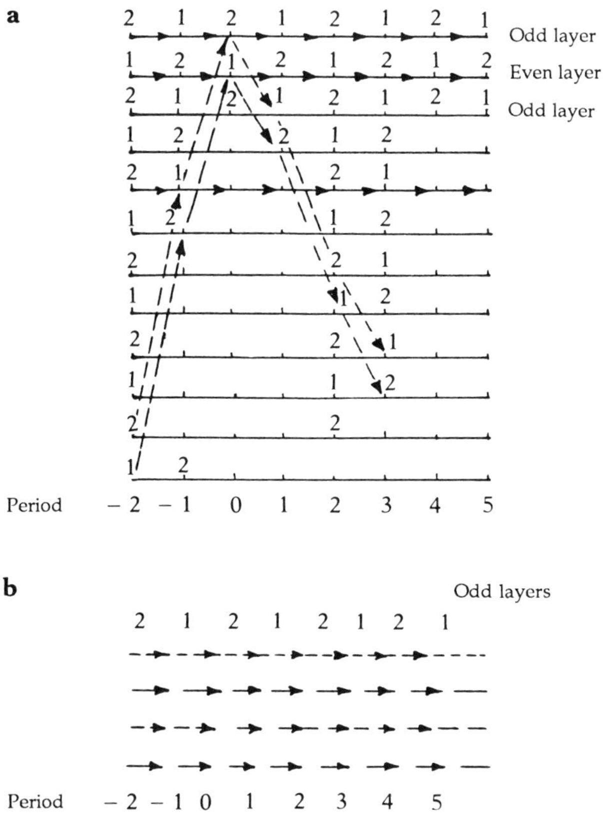

Figure 6.

ii. Acyclicity makes further coordination difficult. In order to check this assertion, assume on the contrary that these infinitely lived agents meet on all markets as in figure 6b. Because of the recursivity of utility functions, finite optimality implies Pareto optimality: it is enough that agents coordinate their trades on every cycle taken alone to get full optimality.

Finally, the Friedmanian policy consisting in decreasing the stock of money through negative lump sum transfers which entail that monetary prices decrease allows implemention of any static C.E. of the model without money. Let $[\overline{p}, \overline{z}]$ be such a static C.E. For each agent and each cycle for this agent, let us keep the relative prices of goods $h \neq 0$ at the levels indicated by $\overline{p}$ and let the monetary prices $(\overline{\pi})$ decrease from cycle to cycle at a rate equal to ρ. For that, a lump sum transfer $c_i(T)$ is taxed on agents of category $i = 2, \ldots, \ell$ at the periods corresponding to the beginning of the cycles traveled by agent of type $i \neq 1$. This transfer is such that the quantity of money owned varies at each cycle by a factor of $1/(1 + \rho)$, i.e.,

$$\text{(L)} \quad c_i(T) = -\rho \sum_{h' < h(i)} \overline{\pi}_{h'}^{T-1} \overline{z}_{ih'}.$$

Facing the sequence of transfers and of prices, each agent of category i will choose a program characterized by the following conditions, if the quantity of money at the beginning of the typical cycle is fixed in an appropriate way:

$$\frac{u'_{ih'}(w_i + \overline{z}_i)}{u'_{ih(i)}(w_i + \overline{z}_i)} = \frac{\overline{\pi}_{h'}}{\overline{\pi}_{h(i)}} \qquad \forall h' \neq h(i).$$

In figure 6a, transfers will concern only agents of category 2. At even periods, agents of category 2 who begin their cycles at even layers are taxed and at odd periods, agents of category 2 who begin their cycles at odd layers are taxed. We can therefore state:

Proposition 7. Consider the reduced form for which each i travels through an infinity of cyles, with utility function (R) and initial allocation which are stationary. Given A1–A4, stationary equilibria different from the initial allocation (price of money different from 0) are characterized by (M) and (I) when the market structure is ${}^1M$, σ_i $(= \sigma)$ is the identity for each i and the rate of discount $\rho > 0$ is the same for each i. This inefficiency can be explained on the basis of the acyclic and directed graph of the pattern of meetings. The Friedmanian policy of negative lump sum transfers (L) allows implementation, in terms of nontrivial C.E., of Pareto optimality.

Remark. We have conceived the dynamics of an economy as the evolution of the distributions of agents' actions on each type of market, knowing that, at each period, there is a large number of markets of each type that are active and that the pattern of meetings is acyclic. In this connection, it is possible to consider what happens at t as the projection on period t of any evolution of these distributions and no longer of only stationary distributions. This leads to a generalization of the approach chosen for the O.G.M. in Geanakoplos and Polemarchakis 1986.

C

Many authors put at the center for their formulations of market coordination failures, monopoly or monopolistic competition. However, these analyses are coherent only if one assumes that the market structure is incomplete, money playing the role of a potential medium of exchange. Actually, the strategy consisting of avoiding the question of the way people trade has odd consequences also in the field of general equilibrium analysis with monopolistic competition. As emphasized many times (see, e.g., Mas Colell 1983) this kind of analysis encounters two difficulties.

i. The concept of equilibrium itself depends on the choice of the numeraire. This is not a defect in itself, but the idea conveyed by this fact is not often analyzed.

ii. When production is taken into account, the profit motive is not necessarily rational for shareholders.

At least in simple models, it is possible to give partial answers (not incompatible with other ones) in terms of an incomplete market structure with money playing the role of means of exchange. In the extensive form, acyclicity allows us to assume that shareholders of a given firm meet only on a "market" called the shareholders assembly, and by varying the number of agents of each category according to the type of markets in order to picture that some type of market is more competitive than another one, to explain in what sense the equilibrium varies with the choice of numeraire.

Conclusion

The main shortcoming of the above analysis is the absence of any true study of the important reasons the market structure and the pattern of meetings have the characteristics we give them. On the one hand, one can analyze the reasons why a market structure is stable, in a similar way to how one analyzes the reasons why an allocation is stable.[8] On the other hand, given the way possibilities of exchanges are defined on each market, one may try to endogenize the choice of order of visits of markets as is done in models in which each agent is choosing between quasimoney (deposits in the banks) and money. In the same way, a more thorough comparison must be made between deterministic and random patterns of meetings. One has worked mainly with the Core because it incorporates in some way the two principles we have emphasized. However, the approach is potentially general. On each market, the chosen concept is applied, given rational expectations of other contracts on other markets and about the conclusions of the bargaining process on other markets. If there is no general bargaining, it is because of acyclicity. In turn, that gives substance to the notion of market by weakening interdependence between markets, without destroying it too much.

A model for which agents can choose the market they are visiting each period may be as follows. In a world where only money can be stored or where only money can be carried from one market place to another one, "barter" can only take the form of reciprocal gifts, and acyclicity makes it unimplementable.

On the contrary, assume that the difficulty of barter comes from the fact that goods can be exchanged only by pairs, that each agent i can visit at most one market per period, and that roundabout patterns of exchanges are costly because of loss of time and the costs of storage of goods. If $r = \ell$, assume that each agent i can own initially only good $h(i) = i + 1$ and desires only good $h = i$ (with the identification $1 \sim r + 1$). i's utility function is

$$\sum_{t \geqslant t_0} \frac{1}{(1 + \ell)^{t-t_0}} u_i(x_i(t)).$$

It is assumed that i gets his initial endowment $w_{h(i)}$ only at the periods when he consumes $x_i(t)$.

The potential market structure is, for each t,

$$M = [(Z^{(h,h')})_{(h,h') \neq 0}, (Z^h)_{h \neq 0}] = {}^2M \cup {}^1M$$

where ${}^2M$ is the market structure for which the last r commodities are exchanged by pairs on each market.

In this setting, a market is in some sense a *local public good* and the stability of an allocation can be tested from this point of view. One can discriminate, at each period, between active markets (there are nonzero trades on these markets), markets that are open (at least one agent is visiting it and thus offers are expected on these markets) but not active, and markets that are not open. In the extensive form, acyclicity forbids agents from cooperating by visiting some markets, in the future, and thus moves consisting in visits to markets are not coordinated ones. Agents are prudent and if they gain by visiting an active market at t rather than not trading, they will do that. However, they do not lose anything in trying to trade on some market (an open one, ex post) if they cannot gain by trading on markets that are active.

Appendix

Proof of Proposition 1

(i) Assume that $(y_k, z_k)_k$ is collectively *rational. Consider generation 0. From Definition 2 and A1, the gradients of all agents' utility functions are colinear. Choose $[\pi^{*0}, \pi^{*1}]$ of norm 1 in $\mathbb{R}^{2r}$ and colinear with these gradients. From Definition 2 and A1, the projections on Z^1 of the gradients of utility functions of k's $\in G(1)$ are colinear with π^{*1}. Now, the gradients of agents k's $\in G(1)$ utility functions are colinear with a vector $\lambda^1[\bar{\pi}^{*1}, \bar{\pi}^{*2}]$ with $\lambda^1 \in \mathbb{R}_{++}$. Choose then λ^1 such that $\lambda^1\bar{\pi}^{*1} = \pi^{*1}$ and define π^{*2} accordingly. In this way, the sequence $(\pi^{*t})_t$ can be built for all $t \in N$. Transfers are then defined by ${}_z d_k^t = \pi^{*t} z_k^t$ and ${}_y d_k^t = [\pi^{*t}, \pi^{*t+1}] y_k$.

(ii) Conversely, consider a C.E. $[(\pi^{*t})_t, (y_k^*, z_k^*)_k]$. With $(y_k^*, z_k^*)_k$, one associates in a unique way sets $[\tilde{Y}_k, \tilde{Z}_k^t, \tilde{Z}_k^{t+1}]_k$. In order to show that condition (2) is satisfied, argue ad absurdum. There exists then a feasible trade $({}^1y_k, {}^1z_k)$ that gives at least as much utility as (y_k^*, z_k^*) for every agent k and strictly more for agent $k_0 \in G(t_0)$. As $(y_k^*, z_k^*)_k$ is a C.E., for each generation t, all agents' utility functions have gradients colinear to (π^{*t}, π^{*t+1}) and $(\pi^{*t}, \pi^{*t+1})\ ({}^1y_k - {}^*y_k) \geqslant 0$ for all t and all $k \in G(t)$ and in particular for $k \neq k_0$. As the gradients restricted to Z^t are colinear to π^{*t} for all agents in $G(t) \cup G(t-1)$, one gets for each $k \in G(t) \cup G(t-1)$ (and in particular for $k \neq k_0$)

$$\pi^{*t}\, {}^1z_k^t \geqslant \pi^{*t} z_k^{*t} = 0, \qquad \text{for } {}^1z_k^t \in \tilde{Z}_k^t.$$

As $({}^1y_k, {}^1z_k)$ is balanced, we have in particular

$$\sum_{k \in G(t_0-1) \cup G(t_0)} {}^1z_k^{t_0} = 0,$$

$$\sum_{k \in G(t_0) \cup G(t_0+1)} {}^1z_k^{t_0+1} = 0,$$

and

$$\sum_{k \in G(t_0)} {}^1y_k = 0.$$

It follows that for agent k_0

$$[\pi^{*t^0}, \pi^{*t_0+1}]({}^1y_k - y_{k_0}^*) \leqslant 0,$$

$$\pi^{*t_0}({}^1z_{k_0}^{t_0} - z_{k_0}^{*t_0}) \leqslant 0,$$

and

$$\pi^{*t_0+1}({}^1z_{k_0}^{t_0+1} - z_{k_0}^{*t_0+1}) \leqslant 0$$

and thus agent k_0 cannot be better off. Q.E.D.

Proof of Proposition 2

First, let us show equal treatment for agents of the same type k, $\forall k$. In order that $(u_{k\tau}, z_{k\tau})_{k\tau}$ belongs to the *Core, it has to be finitely optimal. That entails that there are sets of offers which support it, i.e., for each $(k, \tau) = (t, j, \tau)$.

$$[Y_{k\tau}, Z_{k\tau}^t, Z_{k\tau}^{t+1}]$$

are such that condition (2) of Definition 2 obtains.

Ad absurdum, assume that for some type k_0, one has $u_{k_0}(w_{k_0} + y_{k_0\tau} + z_{k_0\tau}) \neq u_{k_0}(w_{k_0\tau'} + z_{k_0\tau'})$ for some pair (τ, τ'). Consider the infinite coalition S formed of one agent τ_1 for each type having the least utility in his type. The allocation gotten by (k, τ_1), $\forall k = (t, j)$ is

$${}^1z_{k\tau_1}^t = \frac{1}{v}\sum_\tau z_{k\tau}^t \qquad \text{which is equal (normalization) to } z_{k\tau_1}^t$$

$${}^1z_{k\tau_1}^{t+1} = \frac{1}{v}\sum_\tau z_{k\tau}^{t+1} \qquad \text{which is equal to } z_{k\tau_1}^{t+1}$$

$${}^1y_{k\tau_1} = \frac{1}{v}\sum_\tau y_{k\tau}.$$

Obviously, ${}^1z_{k\tau_1}^t \in \tilde{Z}_{k\tau_1}^t$ and ${}^1z_{k\tau_1}^{t+1} \in \tilde{Z}_{k\tau_1}^{t+1}$ for every $k = (t, j)$. Moreover, as at $(y_{k\tau}, z_{k\tau})_{k,\tau}$ (k, τ_1) gets the least utility among agents of his type k, one has $y_{k\tau} \in \tilde{Y}_{k\tau_1}$. Also, for each (k, τ_1)

$$u_k(w_k + {}^1y_{k\tau_1} + {}^1z_{k\tau_1}) \geqslant u_k(w_k + y_{k\tau_1} + z_{k\tau_1})$$

with strict inequality for (k_0, τ_1). Finally, $({}^1y_{k\tau_1}, {}^1z_{k\tau_1})_k$ is balanced as $(y_{k\tau}, z_{k\tau})_{k,\tau}$ is balanced. Thus, S blocks.

Second, because of strict quasi-concavity and collective rationality (the gradients of all agents of type k utility functions are colinear), equal treatment implies that for each k

$$\bar{y}_{k\tau} = \bar{y}_{k\tau'}, \qquad \forall_{(\tau,\tau')}. \qquad \text{Q.E.D.}$$

Proof of Proposition 3

Let us show first that, for each υ, a competitive equilibrium of E^υ belongs to the *Core. Ad absurdum, consider a C.E. $[(\pi^{*t}), (y^*_{k\tau}, z^*_{k\tau})_{k,\tau}]$ and assume that there exists S and a feasible (for S) $({}^1y_{k\tau}, {}^1z_{k\tau})_{(k,\tau)\in S}$ with $\forall (k,\tau) \in S$, ${}^1y_{k\tau} \in \tilde{Y}_{k\tau}$, ${}^1z^t_{k\tau} \in \tilde{Z}^t_{k\tau}$, and ${}^1z^{t+1}_{k\tau} \in \tilde{Z}^{t+1}_{k\tau}$ and which provides at least as much utility as $(y^*_{k,\tau}, z^*_{k,\tau})$ to each (k,τ) in S and strictly more to $(k_0, \tau_0) \in G(t_0)$. For all agents (k,τ) in S and different from (k_0,τ_0), one has

$$\pi^{*t}\,{}^1z^t_{k\tau} \geqslant 0, \quad \pi^{*t+1}\,{}^1z^{t+1}_{k\tau} \geqslant 0, \quad \text{and} \quad [\pi^{*t}, \pi^{*t+1}]^1y_{k\tau} \geqslant 0.$$

From balance, one has

$$\sum_{k\in S\cap[G(t_0-1)\cup G(t_0)]} {}^1z^{t_0}_k = 0,$$

$$\sum_{k\in S\cap[G(t_0)\cup G(t_0+1)]} {}^1z^{t_0+1}_k = 0,$$

and

$$\sum_{k\in S\cap G(t_0)} {}^1y_k = 0.$$

It follows that

$$\pi^{*t}\,{}^1z^{t_0}_{k_0\tau_0} \leqslant 0, \quad \pi^{*t_0+1}\,{}^1z^{t_0+1}_{k_0\tau_0} \leqslant 0, \quad \text{and} \quad (\pi^{*t_0}, \pi^{*t_0+1})^1y_{k_0\tau_0} \leqslant 0,$$

and thus (k_0,τ_0) cannot be better off.

Now, consider a sequence of economies $\{E^\upsilon\}_\upsilon$ with $E^\upsilon \supset E^{\upsilon-1}$ and $\upsilon \to \infty$. $\forall \upsilon$, $*C(E^\upsilon)$ is compact in the product topology and we have $C(E^\upsilon) \supset C(E^{\upsilon+1})$. Let us show that a feasible trade $(y_k, z_k)_k$ which is not a C.E. will eventually be blocked when seen as a trade (equal treatment) in E^υ. Without loss of generality, one can assume that it is collectively rational. There is then $(\pi^{*t})_t$ which supports it. Notice that $(\pi^{*t})_t$ is unique up to a multiplicative real, which is strictly positive.

Assume first that for some t_0, one has for some $k_0 = (t_0, j_0)$

$$\pi^{*t_0} z^{t_0}_{t_0 j_0} \neq 0$$

and for fixing our ideas $\pi^{*t_0} z^{t_0}_{t_0 j} < 0$. That entails, by the convention of normalization, that

$$\pi^{*t_0} z^{t_0}_k < 0, \qquad \forall k = (t_0, j).$$

In figure 7, assuming $r = 2$, an indifference curve II′ is drawn for a type k of generation t_0, keeping trades fixed on Y^{t_0} and $Z^{t_0+1}_{t_0}$. From A1 (differentiability and interiority), there is a point $\lambda_k z^{t_0}_k (\lambda_k \in]0, 1[)$, on the segment $[0, z^{t_0}_k]$ such that

$$u_k(w_k + y_k + z_k) < u_k(w_k + y_k + z^{t_0+1}_k + \lambda_k z^{t_0}_k).$$

Obviously, the argument is true for any finite r.

As there is a finite number of j's for each generation t, one can find a subinterval of $[0, z^{t_0}_k]$ such that each agent $(k, \tau) \in G(t_0)$ gains by choosing the same point on this segment. Now letting υ increase, there exists υ_0 such that by choosing $\lambda_{t_0} = 1 - (1/\upsilon_0)$, each agent of generation t_0 gains by reducing his trade on Z^{t_0} to $\lambda_{t_0} z^{t_0}_k$, keeping trades fixed on other markets Y^{t_0} and Z^{t_0+1}. Consider then the coalition S in the economy E^{υ_0}, built by taking all agents $(t, j; \tau)$ for $t \geqslant t_0$ and for $t < t_0$ all agents $(t, j; \tau)$ except $1/\upsilon$ agents of each type (t, j). Let us show that $({}^1y_{k\tau}, {}^1z_{k\tau})_{(k,\tau)\in S}$ defined by keeping the same trades for all agents in S, except for agents of generation t_o, whose trades on Z^{t_0} are reduced by $1/\upsilon_0$, blocks. Let us verify that $({}^1y_{k\tau}, {}^1z_{k\tau})_{(k,\tau)\in S}$ is balanced for S. First, it is obviously balanced on markets Y^t and Z^t for $t \geqslant t_0$. It is also balanced on markets Y^t and Z^t for $t < t_0$ because all agents of the same type get the same trades.

A symmetric argument can be made if

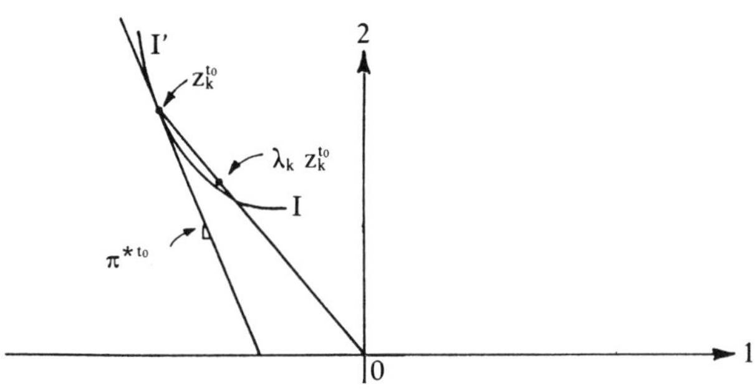

Figure 7.
Market Z^{t_0}.

$\pi^{*t_0} z^{t_0}_{0,j} > 0.$

It follows that $\pi^{*t_0} z^{t_0}_{t_0-1,j} < 0$ and agents of generation $t_0 - 1$ gain by reducing their trades on Z^{t_0}. When v_0 is large enough, they can build a coalition in E^{v_0} by taking all agents for generations $t \leqslant t_0$ and a well-chosen fraction of all agents of generations $t > t_0$.

Finally, assume that for some type $k^0 = (t^0, j^0)$, one has

$[\pi^{*t}, \pi^{*t+1}] y_{k_0} < 0.$

It follows that there exists an interval $]a, 1[\subset [0, 1]$ (with $a < 1$) such that by multiplying y_{k_0} by an element λ_{k_0} of this subset, each agent (k_0, τ) gains, keeping his trades fixed on Z^{t_0} and Z^{t_0+1}. There exists then an economy E^{v_0} and a coalition (in this economy) containing

(i) all agents of type k_0;

(ii) a fraction λ_{k_0} of all agents (k, τ), for each type $k \in G(t_0)$ with $k \neq k_0$; and

(iii) a fraction $\dfrac{\delta_{k_0} = (\ell - 1)\,\lambda_{k_0} + 1}{\ell}$ of the set of agents (k, τ), for each type $k \notin G(t_0)$.

For $k \neq k_0$, one chooses

$${}^1y_k = y_k \qquad \text{and} \qquad {}^1z_k = z_k$$

and for $k = k_0$, one chooses ${}^1y_{k_0} = y_{k_0}$ and ${}^1z_{k_0} = z_{k_0}$. $({}^1y_{k\tau}, {}^1z_{k\tau})_{(k\tau) \in S}$ is balanced and thus S blocks. Q.E.D.

Proof of Proposition 4

(i) Consider some C.E. $[a^*, \pi^*]$ for $M = [Z^1, \ldots, Z^n]$. One shall show that it belongs to the Core* for M. Define $\forall (i, \alpha)$

$${}^\alpha\tilde{A}_i(1) = \{a = [a^1, \ldots, a^\alpha, \ldots, a^n] \in P_i \cap F_i \mid U_i(a) \geqslant U_i(a_i^*) \text{ and } \forall \alpha' \neq \alpha\colon \pi^{*\alpha'} a^{\alpha'} \leqslant 0\}$$

and for each $t > 1$:

$${}^\alpha\tilde{A}_i(t) = \left\{a \in P_i \cap F_i \mid U_i(a) \geqslant U_i(a_i^*) \text{ and } \forall \alpha' \neq \alpha\colon a^{\alpha'} \in -\sum_{i' \in S^{\alpha'}} A_{i'}^{\alpha'}(t-1) \text{ for } S^{\alpha'} \text{ with } i \notin S^{\alpha'}\right\}$$

$\forall t \geqslant 1, {}^{\alpha}\tilde{A}_i(t-1) \supset {}^{\alpha}\tilde{A}_i(t) \supset \{a_i^*\}$ because a_i^* maximizes $U_i(a)$ over the set $\{a \in P_i | \pi^{*\alpha} a^{\alpha} \leqslant 0 \quad \forall \alpha\}$.

Define then ${}^{\alpha}\tilde{A}_i = \bigcap_{t \geqslant 1} {}^{\alpha}\tilde{A}_i(t)$.

(ii) Consider a sequence $\{\tilde{a}(\upsilon)\}$ with $\tilde{a}(\upsilon) \in$ Core* (E^{υ}). As $\tilde{a}(\upsilon)$ is individually rational, the sequence is uniformly bounded from below (A3). As $\tilde{a}(\upsilon)$ is collectively rational*, there is, for each α, a price vector $\pi^{\alpha}(\upsilon)$ such that (A1) $\forall \theta$: grad $U_{\theta}(a_{\theta}(\upsilon))$ is proportional to $\pi^{\alpha}(\upsilon)$. Normalize $\pi^{\alpha}(\upsilon)$ for each υ and each α. In the sequel, one has to keep in mind that sets ${}^{\alpha}\tilde{A}_{\theta}(\upsilon)$ which support $\tilde{a}(\upsilon)$ as an element of Core*(E^{υ}) are such that

$${}^{\alpha}\tilde{A}_{\theta}(\upsilon) \supset {}^{\alpha}\tilde{A}_{\theta}(\upsilon) \equiv \{a \in P_{\theta} | U_{\theta}(a) \geqslant U_{\theta}(\tilde{a}_{\theta}(\upsilon)) \text{ and } \forall \alpha' \neq \alpha\colon a_{\theta}^{\alpha'} = \tilde{a}_{\theta}^{\alpha'}(\upsilon)\}.$$

Ad absurdum, assume that $\tilde{a}(\upsilon)$ is not uniformly bounded from above, while it is from below. One can thus find α, a converging subsequence (keep the same notation) $\{\pi^{\alpha}(\upsilon)\} \to \pi^{\alpha}(0) \in \mathbb{R}_{++}^{q(\alpha)}$ and a subsequence of agents $\theta(\upsilon)$ such that $\sum_j^{q(\alpha)} \tilde{a}_{\theta(\upsilon)j}^{\alpha}(\upsilon) \to \infty$. It follows that

$$\Delta_{\theta(\upsilon)}^{\alpha}(\upsilon) \equiv \pi^{\alpha}(\upsilon)\, \tilde{a}_{\theta(\upsilon)}^{\alpha}(\upsilon) \to \infty.$$

There is, then, υ large enough for coalition S^{α} containing all agents, except $\theta(\upsilon)$, blocks by distributing the net trade $\tilde{a}_{\theta(\upsilon)}^{\alpha}(\upsilon)$ equally among its members, which implies a strict increase of utility for all members of S^{α}, as $\tilde{a}(\upsilon)$ is collectively rational and from A1–A3.

One can thus extract from sequences $\{\pi(\upsilon)\}$ and $\{\tilde{a}(\upsilon)\}$ two subsequences that converge simultaneously toward respectively $\pi(0)$ and $\tilde{a}(0)$ (weakly for $\{\tilde{a}(\upsilon)\}$). Moreover $\tilde{a}(0)$ is absolutely continuous w.r.t. λ. Ad absurdum, assume that $\tilde{\Delta}_i^{\alpha}(0) = \sum_j^{q(\alpha)} \pi_j^{\alpha}(0)\, \tilde{a}_{ij}^{\alpha}(0)$ is not completely 0 for some pair (i, α).

There is then a Borelian $B_i \subset [0, 1]$ such that $\tilde{\Delta}_i^{\alpha}(0)$ is strictly positive on B_i, and for instance pointwise larger than $\beta > 0$ on B_i. From the definition of weak convergence, $\forall \varepsilon > 0$, there is υ_0 such that for each $\upsilon \geqslant \upsilon_0$, we have simultaneously

$$\Delta_{iB_i}^{\alpha}(\upsilon) \geqslant \beta - \varepsilon > 0 \qquad \text{and} \qquad |\mu^{\upsilon}(B_i) - \lambda(B_i)| < \varepsilon.$$

There is then υ such that the coalition S^{α} that includes all agents except a well chosen subset $\bar{B}_i$ of B_i gains by equally sharing the net trade $\tilde{a}_i^{\alpha}(\bar{B}_i)$ because of collective rationality. Q.E.D.

Proof of Proposition 6

1. Consider a C.E. $[a^* \pi^*]$ for which the price of money is 0 and for which for each i, $a_{ih}^{*h} = 0$, $h = 1, \ldots, r$. Define $\tilde{A}_i^h = \{a^h | \exists a = [a^1, \ldots, a^r] \in P_i$ with

$U_i(a) \geqslant U_i(a^*)$ and $\pi_{h'}^{*h} a_{h'}^{h'} \leqslant 0$, $\forall h' \neq h$, $h' \neq 0\}$. Thus, each agent offers the half space of $\mathbb{R}^2$ defined by $a_h^h \geqslant 0$. Thus, no agent would agree to start from a market on which he would be a seller: the above system of offers is stable.

2. Conversely, as one can bound uniformly, without loss of generality, net trades in inside money, one can consider a sequence $\{\tilde{a}(\upsilon)\}$ with $\tilde{a}(\upsilon) \in \text{Core}^*(E^\upsilon)$ that converges weakly toward $\tilde{a}(0)$. If $\tilde{a}(0)$ is such that trades in goods $h \neq 0$ are identically 0, we are home. Thus, assume that $\tilde{a}(0)$ is not such that trades in all goods $h \neq 0$ are identically 0.

i. For every economy E^υ: $\forall \theta$, if $a_{\theta h}^h(\upsilon) < 0$, then $a_{\theta 0}^h(\upsilon) > 0$. If not, θ chooses a coalition $S^h = \{\theta\}$ and blocks on market h.

ii. At $\tilde{a}(0)$, on each active market h, almost all trades are made at the same monetary exchange ratio. Ad absurdum, assume that it is not the case. There is then a market h_0 and a subsequence of υ's (keep the same notation) such that for each υ larger than some υ_0 , a strictly positive fraction of agents either buy (on h_0) at a price above the average or sell at a price below the average. This contradicts Definition 7″ as soon as υ is large enough.

iii. Let N_0 be the set of active markets for $\tilde{a}(0)$. $|N_0| \geqslant 2$. There is thus $\pi^h(0)$ at which almost all trades are made, $\forall h \in N_0$. Let us show that on N_0 marginal rates of substitution are equal to price ratios, for almost every θ. Assume not. There is then a subsequence of υ's, υ_0, two markets h_0 and $h_1 \in N_0$ and some agents $\theta(\upsilon)$ such that for each $\upsilon \geqslant \upsilon_0$

$$\frac{u'_{\theta_{h_0}}}{u'_{\theta_{h_1}}} > \frac{\bar{\pi}^{h_0}(\upsilon)}{\bar{\pi}^{h_1}(\upsilon)} + \varepsilon \qquad (\varepsilon > 0)$$

where one has chosen the above inequality for precision and $\bar{\pi}^h(\upsilon)$ is the average exchange ratio on market h. For υ large enough, there are thus coalitions ${}^\delta S \subset\subset K$ that can block infinitely (and potentially if one wants) through $({}^\delta a_k)_{k \in {}^\delta S}$ by increasing trades on markets h_0 and h_1 (at average prices) and keeping trades fixed on other markets. Now, it is impossible to build a (total) system of offers $(\tilde{A}_i^\alpha)_{i,\alpha}$ that satisfies conditions (i) and (ii) of Definitions 7′ or 7″ and that is stable given these pairs $[{}^\delta S, ({}^\delta a_k)_{k \in {}^\delta S}]$, as in Example 3.

iv. Consider any pair of markets (h_0, h_1) with $h_0 \in N_0$ and $h_1 \notin N_0$. Then for almost all θ, the marginal rates of substitution between goods h_0 and h_1 are the same. Ad absurdum, assume that it is not the case. Extracting a subsequence if necessary, there are two groups of agents $B_1(\nu)$ and $B_2(\nu)$ of nonzero measure such that for each $v \geqslant v_0$:

$$\frac{u'_{\theta_{h_0}}}{u'_{\theta_{h_1}}} > \frac{u'_{\theta'_{h_0}}}{u'_{\theta'_{h_1}}} + \varepsilon\,(\varepsilon > 0), \qquad \forall\theta \in B_1(v), \forall\theta' \in B_2(v).$$

There are thus coalitions $S^\delta \subset\subset K$ that can block infinitely (and potentially) through $({}^\delta a_k)_{k \in {}^\delta S}$; agents who are buying on market h_1 get their additional money by selling more on market h_0 (eliminating some agents who are selling on h_1) and agents who are selling on market h_1 use their additional money by buying more on market h_0 (eliminating some agents who are buying on market h_0), trades being kept constant on all other markets. It is impossible to build a system of offers $(\tilde{A}_i^\alpha)_{i,\alpha}$ that satisfies conditions (i) and (ii) of Definitions 7′ or 7″ and that is stable, given these pairs $[{}^\delta S, ({}^\delta a_k)_{k \in {}^\delta S}]$. Q.E.D.

Acknowledgments

This article is part of a larger study on "Planification à la Française" financed by Commissariat General du Plan. I benefited also from discussions with K. Back, F. Bloch, D. Cass, and G. Mailath. I thank a referee of the French version.

Notes

1. This is not the usual definition of barter. See the conclusion.

2. Referring to credibility of implementation in such a setting raises the question of the relations of this paper with approaches in terms of search (Diamond 1985) and in terms of perfect equilibrium for (pairwise) random patterns of meetings. Obviously, one can redefine the deterministic pattern of meeting in such a way that agents are meeting pairwise and one can assume in models with random patterns of meetings that agents are visiting (in some order) the different markets of the market structure. This is done in Diamond 1985 and Gale 1986 for money in a two-market setting. Note that acyclicity is obtained in these two models for any realization of the process of meetings. They are thus fundamentally different from the O.G.M. and the nonequivalence result in Gale 1986b cannot be gotten in a true O.G.M. structure.

3. Definitions 2 and 3 define notions that are weaker than finite optimality and finite core, respectively. As one wants to emphasize only the consequence of the assumption that the pattern of meetings of the O.G.M. is acyclic in terms of generations, we use the weaker definition 3, which is sufficient, given A1.

4. It is enough to assume that one considers a pair (economy, market structure) such that there exists a C.E. This is generically possible in our general framework

(see Younès 1986). The argument in the text is not fundamentally modified if one makes this more general assumption.

5. The analysis in terms of O.I.1 can be used.

6. It is said in this case that money plays only the role of a store of value. However, the distinction means of exchange—store of value has no theoretical status.

7. Definition 9 provides a notion of "barter," which, because of M^1, boils down to a system of gifts. See, however, the conclusion.

8. This is, for instance, the approach that is chosen when firms decide the market structure by choosing production plans and thus the yields of shares. One can analyze the way imperfect and incomplete information generates an incomplete market structure.

References

Y. Balasko, D. Cass, and K. Shell. 1980. "Existence of Competitive Equilibrium in a General Overlapping Generations Model." *Journal of Economic Theory* 23: 307–322.

Y. Balasko and K. Shell. 1980. "The Overlapping Generations Model, I." *Journal of Economic Theory* 23: 281–306.

O. Blanchard and N. Kiyotaki. 1987. "Monopolistic Competition and the Effects of Aggregate Demand." *American Economic Review* 77(4): 647–666.

D. Cass and M. Yaari. 1966. "A Re-examination of the Pure Consumption Loan Model." *Journal of Political Economy* 74 (August): 353–367.

S. Chae. 1987. "Short Run Care Equivalence in an Overlapping Generations Model." *Journal of Economic Theory* 43: 170–183.

D. Diamond. 1985. "Money in Search Equilibrium." *Econometrica* 52: 1–20.

J. Esteban. 1986. "A Characterization of the Core in Overlapping Generations Models." *Journal of Economic Theory* 39: 439–456.

D. Gale. 1982. *Money: In Equilibrium*. Cambridge Economic Handbooks.

D. Gale. 1986b. A Strategic Model of Trade with Money as a Medium of Exchange. Caress Working Paper, University of Pennsylvania.

J. Geanakoplos and H. Polemarchakis. 1986. "Walrasian Indeterminacy and Keynesian Macroeconomics." *Review of Economic Studies* 53: 755–780.

J. M. Grandmont, G. Laroque, and Y. Younès. 1978. "Equilibrium with Quantity Rationing and Recontracting." *Journal of Economic Theory*.

J. M. Grandmont and Y. Younès. 1972. "On the Role of Money and Existence of a Monetary Equilibrium." *Review of Economic Studies* 39: 355–372.

J. M. Grandmont and Y. Younès. 1973. "On the Efficiency of a Monetary Equilibrium." *Review of Economic Studies* 40: 149–165.

W. Heller. 1985. Coordination Failures under Complete Markets with Application to Effective Demand. Working Paper, University of California at San Diego.

K. Hendricks, K. Judd, and D. Kovenock. 1980. "A Note on the Core of the Overlapping Generations Model." *Economic Letters.*

L. Hurwicz. 1959. "Optimality and Efficiency in Resource Allocation Processes." In *Mathematical Methods in the Social Sciences,* ed K. Arrow, S. Karlin, and D. Suppes. Stanford.

E. Malinvaud. 1953. "Capital Accumulation and Efficient Allocation of Resources." *Econometrica* 21: 233–268.

E. Malinvaud. 1962. "Capital Accumulation and Efficient Allocation of Resources: A Corrigendum." *Econometrica.*

A. Mas Colell. 1983. "The Profit Motive in the Theory of Monopolistic Competition." Presented at Bonn-Harvard Conference on Entrepreneurship.

R. Radner. 1972. "Existence of Equilibria of Plans, Prices and Price Expectation in a Sequence of Markets." *Econometrica.*

J. Roberts. 1987. "An Equilibrium Model with Involuntary Unemployment at Flesible Competitive Prices and Wages." *American Economic Review.*

P. Townsend. 1980. "Models of Money with Spatially Separated Agents." In *Models of Monetary Economics,* ed. J. Kareken and N. Wallace. F.R.B. of Minneapolis.

Y. Younès. 1975. "On the Role of Money in the Process of Exchange and the Existence of a Non-Walrasian Equilibrium." *Review of Economic Studies.*

Y. Younès. 1986. Competitive Equilibrium for Incomplete Market Structures. Caress Working Paper.

Y. Younès. 1985. On the Theory of Incomplete Markets. CEPREMAP Working Paper.

II

Macroeconomic Theories and Models

18

Conventional and New Econometric Models of Investment in France: Do They Fit in the 1980s?

Patrick Artus and
Pierre Sicsic

At the end of the 1970s, economists agreed on the explanation of corporate investment behavior in France (see, for example, Artus and Muet 1984b, 1986). The best econometric equation seemed to be a flexible, accelerator model, that is, a model including an effect of relative factor cost. Such an equation may be compatible either with a putty-clay production function (where the capital-labor elasticity of substitution is close to 1) or with a putty-putty production function (where the elasticity of substitution is much lower, from 0.05 to 0.1). In both cases, the short-run fluctuations of investment caused by cost are equal. The long-run effects, however, are very different. When the entire capital is replaced, the sensitivity of the production technology to cost is 10 times greater in the putty-clay estimates than in the putty-putty ones. The estimates of this standard model yielded broadly constant returns to scale for the production function, and sometimes included an additional production factor (energy) (Artus and Peyroux 1981) or a profit term.[1]

Our purpose here is to verify whether the economists' consensus is still relevant when the early 1980s are included in the sample period. We will show that it is not, and that the explanatory power of the standard model has diminished (section 2). We will then try to explain this decline by examining some additions to the model (section 3). Has there been an increase in the scrapping rate due, for instance, to the rise in the relative energy price, leading to faster equipment replacement (section 3.1)? Has there been a change in the relative weights of the financial constraint and the demand constraint after the worsening of corporate financial positions in the early 1980s and their improvement since 1984? Has the acceleration of inflation and its subsequent rapid slowdown changed firms' perceptions of their profits from a book-value definition to an economic one incorporating inflation-caused depreciation in their debt (section 3.2) (Sterdyniak 1986)? Should we specify profitability effect in a different way? The profitability effect was first introduced using capital adjustment costs (Hayashi 1982; Blanchard and Sachs 1982; Abel 1983; Summers 1981; Abel and Blanchard 1986; D'Autume and Michel 1984), then more realistically via uncertainty on expected demand (Malinvaud 1983; Edwards and Keen 1985; Artus and Migus 1986). It has become customary to explain the weakness of investment by falling profitability or—which is almost the same—by overindebtness (Malinvaud 1987; Levy-Garboua and Maarek 1985). We will try to assess the effect of these phenomena (sections 3.3 and 3.4). In studies on finance, output uncertainty plays a role not only because of short-run stickiness in production technology (Malinvaud 1983) but also because it implies a bankruptcy risk if sales are so low that the firm becomes insolvent (Artus 1985; Baron 1976; Brennan and Schwartz 1978; Turnbull 1979; Warner 1977). This latter effect influences the choice of potential output, the choice of investment, and also the trade-off between debt and equity in the case where bankruptcy entails a cost to the lenders who recover the residual value of the bankrupt firm (section 3.5).

Finally, we will develop a model that combines uncertainty effects on demand and bankruptcy costs. We will show that both profitability and demand variability have an impact on the capital cost and on the expected sales that are factored into the investment decision.

1. The Data and Their Historical Changes

We have constructed series for productive capital in equipment from investment data for French firms excluding the large public-service companies such as utilities and railroads. We have taken a constant scrapping rate of 8%. The initial value is the productive capital of firms in 1963, as given in the national accounts. This procedure enables us to vary the scrapping rate in the estimates.

The accumulation (investment/capital) ratio peaked in late 1973 (3.4% in quarterly data), stayed low until mid-1979 except for a brief rise during the winter of 1975–1976, climbed again from 1980 to 1982 to about 2.9%, declined in 1983–1984, and moved up again in mid-1985. Figure 1 shows that the simplest investment model—accumulation ratio = growth rate + scrapping rate—does not conflict with the investment curve between 1970–1974 and 1976–1979. However, this model—which assumes a constant scrapping rate—fails to explain why the accumulation ratio was higher in the 1980s than between the two oil crises despite a lower growth rate.

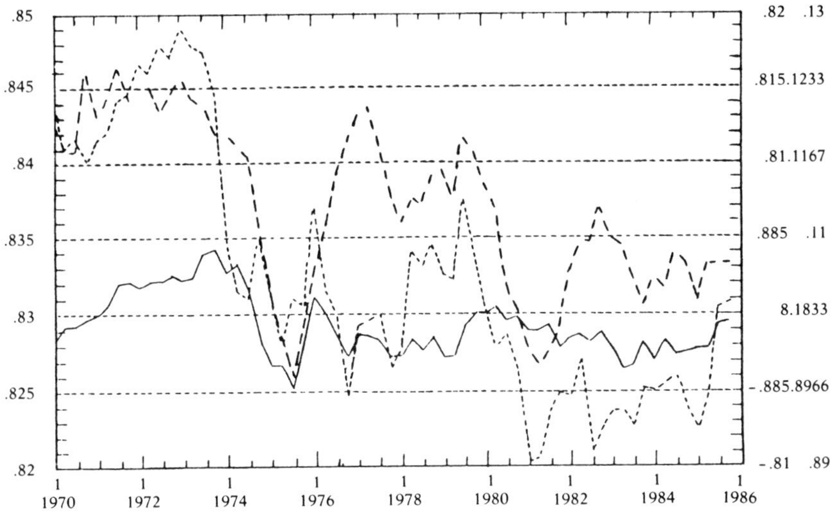

Figure 1.
Accumulation ratio, growth rate, and profit ratio. (———) Accumulation ratio; (– – – – – –) growth rate of value added (first scale on right); (--------) profit ratio (second scale on right).

For our purposes, we refer to a "high" investment level not in an absolute sense, but with respect to its most common explanatory factor: growth. We will say that investment is "high" when the ratio of investment to gross output variation (including the scrapping effect) is high. During "high investment" periods, the ratio of investment to output may be low if the growth rate is low. Any international comparison based on such ratios could be misleading as to the adequacy of investment, since growth-rate gaps are not taken into account. Our aim is therefore to assess not the overall saving effort, but only the investment behavior of firms.

The changes in capital intensity (ratio of capital to value added) raise the same question as for investment. Capital intensity moved down from a level of 4.6 in 1963 (in quarterly data) to 3.2 in 1974. It then remained steady until 1976, decreased slightly in 1979, and rose continuously from 1980 to 1985, returning to its 1966 level of 3.7.

We can therefore observe two clear break-points in the mean productivity of capital in France: (1) between its rise preceding the first oil crisis and its subsequent stability, and (2) between this plateau and its decrease after the second oil crisis. Accordingly, investment in relation to output should have been high between 1980 and 1985. The standard model could explain this trend through changes in the profit ratio or in relative factor prices.

The profit ratio (gross profit to capital value) fell in early 1974 and again in early 1981. Despite a slight upturn in mid-1985, its curve seems inconsistent with the increase of the capital coefficient during the 1980s.

The strong fluctuations in relative cost from 1974 to 1978 (see figure 2), explained by the price term in the real interest rate, afford no insight into the impact of relative cost during this period. From 1980 to 1985, relative cost is broadly constant, growing at an annual rate of about 1%. When we take technical progress into account, we find that relative cost cannot have caused a strong labor-to-capital substitution. The tax incentives introduced in late 1979 stimulated investment.[2] They are therefore the only variable whose curve matches that of capital accumulation, as will be confirmed by our estimate of the standard model.

2. The Standard Model

The standard investment equation found in econometric studies on France links the accumulation rate to

1. the growth rate of output;
2. the growth rate of relative factors cost; and
3. the profit ratio.

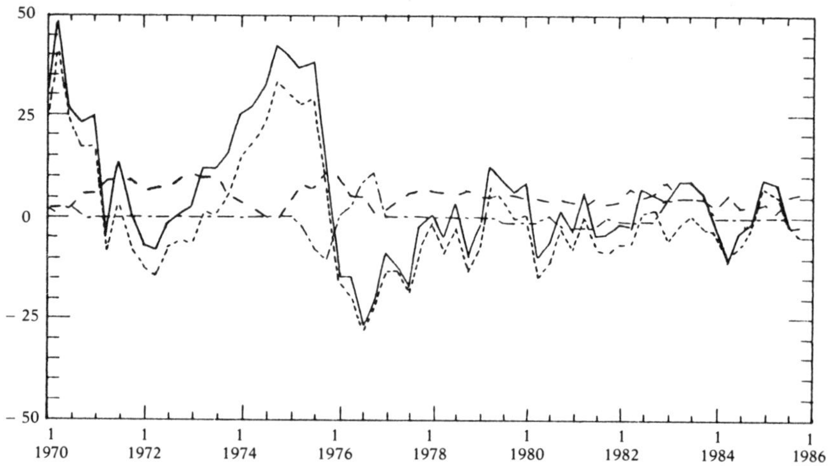

Figure 2.
Relative factor cost. (———) Relative factor cost; (– – – –) wage cost divided by the price of capital goods; (--------) inverse of real interest rate; (— — — —) tax incentive.

This equation will enable us to assess the contribution of each of the different variables discussed in the introduction. With a putty-putty production function, its structure is as follows:

$$\frac{I}{K_{-1}} = a + b\dot{\tilde{Q}} + d(\dot{W} - \dot{C}') + e\dot{F} + k\frac{\pi}{p^k K_{-1}} \qquad (1)$$

where

I/K_{-1} = the accumulation rate,

$\dot{\tilde{Q}}$ = the growth rate of expected output,

$\dot{W}$ = the growth rate of wage cost (including social security contributions),

$\dot{C}'$ = the growth rate of the user cost of capital,

F = tax incentives to investment,

$\pi/p^k K_{-1}$ = the profit ratio (π is gross profits minus interest payments and corporate taxes).

The effect of the tax incentives on the equipment price could be introduced in the capital cost. We believe (as do Avouyi-Dovi and Muet 1987) that this effect is sizable and, at all events, complex; some tax cuts, such as those of 1979–1980, are linked to changes in investment; others are tied to specific conditions, such as those of 1981–1982, which required firms to follow certain employment practices. We therefore choose to estimate the impact of these tax measures separately.

Like Bernard (1977) and Gubian, Guillaumat, Tailliet, and Lecacheux (1986), we write the *user cost of capital* as

$$C = p^k(1 - k_1 - k_2)\left(C_1 - \frac{1 - k_1}{1 - k_1 - k_2} C_3\right) \qquad (2)$$

where

$C_1 = \mu + \delta - \dot{p}^k$ is the standard user-cost variable

and

$C_3 = \dfrac{\mu\tau\delta'}{\mu - \delta'}$ represents the impact of the tax deduction on the user cost,

with

p^k: price of capital goods,

k_1: rate of tax cut reducing depreciation allowances,

k_2: rate of tax cuts not reducing depreciation allowances,

μ: discount rate: here, yield on newly issued bonds,

τ: corporate tax rate,

δ: scrapping rate: here, 8% a year,

$\dot{p}^k$: expected growth rate of the capital goods price: moving average of the actual growth rate over 8 quarters, minus 4% a year, to ensure a positive user cost,

δ': rate of statutory depreciation allowances.

As stated above, we divide the user cost into a pre-tax-deduction component,

$$C' = p^k\left(C_1 - \frac{1 - k_1}{1 - k_1 - k_2} C_3\right),$$

and a tax-deduction component,

$$F = 1 - k_1 - k_2.$$

Expected output $\tilde{Q}$ was calculated as the trend-corrected mean of firms' value added Q, at constant prices, on the last eight quarters—the length was obtained by an iterative procedure:

$$\tilde{Q} = \frac{1}{8} \sum_{i=0}^{7} Q_{-i}(1 + g)^{i+1}$$

where g is the average growth rate of Q over the last eight quarters

$(g = \frac{1}{7}(\text{Log}\, Q - \text{Log}\, Q_{-7}))$.

Equation 1 has been estimated:

- with or without the profit ratio;
- over the periods 1970–1979 and 1970–1984[3] (with quarterly data);
- with an autoregressive formulation or with lags on the explanatory variables.

The results are given in tables 1 and 2.

The autoregressives equations are misleading, because the loss in adjustment quality is concealed by an increase in the autoregressive term coefficient, for instance, when the profit ratio is omitted. If we look at the

Table 1.
Autoregressives Equations

Period	Inter-cept	Lagged endoge-nous	Relative accel-erator	Relative cost	Tax	Profit	R2	DW	SEE[a]
70–79	.004	.846	.082	−.004	−.0114		0.84	1.82	0.97
	(1.8)	(11.5)	(3.4)	(2.1)	(1.4)				
70–79	.001	.731	.051	−.004	−.0082	.056	0.87	1.92	0.89
	(0.6)	(9.3)	(2.1)	(2.4)	(1.1)	(2.8)			
70–84	.004	.840	.067	−.005	−.0123		0.83	2.00	0.88
	(2.4)	(13.8)	(4.0)	(2.8)	(1.9)				
70–84	.003	.757	.036	−.005	−.0010	.037	0.84	2.02	0.85
	(1.7)	(11.1)	(1.8)	(3.1)	(1.5)	(2.4)			

a. multiplied by 1000

Table 2.
Lagged Equations[a]

Period	Intercept	Accel-erator[b]	Relative cost[b]	Tax[b]	Profit	R2	DW	SEE
70–79	.025	.463	.005	−.183		0.69	0.57	1.36
	(41.8)	(8.4)	(0.9)	(4.7)				
		1.9	2.4	2.1				
70–79	.011	.214	−.016	−.131	.153	0.86	1.70	0.95
	(3.3)	(2.9)	(3.2)	(3.7)	(4.5)			
		2.3	0.8	2.0	4.2			
70–84	.027	.299	−.003	−.137		0.57	0.50	1.41
	(82.2)	(8.1)	(0.7)	(4.3)				
		2.2	0.1	2.0				
70–84	.014	.061	−.017	−.075	.142	0.74	0.88	1.12
	(40.6)	(1.0)	(3.7)	(2.5)	(4.4)			
		1.9	1.1	1.9	3.8			

a. Mean lag (in quarters) under the *t* statistic.
b. Sum of the lagged coefficients.

equations with distributed lags, we find

- a general loss of accuracy when the period 1980–1984 is included;
- a strong decrease in the elasticity of capital to expected output ($\tilde{Q}$ coefficient);
- a constancy in the response of investment to profits;
- an insignificant relative factors cost when the tax-credit effect is excluded;
- a strong influence of the tax-credit variable (which weakens when one includes profit increased by the tax deduction; apparently *only the tax deduction part of the relative-factor-cost component plays a role.*

From a theoretical point of view, the difference between the coefficients of the relative factor cost and of the tax variable is surprising, since investment should be equally affected by a direct decrease in the capital-goods price or a decrease due to a tax deduction. In the relative factors cost, the term

$$\frac{w}{c_1 - \dfrac{1-k_1}{1-k_1-k_2}c_3}$$

corresponds to an expectation that applies to the equipment's entire lifetime; $p^k F$, on the other hand, is not an expectation, but defines the purchase price once and for all.

The first term, which corresponds to a long-run expectation, could be incorrectly represented by lags on actual data; morever, this expectation could have been very stable and therefore without effect on investment; this does not rule out a change in investment if the tern suddenly varied. The stability argument is hardly convincing because the fluctuations in the interest rate and in the rate of firms' social security are strong and are probably expected to be permanent.

Because of investment-price sluggishness, an estimation with $p_0^k F$ instead of F alone would yield a coefficient close to ours, thereby eliminating the first objection. Therefore, the proposition that short-run changes in the interest rate or labor costs have very little impact on investment seems robust. We have already observed that in recent years, when investment seems to have been too high relative to growth, the increase in relative factors cost was supposed to brake accumulation, while tax credits were supposed to stimulate investment. The preceding econometric results are therefore not surprising.

The first two findings—loss of accuracy and lower capital-to-output elasticity—should be qualified, as the stability of the coefficients holds up under a Chow test. Nevertheless, the explanatory capacity of the pure accelerator seemingly diminishes in the recent period.

3. Additions to the Standard Model

3.1. Accelerated Depreciation and Rise in Energy Prices

It could be argued that the scrapping rate rose after both oil crises, because some equipment had become unprofitable. This could explain why investment has been so high since 1980. To test this idea, we

1. introduced dummy variables over the periods 1975–1984 and 1980–1984 in the previous equations, and
2. reestimated the equations using different scrapping rates, from 6 to 11%, in the calculation of the capital stock and user cost.

Using the dummy variables in the lagged equations, the results are given in table 3.

These estimates show that, with the accelerator model, accuracy is greatest when the dummy 1975–1984 is introduced. This variable, which has a negative coefficient, replaces the accelerator, since the accelerator coefficient is heavily reduced—from 0.46 to 0.21 when the cutoff date is 1979 and from 0.30 to 0.08 when the cutoff date is 1984. The high returns to scale implied by these estimates with dummies are needed to explain investment fluctuations; however, the economic slowdown then becomes inadequate to account for the fall in the accumulation ratio after the first oil crisis.

When the 1980–1984 variable is introduced, the accelerator coefficient rises, and the positive sign of this dummy variable shows that faster depreciation after the second oil crisis is possible. If we treat the dummy as proxies for the accelerator, then the coefficient of the second dummy—a proxy for the new decrease in growth—should have been negative, if the slowdown in growth were the only new phenomenon after 1980.

The second set of estimates, using the standard accelerator-profits equation, underlines the weakness of investment between the two oil crises (since the accelerator coefficient is very small, this is actually a profit model). When the two dummies are introduced, the accelerator-profit coefficients change slightly, but the 1980–1984 period does not stand out as

Table 3.
Dummy Variables

Period	Intercept	Accel-erator	Relative cost	Tax	Profit	Dummy 75–84	Dummy 80–84	R2	DW	SEE[a]
70–79	.029	.21	−.010	−.12		−.0025		0.76	0.78	1.22
	(19.8)	(2.1)	(1.4)	(2.5)		(3.0)				
70–84	.031	.08	−.019	−.09		−.0033		0.74	0.94	1.1
	(41.4)	(1.6)	(3.9)	(3.6)		(5.8)				
70–84	.026	.39	−.001	−.16			.0015	0.63	0.59	1.3
	(49.1)	(8.3)	(0.1)	(5.2)			(2.9)			
70–84	.030	.16	−.015	−.11		−.003	.0010	0.76	0.96	1.7
	(33.7)	(2.6)	(3.0)	(4.3)		(5.3)	(2.2)			
70–79	.011	.21	−.016	−.13	.15	.0		0.86	1.70	0.6
	(1.9)	(2.5)	(2.9)	(3.6)	(3.3)	(0.0)				
70–84	.024	.04	−.022	−.08	.06	−.0024		0.80	1.25	0.9
	(6.3)	(0.6)	(5.2)	(3.1)	(1.8)	(3.8)				
70–84	.010	.12	−.013	−.09	.17		.0019	0.83	1.25	0.2
	(3.7)	(2.3)	(3.5)	(3.5)	(6.4)		(5.0)			
70–84	.016	.10	−.017	−.09	.12	−.0014	.0015	0.84	1.40	0.2
	(4.1)	(1.8)	(4.2)	(2.5)	(3.4)	(2.2)	(3.7)			

a. multiplied by 1000

an exception, since the sum of the dummy coefficients is nearly zero. This suggests an inadequacy of investment in 1975–1979 with respect to the profit-ratio level.

When different values of the depreciation rate are used, 8% appears to yield the best adjustments for all the estimation periods.[4] This finding does not support the hypothesis of accelerating depreciation. If such a phenomenon has occurred since 1975, its effects have been hidden by those of slower growth.

Many authors believe that a rise in the relative price of raw materials affects investment through

1. depreciation and replacement of old equipment that has become unprofitable, and
2. substitution between capital-labor and raw materials in the choice of technology.

This means that if capital and raw materials are substitutable, a rise in the price of the latter will stimulate investment. If, on the contrary, they are not—that is, if the equipment requires a determined amount of raw materials—the rise will have ambiguous effects. In the nonsubstitutability case, the price of capital should include the price of the energy that will be used. This makes the price of capital rise with the price of energy, thereby reducing investment through capital-labor substitution whereas depreciation accelerates once more. We therefore included in the standard equation (with or without profit ratio) the growth rate of the ratio price of the intermediary-consumption energy price to the user cost of capital. The accumulation-rate specification enables the effects of substitutability and nonsubstitutability discussed above to be represented by this growth rate (table 4).

We eliminated relative factor cost, since its coefficient was always negative. The relative energy price does not seem to improve the equations. This failure, however, could be due to higher depreciation and to the complementarity between capital and energy. For the 1970–1984 period, we obtained the results shown in table 5.

3.2. Changes in the Proportion of Financially Constrained or Demand-Constrained Firms

One interpretation of the accelerator-profits model is that some firms expect to be demand-constrained, and therefore choose their investments accord-

Table 4.
Values of the Scrapping Rate[a]

Period	Scrapping rate (%)	SEE for investment	DW
70–79	6	932	0.51
	7	814	0.56
	8	770	0.57
	9	805	0.54
	10	908	0.48
	11	1057	0.43
70–82	6	1064	0.37
	7	932	0.42
	8	872	0.47
	9	889	0.50
	10	973	0.49
	11	1103	0.47
70–84	6	1086	0.41
	7	945	0.45
	8	873	0.50
	9	880	0.51
	10	954	0.50
	11	1073	0.48

a. As capital K varies with the depreciation rate, we cannot compare the equations on the SEE basis of I/K. We have therefore shown the product of that SEE by the mean value of capital.

Table 5.

Period	Intercept	Accel-erator	Energy relative cost	Tax	Profit	R2	DW	SEE[a]
70–84	.027	.287	.004	−.136		0.58	0.55	1.40
	(82.8)	(7.8)	(1.3)	(4.4)				
70–84	.018	.134	−.004	−.102	.098	0.68	0.68	1.22
	(5.9)	(2.0)	(0.9)	(3.1)	(3.1)			

a. multiplied by 1000

ing to projected demand, while others are financially constrained—which explains the link between profit and investment. There is also a third theoretical case, in which firms are not constrained—that is, are subject to neoclassical investment demand—but this case is consistently rejected by econometric estimates.

In the standard model, the proportions of firms constrained in one way or the other are fixed, since the weights of the accelerator and profit terms are constant. This constancy may explain the lower accuracy of the estimate observed in the most recent period if the actual proportions of constrained firms have changed drastically during those years. Estimations of disequilibrium models for investment (such as Artus and Muet 1984a, 1986, chapter 8) allow the proportions to change from period to period, and therefore make it possible to take into account the effects of growth-rate and profit-ratio changes on the prevailing investment "regime."

We estimated a two-regime model using the CES approximation yielded by aggregation of elementary economic sectors where the strict minicondition prevails (Lambert 1984). Here, profit represents either the effect of a financial constraint or a variable similar to Tobin's q—which appears in models with capital adjustment costs and with no output constraint (Hayashi 1982).

Of these two interpretations of profits, the first seems more plausible for two reasons: (1) actual profits do not necessarily represent expected profits (also, we decided not to use a stock-price index because of the likelihood of bubbles on the share price), and (2) more important, these theoretical models make investment dependent on marginal Tobin's q, which is very difficult to measure and can be very different from average Tobin's q (marginal Tobin's q is the change in the firm's market value divided by the shift in the capital's replacement value that causes the market-value change). Thus, for each elementary sector:

Investment = *Min* (*optimal investment for given output and given relative factor cost; investment permitted by profits*).

Hence, at the aggregated level:

$$\frac{I}{K_{-1}} = \left(\left(\frac{I}{K_{-1}}\right)_D^{-\alpha} + \left(\frac{I}{K_{-1}}\right)_P^{-\alpha}\right)^{-1/\alpha} \tag{3}$$

where $(I/K_{-1})_0$ is the accumulation in the demand-constrained regime and $(I/K_{-1})_P$ the value in the financially constrained regime.[5]

To be consistent with the standard specification, we took

$$\left(\frac{I}{k_{-1}}\right)_D = a + b \sum \beta_i \dot{\tilde{Q}}_{-i} + d \sum \gamma_j (\dot{W}_{-j} - \dot{C}'_{-j}) + e \sum \varepsilon_{-k} \dot{F}_{-k}$$

and (4)

$$\left(\frac{I}{K_{-1}}\right)_P = a' + h \sum \eta_i \left(\frac{\pi}{p^k K_{-1}}\right) \qquad (\sum \beta_i = \sum \gamma_j = \sum \varepsilon_{-k} = \sum \eta_i = 1).$$

The number of lags and their profiles ($\beta, \gamma, \varepsilon, \eta$) are given by independent estimates of the two specifications for each period. There are then fixed in order to limit the number of coefficients in the CES approximate.

Equation 3 is known to be obtained when the spatial error terms—which correspond to the elementary sectors—follow a Weibull law (Gourieroux, Laffont, and Monfort 1984). The larger α is, the closer we get, in the aggregate, to the minimum of the two aggregate values. This corresponds to the case where capital can easily be shifted between sectors when constraints are binding. For instance, if firms are financially constrained in one sector, they will invest more in another. Of course, such transfers are possible only if the elementary firms are free to allocate investment among the goods they produce, which differ in demand and expected profitability (table 6).

These results are not very encouraging. The CES approximation yields less accurate adjustments than the standard, fixed-weights specification. As in our earlier estimates, the coefficient of relative factor cost has a sign opposite to the theoretical one. We therefore estimated our model without the relative factor cost before examining the distribution of the elementary sectors between the two regimes. The proportion of demand-constrained firms is (see Lambert, Lubrano, and Sneessens 1984)

$$\frac{(I/K_{-1})_D^{-\alpha}}{(I/K_{-1})_D^{-\alpha} + (I/K_{-1})_P^{-\alpha}}.$$

This proportion is plotted in figure 3 to the first quarter of 1986. The curve shows that since 1983 the proportion of demand-constrained firms has slightly exceeded its post-1977 level—excluding the 1980 peak, which corresponds to a drop in growth. Two-thirds of the firms still appear to be profit-constrained, and the latest period does not differ very significantly from the one immediately before it. Figure 4, which plots the econometric adjustment, confirms the weakness of investment from 1977 to 1979 with respect to its previously analyzed determinants.

3.3. Effect of the Slowdown in Inflation on the Real Debt Burden

Inflation favors firms because it reduces the real value of their debts insofar as nominal interest rates are not fully inflation-indexed. If firms look at their

Table 6.
CES Approximation

	Demand constraints				Profit constraint					
Period	Intercept	Accelerator	Relative cost	Tax	Intercept	Profit		R2	DW	SEE[a]
70–79	.028	.578	−.002	−.272	.005	.246	6	0.77	0.81	1.15
	(15.7)	(2.1)	(0.2)	(2.2)	(0.5)	(2.1)				
70–84	.029	.568	−0.28	−.254	.014	.148	22	0.70	1.02	1.17
	(32.0)	(3.1)	(1.9)	(2.4)	(7.7)	(9.0)				
70–84	.028	.336		−.186	.013	.162	22	0.65	0.72	1.26
	(46.0)	(5.3)		(3.7)	(4.3)	(5.7)				

a. multiplied by 1000

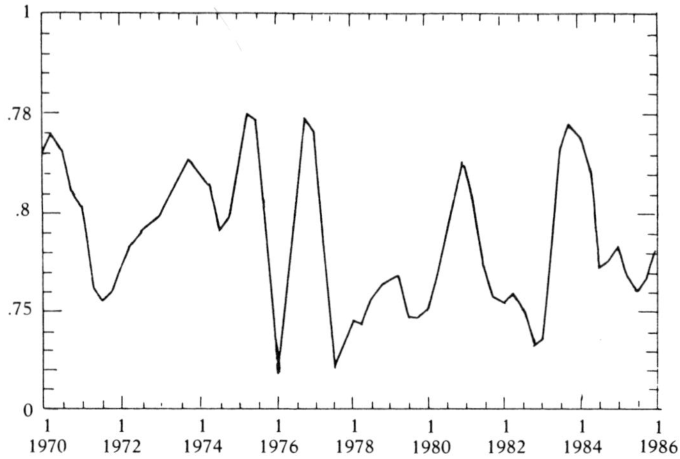

Figure 3.
Proportion of demand-constrained firms.

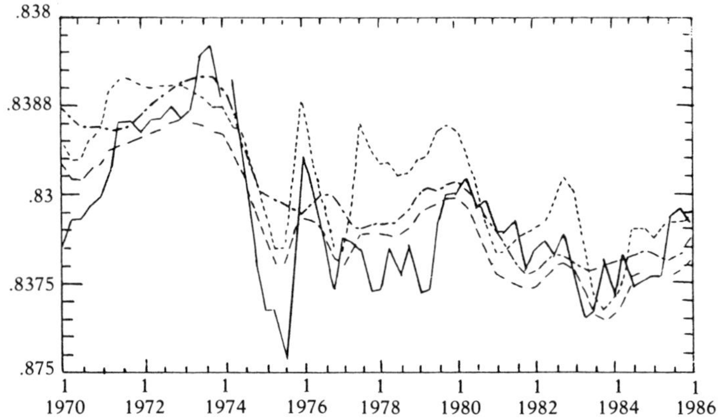

Figure 4.
Adjustment with the CES approximation. (———) Actual; (— —) adjusted; (- - - - -) accelerator; (— - —) profit.

true "economic" profits instead of their "book-value" profits, they should correct the latter for the effects of inflation on debt, that is, by adding $\dot{p}.EN$, where EN is their outstanding debt net of their monetary assets. We reestimated the standard equation 1 with lags, adding the variable

$$\pi = \frac{\dot{p}.EN}{p^k K_{-1}} \quad \text{(and its lags).}$$

No significant effect was obtained. Moreover, the coefficient of this variable is so unstable that the introduction of dummies could change its sign. We were therefore unable to demonstrate any effect of inflation gains on investment.

This result is very surprising, because all econometrics estimations of consumption behavior show that households deduct from their disposable income anywhere from 30 to 40% of the inflationary tax on their monetary assets. This discrepancy would seem to suggest that households are better than firms at calculating their inflation-adjusted "economic" income! If our results are correct, the effect of inflation on demand in the French economy is unambiguous; the current account worsens and personal consumption slackens, while inflation-favored firms do not increase their expenditures. Consequently, all inflationary economic policy measures such as wage rises and devaluations are penalized.

We should point out the dissymmetry between

1. the accelerator term, which incorporates the inflationist gain because the real interest rate is used in the relative factor cost, and
2. the profit, which represents funds available for investment.

We tried to restore symmetry by assuming that firms do not take inflation into account at all. For this, we calculated the user cost of capital with the nominal interest rate. This yielded a coefficient for relative factor cost that was insignificant and had the wrong sign. Hence, taking inflation into account does not seem to bias the relative-factor-cost variable.

3.4. Tradeoff between Productive Investment and Financial Investment

One of the reasons for the weakness of investment in France is the very high yield on financial assets, specially when interest rates are falling.[6] This phenomenon cannot be introduced in the standard model, since the shareholders' discount rate is represented by the coupon rate of newly issued bonds. We tested an alternative version where the discount rate is equal to the yield on a fixed-rate bond. For the period $t - 1$, we get

$$\mu_{t-1} = R_{t-1} + \left(1 - \frac{R_t}{R_{t-1}}\right)\left(1 - \frac{1}{(1 + R_{t-1})^T}\right),$$

with the usual linearization (Shiller 1979), where R = interest rate of newly issued bonds and T = average bond lifetime. Because of its very wide swings, we smoothed the term representing capital gains $(\mu_{t-1} - R_{t-1})$ over eight quarters.

The behavior modeled here is that of managers or shareholders who may spend their corporate or personal funds on productive investment or financial assets. This is not a "Tobin's q" behavior, where shareholders invest in the firm to earn a capital gain on their shares. When the long-term interest rate reverses, the bond-yield rate and the interest rate move in opposite directions (see figure 5). For example, the market rate of return fell in 1980 and rose at the end of 1981 and in 1982.

As the changes in the user cost of capital (excluding tax credits) result from those in the real discount rate (term C_1 in equation 2), the profile of the relative factor costs is very sensitive to the discount rate used. Figure 6 shows that the relative capital cost actually *decreases* in 1979 and 1981 when the market yield is used—despite heavy investment. The results of the estimates using the bond yield as the discount rate are given in table 7.

Again, the figures are disappointing. The equations without profit are slightly better: for 1970–1984 the coefficient of the relative factor cost is significant and—correctly—positive. But this improvement disappears in

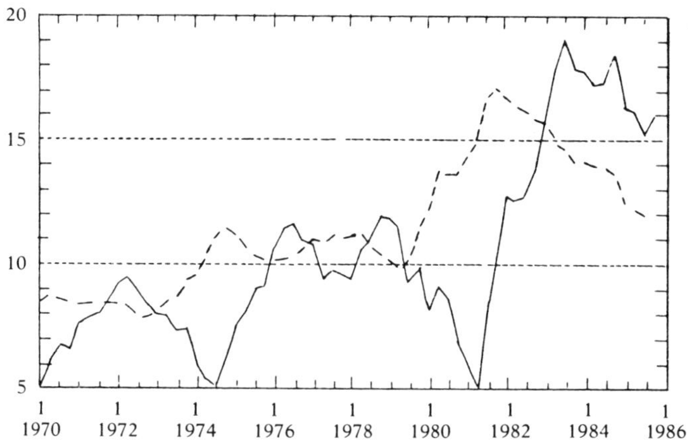

Figure 5.
Yield. (———) Bond yield; (– – – –) interest rate of newly issued bonds.

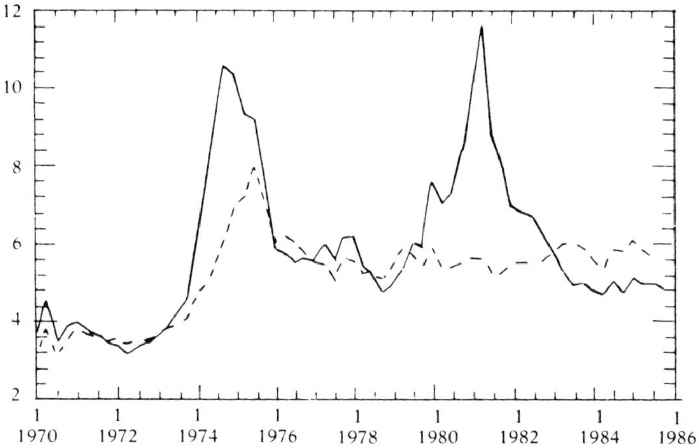

Figure 6.
Relative factor costs. (———) Using bond yield; (----) using rate of newly issued bonds.

Table 7.
Bond Yield Used as Discount Rate[a]

Period	Intercept	Accel-erator[b]	Relative cost[b]	Tax[b]	Profit[b]	R2	DW	SEE[c]
70–79	.025	.436	.005	−.198		0.70	0.66	1.34
	(42.4)	(7.8)	(1.6)	(5.2)				
		1.6	1.4	2.0				
70–79	.016	.356	−.004	−.169	.091	0.82	1.13	1.08
	(5.0)	(4.5)	(1.1)	(4.4)	(2.8)			
		1.8	0.0	2.0	5.9			
70–84	.027	.268	−.005	−.143		0.59	0.63	1.37
	(82.7)	(7.1)	(1.9)	(4.6)				
		1.6	0.8	2.0				
70–84	.018	.126	−.001	−.101	.096	0.67	0.74	1.26
	(5.7)	(1.8)	(0.2)	(3.1)	(2.9)			
		1.2	2.4	1.9	3.9			

a. mean lag under Student's t
b. sum of lagged coefficients
c. multiplied by 1000

the equations with a profit term, where the new discount rate fails to give significance to the relative factor cost. Unfortunately, we cannot answer the question of the effect of financial capital gains on investment. We still do not know which discount rate is correct: the cost of the firm's resources, or the yield of its own assets (or those of its shareholders)—a yield that differs greatly depending on whether the assets are in the form of bank credits or securities. For the moment, the best we can do is to recall the results predicted by theory: if debt is positive and debt constraint maximal, then the user cost is a weighted average of the interest rate on loans and the shareholders' discount rate; if the constraint links the debt to the capital stock, the weights applied are the proportion and equity in the firms' capital (Bernard 1977).

3.5. Uncertainty on Future Demand and Bankruptcy Risk

Uncertainty about future sales implies

1. a link between investment and profitability;
2. a bankruptcy risk.

It also entails a cost, which means that the Modigliani and Miller (1958, 1963) neutrality concerning financial choices does not hold. In the case of bankruptcy, the lenders reimbursed are subjected to the cost of bankruptcy and lose the benefit of the tax deduction on interest payments. The existence of a bankruptcy cost implies that the firm's value does not automatically increase with the debt outstanding, since a high debt engenders a strong likelihood of bankruptcy. Hence, there is an optimal level of debt, and lenders limit their supply of funds to the firm.[7] Credit rationing in these models occurs when, for a given capital, a rise in the interest rate causes an increase in the bankruptcy risk that exceeds the rise in the interest payments. Here, there is no adverse-selection or moral-hazard mechanism of the kind described by Jaffee and Russel (1976) and Stiglitz and Weiss (1981).

The model we use has the following characteristics (the mathematical details are available on request from the authors):

• Random future demand Q_1 is uniformly distributed $(\tilde{Q} - \sigma\tilde{Q}, \tilde{Q} + \sigma\tilde{Q})$, where $\tilde{Q}$ is expected future demand and σ the measure of its uncertainty. An attempt to substitute the empirical standard error of actual demand for $\sigma\tilde{Q}$ did not yield satisfactory results.

• Output is linked to capital K and labor L by the Cobb-Douglas equation $Q_t = (1 + \hat{\rho})^t K_t^a N_t^b$.

- It is possible to define a minimum level of future demand $\bar{Q}_1$ below which the firm goes bankrupt. At this level, assets value and profits are exactly equal to taxes and debt repayment.

If Q_1 is greater than $\bar{Q}_1$, the lenders receive $B_1(1 + R_1)$, where B_1 is the debt outstanding and R_1 is the interest rate; shareholders receive profits minus $B_1(1 + R_1)$ and taxes. If Q_1 is less than $\bar{Q}_1$, the lenders receive profits minus the cost of bankruptcy, while shareholders lose everything. $\bar{Q}_1$ is of course endogenous, and depends on the parameters of the model, which have to be estimated.

- Lenders are risk-neutral and demand that the expected yield on loans be equal to the risk-free interest rate r.

- Shareholders too are risk-neutral. They maximize the expected value of the firm with a discount rate μ by choosing the level of debt and investment—or the level of investment and the probability of bankruptcy, which amounts to the same thing. The optimal probability of "no bankruptcy" is governed by three rules:

1. it decreases with the cost of bankruptcy: if the cost is high, the lenders raise the interest rate, prompting shareholders to increase the probability of bankruptcy, since in that case they would pay no interest;

2. it increases with the shareholders' discount rate: if shareholders have a strong preference for short-term gains, they will want a high-yield investment and seek to minimize the risk of getting no dividends;

3. finally, it decreases with the interest rate: if debt costs more, it is more tempting to go bankrupt in order to avoid paying interest.

Every rise in the probability of no bankruptcy stimulates investment, since the expected output in case of solvency increases, as does the expected value of capital for shareholders.

We end up with a specification of the investment model whose structure is identical to that of the standard model (1):

$$\frac{I}{K_{-1}} = \alpha + \beta\Delta\log\left(\frac{(\tilde{Q} + \sigma\tilde{Q})^{(1+b)/b} - \bar{Q}_1{}^{(1+b)/b}}{2\sigma\tilde{Q}}\right) + e\dot{F}$$
$$+ d\Delta\log\left(\frac{w(1-\tau)}{\left[p^k(1+\mu) - \frac{\tilde{Q}+\sigma\tilde{Q}-\bar{Q}_1}{2\sigma\tilde{Q}}\left(p_1^k(1-\delta) + \frac{p^k(1-k_{-1})}{1-k_1-k_2}\cdot\frac{\mu}{\mu+\delta'}(\tau\delta' - \theta(1-\tau))\right)\right]}\right)$$
$$+ k\frac{\pi}{p^k K_{-1}}. \qquad (5)$$

The notations are the same as in equations 1 and 2. p_1^k stands for the expected capital-goods price, b is the production function's labor coefficient, and $2\sigma\tilde{Q}$, as we have already seen, measures the range of future demand.

There are some difficulties in estimating equation 5, essentially due to the endogeneity of $\bar{Q}_1$ (the minimum demand that ensures solvability). To each set of parameters of the production function $(a, b, \hat{\rho})$ corresponds a value of $\bar{Q}_1$. a and b are also coefficients in equation 5. We calculated b and $\hat{\rho}$ using an iterative procedure: a direct estimation was impossible because $\bar{Q}_1$ is determined implicitly and must be computed separately by means of an iterative algorithm. We therefore set a, b, and $\hat{\rho}$, computed $\bar{Q}_1$, and then estimated equation 5—in particular the coefficient a using the $\bar{Q}_1$ data. Taking this value of a, we computed $\bar{Q}_1$ again, and so on until the value converged on a. We estimated our model for several values of b and $\hat{\rho}$ in order to minimize the standard error of equation 5. Expected output $\tilde{Q}$, which is used in equation 5, is defined as in our previous estimates.

The theoretical model is based on the assumption that the firm goes bankrupt if its net value over one period is negative. This hypothesis, adopted for simplicity's sake, is obviously very strong—all the more so when quarterly data are used. We therefore calculated $\bar{Q}_1$ in two different ways. First, we assumed that the firm goes bankrupt if the cumulated flows of after-tax profits over n quarters plus capital value plus liquidities held are less than the debt. We iterated over n periods—thus applying the notion of effective bankruptcy, which is on average repeated over several quarters. Second, we computed $\bar{Q}_1$ without stock (capital, liquidities, debt, etc.) to see whether the notion of negative profit was more effective than that of negative net value.[8] To our great surprise, the second solution appeared to work better. In other words, the bankruptcy risk would seem to be gauged with respect to profit flows and not to the total accounting picture. In that case, what does the latter specification add to the ones estimated earlier? The following elements should be taken into account:

- The user cost of capital may be written[9]

$$c = p^k(1 - k_1 - k_2)\left(c_1 + (1 - u)c_2 - u\frac{1 - k_1}{1 - k_1 - k_2}c_3\right)$$

where

$$c_1 = \mu + \delta - \dot{p}^k,$$
$$c_2 = 1 - \delta + \dot{p}^k,$$
$$c_3 = \mu\tau\delta'/(\mu + \delta')$$

and where $u = (\tilde{Q} + \sigma\tilde{Q} - \bar{Q}_1)/2\sigma\tilde{Q}$ is the probability that the firm will not go bankrupt (if $u = 1$, we get the conventional user cost). The smaller the probability, the higher the user cost of capital, owing to the greater probability that the firm might be unable to sell its capital. Because of the way in which we calculated $\bar{Q}_1$, the u factor directly introduces profitability in the user cost. This approach differs from the previous specifications, where profit is an added variable. The components c_2 and c_3 are stabler than c_1, which corresponds to the real discount rate. Thus, the changes in user cost closely match the real discount rate.

• The demand variable is

$$[(\tilde{Q} + \sigma\tilde{Q})^{(1+b)/b} - \bar{Q}_1^{(1+b)/b}]^{b/(a+b)} \cdot \frac{1}{2\sigma\tilde{Q}}$$

and not $\tilde{Q}^{1/(a+b)}$ as in the standard model. Hence it includes a profitability effect: if probability diminishes, $\bar{Q}_1$ (the solvency threshold) rises and output (subject to the "no bankruptcy" condition) also shrinks.

• In theory, if demand variability (measured by $\sigma\tilde{Q}$) is greater, u (probability of no bankruptcy) decreases, leading to a higher user cost of capital. Also, the expected output variable when the firm does not go bankrupt is reduced. However, as we have said, our specification deprives us of this last effect.

3.6. Results

Table 8 reports our results for the two estimation periods. For μ, we used a discount rate incorporating capital gains and losses—a choice that yields slightly better results. We applied direct lags to the explanatory variables.

In every case, iteration yielded a b coefficient of 0.80 and a value of σ ranging from 0.52 to 0.55. This is due to the relative insensitivity of the likelihood to these parameters. The theoretical coefficient of the accelerator is $b/(a + b)$. If it is equal to 0.44 (as in the first regression), then a is equal to 0.98. This would entail very high returns to scale—around 1.8—a result found in all our estimates.

The value of σ is surprising, as it suggests that expected output varies around its mean in an interval of 50%. We believe this result is due to the aggregation of microeconomic risks: these are much greater than the fluctuation of aggregate demand alone, because of variations in the market shares.

In the sample period 1970–1979, the equations are clearly more accurate than those obtained with the conventional accelerator (the SEE falls from

Table 8.

Period	Intercept	Acceler-ator[a]	Relative cost[a]	Tax[a]	Profit[a]	R2	DW	SEE[b]
70–79	.024	.447	.016	−.204		0.82	1.13	1.05
	(50.7)	(11.7)	(2.3)	(6.3)				
		2.0	1.7	1.9				
70–79	.016	.319	.011	−.169	.085	0.88	1.60	0.87
	(6.9)	(6.8)	(1.6)	(5.6)	(3.5)			
		1.9	1.8	1.9	3.1			
70–84	.027	.226	−.005	−.132		0.54	0.51	1.46
	(87.5)	(7.5)	(0.6)	(3.8)				
		2.0	2.5	1.9				
70–84	.018	.096	−.009	−.092	.098	0.67	0.73	1.25
	(6.3)	(1.9)	(1.2)	(2.8)	(3.3)			
		0.8	2.2	1.9	4.2			

a. sum of lag coefficients; the mean lag (in quarters) is given under the *t* statistics.
b. multiplied by 1000

0.0014 to 0.0011). The profit coefficient remains significant, suggesting a dual influence of profits:

1. through expected profitability, which, when high, reduces the risk of bankruptcy;

2. through the financial constraint, which links investment to available funds.

In any case, the coefficient of the relative factor cost, corrected by the bankruptcy risk in the present model, is significant and carries the theoretical predicted sign. However, its value is remarkably low, corresponding to an elasticity of substitution of about 2%. These results are encouraging and seem to indicate that the introduction of uncertainty leads to a more realistic model of investment. Nevertheless, when the 1980–1984 period is included, the adjustments are not better than those obtained with the standard model.

Conclusion

We set out with the aim of understanding the changes in investment in France since 1980. Unfortunately, our success has been very limited. We have identified only two elements that seem to improve the existing explanatory model:

1. A discount rate incorporating capital gains and losses on bonds. This leads to a significant—but nevertheless very weak—effect of the relative factors cost. As a result, there appears to be no basis for the often-used argument that underinvestment was due to the excess of financial yields over returns on fixed assets.

2. The introduction of a slight acceleration of depreciation since 1979 rather than 1975 (the impact of this element is less demonstrable).

Despite these corrections, however, some phenomena remain inexplicable, in particular the increase in returns to scale. By contrast, we can enhance our understanding of investment during the 1970s by constructing an innovative model that includes uncertainty on future output and a bankruptcy risk (and cost). Our most interesting findings here—positive and negative—are as follows:

• The influence of investment-specific tax credits is clearly stronger than that of the other components of relative factor cost. It may therefore be possible that the significance of the relative factor cost effect in previous econometric adjustments is solely due to the tax variable. The assumed effects of the real interest rate on investment and on labor demand may be greatly overestimated and the effects of tax credits strongly underestimated. It must be emphasized that a tax credit modifies the user cost of capital—and thus desired capital—but has a purely *transitory* effect on investment, since that effect disappears once the supplementary investment has brought capital up to the desired level.

In all the adjustments, the relative factor cost (tax credit excluded) has a very weak coefficient—often positive when the sample period ends in 1979 and negative when it ends in 1984. The presence of classical unemployment in recent years may have made it more difficult to estimate factor demand, but this assumption needs to be confirmed by disequilibrium estimation.

The average coefficient of the tax-credit variable is about 0.12. Hence a permanent tax incentive equal to 1% of the capital-goods purchase price raises the level of capital by 0.12%. This implies an increase in investment of 1.1% (0.12% times the average ratio of capital to investment) while the supplementary desired capital is being built up, and of only 0.1% thereafter, owing to replacement investment. Even if the tax credits boost investment significantly, the policy's efficiency is not obvious. We should also remember that if the tax credits are removed, the capital stock returns to its former level.

• Firms appear not to adjust their profits for inflationary gains on their debt. As far as inflation is concerned, they are more "myopic" than households and fail to spend this surplus on investment. The explanation may be that profits do not affect investment through the profitability perceived by firms, but represent only the funds available for investment. This interpretation is confirmed by the estimate of the model with uncertainty, which includes both profits and expected profitability.

• The proportions of financially constrained and demand-constrained firms seem to be fairly constant—suggesting a dependence on structural features rather than on cyclical fluctuations of demand or profits.

• The model with bankruptcy risk yields a better understanding of investment in the 1970s when the bankruptcy probability is calculated on *flows* only, and not on the firm's net value. This suggests that indebtedness has no direct effect on investment other than via interest payments. For if we introduce stock mechanisms, the bankruptcy probability becomes very high in the most recent period, leading to weak investment. To test this idea, we estimated the standard model after introducing the net debt ratio (debt + liquidities/capital stock). This variable proves significant only when profit is introduced as well. In that case, however, the accelerator is not significant. The coefficient obtained shows that an increase of 1 unit in debt reduces the annual investment by 0.08 units. The "economic" (inflation-adjusted) debt ratio we used, in which capital is taken at replacement value, decreases from 1979 to 1981, which surprisingly explains the "strength" of investment in the early 1980s. However, the shrinking of the economic debt ratio would contradict the previously described insensitivity of investment to inflationnary gains. We therefore substituted book-value capital for replacement-value capital in the ratio.[10] This new "book-value" ratio is not significant: as figure 7 shows, it rises after 1982 while investment does not decrease.

Notes

1. Economists have debated whether the impact of profits is additive (increasing investment even if the output grows slowly) or multiplicative (hastening the adjustment to the optimal capital level—as in Metric 1981 or Coen 1971).

2. Details of tax cuts from 1966 on are given by Avouyi-Dovi and Muet (1987). We are grateful to these authors for supplying us with their tax-incentive coefficients.

3. Our estimation period begins in 1970 in order to allow a comparison with the available estimates that take the same starting point and include financial variables

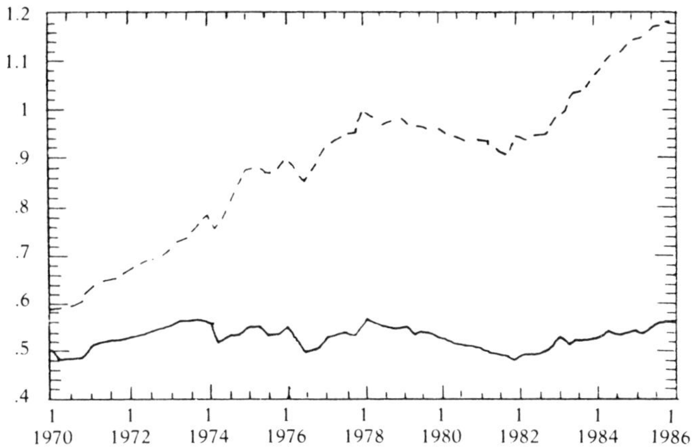

Figure 7.
Debt ratios. (———) "Economic" (inflation-adjusted); (----) book-value.

such as credit; the year 1979 coincides with the second oil crisis and with the end of the sample period used in most of the studies mentioned in the introduction.

4. We accordingly used this value to calculate our capital data.

5. We estimated equation 3 with varying values of α because of the difficulty of estimating this parameter directly.

6. The term "weakness" is appropriate to the absolute level of investment, but not if we measure investment relative to growth (see section 1).

7. On loan contracts of this kind, and models incorporating a bankruptcy risk, see Haugen and Senbet 1978; Van Horne 1986; Diamond 1984; Townsend 1979; Gale and Hellwig 1984; Williamson 1986; Merton 1977; De Angelo and Masulis 1980.

8. In any case, for reasons of accuracy, we have introduced transfer items that appear in the national accounts and are of course omitted from the theoretical model.

9. As before, we estimate the coefficient of the tax variable $1 - k_1 - k_2$ separately.

10. The book-value capital is calculated by cumulating investment, deducting tax depreciation allowances, and incorporating accelerated depreciation.

References

Abel, A. 1983. "Optimal Investment under Uncertainty." *American Economic Review* 73: 228–233.

Abel, A. and Blanchard, O. 1986. "The Present Value of Profits and the Cyclical Movements of Investment." *Econometrica* 54: 249–273.

Artus, P. 1985. "Inventory Investment, Investment and Employment with Uncertain Demand." *Empirical Economics* 10: 177–200.

Artus, P., and Migus, B. 1986. "Dynamique de l'investissement et de l'emploi avec coût d'ajustement sur le capital et le travail." *Annales d'Economie et de Statistique* 2: 75–99.

Artus, P., and Muet, P. A. 1984a. "Investment, Output and Labor Constraints, and Financial Constraints: The Estimation of a Model with Several Regimes." *Recherches Economiques de Louvain* 50(1–2): 33–52.

Artus, P., and Muet, P. A. 1984b. "Un panorama des développements récents de l'économétrie de l'investissement," *Revue Economique*, Septembre, 791–830.

Artus, P., and Muet, P. A. 1986. *Investissement et emploi*. Paris: Economica.

Artus, P., and Peyroux, C. 1981. "Fonctions de production avec facteur énergie, estimations pour les grands pays de l'OCDE." *Annales de l'INSEE* 44.

Avouyi-Dovi, S., and Muet, P. A. 1987. "L'effet des incitations fiscales sur l'investissement." *Observations et Diagnostics Economiques*, January: 149–174.

Baron, D. 1976. "Default Risk and the Modigliani-Miller Theorem: A Synthesis." *American Economic Review*, March: 204–212.

Bernard, A. 1977. "Le coût d'usage du capital productif: une ou plusieurs mesures." *Annales de l'INSEE* 28, October–December: 3–37.

Blanchard, O., and Sachs, J. 1982. "Anticipations, Recessions and Policy: An Intertemporal Disequilibrium Model." *Annales de l'INSEE* 47–48: 117–144.

Brennan, M., and Schwartz, E. 1978. "Corporate Income Taxes, Valuation and the Problem of Optimal Capital Structure." *Journal of Business* 51: 103–114.

Coen, R. 1971. "The Effect of Cash Flow on the Speed of Adjustment." In G. Fromm, ed., *Tax Incentives and Capital Spending*, Brookings Institution.

D'Autume, A., and Michel, P. 1984. "Evaluation du capital en présence de contraintes anticipées sur les achats de biens d'équipement." *Annales de l'INSEE* 54: 101–114.

De Angelo, H., and Masulis, R. 1980. "Leverage and Dividend Irrelevancy under Corporate and Personal Taxation." *Journal of Finance*, May: 453–466.

Diamond, D. 1984. "Financial Intermediation and Delegated Monitoring." *Review of Economic Studies* 51: 1071–1094.

Edwards, J., and Keen, M. 1985. "Taxes, Investment and Q." *Review of Economic Studies* 52: 665–679.

Gale, D., and Hellwig, M. 1984. Incentive Compatible Debt Contracts: The One-Period Problem. Working Paper, London School of Economics.

Gourieroux, C., Laffont, J. J., and Monfort, A. 1984. "Econométrie des modèles d'équilibre avec rationnement: une mise à jour." *Annales de l'INSEE,* July–December: 5–38.

Gubian, A., Guillaumat-Tailliet, F., and LeCacheux, 1986. "Fiscalité des Entreprises et Décisions d'Investissement." *Observations et Diagnostics Economiques,* July: 181–216.

Haugen, R., and Senbet, L. 1978. "The Insignificance of Bankruptcy Costs to the Theory of Optimal Capital Structure." *Journal of Finance,* May: 383–391.

Hayashi, F. 1982. "Tobin's Average q and Marginal q: A Neoclassical Interpretation." *Econometrica* 50: 213–224.

Jaffee, D., and Russel, T. 1976. "Imperfect Information and Credit Rationing," *Quarterly Journal of Economics* 651–656.

Lambert , J.-P. 1984. Disequilibrium Macromodels Based on Business Survey Data. Thèse, Université de Louvain.

Lambert, J.-P., Lubrano, M., and Sneesens, H. R. 1984. "Emploi et chômage en France de 1955 à 1982: un modèle macroéconomique annuel avec rationnement." *Annales de l'INSEE,* July–December: 39–76.

Levy-Garboua, V., and Maarek, G. 1985. *La dette, le boom, la crise.* Paris: Economica.

Malinvaud, E. 1983. Profitability and Investment Facing Uncertain Demand. *Document de Travail,* INSEE, No. 8303.

Malinvaud, E. 1987. "The Legacy of European Stagflation." *European Economic Review,* February–March: 53–68.

Merton, R. 1977."On the Pricing of Contingent Claims and the M. M. Theorem." *Journal of Financial Economics,* November: 241–248.

Metric 1981. *Une modélisation de l'économie française.* Paris: INSEE.

Modigliani, F., and Miller, M. 1958. "The Cost of Capital, Coorporation Finance and the Theory of Investment." *American Economic Review* 48: 261–297.

Modigliani, F., and Miller, M. 1963. "Corporate Income Taxes and the Cost of Capital: A Correction." *American Economic Review* 53: 433–443.

Shiller, R. 1979. "The Volatility of Long Term Interest Rates and Expectations Models of the Term Structure." *Journal of Political Economy,* December: 1190–1218.

Sterdyniak, H. 1986. "Des conséquences patrimoniales de la désinflation." *Observations et Diagnostics Economiques* 17, October: 167–208.

Stiglitz, J., and Weiss, A. 1981. "Credit Rationing in Markets with Impefect Information." *American Economic Review* 71: 393–410.

Summers, L. 1981. "Taxation and Corporate Investment: A q Theory Approach." *Brookings Papers on Economic Activity* 1: 67–127.

Towsend, R. 1979. "Optimal Contracts and Competitive Markets with Costly State Verification." *Journal of Economic Theory* 21: 265–293.

Turnbull, S. 1979. "Debt Capacity." *Journal of Finance,* September: 931–940.

Van Horne, J. 1976. "Optimal Initiation of Bankruptcy Proceedings by Debt Holders." *Journal of Finance* 31: 897–910.

Warner, J. 1977. "Bankruptcy, Absolute Priority and the Pricing of Risky Debt Claims." *Journal of Financial Economics* 4: 239–276.

Williamson, S. 1986. "Costly Monitoring, Financial Intermediation and Equilibrium Credit Rationing." *Journal of Monetary Economics,* September: 159–179.

19

Inefficiency of Private Credit to Sovereign States

Daniel Cohen

The debt crisis of the developing countries has called into question the enthusiastic approval of the commercial banks' recycling of petrodollars. The factors that had contributed to the abundance of the banks' credit supply are now held responsible for the crisis. Overly short-term debt, inadequately diversified in terms of currencies and interest rates, has caused the sharp rise in the dollar and in interest rates to put a stranglehold on the indebted countries. Elsewhere (Cohen 1990) I have indicated the crucial role played in the present crisis by the scissors movement of international interest rates and indebted countries' growth rates. In this paper, I would like to show that even in the absence of fluctuations originating in the international financial markets, bank lending to sovereign debtors is intrinsically inefficient: its duration is too short and it produces a poor diversification of country risk.

The analytical framework employed here rests on the work of Eaton and Gersovitz (1981) and the studies I have carried out with Jeffrey Sachs (Sachs and Cohen 1985; Cohen and Sachs 1986). It is assumed here as in all these papers that a sovereign state can always repudiate its debt if the cost of the repayments demanded by the banks is "too" high. Here, "too" high means that the repayment cost exceeds the retaliatory measures that banks can apply to recalcitrant debtors. As these costs are not infinite, the risk of default cannot be entirely avoided. Now this risk is naturally a variable that countries factor into their optimal strategy calculations. The banks, in their attempt to control country-risk changes, will respond by granting a loan whose duration will be shown to be too short with respect to a potential optimal indebtedness strategy defined *ex ante*. By shortening the debt term, the banks will try to prevent the country from "over-borrowing" in the long run, but the ensuing risk diversification will be suboptimal. In the last section of the paper, we shall see that the origin of this suboptimality is the impossibility of creating a market for marginal loans to a sovereign state.

(This point is also made in Bulow and Rogoff 1988 and Sachs and Cohen 1985.)

In conclusion to this analysis, we can therefore identify a potential role for the International Monetary Fund (IMF) or the World Bank. By centralizing the loans granted to a country and enabling it to precommit itself to a rescheduling strategy, these institutions can help to provide longer-term credit and to spread debt servicing over time, without loss to the banks and for the benefit of indebted countries.

Each of the three periods of the model described will be linked to a specific phase in the country's decision making. Let us look at these in reverse sequence. During the last phase, the country's only alternatives are payment, default, or securing a partial write-off. During the second phase, the options are broader, since the country can return to the international financial markets or, if difficulties arise, obtain a bank rescheduling from the creditors whose loans fall due. I will show that the latter option is not an additional instrument at all, but rather the equivalent of a partial write-off. Finally, during the initial phase, the country is led to choose the level and duration of its debt. It will be demonstrated that the duration is "too" short. Section 1 presents the model. Sections 2 to 4 each deals with one of the country's three decision-making phases. In Section 5, we shall see that the origin of the market failure is associated with the absence of a market for marginal loans.

1. The Model

1.1. Country Resources and Preferences

Let us consider the economy of a country whose economic horizon is composed of three periods: the present (period 1), the short term (period 2), and the long term (period 3). The economy is controlled by a social planner who seeks to maximize a social utility function:

$$U_1 = \operatorname{Max} E_1 \{u(C_1) + \beta u(C_2) + \beta^2 u(C_3)\}$$

where E_1 is the conditional expectation at date 1 of the term in brackets, u is a strictly quasiconcave differentiable utility function such that $\lim_{x \to 0} u'(x) = +\infty$, β is the social planner's time preference rate, and (C_1, C_2, C_3) stand for the consumption streams of a single good (taken as numeraire) to which the country will have access in periods 1, 2, and 3, respectively. (C_2 and C_3 will be two random variables.)

The country's resources are exogenous (for an analysis of capital accumulation see Cohen and Sachs 1986) and measured by a numeraire endowment (Q_1, Q_2, Q_3). Endowment Q_1 is known, but endowments Q_2 and Q_3 are independent random variables whose distributions are $F_2(x)$ and $F_3(x)$ functions, respectively:

$$P[Q_i < x] \qquad F_i(x), \quad i = 2, 3.$$

We will assume that

$$F_i(x) > 0, \qquad \forall x \in]0, \infty].$$

In other words, we never rule out that endowment Q_2 or Q_3 may arbitrarily become as small as possible.

1.2. Country Decisions

The country has access to an international financial market where a risk-free real interest rate r is offered at each of the periods 1 and 2. The creditors are risk-neutral bankers in pure and perfect competition with one another. During period 1 the country chooses to borrow the amount D_1. The debt will be repaid in periods 2 and 3, in installments R_{12} and R_{13}, respectively. In period 2, the country will determine the resources Q_2 at its disposal and will choose to borrow a new sum D_{23}, which will entail a repayment R_{23} in period 3. (For simplicity's sake, I have excluded the case in which the country would choose to lend in period 2.)

If the country was always in a position to honor its commitments, its consumption stream in periods 1, 2, and 3 would be written

$$C_1 = Q_1 + D_1, \tag{1}$$

$$C_2 = Q_2 - R_{12} + D_{23}, \tag{2}$$

$$C_3 = Q_3 - R_{13} - R_{23}. \tag{3}$$

1.3. Risk of External-Debt Repudiation

Let us nevertheless assume that the country was free to repudiate its debt in period 2 or period 3. When the country defaults, its creditors can retaliate by imposing a penalty λQ_i ($i = 1, 2$; $0 < \lambda < 1$) proportionate to its resources and, if the debt is repudiated in period 2, force the country into financial autarky. Thus, a country that defaults in period 2 is constrained to the consumption program:

$$C_{2,a} = (1 - \lambda)Q_2,$$

$$C_{3,a} = (1 - \lambda)Q_3.$$

A country defaulting in period 3 is constrained to consumption $C_{3,a}$ only in period 3.

We postulate that the retaliation costs $(\lambda Q_2, \lambda Q_3)$ demanded of the country cannot be recovered by the creditors. The costs will consist, for example, of a loss of efficiency induced by a trade embargo—a loss that is not directly recoverable. The creditors will therefore have an incentive to negotiate rescheduling agreements with the debtor country in order to recover these costs in part or in full.

2. Equilibrium in Period 3: Default Risk and Debtor Bargaining Power

During period 3, the country—if it has not repudiated its debt by period 2—must repay R_{13} to period-1 lenders and R_{23} to period-2 lenders. At all events, it will prefer default to full repayment if

$$\lambda Q_3 < R_{13} + R_{23} \equiv R_3.$$

When $\lambda Q_3 = R_3$, the country will have an equal incentive to repay or repudiate its debt. For the bankers, however, this choice is not neutral. In one case they will be repaid, in the other they will lose all amounts due—given the assumption that creditors do not recover the repudiation costs. If the debtor has bargaining power, it can exploit the situation and threaten to default unless its creditors grant it a partial moratorium.

In Cohen 1990 I have calculated the Nash equilibrium of this bargaining problem. In the simplest case—where N identical lenders share the outstanding debt R_3 and where the country, like its creditors, is not risk-averse—the creditors obtain $(N - 1)/N\, R_3$ and the country $1/N\, R_3$. When the number of creditors is infinite—that is, when they consist of a myriad small lenders—the country's bargaining power is diluted. The reasoning behind this conclusion is extremely simple: to avoid becoming its debtor's "hostage," a banker will refuse to lend unless there are enough other creditors willing to make loans to the country. Under certain assumptions, this can produce a "bank panic" in which no creditor will be willing to lend for lack of a sufficient quorum of other lenders.

For simplicity's sake, I shall nevertheless assume here that the country has no bargaining power and that the following hypotheses apply. When $\lambda Q_3 < R_3$, the creditors will offer the country a moratorium $R_3 - \lambda Q_3$ to save the country the cost of defaulting. The country's payment λQ_3 will be distributed among the lenders in due proportion to their claims. When $\lambda Q_3 < R_3$, bankers will accordingly receive

$$R'_{13} = \lambda Q_3 \frac{R_{13}}{R_3} \qquad \text{(period-1 creditors)}$$

and

$$R'_{23} = \lambda Q_3 \frac{R_{23}}{R_3} \qquad \text{(period-2 creditors).}$$

The critical threshold of period 3 is written

$$Q_3^* = \frac{1}{\lambda}(R_{13} + R_{23}).$$

The probability that the country will choose not to honor its initial commitments is written

$$\pi_3^* = F_3(Q_3^*).$$

3. Equilibrium in Period 2: Debt Rescheduling

During period 2, the country determines the value Q_2 of its resources and must repay R_{12} to its period-1 creditors. Several options are open to it: (1) it can borrow D_{23} on the international markets and consume $C_2 = Q_2 - R_{12} + D_{23}$; (2) it can repudiate its debt and consume $C_2 = (1 - \lambda)Q_2$; (3) it can turn to its period-1 creditors and demand a rescheduling of payment R_{12}.

If the country chooses to pay R_{12} and borrow again on the international markets, it will have to solve the following problem:

$$\underset{D_{23}}{\text{Maximize}}\, u(Q_2 - R_{12} + D_{23})$$

$$+ \beta \left\{ \int_{Q_3^*}^{\infty} u(Q_3 - \lambda Q_3^*) dF_3(Q_3) + \beta \int_0^{Q_3^*} u[Q_3(1 - \lambda)] dF_3(Q_3) \right\} \qquad (4)$$

where Q_3^* is the threshold $(1/\lambda)(R_{13} + R_{23})$ defined in the preceding section.

R_{23} is determined in such a manner that

$$-D_{23} + \frac{1}{1 + r} E_2 P_{23} = 0 \qquad (5)$$

where

$$P_{23} = R_{23} \quad \text{if } \lambda Q_3 \geqslant (R_{13} + R_{23}) \equiv Q_3^*$$

$$P_{23} = \frac{R_{23}}{R_{13} + R_{23}} \lambda Q_3 \quad \text{if } Q_3 < Q_3^*. \tag{6}$$

Equations 5 and 6 can also be written as

$$(1 + r)D_{23} = [1 - F_3(Q_3^*)]R_{23} + \frac{R_{23}}{R_{13} + R_{23}} \int_0^{Q_3^*} \lambda Q_3 dF_3(Q_3)$$

or

$$D_{23}(1 + r) = (1 - \psi_3^*)R_{23} \tag{7}$$

where

$$\psi_3 = F_3(Q_3^*) - \frac{1}{Q_3^*} \int_0^{Q_3^*} Q_3 dF_3(Q_3).$$

In this form, equation 5 is easy to interpret: credit D_{23} is equal to the present value of the repayment expectation,

$$\frac{1 - \psi_3^*}{1 + r} R_{23},$$

ψ_3^* being interpreted as the "corrected" probability of default in period 3—the "correction" concerns the partial repayment obtained by bankers when $Q_3 < Q_3^*$. The first-order condition of problem 4 then becomes

$$u'(C_2)\left(1 - \pi_2 - R_{13}\frac{d\psi_3}{dQ_3}\right) = \beta(1 + r) \int_{Q_3^*}^{\infty} u'(Q_3 - \lambda Q_3^*)dF_3(Q_3). \tag{8}$$

Let $U_2(Q_2, R_{12}, R_{13})$ be the utility value reached by the country in period 2 if it chooses the program (which I assume to be unique) that solves this equation (which I assume to be sufficient). U_2 is therefore defined by

$$U_2(Q_2, R_{12}, R_{13})$$

$$= \underset{D_{23}}{\text{Max}} \left\{u(Q_2 - R_{12} + D_{23}) + \beta\left[\int_{Q_3^*}^{\infty} u(Q_3 - \lambda Q_3^*)dF_3\right] + \int_0^{Q_3^*} u[(1 - \lambda)Q_3]dF_3(Q_3)\right\}. \tag{9}$$

The country will prefer default to choosing the market solution described by equation 9 if

$$U_{2,a}(Q_2) \equiv u[(1-\lambda)Q_2] + \beta \int_0^{\infty} u[(1-\lambda)Q_3]dF_3(Q_3)$$
$$\geqslant U_2(Q_2, R_{12}, R_{13}). \tag{10}$$

For bankers, unilateral default is a net loss, and they will invariably prefer rescheduling debt R_{12} to allowing the country to default.

The rescheduling of debt R_{12} can in turn take three different forms:

1. The banks offer a partial moratorium $R_{12} - R'_{12}$ and request immediate payment of R'_{12}. Once the moratorium is granted, the country is free to borrow on the international financial markets and to raise a loan D_{23} that will be a solution to equation 9 when R'_{12} is substituted for R_{12}.
2. The banks reschedule the debt by requesting repayments R'_{12} today and R''_{12} tomorrow. Once the rescheduling is agreed to, the country is allowed to borrow on the international markets.
3. As in (2), the bankers reschedule the debt, but the country is *not* free to borrow on the international markets after the agreement has been reached.

In Appendix 1, I demonstrate the following proposition:

Proposition 1. The three rescheduling options are equivalent for the banker. In (2), the bankers will necessarily choose $R''_{12} = 0$.

In other words, the bankers will all receive the same average repayment under each of the three agreements. However, Proposition 1 also indicates that the optimal rescheduling of (2) is the moratorium of (1). *It is therefore suboptimal for a banker to attempt to collect a debt* R'_{13} *in period 3 if the country is free to turn to the international financial markets after the agreement has been reached.* The reasoning behind this statement is extremely simple. Once the agreement has been reached, the country will seek to increase the risk of defaulting in period 3 with respect to the optimal risk that would be calculated by the banker under the terms of a type-(3) agreement. This is because, by increasing the risk, the country indirectly transfers a share of the R''_{12} debt to its new bankers in exchange for a higher credit today. To avoid this risk increase after the rescheduling agreement is concluded, the banks will want to deny the country access to the international financial markets. However, proposition 1 demonstrates that this degree of freedom is illusory. Rescheduling is in fact tantamount to a partial moratorium, followed by the country's free access to international markets. At all events, any agreement between the debtor and creditors—to the extent of our assumption that the creditors can act first and make a firm offer—will be such that the expected utility reached by the country during period 2 will be identical to the utility it would obtain by defaulting. Agreement (1), for example, will therefore be reached by demanding a repayment of R'_{12} such that

$$U_2(Q_2, R'_{12}, R_{13}) = U_{2,a}(Q_2)$$

(U_2 and $U_{2,a}$ are defined in equations 9 and 10).

Let $J_2(Q_2, R_{12}, R_{13})$ be the utility resulting for the country in period 2 after rescheduling (if required), that is,

$$J_2(Q_2, R_{12}, R_{13}) = \text{Sup}\{U_2(Q_2, R_{12}, R_{13}), U_{2,a}(Q_2)\}. \tag{11}$$

For simplicity's sake, we shall assume that there always exists a threshold $Q_2^*(R_{12}, R_{13})$ such that

$$U_2(Q_2, R'_{12}, R_{13}) \geqslant U_{2,a}(Q_2) \Leftrightarrow Q_2 \geqslant Q_2^*(R_{12}, R_{13}).$$

4. Optimal Loan Maturity and Credit-Market Inefficiency

Let us now consider period 1. The decision to borrow a certain amount D_1 can itself be subdivided into two phases. The first consists in seeking the optimal repayment maturity for any amount D_1 borrowed. The second phase is to choose the optimal level D_1 itself. The first phase can be described as the solution of the program

$$J_1(D_1) = \max \int_0^\infty J_2(Q_2, R_{12}, R_{13}) dF_2(Q_2) \tag{12}$$

subject to the constraint

$$D_1 = E_1 \left\{ \frac{P_{12}}{1 + r} + \frac{P_{13}}{(1 + r)^2} \right\}$$

where P_{12} and P_{13} are the actual repayments corresponding to commitments R_{12} and R_{13}, calculated in the manner set out in Section 3; $J_2(Q_2, R_{12}, R_{13})$ is the utility function, defined in Section 3, available to the country when the level of its endowments during the period is Q_2.

The second phase of the country's decision making in period 1 is quite simply

$$\underset{D_1}{\text{Maximize}}\ u(Q_1 + D_1) + \beta J_1(D_1),$$

and we assume in advance the existence of a single solution $D_1^* > 0$ that is the solution to

$$u'(Q_1 + D_1^*) = -\beta J_1'(D_1^*). \tag{13}$$

We propose to demonstrate that the equilibrium thus obtained, which we define as the "market equilibrium," is inefficient.

Proposition 2. The market equilibrium defined above is inefficient.

The market equilibrium is defined by recurrence. In each period, the country's decision is always the best possible one given the constraints imposed by the credit supply. It is also assumed that in subsequent periods the country will also make the best decision subject to the same constraints. We shall demonstrate that the equilibrium thus obtained could be improved with respect to period 1 if the country could commit itself to a borrowing strategy $D_{23}^*(Q_2)$ in period 2 that did not correspond to the market strategy defined in Section 3. The strategy $D_{23}^*(Q_2)$ calculated here will nevertheless leave the country free to choose default. It is therefore not a strategy that would force the country *not* to default assuming it wished to do so. On the contrary, it is a strategy that commits the country to *reducing* its desired borrowing in period 2. By shrinking that amount, the optimal strategy will allow a reduction in debt D_1 risk, and this trade-off will prove to be optimal with respect to period 1.

Insofar as the market strategy is dominated by a strategy that complies with the same constraints—notably the freedom to default—proposition 2 illustrates the "time inconsistency" of economic-policy choices: the optimal *ex ante* policy is not optimal *ex post*. The potential existence of this property has been brought to light by Kydland and Prescott (1977) and Calvo (1978). I have also studied it in a recent joint publication (Cohen and Michel 1988). For an application of this issue to public-debt management, see also Persson and Svensson (1986).

Proposition 2 is demonstrated in Appendix 2. We show that the country can increase its utility by committing itself to reducing its debt $D_{23}(Q_2)$ by a properly chosen amount $\varepsilon(Q_2)$ that will allow it to extend the term of its indebtedness D_1 by increasing R_{13} and reducing R_{12}. In other words, we see that the market equilibrium can be dominated by extending the maturity of debt D_1 and reducing the volume of debt D_{23}. The reasoning that explains this property is identical to the one applied to proposition 1. All outstanding debt is an incentive for the country to increase its subsequent risk. This entails a market equilibrium in which the risk premium on long-term debt is increased in a way that could be avoided ex ante.

5. The Market for Marginal Loans

5.1 Average and Marginal Prices of the Debt

Let us now show that the inefficiency of the credit market is intrinsically a by-product of the public good dimension of the debt. To see this, let us first consider the market value of the debt when the country has reached period 2, owes R_{13} to the senior lenders and R_{23} to the junior lenders.

Call $R = R_{13} + R_{23}$ the overall face value of the country's outstanding commitment. As the end of time 2, the market value of R can be aggregated into

$$V = \frac{1}{1+r}\int_0^{Q^*} \lambda Q_3 \lambda F_3(Q_3) + \frac{1}{1+r}\int_{Q^*}^{\infty} R\, dF(Q_3),$$

in which $Q^* = (1/\lambda)R$.

If all lenders were merging into a single one, the value—to this aggregate lender—of one more dollar due in period 3 would simply be measured as

$$q_m = \frac{\partial V}{\partial R} = \frac{1}{1+r}\int_0^{Q^*} F_3(Q_3) = \frac{1}{1+r}[1 - F_3(R/\lambda)]. \tag{14}$$

This marginal price, however, is not the value of one more dollar accruing to an *individual* lender. It is therefore not the price that is observed on a secondary market. This observed price is the average price, to the extent that all lenders are treated symmetrically at the time when the debt falls due.

This average price is simply

$$q = \frac{V}{R} = \frac{1}{1+r}\left[\int_0^{Q^*} \lambda \frac{Q_3}{R} dF_3(Q_3) + \int_0^{Q^*} dF_3(Q_3)\right]. \tag{15}$$

Taking the value of the marginal price q_m such as it is defined in equation 14, one finds

$$q = q_m + \frac{1}{1+r}\int_0^{Q^*} \frac{\lambda Q_3}{R} dF_3(Q_3).$$

The average price is systematically above the marginal price of the debt.

Why is this discrepancy a source of market inefficiency? In order to answer this question let us see how this discrepancy would be dealt with in the case of corporate debt.

5.2 Average and Marginal Corporate Debt

Let us assume that the nation is a firm that is expected to generate profits $\tilde{\pi} \equiv \lambda \tilde{Q}_3$. If the firm owes R, then the market value of this claim is exactly identical to the one obtained in equation 14. As long as profits are above R, lenders are paid (and the shareholders get the difference). When profits go below R, bondholders take over the company and distribute among themselves however profit π is generated. The basic difference with the debt to a nation, however, is that bondholders may negotiate *ex ante* property rights on the firms' *collateralized* capital in case it goes bankrupt.

It is therefore possible for the senior lenders to design a contract by which they are granted priority on the firms' profits in case it is insolvent. Whatever money the firm borrows at a later time, the new lenders know that they will be paid second. Contrary to what happens in the case of sovereign debt, junior lenders are therefore willing to offer only the marginal price, q_m, for one dollar that the firm may want to promise paying in the future. Because the market for a marginal dollar correctly prices its value, it is easy to see why, in the case of a corporate debt, the lending is efficient.

In the case of sovereign debt, in contrast junior lenders are willing to offer the average value—and not the marginal value—for an additional dollar due by the country. This is a good deal to the country, and this is what explains why the country was shown to "overborrow" in the second period.

Conclusion

We have shown that the equilibrium of the international bank-loan market can be dominated if the debtor is given the option of precommitting itself to the way in which its risk will evolve. This framework allows us to spell out the potential roles of the IMF and the World Bank. By regulating the country's access to international financial markets and laying down rules for country-risk changes, these institutions enable lending periods to be extended and the country's utility to be improved. By contrast, we have also shown that rescheduling agreements under the IMF or World Bank's aegis allowing an already insolvent nation to raise new loans are equivalent to—and conceal—a partial debt moratorium.

Appendix 1: Demonstration of Proposition 1

The partial moratorium consists of claiming R_{12} from the debtor and allowing it to borrow on the international financial markets. The maximum volume R'_{12} obtainable by the bankers is simply defined by

$$U_2(Q_2, R'_{12}, R_{13}) = U_{2,a}(Q_2)$$

(U_2 is defined in equation 9).

This problem's solution can therefore be characterized as follows:

$$u'[Q_2 - R'_{12} + D_{23}] = \beta(1 + r) \int_{Q_3^*}^{\infty} u'(Q_3 - Q_3^*) dF_3(Q_3), \quad \text{(A1)}$$

where

$$D_{23} = \frac{1}{1 + r}[1 - \psi_3]R_{13},$$

$$Q_{23}^* = \frac{1}{\lambda}(R_{13} + R_{23}),$$

$$u[D_2 - R'_{12} + D_{23}] + \beta \int_0^{\infty} u(C_3) dF_3(Q_3) = U_a(Q_2).$$

Let us now consider problem 2. The creditors want to maximize their average earnings:

$$\pi(R'_{12}, R'_{13}) = R_{12}^{(2)} + \frac{1}{1 + r}(1 - \psi_3^*)R_{13}^{(2)} \quad \text{(A2)}$$

subject to the constraint

$$u[Q_2 - R_{12}^{(2)}] + \beta\left[\int_{Q_3^*}^{\infty} u[Q_3 - \lambda Q_3^*] dF_3(Q_3) + \int_0^{Q_3^*} u[1 - \lambda)Q_3] dF_3(Q_3)\right] = U_a(Q_2) \quad \text{(A3)}$$

where

$$Q_3^* = \frac{1}{\lambda}[R_{13} + R_{13}^{(2)}].$$

Let μ be the Lagrangian multiplier corresponding to the constraint A3. The first-order conditions are

$$\mu u'(Q_2 - R_{12}^{(2)}) = 1 \tag{A4a}$$

and

$$1 - \psi_3^* - R_{13}^{(2)} \frac{\partial \psi_3^*}{\partial R_{13}} = 1 - \pi_3^*$$

$$= \beta\mu(1 + r) \int_{Q_3^*}^{\infty} u'(Q_3 - \lambda Q_3^*) dF_3(Q_3). \tag{A4b}$$

Eliminating μ, we get

$$\left(1 - \pi_3 + \frac{R_{13}}{\lambda Q_3^*} \int_0^{Q_3^*} Q_3 \, dF_3(Q_3)\right) u'(Q_2 - R_{12}^{(2)})$$

$$= \beta(1 + r) \int_{Q_3^*}^{\infty} u'(Q_3 - \lambda Q_3^*) dF_3(Q_3), \tag{A5}$$

$$\lambda Q_3^* = R_{13}' + R_{13}.$$

It is clear that

$$R_{12}^{(2)} = R_{12}' - D_{23}$$

and

$$R_{13}^{(2)} = R_{23}$$

where D_{23} and R_{23} are the new loans corresponding to problem 1. As, by assumption, these are loans entailing zero average profit, the two following procedures lead to an identical result for the bankers—and also for the country, since in either case it reaches its autarkic utility level: (1) partial moratorium and immediate repayment of R_{12}', and (2) optimal rescheduling.

Let us now examine problem 3. The creditors, after agreeing to reschedule, allow the country to contract new loans. What is the gain obtainable by the initial bankers? To the extent that the new bankers are, like the earlier ones, risk-neutral agents operating under the assumption of zero profit, there is no advantage in enlisting new bankers in the optimal rescheduling procedure 2. The question this raises is therefore: are the options equivalent or is there a strict worsening? Because procedures 1 and 2 are equivalent, we know that the initial banker, while unable to prevent the debtor from turning to new bankers, can always obtain the same result by granting a partial moratorium. However, I shall now show that the only type-3 rescheduling that maximizes the bankers' debt collection is the type-1 partial moratorium. If the bankers cannot prevent the country from seeking new lenders, then they must grant it a partial moratorium. To demonstrate this, let us consider the problem that the country will solve when the initial creditors have claimed $R_{12}^{(3)}$, $R_{13}^{(3)}$ from it. The country must contract a new loan $D_{23}^{(3)}$. The first-order conditions will be, as before,

$$\left(1 - \pi_3^* + \frac{R_{13} + R'_{13}}{\lambda Q_{23}} \int_0^{Q_3^*} Q_3 dF_3(Q_3)\right) u'(C_2)$$

$$= \beta(1 + r) \int_{Q_3^*}^{\infty} u'(C_3) dF_3(Q_3),$$

$$Q_3^* = \frac{1}{\lambda}[R_{23}^{(3)} + R_{13} + R'_{13}], \tag{A6}$$

$$C_2 = Q_2 - R'_{12} + D_{23}^{(3)},$$

$$D_{23}^{(3)} = \frac{1}{1 + r}(1 - \pi_3^*) R_{23}^{(3)} + \frac{R_{23}^{(3)}}{Q_3^*} \int_0^{Q_3^*} Q_3 dF_3(Q_3).$$

Let us compare the two systems A5 and A6. We see that systems 2 and 3 coincide if and only if $R'_{13} = 0$. In this case, the country achieves the same allocation (C_2, C_3) in both systems. If, instead, $R'_{13} > 0$, we see that the country will tend to increase its marginal utility in period 3 with respect to its marginal utility in period 2. In other words, the country will be inclined to "overborrow" if it is allowed access to the international financial markets *after* the rescheduling agreement. We shall return to this point in Appendix 2. At all events, we can therefore see that systems 1 and 3 will be equivalent to each other—and therefore to system 2—if and only if the bankers abandon all further claims. Moreover, this moratorium system will therefore be equivalent to a debt rescheduling under which the country is denied access to the international markets after the rescheduling is negotiated. This demonstrates our proposition.

Appendix 2: Demonstration of Proposition 2

With respect to the initial market equilibrium, let us increase long-term debt by the amount ε, and reduce the demand for short-term credit in period 2 in such a manner as to leave the risk π_3^* unchanged. Let us also change the volume of short-term debt repayment R_{12} by the amount $(1/(1+r))E((1-E\psi_3^*))\varepsilon$. We will demonstrate that these changes constitute a more than adequate guarantee of repayment of debt D_1 and that they strictly improve the country's position. In period 3, the country's position is by definition unchanged, since we have kept the probability π_3^* constant. The country's consumption accordingly remains

$$C_3 = (\text{Max}\, Q_3 - \lambda Q_3^*, (1-\lambda)Q_3); \qquad \pi_3^* = F_3(Q_3^*).$$

In period 2, the country's consumption is subjected to two modifying influences. First, the volume of indebtedness D_{23} is restricted by

$$\Delta D_{23} = -\frac{1}{1+r}\varepsilon(1-\psi_3).$$

But, at the same time, the repayment R_{12} is reduced by

$$\Delta R_{12} = -\frac{1}{1+r}\varepsilon\, E(1-\psi_3).$$

Hence the new consumption stream in period 2 is written

$$C'_{12} = C_2 + \frac{1}{1+r}\varepsilon[E\psi_3 - \psi_3].$$

We have therefore changed consumption C_2 by a zero-average term that is, however, countercyclical to the original value. As we have assumed that the country is not risk-neutral, the outcome is an improvement in its utility—provided ε is sufficiently small. Also, when $Q_2 = Q_2^*$, the country's utility is strictly greater than the initial level. The country will no longer choose to default on the initial value, but on a lower one. In other words, debt D_1 will be more than repaid by the change

$$\Delta R_{13} = \varepsilon,$$

$$\Delta R_{23} = -\varepsilon\frac{1}{1+r}E(1-\psi_3).$$

In short, the new program is feasible and strictly dominates the one obtained through market equilibrium. This proves our proposition.

Acknowledgments

The author wishes to thank Jeffrey Sachs for the countless discussions to which this paper bears witness.

References

Bulow, J., and Rogoff, K. 1988. "The Buy-Back Boondoggle." *Brookings Papers on Economic Activity.*

Calvo, G. 1978. "On the Time Consistency of Optimal Policy in a Monetary Economy." *Econometrica* 6: 1411–1428.

Cohen, D. 1990. *Private Lending to Sovereign States: A Theoretical Autopsy.* MIT Press.

Cohen, D., and Michel, P. 1988. "How Should Control Theory Be Used to Calculate a Time-Consistent Government Policy?" *Review of Economic Studies* 55: 263–274.

Cohen, D., and Sachs, J. 1986. "Growth and External Debt under Risk of Debt Repudiation." *European Economic Review,* June: 529–560.

Eaton, J., and Gersovitz, M. 1981. "Debt with Potential Repudiation: Theoretical and Empirical Analysis." *Review of Economic Studies* 48, March: 289–309.

Kydland, F., and Prescott, E. 1977. "Rules Rather Than Discretion: The Inconsistency of Optimal Plans." *Journal of Political Economy* 3: 473–493.

Persson, T., and Svensson, L. 1986. "Time Consistent Fiscal Policy and Government Cash Flows." *Journal of Monetary Economics.*

Sachs, J., and Cohen, D. 1985. "LDC Borrowing with Default Risk." *Kredit und Kapital* 8.

20 The Long Run of Macroeconometric Models

Michel Deleau, Cuong Le Van, and Pierre Malgrange

In spite of their weaknesses, macroeconometric models constitute a useful device, without any dominant alternative, for shedding light on the preparation of quantitative economic policy measures (see the introductions of Malinvaud 1980 and 1981). These models aim at providing a simplified numerical representation of the global mechanisms at work in an economy. Inspired by theoretical macroeconomic schemes, they should permit an appreciation of the impact of selected policies. With respect to this ambition, there has been a shift of focus from the short run to the long run both because of the disappointing results of some short-sighted Keynesian policies, and of a better perception of the interactions between the short run and the long run, especially through expectations. There is then a clear need for a careful examination of the picture that macroeconometric models can or cannot give of the long run.

Deriving long-run mechanisms associated with dynamical relationships is not a new quest. Most of the time, however, it has concerned single equations (computation of the long-run propensity to consume, of the long-run demand for money, etc.) and seldom an entire macromodel, with the exception of a small number of studies (see Bergstrom and Wymer 1976; Gandolfo 1981; Currie 1982; Wallis and Whitley 1987). Our contribution aims at giving a synthesis on this question of the long-run properties of standard macroeconometric models. We should first define what will be meant below by "long run," as compared to the usual definitions to be found in macrotheory literature.

In general, the concept of long run does not necessarily reflect the idea of a very distant horizon. It addresses the asymptotic behavior of given economic adjustment mechanisms, when the exogenous forces bearing on the system exhibit some kind of stationarity. In macroeconomic textbooks many embedded "long runs" are indeed considered, according to the purpose retained (see, e.g., Dornbusch and Fischer 1977). Thus, in the IS-LM scheme, it is often assumed that the equilibrium—the long run—on the money market is reached before adjustments on the market for goods take place. Afterward, prices, fixed in the "short run," start moving toward a "long run" perfect flexibility. Lastly, the impact of capital accumulation on productivity becomes significant, paving the way for growth (see the introduction of Malinvaud 1980). This hierarchy between various dynamic adjustments, which gives rise to as many "long run" concepts, is used in macroeconomic theory to split complex phenomena into more tractable dynamic subsystems. In the case of macroeconometric models and, by analogy, it could seem interesting as well to distinguish a "short" long run with prices and capital fixed, a "medium" long run with flexible prices, and a "long" long run involving capital accumulation. Unfortunately, this appealing time hierarchy is not verified for macroeconometric models: all variables move with commensurable speeds (see Le Van and Malgrange 1988). For instance, they exhibit in the short run some price flexibility, whereas quantities are somehow rigid (consumption and investment lags, productivity cycle etc.). It follows that, for macroeconometric models, the only workable concept of long run is the unique "long long run," corresponding to an *equilibrium of all adjustment mechanisms.*

A word now about what is meant by equilibrium. Since the seminal contributions of Harrod and Hicks, it is well known that the best concept of equilibrium adapted to capital accumulation and technical progress is the concept of a growth path at constant rate or *steady-state growth path*—called in the following *SSGP*. Indeed, only such trajectories preserve the invariance of the structure. More especially, they keep stock-flow ratios constant. This imposed definition implies that the economic properties of the long-run equilibrium cannot be set *a priori* but must result from the analysis of the system.

Our study is divided into four sections. The first gives the formal setting of the problem. It amounts to a static simultaneous equations system which sets the initial conditions for an SSGP. In the second section, the SSGP is confronted with the actual working of the original dynamic model, in particular on the historical period. It is shown that SSGPs cannot, in general, be identified with some sample period mean, even if this property is true for the exogenous variables. The third section deals with the economic interpretation of the long-run system. The common assertion "the short run is Keynesian, the long run is Walrasian" is shown to be false for usual macroeconometric models. Indeed, their long run is closer to some kind of monopolistic competition equilibrium. The fourth section is devoted to a short illustration of the methodology for a simplified version of the French model DMS.

1. Methodology

1.1. Formalization

Let us consider a macroeconometric model written as follows:

$$y(t) = f(y(t), y(t-1), x(t); t), \tag{1}$$

with $y(t)\,[x(t)]$, vector $nx1$ $[mx1]$ of the endogenous [exogenous] variables, and t the index of discrete time.

The search for a steady-state growth path (SSGP) amounts to exhibiting particular solutions of equation 1 of the type

$$\begin{aligned} x_i^*(t) &= x_i^*(0)a_j^t \qquad i = 1, \ldots, m \\ y_j^*(t) &= y_j^*(0)b_j^* \qquad j = 1, \ldots, n. \end{aligned} \tag{2}$$

In other words, we look for a set of n initial conditions $y^*(0)$ and n growth rates $(b_1, \ldots, b_n)$ for the endogenous variables, knowing the corresponding exogenous elements $x^*(0)$ and $(a_1, \ldots, a_m)$, so that equation 2 verifies system 1 at each time period.

For a solution of equation 1 of type 2 to exist it is necessary that each equation of this system fulfills some homogeneity conditions. They are imposed by an elementary mathematical property of exponentials: except for pathological cases, a sum of terms evolving through time at constant rates follows an exponential pattern only if all rates are identical. An example is provided by the usual consumption function:

$$C(t) = \beta_1 R(t) + \beta_2 \pi(t) + \beta_3, \tag{3}$$

with real disposable income $R(t)$ and inflation rate $\pi(t)$. A solution of $C(t)$ at a nonzero rate b exists, only if $\beta_2 = \beta_3 = 0$, since in the long run π must be constant. Indeed specification 3 implicitly assumes that the elasticity of consumption with respect to inflation, $\beta_2(\pi(t)/C(t))$, decreases when living standards increase. The same reasoning applies to the constant term β_3, supposed to represent all unexplained factors.

It is then necessary to substitute for the original equation another one as similar as possible which allows for an SSGP. One can, for instance, substitute for formula 3 the consumption function 3′ with time varying coefficients. It coincides with 3 at $t = 0$.

$$C(t) = \beta_1 R(t) = \beta_2 (1 + b)^t \pi(t) + \beta_3 (1 + b)^t. \tag{3′}$$

Our experience of such homogenization corrections shows that distortions with respect to the original form are almost negligible for short-medium-run simulations.

1.2. Determination of Growth Rates

It turns out that the structure of the usual macroeconometric models is such that the long-run growth rates $(b_1, \ldots, b_n)$ for the n endogenous variables can be determined independently from the initial conditions (the reverse being not true; see below). Moreover the m rates (a_i) of the exogenous variables cannot be freely chosen. Actually, all the rates (a_i) and (b_j) derive in a straightforward way from three basic exogenous growth rates:

n: exogenous growth rate of population,

γ: exogenous growth rate of technical progress
(necessarily Harrod neutral),

m: exogenous growth rate of money supply,

or

ρ_e: exogenous growth rate of foreign prices.

The following properties are true, except for very particular specifications seldom encountered:

i. There is a unique rate of growth for all quantities equal to

$$1 + g = (1 + n)(1 + \gamma).$$

For one-sector models, this uniqueness results from supply-demand equilibrium, except for very special cases (the above-mentioned property of sums of exponentials). The same applies to multisectoral models where fixed ratios between quantities of goods are involved, for production (input-output matrix) and/or for consumption (e.g., budget shares). Furthermore, every quantity for every sector must grow at this unique rate. It follows that public expenditures cannot increase at a rate different from g, to preserve the possibility of existence of an SSGP.

ii. The growth rate of prices must also be unique to ensure exponential growth of nominal aggregates. This rate r is determined, either by foreign inflation in an open economy with fixed exchange rates, or by the growth of money supply in the case of flexible exchange rates.

Exceptions to these general rules imply very peculiar specifications, such as an open economy with flexible exchange rates where no nominal aggregate is exogenously fixed, or a smooth homogeneous multisector economy (e.g., of the Cobb-Douglas type) where distortions between quantities can be exactly compensated by opposite distortions between prices.

1.3. Determination of Initial Conditions

The growth rates, including those of the exogenous variables, being determined from the three basic rates (n, γ, ρ), the computation of the initial conditions $y(0)$, knowing $x(0)$, is in principle straightforward. Rewriting the equations of model 1 at time $t = 0$, and substituting the lagged variables by their expression 2, yields

$$y^*(0) = f(y^*(0), (y_j^*(0)/b_j), x^*(0), 0) \tag{4}$$

or, omitting the time index,

$$y^* = \phi(y^*, x^*, n, \gamma, \rho). \tag{5}$$

The system 5, or "long-run system" associated with model 1, consists in a set of simultaneous equations, whose every solution y^*, given the exogenous vector x^*, defines a set of initial conditions for an SSGP.

One can notice that long-run (exogenous) growth rates intervene in this long-run system. The static multipliers associated with 5 correspond to the asymptotic effect of a sustained multiplicative shock on the exogenous variables, which could be obtained through long-run simulations of the initial model 1, provided it is dynamically stable. Let us make a few remarks about this long-run system 5:

i. An equation of model 1 between growth rates yields a long-run relationship between long run growth rates only, without any implication for initial levels.

ii. In a relation involving both rates and levels, only the last ones subsist in the long-run system. For instance, an equation of the following type

$$\mathring{y} = f(z), \qquad z \in \mathbb{R}$$

with " ° " meaning growth rate, implies an autonomous determination of Z^*:

$$z^* = f^{-1}(\mathring{y}^*) = g(n, \gamma, \rho).$$

A typical case is the Phillips curve. It links the growth of wages and prices with the unemployment rate, and thus leads to a long-run determination of the unemployment rate independently from the rest of the system.

iii. In a dynamic progressive adjustment of a variable y to its target Y, $y = \phi(Y)$, a stationary target is generally used for the long-run system—$\phi(1) = 1$. For the long-run system, this leads to

$$y^* = \phi(1/b)Y^* \neq Y^*.$$

This discrepancy between actual and target long-run values is a well-known phenomenon (see for instance Friedman 1957, p. 144). It has been intensively studied in recent years under the headings of error correction mechanisms and cointegration (see, e.g., Davidson et al. 1978 or Hendry 1986). Even if the long-run system 5 admits a mathematical solution y^*, the associated SSGP is not necessarily economically meaningful, unless this phenomenon has been taken care of at the very specification stage of 1.

2. Long-Run System and Historical Simulation

Being static, system 5 is much easier to handle than the original dynamic system 1. In particular, eliminating variables and equations of secondary importance is straightforward because of the absence of lags. One important characteristic of this system is the possible presence of implicit relations when endogenous variables appear in the original model in terms of growth rates (e.g., wages in the Phillips relation). The structure of the interdependencies can thus be substantially different from the structure associated with the dynamic model 1. It can lead to total inefficiency of a Gauss-Seidel type resolution algorithm devised for this original model.

It is interesting to compare the solution of 5 for given values of the exogenous variables with historical data. One can be tempted, in particular, to try to relate the SSGPs with some mean of the sample trajectory. For convenience we deal in this section with the case of a unique linear equation, though generalizing would add no serious difficulty. For this case, the equations corresponding to 1 and 5 would be written

$$y(t) = \beta y(t-1) + \gamma x(t), \tag{6}$$

$$y^*(t) = \beta y^*(t-1) + \gamma x^*(t) = \beta/a y^*(t) + \gamma x^*(t), \tag{7}$$

a being the common long-run growth rate. If model 6 has been estimated by OLS on the sample period $(0, T)$, the following property holds:

$$\overline{y} = \beta\overline{y} - 1 + \gamma\overline{x}, \tag{8}$$

$\overline{y}$ and $\overline{x}$ being the means of $y(t)$ and $x(t)$ on the period $(1, T)$, and $\overline{y} - 1$ the mean of $y(t)$ on the period $(0, T - 1)$.

Combining equations 7 and 8 gives

$$y^* = (1 - \beta/a)^{-1}[(1 - \beta\overline{y} - 1/\overline{y})\overline{y} + \gamma(x^* - \overline{x})]. \tag{9}$$

Hence the following comments:

i. Let us set x^* at its historical mean $\overline{x}$. When $\beta \neq 0$, y^* and $\overline{y}$ coincide only if

$$\overline{y} = a\overline{y} - 1, \tag{10}$$

that is, if the average growth factor $\hat{a}$ of $y(t)$, the OLS estimator of

$$y(t) = \hat{a}y(t - 1) + \varepsilon,$$

is equal to the theoretical growth factor a. In other words, if condition 10 holds true, then the SSGP associated with the exogenous value $x^* = \overline{x}$ coincides with the mean $\overline{y}$ of the sample. A failure of 10 implies a gap between the mean trajectory and the SSGP, which is smaller the lower β is. It can be large for values of β close to a, a common occurrence in practice (β slightly less than 1 and a slightly greater than 1).

ii. Even if $\hat{a} = a$, y^* may diverge from $\overline{y}$ if x^* is not equal to $\overline{x}$ with a greater multiplier effect the closer β is to a. Occurrences of this are shown in the numerical illustration below.

iii. In the case of a relation between a growth rate and a level of the type

$$\mathring{y} = az + b,$$

the mean point condition amounts to checking whether the historical growth of y is consistent with its long-run theoretical value.

It follows from these remarks that trying to derive the SSGP from some averaging operation over the historical period is far from obvious. An empirical and "common sense" approach of this kind of the long run of a given macroeconometric model can be quite misleading.

3. The Economics of the Long-Run System

3.1. A Reference Core Model

We turn now to the economic properties of a typical long-run system. We use a representative core model derived from the analysis of the long run of several macroeconometric models, in particular the French METRIC and

DMS models, as well as of the CEPREMAP "maquette" (see Brillet 1987; Brillet et al. 1986; Deleau et al. 1984; Kuh et al. 1984; Malgrange 1983, 1985). This core model describes the long-run structure of a Keynesian open economy with fixed exchange rates. All variables below refer to long-run equilibrium values in the sense of section 1.3. The asterisk is omitted for the sake of simplicity, as well as the explicit presence of long-run growth rates.

Firms, equipped with constant return to scale technology, derive their demand for labor N^d and for investment I from cost minimization at given demand for output Q and given capital-labor price ratio. (The present specification is consistent with putty-clay as well as with putty-putty by transforming the variable "capital" K into I using the long-run relation $I = (g + \mu)K$, with μ rate of capital evaporation.) They set the supply price p for their output through mark-up on unit costs. Workers supply a fixed amount of labor $\bar{N}$ and consume a fraction of their disposable income-wage plus nonwage income. Foreign trade—exports X, imports M—depends on domestic demand Q, foreign demand $\bar{Q}_e$, and competitiveness $p/\bar{p}_e$, with $\bar{p}_e$ foreign general price level in domestic currency. The prices of the different demands are given by the usual formulas $p_u = p^{1-\alpha}\bar{p}_e^{\alpha}$, where α corresponds to the import share in the relevant aggregate demand. Wages deflated by p_u can then be written

$$W/p_u = W/p[p/\bar{p}_e]^{\alpha}.$$

Lastly, the interest rate is assumed exogenously fixed.

According to our experience, this representation describes rather well the long-term structure associated with most usual macroeconometric models (see the aforementioned references). It can be synthetized by a three-equation system:

(M1) (demand)

$$Q = \underbrace{(\beta_1 WN^d + \beta_2 pQ)/p_c}_{C} + \underbrace{Qi(W/p_I)}_{I} + \underbrace{\bar{Q}_e \times (p/\bar{p}_e)}_{X} - \underbrace{Qm(p/\bar{p}_e)}_{M} + \bar{G},$$

(M2) (supply price)

$$p = \beta_3 WN^d/Q,$$

(M3) (equilibrium on labor market)

$$\bar{N} = \beta_4 Qn(p_I/W) = \beta_4 N^d,$$

with $p_I = p^{1-\alpha_1}\bar{p}_e^{\alpha_1}$ and $p_c = p^{1-\alpha_2}\bar{p}_e^{\alpha_2}$,

and $i(\cdot)$, $n(\cdot)$ optimal investment and labor demand per unit of production. It is supposed that $\beta_1 + \beta_2 \leqslant 1$, $i' > 0$, and i', n', x', $m' > 0$.

The first equation describes equilibrium of supply and demand on the market for goods in a quite traditional manner except that the various elements of the aggregate demand are here supposed to correspond to an SSGP. The two other relations correspond, respectively, to the long-run outcome of the dynamics of prices and wages, with β_3 the mark-up rate and β_4 the predetermined unemployment rate (deriving from the Phillips curve as noticed in Section 1.3). Substituting in relations M1 and M2 the labor demand N^d by its expression in terms of p_I/W and p_c, and eliminating p_c and p_I, give the following system with the three variables Q, $p/\bar{p}_e$, and W/p:

(M1′)

$$Q = Qd(W/p, p/\bar{p}_e) - Qm(p/\bar{p}_e) + \bar{Q}_e \times (p/\bar{p}_e) + \bar{G}, \qquad d_1', d_2' > 0$$

(M2′)

$$(p/\bar{p}_e)^{\alpha_1} = h(W/p), \qquad h' > 0$$

(M3′)

$$(W/p) = (p/\bar{p}_e)^{-\alpha_1} t(Q/\bar{N}), \qquad t' > 0.$$

In the first equation, the propensity to spend depends positively on the real wages and on the relative prices. It is worth noting that the autonomous expenditure multiplier *at given prices* is $(1 - d + m)^{-1}$. The second relation links relative prices with the real wages, given the labor demand function. When $\alpha_1 = 0$ (no import content in investment), W/p is fixed independently of the other variables Q and $p/\bar{p}_e$.

The model includes four exogenous variables: government expenditures, $\bar{G}$, foreign demand, $\bar{Q}_e$, labor force, $\bar{N}$, and foreign prices, $\bar{p}_e$.

3.2. The Working of the Model

We first observe that a variation of $\bar{p}_e$ implies a proportional shift in prices and wages, without any effect on real variables. In the same way, simultaneous proportional shocks on $\bar{N}$, $\bar{G}$, and $\bar{Q}_e$, affect Q only and leave prices and wages unchanged. Two important cases can be distinguished:

i. $\alpha_1 = 0$. No import content in investment. In this case, real wages result from M2′ independently from the exogenous variables. The relation M3′ then gets the production Q which does not depend on demand but only on the labor force $\overline{N}$.

In this classical regime, variations of $\overline{G}$ and/or $\overline{Q}_e$ affect prices only; the greater the effect, the lower the price elasticities of foreign trade and the greater the import content of consumption (α_2). The case of a Leontief technology, $Q = \overline{n}N$, where output results obviously from the predetermination of N, can be put in this category.

ii. General case, $\alpha_1 > 0$. The system is now interdependent. If we eliminate wages through relation M2′, we get a traditional aggregate demand-aggregate supply system:

(M1″)

$$Q = Q\overset{(+)}{\hat{d}(p/\overline{p}_e)} - Q\overset{(+)}{m(p/\overline{p}_e)} + \overline{Q}_e \times \overset{(-)}{(p/\overline{p}_e)} + \overline{G}$$

(M2″)

$$(p/\overline{p}_e)^{\alpha_1} = \overset{(+)}{\hat{t}(Q/\overline{N})}.$$

It can be observed that the aggregate demand relation (M1″) is not necessarily downward sloping with respect to prices, because of their positive influence on domestic demand *d*. This positive relative price effect, direct, and indirect through the real wages, called the "Laursen-Metzler effect," expresses that an adverse inflation gap w.r.t. foreign prices mechanically implies a smaller increase in relative user price because of the import share, and acts then as a lever on real income. The aggregate demand function is less decreasing when the economy gets more open (α_1 and α_2 larger). This phenomenon is reinforced if the constant price multiplier is small.

The second equation M2′ corresponds to the traditional aggregate supply function of textbooks. It incorporates three basic elements: description of the labor market, labor demand function, and supply price relation. The only, but important, difference lies in the replacement of the Phillips curve by a fixed unemployment rate, which is its long-run counterpart.

The main comparative static results can be briefly summarized:

1. A positive shock on $\overline{G}$ or on $\overline{Q}_e$ induces a translation of the demand curve, i.e., a move of the equilibrium along the supply curve, and then an increase in both prices and quantities, the greater the price increase the less open the economy.

2. An exogenous increase in labor force $\bar{N}$ shifts the supply function upward and generates a rise in production and a drop in prices.

3. A movement in foreign prices $\bar{p}_e$ generates an equal variation of domestic prices, without any effect on the quantities.

The following table gives as an illustration the multipliers (expressed in terms of elasticities) of government expenditures and of labour supply for the French models MICRO-METRIC (Malgrange 1983) and MICRO-DMS (Deleau et al. 1984).

	Shocks			
	$\Delta\bar{G}/Q = 1\%$		$\Delta\bar{N}/\bar{N} = 1\%$	
	METRIC	DMS	METRIC	DMS
$\Delta Q/Q\%$	1.02	0.	1.50	1.41
$\Delta p/p\%$	6.20	6.70	−16.23	−7.30

This table reveals a price elasticity for the supply function of about 1/6 for METRIC and 0 in the case of DMS. The price elasticity of the demand function amounts approximately to − 1/10 and − 1/5, respectively.

3.3. The Long-Run Core Model and Macroeconomic Theory

In this section, the specification of this core model is confronted with the suggestions that would emerge from traditional macroeconomic theory.

i. The Phillips curve implies, in the long run, an involuntary unemployment equilibrium rate independent from the state of the economy. This rate may be greater than its mean historical value if the progression of wages has been actually higher in the sample period than the productivity growth (see below the case of MICRO-DMS). Furthermore, on the goods market, the hypothesis of monopolistic competition between firms leads to a mark-up pricing corresponding to an excess supply of output *at given prices.* Hence the following remarks:

1. It is clear that the long run of macroeconometric models is not Walrasian: it would be advantageous for firms to produce more and for consumers to work more *at equilibrium prices;* this is blocked by the monopolistic behavior of the agents.

2. The black-box nature of the Phillips curve already discernible for short-run analysis becomes impeding in a long-run setting. The representative

core model would gain much in explanative power from a real dynamic theory of wages and employment. In the present state of macrotheory and macromodeling, the long run of macroeconometric models heavily rests on an unemployment rate determined only by a black-box relation, very often of rather poor econometric quality.

3. In the core model, the elasticity of the demand perceived by firms is directly linked with the value of β_3, while the realized demand function is given by M_1 or M_1'. The underlying monopolistic competition scheme would gain from being stated more explicitly (see, e.g., Dixit and Stiglitz 1977).

ii. Another important problem consists in the limits to be drawn between the exogenous and endogenous domains. In a short-run perspective, it is usual to leave aside some phenomena that look largely pre- or post-determined with respect to the system under consideration. This practice may affect the long-run properties and consistency of the model. The internal and external debt intertemporal constraints are typical examples. In the previous core model, a sustained increase of public expenditure leads to a permanent deterioration of the government budget, and an unbounded increase of the public debt. The so-called long-run public spending multiplier thus has a dubious meaning. This phenomenon is well known since Christ (1968). This same policy exercise implies a permanent worsening of the balance of payments, with an infinite foreign debt in the long run. Taking into account these two constraints would enhance the economic relevance of the long-run core model. It would also lead to substantial extra complexity, money and public bonds, interest rate, exchange rate, and capital movements being then endogenous variables.

To summarize, macroeconometric models have long-run economic properties that parallel some macro-theory models. They do not correspond, however, to what is often claimed (short-run Keynesian, long-run Walrasian). Furthermore, the long run magnifies the ambiguities of the theory (functioning of the employment market, correct description of the intertemporal constraints and choices).

4. Illustration: The Case of MICRO-DMS

4.1. Presentation of MICRO-DMS

DMS is a multisectoral annual model of about 2500 equations built and run by INSEE. It is used for medium-run planning and forecasting. A miniaturized version of DMS, MICRO-DMS, was first elaborated (Brillet 1982) as a pedagogical tool. This core model has been slightly modified in order to admit SSGPs (Deleau et al. 1984), as explained in the first section, and reestimated by OLS for the sample period (1960–1978). The equations are listed in table 1.

Equation 1 defines desired nonagricultural employment *ND* as a linear function of production (Leontief technology), and equation 2 defines actual nonagricultural employment *NA* by a progressive dynamic adjustment toward *ND*. Total employment *N* is given by equation 3. Job demand *PD* is given by equation 4—$\bar{N}_0$: exogenous working force; hence the unemployment rate *UN* given by equation 6. Equation 5 is a measure of the capacity utilization rate *TU*; equation 7 is a Phillips curve without money illusion (*WA* being the *real* wage rate). Equation 8 provides a definition of the profit rate *TP*, and equation 9 is the standard consumption function *C*. As in the original model, investment *I* is determined by a combination of accelerator and profitability mechanisms (equation 10). Equation 11 defines

Table 1.
MICRO-DMS: Equations. Source: Deleau et al. 1984.

[1] $ND = (Q - \overline{QZ})/\overline{PRODT}$

[2] $\text{Log}\dfrac{NA}{NA_{-1}} = 0.326\,\text{Log}\dfrac{ND}{NA_{-1}} + 0.00882$

[3] $N = NA + \overline{NZ}$

[4] $PD = -0.55\,(N - \bar{N}_0) + 797 \times (1 + n)^t$

[5] $TU = 1.37\,Q/K$

[6] $UN = PD/(PD + N)$

[7] $\text{Log}\dfrac{WA}{WA_{-1}} = -0.994\,UN + 0.0803$

[8] $TP = [(Q - \overline{QZ})(1 - \overline{TAX}) - WA \times NA]/K$

[9] $C/(WA \times N + \overline{RDX}) = 0.877$

[10] $I/K = 0.658(I/K)_{-1} + 0.149\,TP + 0.056(Q/Q_{-1} - \overline{TU}/TU) + 0.0145$

[11] $DI = C + I + \overline{DA}$

[12] $\text{Log}(M/DI) = -0.265\,\text{Log}(1 - TU) + 1.744\,\overline{OUV} - 3.7$

[13] $\text{Log}(P/P_{-1}) = 0.562\,\text{Log}\left[\dfrac{P \cdot WA \cdot N}{Q} \Big/ \left(\dfrac{P \cdot WA \cdot N}{Q}\right)_{-1}\right] - 1.143(TP - \overline{TP})_{-1}$
$+ 0.239(TU - \overline{TU}) + 0.022$

[14] $\text{Log}(X/\overline{DM}) = -1.355\,TU + 0.717\,\log(\overline{PE}/P) + 0.387\,\overline{OUV} + 12.6$

[15] $Q = DI + X - M$

[16] $K = 0.963\,K_{-1} + I_{-1}$

domestic demand *DI*, and equations 12 and 14 are standard imports *M* and exports *X* functions. The price equation 13 describes a dynamic adjustment of prices *P* to costs, with some influence of capacity utilisation and profits. Finally, equation 16 defines capital accumulation.

4.2. The Long-Run System: Numerical and Statistical Analysis

Table 2 gives the associated long-run system. The different ordering of equations from Table 1 reflects the strong hierarchical structure of this system. The same numbering has been kept to allow for comparisons.

Three variables defined by their growth rate—*WA*, *P*, and *K*, equations 7, 10, and 13—give three implicit long-run relations with predetermination of UN^* and codetermination of TU^* and TP^*. The supply of output Q^*, because of complementary factors, is fixed independently of demand and the adjustment of the latter takes place through exports shift, implemented by prices variation—equations E14 and E15. In other words, we get here a "supply model" in total contrast with what happens in the short run where supply adjusts to demand through the traditional multiplier mechanism with sluggish prices.

Table 2.
MICRO-DMS: The Long-Run System. Source: Deleau et al. 1984.

[7]	$\mathrm{Log}(1+\gamma) = -0.994\, UN^* + 0.0803$
[E10]	$(1-0.658)(g+0.037) = 0.149\, TP^* + 0.056(1 + g - \overline{TU}/TU^* + 0.0145)$
[E13]	$(1-0.562)\,\mathrm{Log}(1+\rho) = -1.143(TP^* - \overline{TP}) + 0.239(TU^* - \overline{TU}) + 0.022$
[E6]	$PD^* = N^*\, UN^*/(1 - UN^*)$
[E4]	$N^* = \bar{N}_0^* - (PD^* - 797)/0.55$
[E3]	$NA^* = N^* - \overline{NZ}^*$
[E2]	$ND^* = NA^*[\exp(-0.00882)(1+n)^{1-.326}]^{1/.326}$
[E1]	$Q^* = \overline{QZ}^* + ND^* \times \overline{PRODT}$
[E5]	$K^* = 1.37\, Q^*/TU^*$
[E16]	$I^* = (g + 0.037)\, K^*$
[E8]	$WA^* = [(Q^* - \overline{QZ}^*)(1 - \overline{TAX}) - K^*\, TP^*]/NA^*$
[E9]	$C^* = 0.877(WA^*\, N^* + \overline{RDX}^*)$
[E11]	$DI^* = C^* + I^* + \overline{DA}^*$
[E12]	$\mathrm{Log}\, M^* = \mathrm{Log}\, DI^* - 0.265\, \mathrm{Log}(1 - TU^*) + 1.744\, \overline{OUV}^* - 3.7$
[E15]	$X^* = Q^* + M^* - DI^*$
[E14]	$P^* = \overline{PE}^* \times [(\overline{DM}^*/X^*)\exp(12.6 + 0.387\, \overline{OUV}^* - 1.355 \times TU^*)]^{1/0.717}$

It is interesting to compare the mean point of the sample period to the numerical results of the long-run model. We first observe that the original model includes five dynamic equations generating as many relationships between the long-run growth rates and the levels. If in the long-run system we set the levels of variables at their mean values of the historical period, we end up for these five equations with the following relations:

(E7′) implies $\gamma = 0.0548$

(E10′) implies $g = 0.0502$

(E13′) implies $\gamma = 0.0515$

(E2′) implies $n = 0.0138$

(E16′) implies $q = 0.0515$

If these five relations had a solution in the three basic rates (n, γ, ρ), then *giving to the exogenous variables their mean historical values would lead to a solution of the long-run system with also the mean historical values for the endogenous.* In the present case, it is clear that such a solution does not exist. In particular, the constraint $1 + g = (1 + n)(1 + \gamma)$ is obviously violated. As a matter of fact, the productivity growth rate is given exogenously in the model at 3.68% while condition (E7′)—derived from the Phillips curve—gives a compatibility value of γ w.r.t. the past average growth rate of wages equal to 5.48% during the sample period.

Table 3 gives, in columns 1 and 2, the mean level and the average growth rate of the sample period. In Deleau et al. (1984) the following growth rates were chosen:

$$n = 0.0131; \quad \gamma = 0.0379; \quad \rho = 0.0631; \quad g = 0.0515.$$

This generates a gap between values given by the long-run system and actual mean historical values of -3% on employment, -4.3% on output, and $+30\%$ on the price level—see column 3 of table 3. Such a distortion for the last value comes from the long-run structure. Indeed a downward shock of 1% on supply, keeping everything else constant, imposes a drop of exports of 7% through a price increase of almost 10% (relations E15 and E16). If, in the long-run model, the relation E7 is replaced by the identification of the unemployment rate to its mean historical value, the gap is reduced to -0.3% for output and $+6\%$ for prices as shown from the last column of table 3.

To summarize, it can be seen from this particular example that the long-run model is able to reproduce the mean historical data only if very

Table 3.
MICRO-DMS: Numerical Values

	Sample set			LR with corrected U_n
Variables	Mean	Growth rates	LR (DLM)	
UN^*	.0271	0	.0434	.0271
$\overline{TU}$	.843	0		
$\overline{TP}$	.0836	0		
TU^*	.843	0	.856	.856
TP^*	.0836	0	.0813	.0813
N^*	21,280	.59	20,628	21,254
PD^*	.588	.70	.936	.588
$\overline{NO}$	20,881	.98		
NA^*	14,430	1.44	13,778	14,404
$\overline{NZ}$	6,850	−1.05		
ND^*	14,458	1.53	13,778	14,404
$\overline{QZ}$	51,202	.91		
$\overline{PRODT}$	38.548	3.68		
Q^*	608,531	5.03	582,336	606,447
K^*	984,681	4.97	932,009	970,600
I^*	85,465	5.42	82,483	85,900
WA^*	13.28	5.48	13.44	13.46
$\overline{TAX}$	.5087	0		
C^*	463,569	5.21	458,633	466,393
$\overline{RDX}$	245,720	4.87		
DI^*	604,122	5.09	596,197	607,374
$\overline{DA}$	55,083	4.12		
M^*	112,455	9.95	108,798	110,837
$\overline{OUV}$	.8517	3.52		
X^*	116,876	9.02	94,937	109,910
P^*	1.101	6.05	1.432	1.168
$\overline{PE}$	1.089	5.91		
$\overline{DM}$	.8937	8.86		

restrictive conditions on the average growth rates during that period are verified. If the analysis of the distortions may bring useful pieces of information on the robustness of the specification of the model, this result implies that one must be extremely careful when interpreting the numerical solution of the long-run model.

4.3. Reduction of the Long-Run System

We turn now to the three equations representation given in Section 3.2. Keeping in mind that TU^*, TP^*, and UN^* are determined by E10, E13, and E7 before the rest of the system, we get the following equation for the equilibrium of the goods market from the combination of the last eight equations plus E1 to E3:

(M1)

$$Q^* = (1 - m)\left[.877\left(WA^*\left\{\frac{Q^* - \overline{QZ}}{\lambda} + \overline{NZ}\right\} + \overline{RDX}\right) + (g + .037)\frac{1.37}{TU^*}Q^* + \overline{DA}\right] + \mu\overline{DM}(\overline{p}_e/p^*)^{.717}$$

with

$$m = (1 - TU^*)^{-.265}\exp(1.744\,\overline{OUV} - 3.7),$$

$$\lambda = \overline{PRODT}[\exp(-.00882)(1 + n)^{1-.326}]^{1/.326},$$

$$\mu = \exp(-1.355\ TU^* + .387\,\overline{OUV} + 12.6).$$

The relation E8 gives

(M2)

$$WA^* = \lambda\left[1 - \overline{TAX} - 1.37\cdot\frac{TP^*}{TU^*}\frac{Q^*}{Q^* - \overline{QZ}}\right].$$

At last, combining job market equations E6 and E1 to E4, we get

(M3)

$$(Q^* - \overline{QZ}) = \lambda\left[\frac{797 + .55\overline{N}_o}{UN^*/(1 - UN^*) + .55} - \overline{NZ}\right].$$

The following comments can be made:

i. If K^* were proportional to $(Q^* - QZ)$ instead of Q^*—i.e., "true" Leontief technology, see equations E1 + E5—WA^* would become independent of Q^*, corresponding to the case $\alpha = 0$ of Section 3.2.

ii. The relation M2 may be interpreted as the price to be fixed by firms at fixed nominal wages $(P^* W^*)$ and output Q^* in order to realize a given equilibrium profit rate.

We are ready now to get the "aggregate demand-aggregate supply" representation. Keeping only the exogenous variables DA, DM, P_e, N_o, and substituting for the other exogenous variables their average historical values as given in table 3, column 1, we get

$$(\text{M3}) \Rightarrow Q^* = 35,61 \cdot \overline{N}_o - 161250$$

$$(\text{M2}) \Rightarrow WA^* = \lambda\left(.4913 - .13 \frac{Q^*}{Q^* - 51202}\right).$$

Substituting this expression of WA^* in M1, we obtain the long-run *aggregate demand* of the MICRO-DMS model, which cannot be put in a simple form because of the specific shape of both M2 and the consumption function:

$$(\text{M1}) \Rightarrow P^*/\overline{P}_e = \left[\frac{\mu\overline{DM}}{.625\, Q^* - 226100 + \dfrac{1.26 \times 10^9}{Q^* - 51202} - .817\overline{DA}}\right]^{1.39}.$$

Figure 1 plots this demand curve as well as the supply curve deduced from M3.

The (log)linearization of M1 around the equilibrium gives approximately

$$\frac{\Delta P^*}{P^*} = -5 \cdot \frac{\Delta Q^*}{Q^*} + \frac{\Delta \overline{P}_e}{\overline{P}_e} + 1.39 \frac{\Delta \overline{DM}}{\overline{DM}} + 7.4 \frac{\Delta \overline{DA}}{Q^*}.$$

We find again the relative price rigidity of demand $(-1/5)$, described above at a theoretical level, and the highly inflationist character of the public expenditure.

Conclusion

The previous analysis leads to a certain number of conclusions, negative as well as positive, about the long run of macroeconometric models.

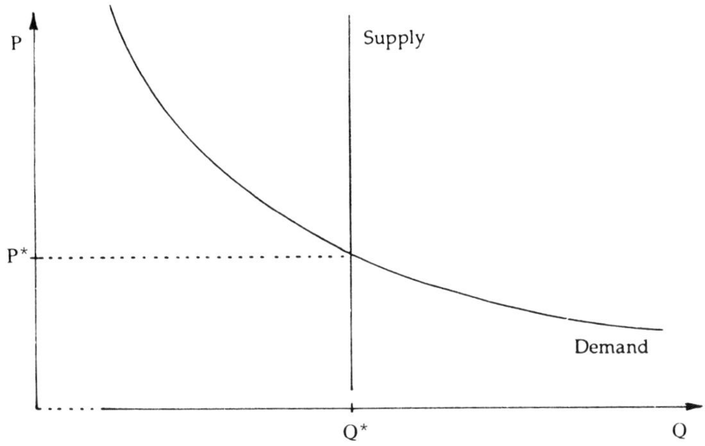

Figure 1.
MICRO-DMS, long-run equilibrium.

The negative conclusions consist in the numerous prerequisites that a given macroeconometric model has to satisfy in order that an acceptable long run can be associated with it. These prerequisites refer to the specification of the model (Section 2), its estimation (Section 3), and the economic relevance of the relations obtained (Section 4). The example of MICRO-DMS proves that, even after adjustment to specification constraints, the long run associated with a given macroeconometric model may substantially diverge from average historical data. Furthermore, the long-run analysis of macroeconometric models is a very acid test for applied macroeconomics. The limitations of black-box approaches or approximations, which can be considered tolerable for short-run simulation, appear strongly binding when put in a long-term perspective.

On the positive side, our study offers a methodology to incorporate long-run considerations in the elaboration of macroeconometric models. In this respect, it points out potential improvements. Some are linked with research in progress. If, clearly, existing macroeconometric models should be considered with extreme caution for interpreting long-run phenomena, macroeconometric modeling should in the future benefit from fruitful lines of research.

Acknowledgment

This research was partly financed by the Direction de la Prévision.

References

Bergstrom, A. R., and Wymer, C. R. 1976. "A Model of Disequilibrium Neoclassical Growth and an Application to the United Kingdom." In Bergstrom, A. R., ed., *Statistical Inference in Continuous Time Economic Models*. Amsterdam: North-Holland.

Brillet, J. L. 1988. L'équation de Phillips: comparaison sur un maquette de plusieurs formulations alternatives. Mémoire INSEE, Service des Programmes.

Brillet, J. L. 1988. "Propriétés à long terme de la maquette de MICRO-DMS." In Demongeot, J., and Malgrange, P., eds., *Biologie et Economie: Les Apports de la Modélisation*. Presses Universitaire de Dijon.

Brillet, J. L., Le Van, C., and Malgrange, P. 1986. Stabilité structurelle des modèles macroéconométriques: optimisation dynamique et incertitude. Mémoire CEPREMAP.

Christ, C. F. 1968. "A Simple Macroeconomic Model with a Government Budget Restraint." *Journal of Political Economy* 76: 53–67.

Currie, D. A. 1982. "The Long-Run Properties of the Bank of England's Small Monetary Model of the UK Economy." *Applied Economics* 14: 63–72.

Davidson, J. E. H., Hendry, D. F., Srba, F., and Yeo, S. 1978. "Econometric Modeling of the Aggregate Time Series Relationship between Consumers' Expenditure and Income in the United Kingdom." *Economic Journal* 88: 661–692.

Deleau, M., Le Van, C., and Malgrange, P. 1984a. "The Uncertainty Frontier as a Global Approach to the Efficient Stabilization of Economic Systems: Experiments with the MICRO-DMS MODEL." In Hughes-Hallett, A., ed., *Applied Decision Analysis and Economic Behaviour*. Dordrecht: M. Nijhoff.

Deleau, M., Malgrange, P., and Muet, P. A. 1984b. "A Study of Short Run and Long Run Properties of Macroeconometric Dynamic Models by Means of an Aggregative Core Model." In Malgrange, P. and Muet, P. A. eds., *Contemporary Macroeconomic Modelling*. Oxford: Basil Blackwell.

Dixit, A. K., and Stiglitz, J. E. 1977. "Monopolistic Competition and Optimum Product Diversity." *American Economic Review* 67 (3): 297–308.

Dornbusch, R., and Fischer, S. 1977. *Macroeconomics*. New York: McGraw-Hill.

Friedman, M. 1957. *A Theory of the Consumption Function*. National Bureau of Economic Research, Princeton University Press.

Gandolfo, G. 1981. *Qualitative Analysis and Econometric Estimation of Continuous Time Dynamic Models*. Amsterdam: North-Holland.

Hendry, D. F. (ed.) 1986. *Econometric Modelling with Co-Integrated Variables. Oxford Bulletin of Economics and Statistics*, special number 48.

Kuh, E., Le Van, C., and Malgrange, P. 1984. "Une étude de la dynamique structurelle des modèles macroéconomiques." Mémoire CEPREMAP.

Le Van, C., and Malgrange P. 1988. "Hiérarchie temporelle dans un modèle macroéconomique—Application à une maquette du modèle METRIC." In Demongeot, J. and Malgrange, P., eds., *Biologie et Economie: Les Apports de la Modélisation*. Presses Universitaires de Dijon.

Malgrange, P. 1983. "Steady Growth Paths in a Short Run Dynamic Model: The Case of the French quarterly Model METRIC." Mémoire CEPREMAP No. 8321.

Malgrange, P. 1985. "Sentiers stationnaires des modèles macroéconomiques: leçons de la maquette du CEPREMAP." In Ritschard, G., and Royer, D., eds., *Optimalités et Structures*. Paris: Economica.

Malinvaud, E. 1980. *Profitability and Unemployment*. Cambridge University Press.

Malinvaud, E. 1981. "Econometrics Faced with the Needs of Macroeconomic Policy." *Econometrica* 49(6): 1363–1375.

Wallis, K. F., and Whitley, J. D. 1987. "Long-Run Properties of Large-Scale Macroeconometric Models." *Annales d'Economie et de Statistique* 6–7: 207–224.

21 Employment and Fiscal Policy with a Realistic View of the Social Roles of Wages

Serge-Christophe Kolm

1. Wages and Work in Society: A Realistic View and Its Consequences[1]

1.1. The Classical vs. Keynesian Debate in the Face of the Effective Roles of Wages in Society

The protracted dispute between various brands of "classics" and "Keynesians," with its vast policy consequences, does not survive a realistic view of labor markets. We shall see that the crucial peculiarities of these markets lie on the supply side, and that they nevertheless lead to requiring a fiscal policy. This policy, however, is not simply "deflate" or "reflate": its taxes, subsidies, and expenditures are more specifically defined as to their bases, rates, and mix. This view of the labor market blurs the distinctions between the various kinds of unemployment (like "involuntary" and "voluntary," etc.). Malinvaud's (1983) view that an economy can be at once "Keynesian" and "classical" (*Essais sur la théorie du chômage*), which is also Keynes' own position (*General Theory*, 1936, Chapter XXI, Section IV-3°), is in a sense even more true than these authors suggest: not only different sectors can be of different kinds, but, still more, the same labor market can present together Keynesian and classical features. In the end of the analysis all these traditional distinctions fade away. We need not mourn them, though, since by the same token they lose their usefulness. Indeed, the basic question is about policy rather than classification, and these categorizations and their policy implications are bypassed when one deduces the *good fiscal policy* directly from the basic characteristics of the wage (and price) determination process, i.e., as a problem in "*optimal taxation*" (these two homonyms should become synonyms). The relevant structures of the labor market are observed directly everywhere, but they are also shown by a vast empirical literature in the fields of "labor" or "industrial" relations, psychology and sociology of labor, and various schools of institutional economics. When translated into the language of classical economic theory, they lead to the introduction of wages directly in utility functions.

Indeed, to explain wage levels and, thus, employment in modern society, Durkheim and Tarde may be more helpful than Walras, Cournot, and Bertrand. This remark does not seem inconsistent with the general spirit of Malinvaud's remarks on the causes of wage rates, although he does not express it in these terms. At any rate, disciplines other than theoretical economics which have abundantly studied this question lean strongly in this direction. The most impressive it probably the field of "labor" and "industrial relations," because it looks at the phenomenon globally and empirically, it specializes in it, and it is devoid of methodological prejudices (whereas psychologists prefer experimentation, sociologists use case studies, and economists especially like *a priori* hypotheses on behavior). In particular, the sociological concept of a "wage norm" is the most frequent idea. But since economists are also strongly interested in this question and derive very important consequences from it, and since they study it with intellectual tools which have their own strong points, we must try to establish a link and to build up a fruitful integration of these various views.

One of the reasons of this interest for economists is that the important theory of unemployment of Malinvaud and of the other economists who take the same approach had to face the objection that it takes prices and wages as exogenous variables. It was argued that the least that a global economic theory should do is to provide an explanation of price and wage levels. Unfortunately, these reservations were voiced by certain American economists who proposed instead models in which the labor market is in a state of classical perfect competitive equilibrium (and even, sometimes, where this perfect competition is the doing of a single agent!), a too unrealistic vision. In response to these "new classical" views of the labor market, economic theories aiming at explaining wage rigidity began to flourish. But have some fifteen years and a few dozen imaginative articles solved the problem?

1.2. Some Difficulties in the Economic Theories of Wage Rigidities

The literature on the theory of "implicit contracts," for example, contains its own evaluation. But the essential is perhaps to ask if it responds sufficiently to the naive question: If these contracts are so important, why do they remain implicit? They concern agreements on future employment and wages according to the business situation. Such agreements are possible. In every country, one finds numerous examples of accords in which wages vary according to the performance of the firm (profit sharing in various forms, indexation on productivity, bonuses, etc.). Furthermore, in certain countries or, more specifically, certain cultures, the "implicit contract" leads to a policy of not laying people off and lowering wages when times are hard (the "scandinavo-nippo-alpine" model of Sweden, Finland, Switzerland, Austria, and Japan). The answer either requires the introduction of other phenomena which become the explanation or suggests that one abandon this theory.

The "efficiency wages" theory is based on the idea that an individual works harder (or better) if his wage is higher. This certainly is a possibility, and perhaps more so in the inverse case where one works less (or poorly) following a wage cut. The general theory of the effect of wages on productivity will be presented in Section 13 below. But the purely economic explanations that have been offered—threats against shirking, stabilization of work rotation, adverse selection—run up against the same question as above: it would be possible to remedy the situation with more finely tuned contracts, the absence of which has to be explained (Yellen 1984 reviews the literature and sums up the results). And the other explanations have to rely on the fact that one works more or better to reestablish an equilibrium if one feels overpaid (experiments by Adams 1965a), or on "morale," or gratitude, or return gift behavior (Akerlof 1982), etc., thus abandoning the "homo economicus" model in the strict sense (nutritional effects are limited to the poorest countries). One could furthermore wonder about the importance and extent of this phenomenon—given the necessity to explain mass unemployment. In fact the inverse relation also exists: it is sometimes necessary to keep workers on the lean side so that they are attentive, energetic, hard-working, and obedient (easy going work and a higher wage can also be consequences of the same victory in labor disputes concerning together working conditions and remunerations). In reality, some studies in experimental psychology on work motivation conclude the validity of the latter relation, explained by the theory of *cognitive dissonance*: an individual who is less well paid convinces himself that his work is more interesting, as a compensation in order to maintain a balance in his psychic evaluation of his work and to maintain his self-esteem (and he better performs a task that interests him more). Other experiments show that a higher wage by piecework leads a worker who then feels overpaid to work either more slowly, or better, to reestablish equilibrium, with thus a total productivity which can either increase or decrease (Adams 1965a). As one can see, the effect depends essentially on the way in which the wage is established and the entire psycho-social context.

But even the simple logic of the phenomenon poses a problem since, in order for "efficiency wages" to explain "involuntary unemployment," the effect of the wage rate on production must have a special form. For example, this literature, following Solow (1979), writes the production function as $\varphi[e(w)\cdot\ell]$ where φ is the product, w the wage, ℓ the employment, and φ and e are increasing functions. $e\ell$ is the labor in "efficiency units." This literature considers that the firm minimizes its cost $w\ell$ at a given level of production $\varphi(e\ell) = q$. But we must also consider the case where it maximizes its profit $P = \varphi - w\ell$ without a sales constraint. And we must equally consider the case—which is more general and pertinent in macroeconomic analysis (i.e., with aggregate variables) than that of a given level of output—where the product demand is $D(w\ell, P) + x$, where D is a nondecreasing function of wage income $w\ell$ and of the profit P (perhaps by their sum φ as in Keynes' own theory) and x is an autonomous demand. Denoting $c = w\ell$ the cost, we can check that all these three structures lead, with the relevant and well-known conditions on the function D, to the choice of ℓ and w which can be equivalently described by the maximization of P or φ at a given c or D, or by the minimization or c or D at a given P or φ. For example we minimize c at a given level of φ, thus at a given $e\ell = c\cdot e(w)/w$, that is *we choose the w that maximizes $e(w)/w$*. This result is independent of the structure of the functions D and φ and of the level of x. We see that *it holds under a much larger set of settings* than the problem to minimize c for a given q which led Solow to the condition $we' = e$ (implied by the maximum of e/w) and which has been considered by the ulterior writers. (In Sections 10 and following we shall discuss the possibility that labor supply constrains this choice, with also a more general structure of the effect of w on the production.) Now if $e(0) > 0$, or if, when $e(0) = 0$, the function $e(w)$ is concave because of the ordinary diminishing returns to scale of wage productivity, $e(w)/w$ is maximum for $w = 0$ [as is for instance clear on a figure of the graph $e = e(w)$]. But at a zero wage certainly the demand for productive labor (i.e., with $e(0) > 0$) exceeds the labor supply (for example, with common assumptions demand is infinite and supply is zero, but the excess is likely to hold even if demand is finite and if supply is positive), and the "efficiency" solution is not reached—for $e = w = 0$, labor demand is not determinate and supply may not be either. The existence of a non zero efficiency wage, and thus the possibility of this "efficiency" solution and by consequence of the involuntary unemployment which results, necessitates therefore $e(0) = 0$ and $e'(w)$ initially increasing or zero, then decreasing. The increasing returns section of this wage productivity is peculiar and requires careful explanation. It is observed, for example, in some cases in developing countries where workers acquire an "industrial mentality" which they did not previously have—labor productivity reacts to wage increases first more and more by increasing sensitivity or awareness or by an addiction-like effect, then less and less by a satiety structure (decreasing returns) of the effect (this has been studied in some Algerian firms). But can one sufficiently explain unemployment by this peculiar structure of "enthusiasm for work"? Furthermore, the effect of w on the production function can take on forms other than this "labor-augmenting" one, but then problems of the same kind remain and may even get worse.[2] However, the wage rate w certainly has a positive lower limit if there is employment, for a number of possible reasons—subsistence, alternative occupation or minimum-wage law—and that resolves the problem considered.

But above all, the theory of efficiency wages by itself leads to the exact opposite conclusion of the one it wishes to demonstrate *in fine*. The original intention was to find a base from which to counter the "new classical" assertion that "the government should not intervene (with Keynesian policies) because the labor market is in competitive equilibrium and is thus Pareto-efficient." The "efficiency wage" does yield a labor market in disequilibrium and "involuntary unemployment." But the situation it describes is Pareto-efficient since it corresponds to an unconstrained profit maximization in the labor market by the firms choosing both employment and wages. This theory does not justify therefore government intervention to improve the efficiency of the economy. Such a justification thus requires one to introduce other non-classical "market imperfections" (such as constrained output due to imperfect futures markets).

As we shall argue below, both for policy conclusion and for explanation, it is more important to introduce wages in utility functions than in production functions (which "efficiency wage" theory does, and we shall do both).

The various explanations that put forward the role of unions' monopoly of labor supply, considered by authors too numerous to be quoted here, and the insiders-outsiders models of Lindbeck and Snower (1989), Shaked and Sutton (1984), and Sabourian (1988) pinpoint a much more important cause, already mentioned by Keynes himself. We must note however that the early 1980s, in almost all countries, show at once a decrease in the role and importance of unions, and a marked increase in unemployment. Furthermore, these models come up against a series of difficulties. Those that explain wage formation by sequential bargaining (Shaked and Sutton 1984, for example), or the collusion between workers and the wage by sequential markets (Sabourian 1988), are as of yet only interesting examples with very "ad hoc" hypotheses. And more general models with constituted unions struggle over the choice of hypotheses as to the objectives of these organizations—are they only concerned with wages, or do they consider both wages and unemployment, do they neglect the unemployed, etc.? The only way to respond properly to these questions is to enter into the sociology and psychosociology of labor.

1.3. The Causes of Wage Preferences

1.3.a. A Multiplicity of Causes

We argue that wages are importantly objects or determinants of preferences (hence, that they should appear in utility functions as variables or parameters) for reasons other than the income specifically yielded by this wage. We call "wage preference" this property and "preferred wages" the wages which have it. The reasons for the existence of wage preference are very numerous and diverse. They belong to the realms of psychology, sociology or economics (yet all these reasons have economic effects). They can lead one to have preferences on, or influenced by, one's own wage or others' wages. These reasons can be classified as follows:

- *psycho-social*, a very vast field, including questions of *wage-norm; status wages; merit wages; fair, just, equitable wages*; maintenance of "*wage contours*" (for example, relative wages); wage *inequalities*; wage *envy* or *jealousy; normal*, correct, adequate, usual *wages*; etc.;
- *freedom* as an end-objective (rather than only welfare);
- *signaling of labor demand and opportunities*, which affects labor supply behavior;
- *inducing job search activity;*
- *influencing future preferences;*
- *influencing future wages and incomes through the following:*
    - *influencing future labor supply behavior,*
    - *psycho-social wages and income maintainance schemes,*
    - *signaling labor productivity,*
    - *keeping or losing other workers' support* in a labor collusion.

We now explain more in detail these causes of wage preferences.

1.3.b. Norm, Status, Sign, Merit, Fair, Just or Customary Wages

In the past year in the country where I am writing, a number of important labor conflicts about wages came into the domain of public information. Firstly, a major television network went on strike because it had hired a star newscaster at a very high wage, and, as a consequence, other employees of all qualifications demanded a raise. Then, the nurses nationwide went on strike, claiming a higher wage because their job is very painful and thus deserves a higher compensation. Then the anaesthetists went on strike because, since they study one year more than the others, they deserve a higher wage. Then the teachers went on strike because their present wages do not respect the dignity of the function. These strikes went with marches and public manifestations, and the mentioned reasons were voiced repeatedly and loudly. In all cases the demands were partly met. The fact that they were considered as justified and fair by the general opinion were doubtlessly influential in the determination of the strikers and in the final outcome. Is it the case that these persons just wanted a higher income and that the specific reasons which they took great care to present were just a make up while they were using their market power? If it were so, why did they take the pain to present these reasons, why did the TV network go on strike at this very moment, why did not the other networks also demand wage raises? Finally, the reasons for these wage raises have been justice as a limit of the inequality of wages (in the same workplace, a reason analyzed in general by Frank, 1984, 1985), deservingness, and social status.

Similar motivations are present in more private and discrete forms of wage and employment determination. Indeed, when someone refuses a wage that he judges to be too low, when he demands a certain wage in exchange for his work, the satisfaction that he enjoys from the consumption permitted by this income is rarely his only consideration—with the diminution of his leisure time and other effects of working. Most often, in the present day, he does not even have this satisfaction and this consumption on his mind and he doesn't even know precisely at that time on what he will spend all this income. This person is on the contrary fully aware of other facts that enter into his calculations and determine his choice and his behavior, and he is perfectly informed of a certain number of these facts. For example, he does not like, and eventually he refuses, a wage which is lower than the one he previously received because this would lower his self-esteem or his status in others' eyes; or a wage which is short of the one he thinks he is entitled to because of his education, his degrees, his experience or his seniority; or a wage which is not high enough compared to the wages of other persons to whom he compares himself because he thinks he deserves as much as them or because the lower wage would impair his status in others' and especially in his own eyes, or because the others' wages determine what he thinks is a normal and correct wage, or because of envy or jealousy, etc. A wage level is important not only *for* consumption but also *as* a conspicuous consumption (man's main consumption is others' view of him) and for pride, dignity, sentiments of justice, and honor as well as glory or vanity. It is the main measure of individual achievement in our societies. An individual's wage is not only the price of his work productivity, but also the label that society puts on him indicating the value it attributes to him. The common American expression "I'm worth so many thousands of dollars," said with a certain pride, is very revealing. The wage judges not only the market value of the flow of services but also the social value of human capital. To offer one's labor at a lower price is literally to make oneself cheap. It could be to derogate, or to break a norm or a solidarity.[3] Motivations of this kind have often led men to undergo serious material hardship. At the very least such motivations can slow down a lowering of wages in so far as the labor supply is not perfectly competitive (or that these wage effects are discontinuous at least at the margin—see below). And they come into play all the more that the material hardship of unemployment is attenuated by insurance, social security and general assistance, second incomes in the family, etc.

Furthermore, a worker can refuse or abstain from proposing a lower wage because the previously attained level had been so difficult to conquer collectively in labor conflicts, or by a sentiment of solidarity so as not to see his colleagues unemployed or forced to bid for lower wages ("class consciousness" and resulting behavior which is not strictly individualistic just happen to exist, and while they usually imply self-interested mutual support, there generally is more to them in terms of shared vision, brotherhood-like benevolence, etc.). One sees, moreover, that many of these motivations are intensified if they lead to an action which is public and known to other people.

The social norm aspects of wages, and their importance in the determination of wage levels beyond strict considerations of net productivity and disutility of labor, are quite obvious both in the direct observation of the labor market and in the numerous systematic studies mentioned below. Some of the most current expressions are those about wage norms and of what wages are normal, habitual, customary, traditional, correct, fair, just, equitable, suitable, honest, etc. In particular, ideas of distributive justice cannot help but influence the structure of wages, since wages make up the principal source of income in our societies. These norms are motivated sometimes by the wage income and the purchasing power that it gives, sometimes by the unit rate of compensation of labor (more by the latter when labor time is freely chosen by the worker by individual or collective-unionized decision).

In particular, the *comparison of wages* is very important for a whole series of reasons beyond the relative productivities and the disutilities of labor. This may lead to preferences on ratios of wages ("relative wages"), or on differences of real wages, etc. The desires for relative status and individual distinction, as well as jealousies or envies, of the wage earners are firstly concerned with the comparison of wages. Wages are, in part, "positional goods" in Harrod's sense. Correlatively, collective desires for peace, harmony, and a certain justice tend to the restraining of wage disparities. The wages of others are an essential determinant in wage norms. The fact that a wage earner has preferences regarding the comparison of wages can introduce four non classical aspects since these preferences then may bear upon (1) *one's own wage for a reason other than the direct satisfaction derived from the wage income*, (2) the *wages of others and not only one's own* (it is in this sense a kind of external effect), (3) the *wage rates and not only the wage incomes*, and, (4), since this effect can eventually be described as *relating to nominal wages and not necessarily to real wages*, in particular if relative wages are the relevant variables. If a wage earner wishes that his wage were higher compared to others' wages, and if *a non-cooperative labor market* causes him to take the wages of others as given (à la Nash-Cournot-Bertrand), he behaves with respect to his labor supply as if he preferred having a higher wage independently of the wage income he draws. Cooperation between wage earners who are preoccupied with the comparison of wages, making them agree to lower their wages so as to have more work, does not run only into the difficulties and costs of a collective agreement. It is above all hampered by the fact that unemployment manifests itself first by the existence of completely unemployed people on one hand and employed ones on the other, so that the former, who would obtain jobs, do not have a wage cut to offer in return because they don't have a wage. Of course, the wages which are thus compared are those of "reference groups" more or less extended (groups of the same profession, training, seniority, company, family, place of work or residence, etc.). For example, labor economics has long recognized the importance of the maintenance of "wage contours" as an objective of labor claims and in wage disputes and settlements (Dunlop, Piore, and many others). And Frank (1984, 1985) shows that the wages of the members of a work group are less dispersed than their individual productivities (as far as a single individual's productivity can be distinguished), and this certainly results from the group members' opinions in comparing wages.

The norm and status reasons for and effects of wages are indeed not surprising, since a wage provides an income for labor, and both income and the consumption goods bought with it on the one hand, and labor on the other hand, substantially follow norms, determine statuses, and are chosen for these purposes. Indeed, many an expense also has for object conformity to consumption norms or maintenance or promotion of one's status, and not only for the extreme case of "conspicuous consumption" but for a large part of the income.

This is still more striking for labor which gives rise to the wage. Its consideration—and hence that of unemployment and of wages—by current economic analysis remains silent about motivations other than those to obtain purchasing power, and in important cases these motivations cannot be considered as being treated implicitly by the analysis and this entails serious consequences for the conclusions. Voltaire says in *Candide*: "Work removes from us three great evils: boredom, vice and need." Remark that "need" comes only in third position. In most cases man does not want a job and a wage only for the necessity or the pleasure of consuming the income. Even at a zero wage, labor supply would be far from negligible (in supposing that basic needs are catered to by assistance or other resources). Many unemployed people despair even though they receive unemployment compensations which are close to their former wage. Both lucid observation (which introspection can help) and the results of numerous studies on work motivation show that one wants a job not only to earn a living, but also because work gives a social identity (by the "profession"), a social status, an activity, a rhythm to one's time, social relations, a community, the sentiment of being wanted and appreciated and of not being rejected or excluded or left by the wayside, a possibility to contribute something to society and to be useful, sometimes an interest in itself or for the responsibility it gives, the possibility to express one's creative capacities, the esteem of others and of oneself, self-actualization, etc. Certainly these various aspects depend on the particular case, but these extra-remunerative reasons for working are certainly more and more important on the whole in the current orientation of our world. This is due as much to certain tendencies in the transformation of labor (a great increase in the qualification levels, mechanization reducing the physical difficulty of labor, a deliberate movement toward the enrichment of individual tasks, an increased participation in decision making and greater responsibility, etc.), than because some needs are assured by other means (savings and wealth, public services, social security, other incomes in the family). In other societies these individual "extra-economic" reasons for work activity are often still more important (the minimum importance of the extra-economic interest in working must have been reached by industrial workers in the nineteenth century, the example of which seems to have strongly influenced economic thought). And to the degree in which these reasons decrease the *net* marginal disutility of labor, if, for a given quantity of labor, the wage does not similarly decrease, that implies that it is boosted by noncompetitive means which create a "wage gap" and the corresponding "involuntary unemployment."

The necessity for considering such psycho-social wage preferences does not only result from *prima facie* observation of the motivations. It also results from very numerous systematic scientific observations of the labor market by all the disciplines which study it empirically.

One of them is labor economics where, for example, workers' preferences for maintaining or restoring "wage contours" not only are directly observed (numerous authors, among them Dunlop, Piore, Frank), but are the only possible way to explain the observed influences of wage agreements in one sector over those in another and the wage-hike contagions and wage sprees (Dunlop, Piore, et al.).

Psycho-social wage preferences are also the most common and central phenomenon encountered in the empirical studies at firm or sectorial level performed within the field of "labor relations" or "industrial relations" (which have developed into a proper discipline in itself), in the experimental studies of labor psychology, and in the case studies (often at workshop level) of the micro-sociology of labor. History, anthropology, macro-sociology also provide informations in this sense. On the whole, these scientific observations and experimentations constitute a huge volume of convergent evidence which it is impossible to ignore. As a mere sample, let us mention the books by Annable, Behrend, Brown, Fogarty, Jaque, Lupton and Bowey, Patchen, Richardson, Salais and Thévenot, White, Williams, in the field of industrial relations, the studies of Adams, Adams and Rosenbaum, Andrews, Argyle, Lawler, Ribeaux and Poppleton, Pritchard, Dunnette-Jorgensen, Runciman, Taylor, Vroom for psychological experiments, or the case studies like those of Homans.

Psycho-social wage preferences are very often described by the objective and desire that wages be as close as possible to a "wage norm" (for absolute or relative wages), and by the corresponding behavior. None of the above mentioned studies fails to use this expression abundantly, in contexts which fit well with the usual observations of the question. On the contrary, the term and the idea of a wage norm are relatively very rare in the economic literature. It is interesting, though, to note that they are not completely absent either. A few general economists mention it, such as Hicks, Kaldor, Solow, Lindbeck, Malinvaud, whereas Okun speaks of the norms of wage increases. Akerlof (1980) goes beyond mere mention and constructs a model. Most of these references, and the model, however, consider wage norms for the firm, for labor demand, and not for labor supply and for the workers, one exception being Malinvaud who more correctly mentions the wage norm generally without specifying to which side of the market it applies. In contrast, Hahn (1982), inspired by Keynes' remarks on relative wages, writes the workers' utility as a discontinuous function of the ratio of the workers' wage over the prevailing wage, and he convinces himself of this discontinuity by introspection about the effect of this "social norm." Furthermore certain economists have discovered the other studies and are looking at the supply side. Oswald (1986), draws from psychology the idea of a utility that is a function of wage income which has an angle at the level of a wage norm. Akerlof (1982), inspired by micro-sociology and anthropology, considers the supply of work-effort, with concepts of norm but perhaps not precisely of wage norm.[4] The wage norm that the workers follow in Sabourian's (1988) interesting (but in its present form still particular and very simplified) example-model expresses their tacit collusion and results from the repeated game constituted by a sequential labor market (note that it is classic, in sociological theory, to explain certain types of norms by a game of repeated "prisoner's dilemma"—cf. Ullman-Margalit, Coleman, etc.—although the present lesson of the field is that this is bound to explain only a small fraction of norms and not the most interesting one, and not the most important and interesting aspects of norms, since norms mobilize emotions and more complex psychic structures and social interactions, as is true in particular in the case of wage norms). The references to wage norms are more frequent as one moves away from "pure theory." It is the object of the statistical studies by Perry and Mitchell, and it is a usual concept for French economists with an explicit sociological culture, such as Aglietta, Boyer, Lipietz, Petit, Reynaud, Salais, Thévenot, and others. Finally there are historical examples: Marx explains the wage by the workers' consumption norm, and among the causes of the downward rigidity of wages suggested by Keynes, one finds the attachment to relative wages which certainly has some of the characteristics of norms.

Since the various disciplines which consider labor and wages use different paradigms (different conceptual glasses to make sense of the world, different models of models), there may be problems in translating psychologists' or sociologists' explanations into the economist's language of preferences and "utility." This translation is always more or less possible theoretically, eventually in introducing new types of variables, but it may or may not be a meaningful exercize, that depending on the use which is made of the theory.[5] For wages, the exercize often leads precisely to the introduction of wage preferences. Norms are one such psycho-social concept. The normed behavior can often be described by a preference for lowering some "distance" between the wage and the norm, but the norm may be either taken as given, or described as a function of what it depends, or more or less explained. The full exercize may eventually be quite complex, even for the simplest of social phenomena. For example, behavior driven by norm or by status may have to be explained by an actor's preference on others' judgments bearing on his wage situation or his actions; these judgments may eventually be held and expressed by others because still others (usually the same ones) have opinions on these opinions, and so on; the structure is one of preferences on preferences on preferences, etc., with a theoretically infinite regress, which is yet *de facto* rapidly vanishing, characteristic of what norms and sociology really are. Yet, when applied to wages the final conclusion may just be (indirect) wage preferences. Another case is "minimizing *cognitive dissonance*" which happens to be directly a maximizing behavior, although not of the simplistic "self-interest" type. For example, I may experience "cognitive dissonance" because I think highly of myself while my wage is low. Then, Leon Festinger says, either I revise downwards my view of myself towards a more modest evaluation, or I try harder to raise my wage (by working harder, formation, search, strike, collusion, persuasion, etc.). The second case is behavior from a wage preference.

1.3.c. Freedom Wages

Individuals often have preferences about their (or others') freedom *not only* for the situation resulting from the specific choice that this freedom permits. Freedom is described by the possibility set. It is unambiguously increased or decreased when this set expands or is amputed. The most common case is a preference for more freedom, although the converse opinion sometimes results from costs of information and of choosing and from "choice anxiety" (or anguish). Now, a worker choosing his consumption-income y and his employment in quantity of labor ℓ in a labor market where he faces the given wage w and no employment constraint has the corresponding possibility set defined by $0 \leqslant y \leqslant w\ell$ (he happens to choose a $y = w\ell$ if he prefers more consumption-income or less work). This possibility set expands when w increases. Hence, it all depends on what one expects from the labor market. If one wants freedom to choose *per se*, one is interested in w. If one wants welfare, one is interested in y and ℓ (and only indirectly on w by the intermediary of the choice made). If one is concerned by both, one is interested in the three variables y, ℓ, w. Therefore, for a "rational" maximizer, the utility function is, in these three cases respectively, $u(w)$, $u(y, \ell)$, $u(y, \ell, w)$. The third argument of the latter function is a "preferred wage" called a "freedom wage" (similar reasonings on other markets yield preferences for "freedom prices").[7] If the individual is furthermore constrained in his employment by $\ell \leqslant \bar{\ell}$ with given $\bar{\ell}$, the same reasoning still holds.[8] Finally, an individual may care about his own freedom, or about the freedom of others and hence about others' wages, or both (he may in particular care about interindividual relative freedoms for equity reasons).[9]

1.3.d. Others' Wages Signaling Labor Supply Opportunities

Observed wages of others are usually taken by individual workers as important indications about the wage that they could obtain on the labor market, given their uncertainty about labor supply and possible wage-job opportunities. These wages of others thus influence the individual's search behavior, the time, energy, costs and income foregone he spends at it, his "reservation wage" at each time, and the wage and labor situation he finally settles for. For all these reasons, others' wages influence the individual's welfare and utility. This influence on behavior and utility can be modeled in detail by the classical models of search behavior. The effects of many of the outcomes are pecuniary: final income, income forgone, various material and money costs, etc. This however is not the case for all; for instance it is not the case for sentiments of hope, disappointment, frustration, surprise, etc. Through the latter, others' wages enter the utility function otherwise than by the intermediary of disposable income. In both cases, through elements additive to income (or subtracted from it) and otherwise, others' wages are in this manner parameters of the individual's utility.

For given employment prospects of the considered individual, the effect of these wages of others on utility for this reason is not likely to be monotonous. Indeed, other things being equal, the higher the observed relevant others' wages, the longer the search and the higher the finally accepted wage. Hence, too high others' wages induce too long a search and too low others' wages induce a too short one. Thus when the others' wages increase, they induce first a higher, then a lower utility.

1.3.e. Own Wage Inducing Search Activity

The decisions relative to search on the labor market also depend on one's own wage: one tends to search more when it is low and less when it is high, in relation to the wage one hopes to obtain (which may in particular be influenced by others' wages as just remarked and thus vary like them). Then the effects of this search, whether pecuniary (obtained wage, search costs and income forgone), or more directly psychic as described above, which depend on the individual's present wage, make this wage influence the individual's utility through them.

1.3.f. Present Wages Influence Future Preferences

An individual psycho-social wage preference at a given date often depends on his past wages, for reasons of habits, norm formation and sentiments of normalcy or of what is due, variations in status, comparison with others' present wages, (for example, I may be all the more jealous of their high wages that I had a high wage before myself), etc. Furthermore, a rational wage earner discounts his future utilities for his present choices and evaluations. Since his future utilities depend on his present wage for the reasons mentioned, that creates another reason for a wage preference on the current wage. This refers to sentiments and behavior concerning habit formations, progress, regrets, etc. We remark that these phenomena give essentially reasons for having a lower present wage.

1.3.g. Present Wages Influence Future Wages

Present wages influence future wages or incomes for a number of reasons. Then time discounting translates this effect as a wage preference. Future wages may be desired for all the reasons for which wages are desired, both for the income they directly allow and for all the other reasons considered here (in particular for their eventual influences on still later wages). We have already considered several reasons by which wages have this effect: search behavior induced by one's present wage, influence of the present wage on future preferences and norms and hence on future labor supply behavior on the labor market. There are still other reasons which we will consider.

1.3.h. Present Wages Influence Future Incomes Through Psycho-Social Considerations and the Ensuing Wage and Income-maintenance Policies

A widespread opinion holds that it is better that a wage-earner is not forced to decrease his consumption levels in a way which would notably modify his habits, lifestyle, and status. This is an opinion on variation and not on level only. It often influences wage settlements through decisions, arbitrations or compromise of various types. Furthermore, an individual who involuntarily ceases to work is often helped by an income maintenance scheme such as unemployment or disability compensations and old-age pensions. These incomes are usually related to past wages for the mentioned reasons (we do not consider here pure individual insurance or savings, either private or publicly implemented according to the individual's preferences). In all these manners, the present wage influences future wages and incomes and it thus influences forward-looking present utility.

1.3.i. Wages Signaling Productivity for Future Wages

A future employer who is uncertain about the worker's productivity may consider past wages as signalling the required capacities and motivations and adjust his offer of a wage (and employment) accordingly. This is a special case of taking a price as a quality indicator, a phenomenon which economists have considered since long (the references will be provided below). This specific application is also present in Greenwald's adverse selection models. However, since wages are also determined by fairness, custom, comparison with others' and past wages, and labor supply monopolizations (in particular unions), do they measure productivity? The answer is that they nevertheless do if the employers were wage takers free to hire and fire (as in most of the model presented below).

1.3.j. Collusion Wages

Another case where to accept too low a wage lowers future wages results from the sequential game theoretic structure of labor supply collusion. If a worker accepts a wage lower than others', he gains employment at the expense of others or he forces them to also accept lower wages. Then the others retaliate by withdrawing their support for the negotiation of this worker's future wage, which thus becomes lower than it would have been. This support is by collective action which could be explicit or tacit, and unionized or not. This situation is for example the structure of Sabourian's model (1988). It is but the inter-temporal manifestation of an explicit or implicit entente or collusion between workers, a detailed specification of the labor monopoly model.

To conclude the paragraph, a description of the wage-earners' satisfaction and behavior on the labor market which rests *only* on the substitution between income-consumption and leisure misses causes of satisfactions and of behavior which are crucial in the determination of wages and of employment, and it is an erroneous description of the relevant psychology, sociology, and economy. Wages are determined by ethics and status and not only by the economy, for freedom and not only for income, by reference to past wages and not only by forward-looking motivations, by others' wages not only because of substitutabilities and complementarities of labors in production, by their "sign" effects demonstrating success or rank and by their "signaling" of labor demand opportunities and labor supply productivity and not only for the income they procure directly. The addition of preferred wages is the minimal and first step correction of the classical model; it enables, by a simple and restricted complement, a notable progress towards realism.

1.4. "Voluntary" and "Involuntary" Unemployment: A Dubious and Useless Distinction

Unemployment resulting from such brakes in wage reductions or pushes in wage increases might not be called "involuntary." Now, the economic debate since Keynes has been polarized on this notion according to the principle that only "involuntary unemployment" eventually justifies public intervention, notably macroeconomic, to reduce it, with the implication accepted by all the protagonists that such measures would be unfounded if the unemployment were only "voluntary." Now this kind of idea cannot be maintained for a series of reasons which can be grouped in two categories.

On the one hand, it is possible that no unemployment is classified as "involuntary," or that the unemployment could be classified as voluntary, and that a *public action*, notably by a general reflation of the economy, could *improve the lot of everyone*. This is the case, for example, if there is equilibrium in the labor market and an excess supply in the goods market (with a reflation which will increase real wages). Or, again, if a wage threshold is considered as being part of the labor supply curve and if the labor demand curve intersects the former in this zone. And the model presented below shows other examples in this category.

Furthermore, we shall see that unemployment resulting from the behaviors described above cannot in general come from the individual behavior of the workers if they compete with one another. It can arise only because of an agent disposing of market power (for example, a union) or because of the government. This unemployment thus at once is the realization of the desires of the workers (thus it is "voluntary") and is imposed by force on the individual workers (thus it is "involuntary").

Indeed, the term "voluntary" or "involuntary" is totally *ambiguous for several reasons*. To start with, a *union* might maintain a monopoly wage with the unanimous accord of the workers each of whom could be fully employed or partially or totally unemployed (and could receive unemployment transfers from the union or from other sources instigated by union pressure); the corresponding unemployment is thus involuntary by individual action and voluntary by collective action; public intervention can only restrain the wastage caused by the price-fixer monopoly, and this waste does not even exist if the union and the firms cooperate by efficient negotiation on wages and employment. Equally, theories of "implicit contracts" aiming to explain wage rigidities are led to consider *ex post* involuntary unemployment which isn't involuntary *ex ante* (that is, in the implicit contract). More profoundly, the idea in question derives a *normative* conclusion on what the government *should* do from consideration of what is or is not *voluntary*. Now, such reasoning must be sufficiently clear, explicit, and justified as much on the ground of the *social ethics* retained as on that of the underlying *psychology*. This is not the place to elaborate these considerations which are nonetheless fundamental. Let us just recall that the conclusion can depend on whether the objective is, for example, welfare or freedom and on the distribution of this welfare or on the specific definition of this liberty. Furthermore, any act has both voluntary and involuntary causes, and the modes of social influence are indeed particularly rich, complex, ambiguous, and subject to discussion when it concerns questions of norms or status. In particular, if an unemployed person refuses a job because he compares with wages of others, his unemployment is in a sense voluntary, but on the other hand his choice depends on the wage levels that serve as a reference and that are given to him. More subtly, the ways in which others form their opinions on the activity and wage of a person seeking recognition, approval, or status are a given for this individual. And more intimately, even, an individual's preferences are in general "involuntary" for him (especially in the West).[10]

It is not negligible to note that Keynes himself, who launched this debate (which remains, 50 years later, the fundamental debate of economic policy and has strongly marked these policies and thus the world), seems to contradict himself within a few lines on this subject. In Chapter 2 of the *General Theory*, he says "*the equality of the real wage and of the marginal disutility of labor corresponds to the absence of "involuntary" unemployment*" (pp. 37–38 of the first French edition), after having said that " "*voluntary" unemployment, due to legislation, social uses, worker coalitions, slow adaptations, or to the simple obstination of human nature leads to a wage which is higher than the marginal disutility of labor*" (p. 28) and having repeated that "*when a workers' corporation refuses to work at a wage lower than a certain real wage, that does not constitute involuntary unemployment*" (if "corresponds" means "if and only if," as it seems, there is contradiction, whereas there is not if it just means "implies"—since the text obviously sees the adjectives "voluntary" and "involuntary" as logical contradictories). This can only reinforce our argument that these notions should be abandoned in this context.

1.5. Modeling Objectives and Strategy

We will remain here as close as possible to the most usual concepts in economic analysis. The above considerations show that strict classicism is seriously lacking in realism, but they also indicate that the minimal non-classical trait, which permits description of a whole series of important and pertinent psychosocioeconomic facts and to analyze their economic consequences, consists in considering preferences on wages rates or influenced by them, in introducing wage rates into utility functions. More generally similar considerations lead to the introduction of prices directly into utility functions (many of the effects of norm, sign, signaling, status that we have described for wages also exist for certain prices, notably for the sellers).[11] This by itself entails drastic consequences for the relations between equilibrium and the normative aspect. Indeed, *market equilibria are no longer Pareto-efficient* (even if each wage earner has such preferences only on his own wage, without "externalities"). Thus, the efficient states are disequilibria. In particular, with preferences for higher wage rates at a given income, *efficiency implies the existence of a certain unemployment at given wages, and which in this sense seems to be "involuntary."*

The objective of this paper is to derive the consequences for employment and policy of those phenomena mentioned above that can be sufficiently described by introducing wage rates in utility functions. It is not to analyze in detail the structure and origins of these influences of wages on present behaviors and evaluations. Such a task would be enormous. For an overwhelming majority of the mentioned phenomena it would concern preference formation in the realm of psychology and socio-psychology (not economics). The cases, mentioned above, where standard economic analysis can provide an important part of the explanation of this relation, for wages signaling the opportunities or the productivity, are on the whole far less important than the others, as the general overview shows. In addition, we have noticed that in reality these "purely economic" relations are closely intermingled with other psychic and social ones which cannot be reduced to such a naked and simplistic self-interest. And it would be a sterile exercise to take one very specific reason of influence and try to infer from it rather general conclusions concerning fiscal policy—which is the objective. Finally, introducing wages in present utility functions either can sufficiently describe the specific case (sometimes under assumptions such as a stationary state) or can provide general indications and a reference and starting point for a more detailed and specific study.

2. The Model

The simplest model which permits us to analyze the logic of this question is macroeconomic (the microeconomic model adds and makes explicit a certain number of phenomena but its exposition is lengthy and it will be published by itself elsewhere[12]). We must, however, retain certain microeconomic traits such as a variable real wage and especially the utility function—if only to obtain the optimality properties. ℓ is the quantity of labor, w the wage rate, and $w\ell$ the wage income. The suppliers of labor, or wage earners, or employees, will be called "workers" (whatever the qualification and type of their work). y is their income and $u(y, \ell, w)$ is their utility function. The price of goods is taken to be equal to 1 (w is therefore the real wage), and the labor ℓ produces the quantity $f(\ell)$ (we will introduce later on a productivity effect of the wage in noting the production $f(\ell, w)$). The functions u and f are assumed to be differentiable to the second order. We denote $a = -u'_\ell/u'_y$ and $b = -u'_w/u'_y$. We remark that b—a marginal willingness to pay for a wage rate—has the *dimension of labor* or of *unemployment*; as a result it will in general appear in the formulas through the sum $\ell + b$ or the ratio b/ℓ which is comparable to a *rate of unemployment*. We have $f' > 0$ and we assume $f'' < 0$ (we may consider that a second factor of production—the capital—is fixed in this study).

The fact that u depends on y (which is, for example, also the consumption of the workers) and on ℓ is classic with $u'_y > 0$ and $u'_\ell < 0$ and thus $a > 0$. The third argument of u describes various effects of norm, status, sign, and signaling etc., of the wage rate described in the previous section. When such effects pass by the wage income $w\ell$ rather than by w, we include them in the effect of $w\ell$ on u through the intermediary of y (this implies that when y contains other elements such as the addition of profits or the withdrawal of taxes—see below—this effect concerns in fact y). Similarly, along with the most classical effect of ℓ on u resulting from the occupation of time by working (less time for leisure), the formulation can also describe the effect of the painfulness of labor and also, inversely, any desirable effect of work, examples of which are described above (all in all therefore we could have $a > 0$). The preferences concerning the wage rate for the reasons indicated above tend to favor a higher wage. But three categories of important facts and variables, which the corresponding microeconomic model explains completely, remain necessarily implicit in the global version presented here: relative wages, the sharing of total work, and, when necessary, the relations between workers and their union (and similarly a situation of monopoly among firms).

The preferences concerning the *comparison of wages* cannot be presented explicitly here because there is only one wage rate, w. This influence of w on u can however describe such preferences, but we must then distinguish according to whether the kind of externality constituted by the fact that the wage of one person concerns another (whoever determines the wage) is internalized or is not. This distinction cannot explicitly appear with the aggregated variables considered here, but it leads to different values for b. For instance, if the workers act in an individualistic fashion in attempting to press for increases in their wage while taking the others' wages as given, the preferences on relative wages to be used for explaining behavior lead in total to $b > 0$. But if all the wages are adjusted proportionately together, preferences concerning only relative wages remain indifferent from this viewpoint so that $b = 0$ (but the preferences may bear on other variables than only ratios of wages, and other wage preferences may also exist in addition and lead to $b > 0$).[13] These collective internalizing actions could be due to a union or to a public policy (including fiscal incentives). This distinction, however, will not pose any problems below, since the individualistic behavior (without a labor union or a specific public policy) that we shall consider is that of perfect competition, and we will show that in this case the variable b as such does not intervene in the result, whether this be competitive equilibrium (on condition that b is a continuous function of the wage), or the "efficiency" choice by firms the possibility of which is introduced from Section 10 onward (cf. section 11). We will also see symmetrically that b does not intervene as such in the optimal fiscal policy in the presence of a general union monopoly. It will thus intervene only in the optimal fiscal policy in a situation of competition, and in monopolistic union behavior without public intervention, and in both these cases the relevant b will be the "internalized" one.

Only the disaggregated model allows one to distinguish which persons *work more or less and which ones do not work at all.* The aggregated model can suppose $\ell > 0$, with also $w > 0$. And since the relevant cases for $b \neq 0$ are with $b > 0$, we can assume $\ell + b > 0$. Furthermore several cases can arise concerning the existence of an effective constraint $p \geqslant 0$ (nonloss or nonfailure). It is possible that such a constraint would not be effective in the encountered states. Moreover, a $p < 0$ could be possible with a deficit covered by the owners, or by savings or public transfers, according to the case. However, such a constraint can also be real, profit maximizing firms then choosing $\ell = f = p = 0$ rather than incurring a loss. Finally, for simplicity, we will consider only the first-order conditions of behaviors and optimalities. The definitions of optimality and the variables of the fiscal policy will be introduced further below.

We will consider *four structures of the labor market*, according to whether supply and demand are in a state of perfect competition or of monopoly (one case being thus the bilateral monopoly which is supposed efficient). A competitive labor supply is represented by the supply of ℓ that maximizes u at a given w. The monopolization of the labor supply is considered to be done by a union that maximizes u where ℓ and w are variable. The microeconomic basis of this structure is what we call an "efficient or rational union," that is to say a union that defends a group by not making a decision if another alternative exists in which each member of the group would be better satisfied (with the possibility that some members may be left indifferent). This can represent either just cooperative behavior within this group, or the institution of a labor union which cannot be defeated by unanimous vote among the members of the group. We assume also that this group—which is in fact always larger than strict union membership—consists of all the suppliers of labor, and that this union can effect or ensure transfer payments between them, notably from those who have a job to the unemployed (this could come from solidarity contributions, or unemployment insurance premiums collected by the employer or the government according to a procedure put in place in particular under union pressure).

An important question that arises is what becomes of the *mechanisms and outcomes of competition*, and, in particular, *perfect competition, when prices (or wages) figure directly in the preference or production functions*. Consider, for example, a worker who is partially unemployed, i.e., he would like to work more at the existing wage rate. Consider also that he has a direct preference on his wage rate for any of the reasons indicated above, a preference that makes him prefer a higher wage rate (at a given income). Can this former preference not prevent the worker from proposing to work at a lower wage, or from accepting such a proposition, which would result in the existence of some unemployment? One conclusion is that such a consequence does not normally occur in the conditions of perfect competition if the effect of the wage on the utility is smooth. And as a consequence, perfect competition is inefficient because it prevents the outcome from being influenced by this effect of wages.

This question will be analyzed in Section 11 only, in order to include at once the preference and productivity effects of wages which have from this viewpoint a similar logic. It will be shown that properly defined competitive conditions can lead to *two types of situations* and that if there is *in effect competition on both sides* of the market we obtain the classical *equilibrium* of perfect competition in the sense of equality between supply and demand at parametric prices (wages). But there might also be a situation without effective competition on one side of the market (without there being either monopolistic collusion to any degree), because the corresponding agents choose without constraint the prices (wages) and quantities (of labor) that maximize their utility or profit. This implies that the other agents accept these prices and quantities (for example, they do not collude to threaten complete withdrawal and negotiate from this point). For instance, if there is a productivity effect of wages, such a situation is the "efficiency wages" equilibrium resulting from the firms' choice unconstrained by the labor supply (thus with employment not larger than labor supply at this wage if the workers are wage takers). The second category of situations of this type would be a symmetrical unconstrained choice of wages and employment by the workers. But that would imply $\ell + b > 0$, which is impossible with $\ell > 0$ and $b \geqslant 0$, and thus this case is excluded. In particular, with no productivity effect of wages and $b > 0$, only the competitive equilibrium can exist. The essence of the reason why the effects of competitive mechanisms may remain unchanged is that if one agent who cannot buy or sell all that he wishes at the given prices moves his prices slightly toward equilibrium levels without his competitors acting likewise, the possibility that he subsequently acquires to buy or sell the quantities he wishes, or to crowd out his competition, procures an advantage for him that is of a higher order of magnitude than that of the variation in price, whereas the preference or productivity effects of wages and prices, supposed continuous, are of the same order of magnitude as this variation.

3. The Private Economy Equilibria

Let us consider in this situation the behavior of the private economy (no public finance) in the four cases of the labor market structure. We have $y = w\ell + y_0$ (where y_0, which can be zero, is a given income for the workers).

The labor supply maximizes u at a given w: it is $\ell = \ell_s(w)$, which verifies $a(\ell, w) - w = 0$ for $\ell_s > 0$.

The labor demand maximizes the profit P at a given w: it is $\ell = \ell_d(w)$, which verifies $w = f'(\ell)$, with $\ell'_d = 1/f'' < 0$, for $\ell_d > 0$. Depending on the case, a condition $p \geqslant 0$ might have to be added (with $\ell_d = 0$ if $\max_\ell p < 0$).

The four cases of labor market structure are the following:

1. The perfect competition equilibrium is ℓ and w, which verify $\ell = \ell_d(w) = \ell_s(w)$, and thus $w = a = f'$.

2. The monopoly of the labor supply maximizes u under the constraint $\ell = \ell_d(w)$ (if there is not an effective relevant constraint $p \geqslant 0$). The solution thus verifies

$$(w - a)\ell'_d + \ell + b = 0. \tag{1}$$

The signs of $\ell + b$ and ℓ'_d imply that $w > a$.

We can specify the effect of the preferences on employment and on unemployment by that of b taken as an independent parameter on ℓ and on $\ell_s - \ell$. Assuming, at least locally, that the marginal disutility of labor a depends only on labor ℓ and not on y or w (thus on the preference effects of wages), the differentiation of (1) gives

$$d\ell/db = -[2 - a'\ell'_d - (\ell + b)\ell''_d/\ell'^2_d]^{-1},$$

and we have $d(\ell_s - \ell_d)/db = (f''/a' - 1)\cdot d\ell/db$ if $a' \neq 0$ (since ℓ_s is defined by $a(\ell_s) = w = f'(\ell)$). The case $a' = 0$ is the structure where labor supply consists in $a =$ constant for $\ell \leqslant \bar{\ell}$ where $\bar{\ell}$ is full employment at $w = a$.[14] The case $a' \geqslant 0$ is the normal hypothesis. Then $d\ell/db < 0$ and $d(\ell_s - \ell_d)/db > 0$ if $\ell''_d \leqslant 0$. But $\ell''_d = -f'''/f''^2$. Therefore $d\ell/db < 0$ and $d(\ell_s - \ell_d)/db > 0$ if $f''' \leqslant 0$: *Wage preferences reduce employment and increases unemployment if* $f''' \leqslant 0$.

Let us say that we are in the linear case when $u = u(y, \ell, w)$ has a linear specification in ℓ and in y and when ℓ_d is linear. Then $a' = 0$ and $\ell''_d = 0$, from which $d\ell/db = -1/2$. If then $\ell_d = -\alpha w + \beta$ where α and β are positive constants, we have $\ell = (\beta - \alpha a - b)/2$. A $b \neq 0$ measures the preference effect of wages. Therefore, *the preference effect of wages reduces employment by half the value of this effect*. If labor supply is of the type $\ell \leqslant \bar{\ell}$, unemployment is increased by this amount.

3. The monopoly of the labor demand maximizes the profit $p = f - w\ell$ under the constraint $\ell = \ell_s(w)$, from which $f' - w = \ell/\ell'_s$, which implies $w < f'$ with a normal $\ell'_s > 0$ (if there is not an effective relevant constraint $p \geqslant 0$).

4. The efficient bilateral monopoly gives

$$\frac{du}{d\ell}\bigg/\frac{du}{dw} = \frac{dP}{d\ell}\bigg/\frac{dP}{dw},$$

from which we deduce

$$\frac{b}{\ell} = \frac{f' - a}{v - f}.$$

A particular case is the one in which the union monopoly of labor supply dominates the global labor demand but cannot put the firms into failure because they would choose $\ell_d = 0$; the solution then is max u under $P = 0$. Furthermore, the general condition obtained shows that if $b = 0$, $f' = a$. And if $b > 0$, $w > f' > a$. We have then $\ell_d < \ell < \ell_s$, which is to say there is at once an excess supply of labor and an excess employment in the firms (given the wages), in this sense simultaneously underemployment and overemployment.

This excess employment $\ell > \ell_d$ can occur when there is only one firm or when a union of employers can impose this overemployment on its members (this condition being part of the agreement between them). But in reality such a situation of overemployment arises sometimes under the pressure of employees and their unions, or of public authorities, or of public opinion. This scenario seems to be very rare in North America; it exists in a number of European countries but only to a very limited extent if of a durable nature and short lived if the phenomenon is relatively important (this overemployment may be more common in socioeconomic systems of the liberal corporatist kind—Scandinavia and Austria—or of the "communitarian" kind of various types—from Switzerland to Japan—but even this is not sure since wage rates are also more flexible in these countries than in most other European ones). The usual situation encountered in market economies, however, is the exercise of the *right to hire and fire* by individual firms, whence, if they take the wage rate w as given, $f' \geqslant w$. We will assume in the rest of this study that this is the case. A symmetrical condition that excludes forced labor at given wages, $\ell \leqslant \ell_s$, and thus $w \geqslant a$, would not be effective in the analyses that follow up to Section 10, and we can thus abstain from writing it (it will have to be explicit only in Section 10).

4. The General Model

We want to know if, in these situations, the government should intervene, and, if affirmative, what policy should be implemented. In particular, the existence of unemployment at given wage rates poses the question of the utility or the necessity of a fiscal policy. On the other hand if this unemployment is indeed "voluntary," that suggests that this policy would be unnecessary or damaging. These at least are the conclusions that one can draw from current discussions in economics. We shall see that a certain fiscal policy must exist, even in a situation of perfect competition. We shall see, furthermore, that what ordinarily thwarts the possibilities of fiscal policies, public budget constraints and nonzero marginal tax rates (or subsidies), on the contrary in this case allows this policy to achieve the first best optimum (under the constraint of freedom to hire).

The model presented here describes together different possible types of societies which differ according to which agents matter and to the distribution of profit. There are four possible types of agents. (1) The "workers," who could eventually receive some profit. (2) The nonworkers, who may not be present. (3) The firms, which maximize their net profits (after transfer payments and taxes) and are free to hire and fire. (4) The government, which can take money from certain agents and distribute it to others directly or by buying the production of some goods (in particular public ones) which benefits them. But only the workers and the nonworkers can be final agents. The government is the optimizing agent, which implies a definition of the optimum (section 5) and of the policy instruments (section 7).

The production function will be temporarily written as $f(\ell, w)$ instead of $f(\ell)$ so that we can apply the results to the case where wages have a productivity effect which we will be considering in sections 10 and 11 (note that this productivity effect of wages is more general than the particular effect on labor-augmenting effort $f = \varphi[e(w) \cdot \ell]$). We designate by τ, with indices, the transfers relative to the three types of agents: firms τ_p, workers τ_w, and nonworkers τ_c. These will be in section 5 the lump sum transfer payments defining optimality, and in section 6 taxes, subsidies, or public expenditures, functions of the other variables of the model (based on them). τ can have any sign and we count $\tau > 0$ as taken from the agents' income, as a tax, so that $\tau < 0$ is a transfer of $-\tau$ in their favor.

The profit is distributed with amounts P_c going to nonworkers and P_w to workers, and $\tau_p(\gtrless 0)$ is taken from it, so that before-transfers profit is

$$P = f(\ell, w) - w\ell = P_c + P_w + \tau_p.$$

The final income of the nonworkers is

$$r = P_c - \tau_c.$$

The final income of the workers is

$$y = w\ell + P_w - \tau_w,$$

and their utility is $u(y, \ell, w)$.

This can describe different types of societies and each type can have three sorts of ethical status. Its existence can be considered as a social fact which is given to the optimization and the policy under consideration. It can also be considered *a priori* as optimal. Or yet again this type of society can result from the optimization. In a *pure wage society*, the nonworkers do not exist (pure capitalists, owners, or "rentiers") and $P_c = \tau_c = 0$. In a *pure class society*, the workers receive no profit, $P_w = 0$—and the τ's may be all zero (no government intervention) or may not be so. In a *pure state socialist society*, no profit is distributed privately, and there are no nonworkers, $P_c = P_w = \tau_c = 0$. In a a society of *pure people's capitalism* or of *pure self-management*, $P_c = \tau_w = \tau_p = \tau_c = 0$, thus $P = P_w$ (the difference between these two is that in the case of self-management the workers receive the profit of their own firm).

We have in addition the four following possible constraints:

1. We consider cases where the firms maximize their profits (or minimize losses), are wage-takers as a result of competition or because a monopoly of labor supply imposes it, and are free to hire and fire. This freedom to hire and terminate employment can be, from a normative perspective, either a de facto constraint on optimization, of a political or sociological nature (or perhaps out of necessity for economic efficiency), or else an ethical priority because it is a manifestation of the freedom to exchange. Consequently, $f_1(\ell, w) = w$.

2. We may or may not have a constraint $P - \tau_p = P_w + P_c \geqslant 0$. Its presence is the condition of nonfailure or nonloss after transfers. But it might not be effective, or the financing by the owners of firms or from savings can permit $P_w + P_c < 0$.

3. We may or may not have the restriction $r \geqslant 0$. It indicates that the income of the nonworkers cannot be negative. It might not be effective. The case $r = 0$ or $P_c = \tau_c$ could imply the *disappearance* of the category nonworkers (then $P_c = \tau_c = 0$). But if the nonworkers possess other wealth or other revenues not considered explicitly here, $r < 0$ could be possible.

4. We may or may not have a constraint $y > 0$. A $y \leqslant 0$ implies that the workers have other sources of revenue not considered explicitly here. If this is not the case, $y > 0$ is a necessary condition for the survival of the workers. This is in fact a condition for the maximand.

We must now consider two questions. On the one hand the definition and characterization of the optimum optimorum (under the above conditions) and on the other hand the existence of specific market structures and the optimal public policy with instruments which can be functions of the state of the economy.

We also consider a "social welfare function" or "social maximand," a function of the utilities of the final agents, $W(u, r)$, with the derivatives $W_1 > 0$ and $W_2 \geqslant 0$. The case $W_2 \equiv 0$ means that no value is attached to the revenue of the the nonworkers (which leads to $r = 0$ and in fact to $P_c = \tau_c = 0$). Let us note that this maximizing criterion is not necessarily "welfarist" since the outcome can also represent that of a putative agreement between agents using their legitimate rights which is the principle of a social ethic based on liberty (liberal social contract).[15]

5. General Optimality

The criterion we retain for first best optimality is the maximization of W under the conditions indicated in the previous section and for the variables ℓ, w and the lump sum transfers between agents (workers, nonworkers, and firms). The lump sum transfers are denoted θ, replacing the τ of the previous section, with $\theta_p + \theta_w + \theta_c = 0$.

The optimum is thus defined by the *Program* Ω:

$$\max_{\ell, w, \theta_p, \theta_w, \theta_c} \quad W[u(y, \ell, w), r]$$

under

$$y = w\ell + P_w - \theta_w$$

$$r = P_c - \theta_c$$

$$P = f(\ell, w) - w\ell = P_c + P_w + \theta_p$$

$$\theta_p + \theta_w + \theta_c = 0$$

$$f_1(\ell, w) - w = 0$$

$r \geqslant 0$ or absence of this condition

$y > 0$ or absence of this condition

$P_w + P_c = P - \theta_p \geqslant 0$ or absence of this condition.

If $r = 0$, the conditions give

$$y = w\ell + P_w - \theta_w = f - P_c - \theta_p - \theta_w = f - \theta_c - \theta_p - \theta_w = f,$$

and if a constraint $r \geqslant 0$ is binding or if $r \equiv 0$, the maximand becomes

$$u[f(\ell, w), \ell, w].$$

If there is no such constraint attained, and in particular if $r > 0$ at the optimum, a small increase of θ_w by $\epsilon \lesseqgtr 0$ and a small diminution of θ_c by ε, with $|\varepsilon|$ being sufficiently small so that the conditions $r \geqslant 0$ and $y > 0$ remain respected, on the one hand respect all constraints, on the other increase W by $(W_2 - W_1 u_1) \cdot \varepsilon$. Since ε can have either sign, at the maximum of W we have $W_2 = W_1 u_1$. Therefore the first order conditions of the program Ω are the same as those of the maximization, for the same variables and under the same conditions, of

$$u(y + r, \ell, w) = u(f - \theta_p - \theta_c - \theta_w, \ell, w) = u[f(\ell, w), \ell, w],$$

which is the same result as in the previous case.

Proposition. In all the cases considered, the optimum maximizes

$$u[f(\ell, w), \ell, w].$$

6. The Optimality Condition

Let us go back to the absence of productivity effect of wages: $f = f(\ell)$, $w = f'(\ell)$.

In all the cases considered the optimum is the maximum of $u[f(\ell), \ell, f'(\ell)]$. Hence the condition

$$f' - a + bf'' = 0 \tag{2}$$

which shows the optimal wage gap

$$w - a = -bf''. \tag{2'}$$

$b > 0$ and $f'' < 0$ then give $w > a$.

Thus, with a norm-status-sign role of wages *the optimum requires the existence of "involuntary" unemployment.* The intuitive reason is that this unemployment allows a higher wage rate w, and a higher wage rate is also desired per se by the workers.

This shows that the *competitive equilibrium* ($w = f' = a$) *is not optimal.* But the *monopoly of the labor supply is not either* since in this case, according to equation 1,

$$w - a = -(\ell + b) f''. \tag{1'}$$

These results have a straightforward geometric representation in a plane (ℓ, w). Call A and B the points on the labor demand curve and on the labor supply curve, respectively, with the same employment ℓ. Call C the point where the tangent to the labor demand curve at A intersects the line at constant w passing through B. Then, at the optimum $CB = b$, with the labor union monopoly $CB = \ell + b$ [and, in the case considered below with a productivity effect of wages $f(\ell, w)$ with $\delta f/\delta w = f_2$, at the optimum $CB = b + f_2$].

These conditions imply the following results.

Proposition. Let us consider a positive wage preference effect $b > 0$, $w = f'(\ell)$, $f'' < 0$ and an $a[f(\ell), \ell, f'(\ell)]$ which is a nondecreasing function of ℓ (for example, a depends only on its second argument and this inverse labor-supply function is nondecreasing). Then the optimum requires "involuntary" unemployment, and a lower employment and a higher wage than at full employment. And if $f''(\ell)$ does not increase too fast (in particular if $f''' \leqslant 0$—a concave demand curve—with a constant b), employment is higher, the wage rate is lower, and "involuntary" unemployment is lower at the optimum than with a monopoly of labor supply.

Let us consider, for example, the linear case where a and b are constants and $\ell_d(w) = -\alpha w + \beta$ where α and β are positive constants. In using c, o, and m as indices for competitive, optimal, and monopoly of labor supply, we obtain

$$w_c = a, \qquad w_0 = a + b/\alpha, \qquad w_m = [a + (b + \beta)/\alpha]/2,$$

$$\ell_c = \beta - \alpha a, \qquad \ell_0 = \beta - \alpha a - b, \qquad \ell_m = (\beta - \alpha a - b)/2.$$

We remark that, in this case, $\ell_0 = \ell_c - b$: *the competitive employment level is too high by an amount equal to the wage preference effect.* (We also have $\ell_0 = 2\ell_m$, this very small ℓ_m in this case resulting from an extreme trait which is the constancy of a—that is to say a horizontal labor supply "à la Marx.")

As for economic policy, the results obtained show that the optimum can be realized by a *minimum wage* in the case of competition, and in the indicated case by a *maximum wage* in a situation of monopoly. But fiscal policy is more commonly used to influence employment. What can it do? Can it achieve the optimum? And what should it be?

7. First Best Optimality of the Distortionary Fiscal Policy with a Balanced Budget

We consider now a group of public expenditures, subsidies, and taxes. In traditional Keynesian macroeconomics, when there is involuntary unemployment in the Keynesian sense, the optimal fiscal policy that should be applied tends to imply a budget deficit. In microeconomic analysis of efficiency, nonzero marginal tax rates prevent the realization of optimality ("first best," in the absence of external effects). Now, we shall see that under the usual conditions, with the "involuntary" unemployment encountered here, *fiscal policy* can reach the *(first best) optimum*, not only with a *balanced budget* and with *nonzero marginal tax rates*, but indeed thanks to this balanced budget and these nonzero marginal tax rates.

The τ of the general presentation of Section 4 becomes taxes-subsidies-expenditures T. A tax or a subsidy is subtracted from or added to an income, whatever the tax base (which always has a certain relation with the receiver of this income). Given an *income* x, we will denote T_x a tax subsidy deduced from or added to the income x, the after tax subsidy income being $x - T_x$, so that $T_x > 0$ measures a tax and $T_x < 0$ measures a subsidy of $-T_x$. Another public expenditure benefiting the corresponding agents will be counted here as a subsidy.

If z is a tax *base* of T_x, we have $T_x(z)$. $T_x'(z)$ is the marginal tax subsidy which is a marginal tax if $T_x'(z) > 0$ and a marginal subsidy of $-T_x'(z)$ if $T_x'(z) < 0$. Similarly, $T_x(0)$ is a lump sum tax subsidy which is a lump sum tax if $T_x(z) > 0$ and a lump sum subsidy of $-T_x(0)$ if $T_x(0) < 0$.

The *incomes from which T_x is deducted or to which $-T_x$ is added* are here the profit P, with a T_x that we denote T_P; the workers' income $w\ell + P_w$, with a T_x that we denote simply as T; and the nonworkers' income P_c, with a T_X denoted as T_c. That does not prejudge for the moment the tax bases.

The after tax or subsidy incomes are $y = w\ell + P_w - T$ for the workers, and $r = P_c - T_c$ for the nonworkers, and the after tax or subsidy profit is $\Pi = P - T_P = f - w\ell - T_P = P_w + P_c$.

The balance of the public budget is $T + T_c + T_P = 0$. But, in fact, the government is submitted here to the constraint $T + T_c + T_P \geqslant 0$ (it might not spend some of the fiscal returns). We discuss questions of money and of the public debt in Section 9. The taxes-subsidies are *a priori* based on the corresponding incomes. $T_P = T_P(P)$, $T_c = T_c(P_c)$, $T = T(w\ell, P_w)$. This last case allows representation of a different taxation of the workers' income coming from wages and from profits, but the tax base can in particular be written as $w\ell + P_w$, or it can contain the three variables $w\ell$, P_w, and $w\ell + P_w$ as is the case in reality, or it can contain only two of these variables. We consider, since it is a faithful representation of reality, that P_w *is parametric for the behavior of individual workers or of their unions in the labor market*. A different hypothesis would signify that the workers or their unions take into account, in these behaviors, their effects on the profit P

because of the part P_w of P which eventually goes to the workers. Now this in fact does not take place except in the case, which we exclude, of collective actions at the firm level by workers who receive a share of the profits of their company (profit-sharing schemes or self-management systems). Let us note furthermore that $P_w = 0$ is often a good model, that interest revenus (from bonds) included in P_w do not depend on P (except in the case of failure), and in any case the individual choice of a worker regarding his job and his wage has no appreciable effect on the fraction of the global profits that he receives. We denote $t = \partial T/\partial(w\ell)$.

Fiscal policy can *a priori* intervene in the optimization by two different structural paths. (1) Its taxes and expenditures can influence the situation obtained, characterized here by ℓ and w. (2) They can directly influence the maximand W. To take an example, with the taxes-subsidies based on the mentioned incomes, $W\{u[w\ell + P_w - T(w\ell, P_w), \ell, w], P_c - T_c(P_c)\}$ depends on the functions $T(\;)$ and $T_c(\;)$ not only through their effects on the ℓ and w realized, but also directly because these functions figure in the maximand. We are going to see, however, that this second effect disappears.

In the rest of this section we return to the production function $f(\ell, w)$ instead of $f(\ell)$ to take into account the possibility of a productivity effect of wages which will be introduced from Section 10 and following.

The problem is to determine the optimal fiscal functions $T(\;)$, $T_c(\;)$, $T_P(\;)$. They are the solution to the following program, which is discussed further below.

Program Ω':

$$\max_{T(\;),T_c(\;),T_P(\;)} W\{u[w\ell + P_w - T(w\ell, P_w), \ell, w], P_c - T_c(P_c)\}$$

under the conditions

1. *either* (α)

$$\ell = \arg\max_{\ell \geqslant 0} u[w\ell + P_w - T(w\ell, P_w), \ell, w]$$

$$= \arg\max_{\ell \geqslant 0} \{f(\ell, w) - w\ell - T_P[f(\ell, w) - w\ell]\}$$

$$\text{eventually if } f(\ell, w) - w\ell - T_P[f(\ell, w) - w\ell] \geqslant 0$$

or (β)

$$(\ell, w) = \arg\max \mathrm{u}[w\ell + P_w - T(w\ell, P_w), \ell, w]$$

$$\ell \geqslant 0, w \geqslant 0$$

$$\ell = \arg\max_{\ell \geqslant 0} \{ f(\ell, w) - w\ell - T_P[f(\ell, w) - w\ell] \}$$

eventually $f(\ell, w) - w\ell - T_P[f(\ell, w) - w\ell] \geqslant 0$

2. $f(\ell, w) - w\ell = P_c + P_w + T_P[f(\ell, w) - w\ell]$
3. $T(w\ell, P_w) + T_c(P_c) + T_P[f(\ell, w) - w\ell] \geqslant 0$
4. $P_c - T_c(P_c) \geqslant 0$, or absence of this condition
5. $w\ell + P_w - T(w\ell, P_w) > 0$, or absence of this condition
6. $W_1 > 0$, $W_2 \geqslant 0$, $u_1 > 0$, plus the properties of concavity required for W and u.

One result is the following property:

Proposition. If there exists a function F from R to R with $F' > 0$ and a function v from R^2 to R, such that

$$F[u(y, \ell, w)] \equiv y + v(\ell, w) \quad (3)$$

the program Ω' is equivalent to

$$\max_{T(\,), T_c(\,), T_P(\,)} \quad u[f(\ell, w), \ell, w]$$

under the conditions (1) to (6) for the first-order conditions.

The conditions and this result have the following meanings. The conditions 1 represent the two structures of the labor market considered: competition (α) or a rational union monopoly of labor supply (β). Condition 2 describes the profit and its distribution. Condition 3 is the public budget constraint. Condition 4 is the nonnegativity of the nonworkers' income. Condition 5, $y > 0$, is a minimal requirement for the *survival* of the workers. The condition (3) of the proposition is the classical "constancy of the marginal utility of income" (we have $v_1 = -a$ and $v_2 = b$). The proposition shows that *the fiscal functions no longer figure directly in the maximand,* that is to say they act only by their role of incentive in the realization of ℓ and w, and that *this maximand is that of the first best optimum;* thus the optimal fiscal policy is one that achieves the first best optimum (under freedom to hire and fire) if it can incite the agents to choose the corresponding ℓ and w.

Proof.

1. With the form (3), the conditions imply at the first order

$$f_1(\ell, w) - w = 0$$

for $\ell > 0$ and $T_P' < 1$, and, for $t < 1$, for (1α)

$$[1 - t(w\ell, P_w)] \cdot w + v_1(\ell, w) = 0,$$

and for (1β)

$$\frac{[1 - t(w\ell, P_w)] \cdot w + v_1(\ell, w)}{f_{11}(\ell, w)} = \frac{[1 - t(w\ell, P_w)] \cdot \ell + v_2(\ell, w)}{f_{12}(\ell, w) - 1}$$

or eventually $f(\ell, w) - w\ell - T_P[f(\ell, w) - w\ell] = 0$. These conditions determine ℓ and w in these two cases of market structure. We note that they depend on the fiscal functions only by $t(\ )$ and eventually $T_P(\ )$. This is therefore also true for these ℓ and w. In particular they do not depend on the addition or the subtraction of a constant to T or to T_c.

2. If the public budget constraint is not reached, that is, if condition 3 is verified with inequality $>$, let us reduce T by a small positive constant ε. According to the previous result that will not change the ℓ and w attained in the two market structures. Let us take a sufficiently small ε so that condition 3 remains respected. The maximand W is increased by $W_1 u_1 \varepsilon > 0$. Thus, at the optimum, condition 3 is with an equality, i.e., the public budget is balanced.

3. If the solution is with $r = 0$, then $P_c = T_c$ (whether or not they are equal to zero), and

$$y = w\ell + P_w - T = f - T_c - T_P - T = f(\ell, w)$$

according to condition 2 and to the preceding result. Thus, if a constraint $r \geqslant 0$ is binding (or if $r \equiv 0$), the optimum is the maximum of $W\{u[f(\ell, w), \ell, w], 0\}$ and thus that of $u[f(\ell, w), \ell, w]$.

4. If there is no constraint $r \geqslant 0$ binding (or $r \equiv 0$, thus in particular if $r > 0$, or $r < 0$ if it is possible), let us add to T, and subtract from T_c, a small constant ε of any sign. This transformation does not affect the functions $t(\ )$ and $T_P(\ )$, and, thus, according to the result of paragraph 1, the ℓ's and w's determined by the markets in the considered cases are not affected either. It respects condition 3 with equality. And we can thus choose a sufficiently small $|\varepsilon|$ so that constraints 4 (starting off from inequality) and 5 are respected. This transformation is thus compatible with the constraints, and it increases the maximand by $(W_2 - W_1 u_1) \cdot \varepsilon$. There-

fore at the optimum $W_2 = W_1 u_1$. It then follows that for the first-order conditions, the optimum maximizes

$$u(y + r, \ell, w) = u(w\ell + P_w + P_c - T - T_c, \ell, w)$$

$$= u(f - T_P - T - T_c, \ell, w) = u(f, \ell, w),$$

from condition 2 and the obtained result that the budget should be balanced.

Proposition. If the function $u(y, \ell, w)$ has a specification of the form $u = y + v(\ell, w)$, the optimal fiscal policy maximizes $f(\ell, w) + v(\ell, w)$. It follows that

1. The tax and expenditure functions do not figure directly in this maximand, they only intervene through their effects on the ℓ and w obtained.
2. The maximand is also that of the first best optimum (with free hiring and transfers), $u[f(\ell, w), \ell, w]$.
3. Therefore, if the fiscal policy can incite the ℓ's and w's chosen by the markets to be those of the first best optimum, it can assure this optimum.

The following section considers this capacity. We remark that this first best optimality of the fiscal policy is obtained *despite the constraint of a balanced public budget,* and *in spite of the possibility of nonzero marginal rates of taxes and subsidies.* Indeed, it is obtained *thanks to the balanced budget constraint,* as we have seen, and *thanks to nonzero marginal rates of taxes and subsidies,* as we shall see.

8. Effect of the Fiscal Policy and the Optimal Policy

Let us return in this section to the case of the $f(\ell)$ production function, with the condition of freedom to hire $w = f'(\ell)$. The workers maximize $u[w\ell + P_w - T(w\ell, P_w), \ell, w]$ with a parametric P_w. The resulting first best conditions are, in the case of competition,

$$(1 - t) \cdot w - a = 0,$$

and in the case of a monopoly of labor supply

$$(1 - t) \cdot w - a + [(1 - t) \cdot \ell + b] \cdot f'' = 0,$$

or

$$(1 - t)(f' + \ell f'') - a + bf'' = 0,$$

if there is no constraint $P - T_P \geqslant 0$ or if such a constraint is not binding. If such a constraint can exist, another solution in the situation of a monopoly union consists in adjusting T_P so that $P - T_P = 0$ at the optimum, and the best t is then indeterminate within the relevant limits; we now consider the other, first-mentioned solution, which is applicable in all cases and is more "decentralized" and "incentive"-using. Comparing the above results with the optimality condition (2), and denoting $\eta = w\ell_d'/\ell = w/\ell f''$ the elasticity of the labor demand, we obtain the optimal marginal tax rates or subsidies $t = t_c$ for competition and $t = t_m$ for the monopoly case,

$$t_c = -b/\ell\eta \tag{4}$$

and

$$t_m = 1/(1 + \eta) \tag{5}$$

where w and ℓ have their optimal values.

We have $t_c > 0$ since $\eta < 0$ and with $b > 0$, that is to say *the fiscal policy in a situation of competition should include a marginal tax*. Budgetary equilibrium implies then that there is also *lump sum public spending or transfers*.

Furthermore, since $\eta < 0$ and $t_m < 1$, the expression of t_m shows that we should have $t_m < 0$, meaning that *fiscal policy in the case of a monopolization of labor supply should include a marginal subsidy*.

We remark finally that t_c depends directly on b and is zero when b is. In contrast t_m does not depend directly on b (nor on a), and it depends on the function u only through the intermediary of ℓ and w.

This can doubtlessly be explained in the following manner. The working of competition forces the workers to take the equilibrium wages (with taxes if need be) as parameters (see section 10), so that they cannot manifest their wage preferences, and the fiscal policy must thus take these preferences into account. In contrast, a monopoly of labor supply chooses wages and thus takes into account these preferences, the result obtained shows that it takes them into account to a sufficient extent, and the fiscal policy can then content itself with the correction of the wastage effect caused by the monopolistic situation.

Proposition. The optimal fiscal policy in the presence of wage preferences and of the corresponding unemployment allows, in the indicated conditions, realization of the first best optimum in correcting both the corresponding inefficiencies of the markets (even competitive ones) and monopolistic inefficiencies. In the case of competition, it includes public expenditures or a lump sum transfer payment, and a marginal tax on the income of the workers at the rate of $-b/\ell\eta$, where b is the wage preference effect, ℓ is employment—thus b/ℓ is the relative wage preference effect on employment—and η is the elasticity of labor demand. In the case of a monopoly of labor supply, this policy includes a subsidy at the rate of $-1/(1+\eta)$, independent of the wage preference effect, which corrects the monopoly (which takes this effect into account spontaneously).

(In practice, such a subsidy increasing with income could consist in the reduction of already existing taxes.)

9. Introduction of Money and of the Public Deficit

The phenomena considered here are purely real but the macroeconomic viewpoint suggests consideration of the quantity of money. This can be an already existing stock, or credit money that monetizes the stock of capital (implicit) or a debt that might eventually adjust itself to the demand for money, and the general price level and this quantity may adjust to each other. We can also consider that the government issues the quantity of money m, measured in real value, necessary for the transactions and for the corresponding cash balances. This necessary m is for example function of the total production $f(\ell)$ (in the following section $f(\ell, w)$), perhaps also of the total wage income paid $w\ell$, etc. In all it is a function of ℓ and w, $m(\ell, w)$. Since the State issues this m, what changes is the public finance constraint which becomes $T + T_P + T_c + \mathrm{m} \geqslant 0$, where equality will be attained at the optimum. m appears then as a public *budget deficit* financed by an increase in the money supply, according to the usual accounting. By replacing, in the program Ω', the budget constraint (3) by this form, we find that the fiscal policy should maximize $u[f(\ell, w) + m(\ell, w), \ell, w]$. (Of course, more complete models would introduce cash balances in the utility or production functions, and the handling of the debt would have to be considered, which requires the introduction of temporality and dynamics.) The determination of the fiscal policy thus leads also to that of the optimal quantity of money and of the optimal public deficit.

10. Addition of a Productivity Effect of Wages: The Possible Cases

We call productivity effect of wages an effect of the wage rate on employees' working behavior and thus on the output for a given work force (and given other inputs). This phenomenon has been studied extensively by labor psychology and in sociological and labor relations studies and it has recently received some attention in economic theory in the discussion of "efficiency wages." The general formulation of this effect consists in writing the output as $f(\ell, w)$. The form $f \equiv \varphi[e(w) \cdot \ell]$ with an increasing $e(w)$ is used in recent economic discussions, but it is only a special case, the case of a "labor-augmenting productivity effect of wages," where a higher wage induces a change in working behavior the effect of which is equivalent to faster work if ℓ is measured by work time or to a larger work force if ℓ is measured by a number of workers. We write $f_1 \equiv \partial f/\partial \ell$, $f_2 \equiv \partial f/\partial w$, $f_{12} \equiv \partial f/\partial \ell\, \partial w$. We have $f_1 > 0$. We have seen in Section 1 that f_2 can have either sign, but we shall consider here $f_2 > 0$.

It is *a priori* possible that firms can choose $\ell = \bar{\ell}$ and $w = \bar{w}$ which maximize their profit $P = f(\ell, w) - w\ell$ without constraints. This "unconstrained efficiency" point $E = (\bar{\ell}, \bar{w})$ thus satisfies $f_1(\bar{\ell}, \bar{w}) = \bar{w}$ and $f_2(\bar{\ell}, \bar{w}) = \bar{\ell}$: *labor and the wage rate are each equal to the marginal productivity of the other*, and, in particular, *labor is equal to the marginal productivity of the wage rate*. If the firms can, they choose $\bar{\ell}$, $\bar{w}$ whether they are monopolistic or in competition. If $\bar{\ell} < \ell_s(\bar{w})$, this efficient choice of the firms brings in involuntary unemployment of $\ell_s(\bar{w}) - \bar{\ell}$, *even though the firms are not constrained either by the demand of their product or on their choice of wages*. But this maximization of P could be constrained either by the labor supply and the no-forced-labor condition—if the workers are price takers this happens when $\bar{\ell} > \ell_s(\bar{w})$, that is to say $\bar{w} < a(\bar{\ell}, \bar{w})$—or by product demand, or by monopolistic behavior of labor supply or of product demand. We will also denote $C = (\ell_c, w_c)$ the "competitive point," intersection of the labor supply and demand curves, with $w_c = f_1(\ell_c, w_c) = a(\ell_c, w_c)$.

We must thus move away from, or complete, the classical theory of efficiency wages (for example, Solow's original of 1979) for several reasons. On the one hand, it considered a constrained output, which would here be $f(\ell, w) = q$ at a given q, with the firm minimizing its cost $w\ell$, to show that, as a result of the productivity effect of wages, w could vary only by a little or not at all in response to variations of q. However, the case noted above, without this output constraint, and which nevertheless leads to involuntary unemployment, is an interesting one. Moreover, when the production is limited by the demand, for a macroeconomic model the interesting form considers that this demand depends on incomes, which gives a constraint $f = D(w\ell, P) + x$ (where x is an exogenous demand), of which we indicate the consequences below. Finally, the particular form of wage productivity $f = \varphi[e(w) \cdot \ell]$ is usually retained. It is this form that gives a w maximizing P, which is independent of the structure of the function D and thus of x (and therefore in particular independent of q, Solow's result). But this w (which is the unconstrained efficient w obtained when P is maximized without constraint on output) maximizes e/w as we have found in Section 1 (this result is usually presented for the case $f = q$, but it also applies to the more general case $f = D(w\ell + P) + x$ and to the unconstrained case). Even if labor supply prevents the occurrence of an "efficiency" solution unconstrained on the labor market, a productivity effect of wages giving $f(\ell, w)$ may be important.

The discussion of the various possible cases requires consideration of the following loci in the plane (ℓ, w), of which we indicate the meaning, the equation, properties, and the equation in the case where

$f(\ell, w) = \varphi[e(w)\cdot\ell]$ (thus $f_1 = e\varphi', f_2 = \ell e'\varphi'$).

10.1. Maximization of $P = f(\ell, w) - w\ell$

1. At a given w: $f_1 = w$, *the labor demand curve* $\ell = \ell_d(w)$, passes through C and E.

2. At a given ℓ: $f_2 = \ell$, *the wage efficiency curve at a given employment* passes through E; $e'\varphi' = 1$.

3. At $f = D(w\ell, P) + x$ where D is the demand for goods function of wage income $w\ell$ and of profit P and x is an autonomous demand: $w/f_1 = \ell/f_2$; the curves $f =$ constant, $P =$ constant, $D =$ constant, $w\ell =$ constant are tangent in this point where their slope is $-w/\ell$; when $D + x$ varies, whatever the deformation of D (and in particular when x varies), this point traces the *efficiency curve at product supply restricted by demand*; it passes *through* E; the same result is obtained if D depends only on the sum of its arguments, f, or depends only on one of them, or is constant (which describes the usual choice of individual firms for which the sales do not depend on the revenue they distribute); with $f = \varphi[e(w)\cdot\ell]$, $e(w)/w$ is maximum from which $e'w/e = 1$ (Solow's 1979 case was one of a firm with a given level of production).

4. At a given $u(w\ell, \ell, w)$: $(w - a)/(f_1 - w) = (\ell + b)/(f_2 - \ell)$, *bilateral monopoly contract curve*, passes through C, E, Δ (see below), but the effective part ends in E; $1 - a/w = (1 + b/\ell)(e\varphi'/w - 1)/(e\varphi' - 1)$.

5. At $w = a(\ell, w)$: $a_1/(f_1 - w) = (a_2 - 1)/(f_2 - \ell')$, *monopoly of labor demand.*

10.2. Maximization of $u = (w\ell, \ell, w)$

1. At a given w: $w = a$ *labor supply curve* $\ell = \ell_s(w)$, passes through C.

2. At a given ℓ: $\ell + b = 0$, *wage satiety*, inexistent if $b > 0$ throughout.

3. At $f = D(w\ell, P) + x$ defined as above:

$$\frac{w-a}{\ell+b}=\frac{(1-D_2)f_1-(D_1-D_2)w}{(1-D_2)f_2-(D_1-D_2)\ell}, \quad \text{and} \quad \frac{w-a}{f_1}=\frac{\ell+b}{f_2}$$

if D depends on $w\ell$ and P by their sum f as in Keynes or is constant; in these latter cases, if the autonomous demand x varies, this point describes the *curve of the best* (ℓ, w) *for the workers at Keynesian equilibria or at constrained demand*; with $f = \varphi[e(w)\cdot\ell]$ and $D =$ constant, we have $1 - a/w = (1 + b/\ell)\cdot e/e'w$.

4. At a given P: $(w - a)/(f_1 - w) = (\ell + b)/(f_1 - \ell)$, *bilateral monopoly contract curve*, passes through C, E, Δ: cf. supra.

5. At $f_1 = w$: $(w - a_1)/f_{11} = (\ell + b)/(f_{12} - 1)$, *labor supply monopoly*; $w - a = (\ell + b)e^2\varphi''/(\ell ee'\varphi' + e'\varphi' - 1)$.

6. At $f_2 = \ell$: $(w - a_1)/(f_{12} - 1) = (\ell + b)/f_{22}$, *labor supply monopoly fixing employment*; $w - a = (\ell + b)(\ell ee'\varphi' + e'\varphi' - 1)/\ell\cdot(e''\varphi' + \ell e'^2\varphi'')$.

Furthermore, when a constant $p \geqslant 0$ exists (with, for example, firms that choose $\ell = 0$ rather than $P < 0$), the intersections of the locus $P \geqslant 0$ and of the curve $P = 0$ with all the loci defined above can be relevant. For example, the pertinent point of the contract curve, where $P = 0$, Δ, represents the domination of workers unions, and the effective part of the contract curve is then $E\Delta$. Or the labor supply monopoly with wage-taking firms may have to stop at the pertinent point where the labor demand curve cuts $P = 0$. Similarly $P = 0$ can be the effective limit of a production with product supply limited by demand, or of a monopoly of labor demand, and a condition $P \geqslant 0$ can prevent competitive equilibrium.

In the plane (ℓ, w), these curves, their intersections, and these points are traced from the networks of the iso-profit curves $P =$ constant (centered at E), iso-utility curves $u =$ constant, and iso-product curves $f =$ constant. We deduce from this a series of possible situations according to the behaviors (monopoly or competitive), the existing constraints, and effective ones. For example, we can have a behavior of firms max P under two or three constraints, the effective demand $f \geqslant D + x$, labor supply $w \geqslant a(\ell, w)$, and eventually nonfailure $P \geqslant 0$, and one or the other can be effective. We will not present the entire discussion here but the following remark is necessary.

11. Competition with Prices or Wages in Utility or Production Functions

A partially unemployed worker may refuse to obtain more work at a lower wage if he has a direct preference for a higher wage. And a firm facing an excess supply of labor may refuse to lower its wage because of a productivity effect of wages. That shows that the working and the consequences of competitive mechanisms in the presence of preferences on wages and of productivity effects of wages require a special study. More generally, one has to investigate the working and consequences of competitive mechanisms when there are prices in utility or production functions. Let us note that there does not exist a complete and general theory of a perfectly competitive process (eventually leading to equilibrium) in the absence of the specific price effects which we consider here. We thus do not provide here such a complete and general theory. We intend only to show the crucial phenomena at work and their consequences. In particular, the conditions and reasons of the following proposition should be made somewhat precise.

Proposition. With twice differentiable effects of the wage on the otherwise well-behaved utility and production functions, a positive wage preference effect b, and an excess supply at wage level w having the sign of $w - w_c$, competitive mechanisms lead to the highest of the two wages: the equilibrium wage w_c and the efficiency wage $\bar{w}$. Thus, if the labor demand function is decreasing, the competitive mechanism leads to the smallest of the two employment levels: the equilibrium level ℓ_c and the efficiency level $\bar{\ell}$. In particular, if wages have only a preference effect and no productivity effect, which implies a decreasing labor demand function and $\bar{w} = 0$, with a nondecreasing labor supply function the competitive mechanisms lead to equilibrium.

One underlying phenomenon, which we shall make precise, is that price competition undercuts the behavioral manifestations of the preferences on the wage rate. This produces efficiency if preferences on the wage rate only pass through $w\ell$, and inefficiency if they also bear on w alone.

We now consider several firms, and several workers, with still a single type of labor and a single type of product with a price of 1. To simplify the presentation, we suppose that the norm-status-sign effect for a worker depends only on his own wage, that a firm pays the same wage rate to all its workers, and that the wage productivity effect for the firm depends only on this rate. The firm i employs the labor ℓ_i at the unit wage of w_i, it produces $f^i(\ell_i, w_i)$ and earns the profit $P^i(\ell_i, w_i) \equiv f^i(\ell_i, w_i) - w_i\ell_i$ (from which other costs not depending on these variables can be subtracted). The worker j works ℓ_j for a wage w_j and has a utility $u^j(w_j\ell_j, \ell_j, w_j)$. The f^i's and u_j's are twice differentiable (these functions and the supply and demand functions thus are continuous). f^i is a strictly concave function of ℓ_i

(because of other implicit factors of production); hence the same holds for P^i. u^j is increasing in $w_j\ell_j$ and strictly quasiconcave for $w_j\ell_j$ and ℓ_j. We define

$$(\bar{\ell}_i, \bar{w}_i) = \arg \max_{\lambda \geqslant 0, \mu \geqslant 0} P^i(\lambda, \mu)$$

$$\ell_i(w_i) = \arg \max_{\lambda \geqslant 0} P^i(\lambda, w_i)$$

$$\ell_j(w_j) = \arg \max_{\lambda \geqslant 0} u^j(w_j\lambda, \lambda, w_j)$$

$$U_j(w_j) = \max_{\lambda \geqslant 0} u^j(w_j\lambda, \lambda, w_j) = u^j[w_j\ell_j(w_j), \ell_j(w_j), w_j]$$

$$\Pi_i(w_i) = \max_{\lambda \geqslant 0} P^i(\lambda, w_i) = P^i[\ell_i(w_i), w_i]$$

$$\ell_d(w) = \Sigma \ell_i(w)$$

$$\ell_s(w) = \Sigma \ell_j(w)$$

$$(\ell_c, w_c)\colon \ell_d(w_c) = \ell_s(w_c) = \ell_c.$$

We assume $\ell_d(w) \lesseqgtr \ell_s(w) \Leftrightarrow w \gtreqless w_c$.

We can have the following cases.

I. If all firms choose $\ell_i = \bar{\ell}_i$ and $w_i = \bar{w}_i$ without constraint, we have a general "efficiency" solution. Then $f_1^i(\bar{\ell}_i, \bar{w}_i) = \bar{w}_i$, $f_2^i(\bar{\ell}_i, \bar{w}_i) = \bar{\ell}_i$ if $\bar{\ell}_i > 0$, $\bar{w}_i > 0$, for all i's. If $\bar{w}_i = \bar{w}$ is the same for all i's, $\partial \Sigma f^i(\bar{\ell}_i, \bar{w})/\partial w = \Sigma f_2^i(\bar{\ell}_i, \bar{w}) = \Sigma \bar{\ell}_i = \ell_d(\bar{w}) = \bar{\ell}_d$. It is the efficiency point E. If workers are free wage takers, this solution implies $\ell_d(\bar{w}) \leqslant \ell_s(\bar{w})$, thus $\bar{w} \geqslant w_c$.

But in this case there is no *effective* competition between the demanders of labor. And there is not either between the suppliers (ruling out, however, cases of labor supply collusion threatening to offer only $\ell < \bar{\ell}_d$, for example $\ell = 0$). For the other cases, this competition should be defined. We retain here the following formulation which assumes for simplicity the realistic situation where a worker cannot satisfy all the labor demand and works at only one firm. Consider a situation where all wages are the same: $w_i = w_j = w$ for all firms i and workers j. The following properties then are assumed with respect to rationing of supply or demand on the labor market.

1. If at wage w an agent is rationed, then

a. no agent on the other side of the market is rationed, and

b. this agent is not alone on its side of the market (already assumed for workers).

2. If the firm i can hire only $\tilde{\ell}_i < \ell_i(w)$, if it offers the wage $w + \varepsilon$ while the wages paid by the other firms do not change, it can obtain $\ell_i = \min[\ell_i(w + \varepsilon), \ell_s(w + \varepsilon)]$, however small $\varepsilon > 0$ may be, if enough workers prefer this wage to the one they had.

3. If the worker j can obtain only the employment $\tilde{\ell}_j < \ell_j(w)$ ($\tilde{\ell}_j = 0$ is a possibility), if he asks for the wage $w - \varepsilon$ he can obtain the employment he desires $\ell_j(w - \varepsilon)$, however small $\varepsilon > 0$ may be, if one firm prefers the wage $w - \varepsilon$ to the wage w, given that a sufficient number of workers do not change their wage demands, and assuming that a sufficient number of other workers are also rationed at wage w and also offer wage $w - \varepsilon$, so as to staff this firm (a condition made necessary by the simplifying assumption that a firm pays a single wage rate).

We can then have the two following situations:

II. If the firm i obtains only labor $\tilde{\ell}_i < \ell_i(w)$, consider that it offers wage $w + \varepsilon$ with $\varepsilon > 0$ and arbitrarily small.

If $\ell_s(w + \varepsilon) > \ell_i(w + \varepsilon)$, P^i becomes

$$P^i[\ell_i(w + \varepsilon), w + \varepsilon] = P^i[\ell_i(w), w] + \eta(\varepsilon) > P^i(\tilde{\ell}_i, w)$$

where $\lim_{\varepsilon \to 0} \eta(\varepsilon) = 0$, if ε is sufficiently small and by definition of $\ell_i(w)$.

If, on the other hand, $\ell_s(w + \varepsilon) \leqslant \ell_i(\mathrm{w} + \varepsilon)$, P^i becomes

$$P^i[\ell_s(w + \varepsilon), w + \varepsilon] = P^i[\ell_s(w), w] + \eta_1(\varepsilon) > P^i(\tilde{\ell}_i, w)$$

where $\lim_{\varepsilon \to 0} \eta_1(\varepsilon) = 0$, if ε is sufficiently small. Indeed, this inequality results from $P^i[\ell_s(w), w] > P^i(\tilde{\ell}_i, w)$. This holds for the following reason. First, $\ell_s(w) > \tilde{\ell}_i$ since firm i is rationed at uniform wage w and from assumptions (1a) (labor supply is not rationed) and (1b) (other firms receive labor). Second, $\ell_s(w) \leqslant \ell_i(w)$ since $\ell_s(w + \varepsilon) \leqslant \ell_i(w + \varepsilon)$ however small ε is and since the functions ℓ_s and ℓ_i are continuous because of the differentiability to the second order of utility and production functions. Thus, $\tilde{\ell}_i < \ell_s(w) \leqslant \ell_i(w)$. Now these inequalities, the definition of $\ell_i(w)$, and the strict concavity of $P^i(\lambda, w)$ in λ imply $P^i[\ell_s(w), w] > P^i(\tilde{\ell}_i, w)$.

Thus, in both cases *the firm benefits from raising its wages* from w to $w + \varepsilon$.

On the other side of the market, the worker j is not rationed and prefers a higher wage if $U_j'(w) > 0$. Now, from the definition of $\ell_j(w)$ and the envelope theorem, and denoting $b^j = u_3^j/u_1^j$,

$$U_j'(w) = u_1^j\{[w\ell_j(w), \ell_j(w), w] \cdot \{\ell_j(w) + b^j[\ell_j(w), w]\}$$

which is > 0 if $\ell_j + b^j > 0$ and in particular if $b^j > 0$.

Therefore, the rationed employer wishes to pay the higher wage and the workers prefer this higher wage. Competition raises wages, until no labor demand is rationed.

III. If on the contrary the supplier of labor j can be employed only for $\tilde{\ell}_j < \ell_j(w)$ ($\tilde{\ell}_j = 0$ is possible), if he offers instead to work for $w - \varepsilon$ with $\varepsilon > 0$ and arbitrarily small, by assumption he can work at the employment he prefers $\ell_j(w - \varepsilon)$. u^j then becomes

$$u^j[w - \varepsilon) \cdot \ell_j(w - \varepsilon), \ell_j(w - \varepsilon), w - \varepsilon] = u^j[w\ell_j(w), \ell_j(w), w]$$

$$+ \eta_2(\varepsilon) > u^j(w\tilde{\ell}_j, \tilde{\ell}_j, w)$$

where $\lim_{\varepsilon \to 0} \eta_2(\varepsilon) = 0$, if ε is small enough and from the definition of $\ell_j(w)$. This worker thus offers to work at a lower wage rate (despite the positive preference effect of its wage rate).

On the other side of the market, a firm i is not rationed, and from the definition of $\ell_i(w)$ and the envelope theorem,

$$\Pi_i'(w) = P_2^i[\ell_i(w), w] = f_2^i[\ell_i(w), w] - \ell_i(w).$$

Hence $\Pi_i'(w) \lesseqgtr 0$ according to whether $w \lesseqgtr \overline{w}_i$. Assume again that $\overline{w}_i = \overline{w}$ is the same for all firms i.

If $w > \overline{w}$, the firms wish to lower their wages. The wage cutter rationed workers thus find an employer at the lower wage they propose or accept. This ceases to happen when either labor supply is no more rationed thus at $w = w_c$, or $w = \overline{w}$.

If, however, $w < \overline{w}$, $\Pi_i'(w) > 0$, the firms wish to raise their wage rates, while the rationed workers supply their labor at lower wage rates. There is no agreement, but the freedom of exchange entails that the choice is made by the firms who finally choose $(\overline{w}, \overline{\ell}_i)$.

This second case does not exist if $\overline{w} \leqslant w_c$ since excess supply implies $w > w_c$. And with $\overline{w} \leqslant w_c$ the first case causes wages to decrease to w_c.

Finally with $\overline{w} = \overline{w}_i$ for all i's, if $\overline{w} < w_c$ the mechanisms of competition lead to equilibrium $w = w_c$ whatever the starting situation, and if $\overline{w} > w_c$ it is $w = \overline{w}$ that is attained. Thus, with productivity and norm-status-sign effects of wages, competitive equilibrium is not a state that is not realized: it is the one that occurs in a competitive setting when the unconstrained-efficiency wage $\overline{w}$ is lower than the competitive equilibrium wage w_c. One can also say that it is the one that arises when there is *effective* competition. We remark that the wage preference effects do not intervene in this discussion (this would not be so if $\ell_j + b^j = 0$ were possible or if u^j were not continuous in its third argument w_j).

We must finally note the effect of three crucial phenomena on this situation.

The nonfailure constraints $P_i \geqslant 0$ can block the process. Consider the aggregate level and denote $w_f = w$ such that $P[\ell_d(w_f), w_f] = 0$, with $P_2[\ell_d(w_f), w_f] < 0$. Then $w_f > \bar{w}$ if some production is profitable. If $\bar{w} > w_c$ or if $w_f > w_c > \bar{w}$, the above conclusions are unchanged. But if $w_c > w_f$, the competitive process ends with an excess demand at $w = w_f$.

Furthermore, all the preceding discussion extends immediately to the case where there are taxes or subsidies.

Finally if the production is limited by effective demand, that is, in aggregate form, $f(\ell, w) \leqslant q$, it is necessary to replace in the previous analyses $\ell_d(w)$ by $\min[\ell_d(w), \psi(w, q)]$ where $\psi(w, q)$ is the inverse function in ℓ of $f(\ell, w) = q$ (a similar remark treats the problem if the output limitation is $f(\ell, w) \leqslant D(w\ell, P) + x$).

12. Optimality and Good Fiscal Policy with Norm-Status-Sign and Productivity Effects of Wages

According to Section 5, the optimum maximizes $u[f(\ell, w), \ell, w]$. We still consider an unconstrained production, with an ethical or political or decentralization condition of freedom to hire and fire at a given wage, and thus the constraint $f_1(\ell, w) - w = 0$. Optimality then adds the condition

$$\frac{f_1 - a}{f_{11}} = \frac{f_2 + b}{f_{12} - 1}. \tag{6}$$

We remark that $w = f_1 < a$ is possible in the case of a union monopoly that chooses both employment and wages, but not in the case of free employment (no forced labor) of individual workers who are wage takers. This last case is in particular the one of free competition in the labor market, and the one of a union monopoly which contents itself to set wages. Now, in the usual case where $f_{11} < 0$ and $f_2 + b > 0$, $f_1 - a$ given by condition (6) has the sign of $1 - f_{12}$. And, $f_{12} \lesseqgtr 1$ according to whether the demand curve defined by $f_1(\ell, w) - w = 0$ is decreasing or increasing, since its slope is $dw/d\ell = f_{11}/(1 - f_{12})$. We thus assume that this curve is decreasing as in the classical case, that is to say $f_{12} < 1$, which gives $f_1 - a > 0$ at the optimum, therefore unemployment.

We now consider fiscal policy from the concepts, notations, and results of Section 7. We note that here also a tax subsidy on the firms' profit P,

$T_p(P)$, which leaves the after tax profit $P - T_p(P)$ an increasing function of P, does not change a profit maximizing behavior of firms (when particular problems of risk or failure do not intervene)—this holds when the firms choose the efficiency employment and wage levels E or with any other competitive or monopolistic behavior. Fiscal policy can, however, act through the labor supply. When this supply is competitive, all the reasoning of the preceding section is still valid with the new labor supply curve defined by $[1 - t(w\ell)]w - a(\ell, w) = 0$ (where t is the marginal tax or subsidy rate and where P_w, assumed to be parametric for the reasons indicated above, is not noted explicitly here). In particular, when the efficiency wage and employment levels E are chosen, fiscal policy cannot change this state, but it can reduce the corresponding unemployment, or increase it, and, with $t > 0$ and sufficiently high it can bring an end to this choice in shifting the labor supply curve with taxes so that point E is on the other side of it; similarly, if E is not chosen, a sufficient marginal subsidy can, in the absence of supply collusion, shift the labor supply curve so that E is on the other side of it and bring into existence this "efficiency choice" of firms. We now still consider two market situations, *competitive equilibrium*, and the *rational union monopoly of labor supply* fixing the wage w under the constraint of freedom to hire by the firms, and the cases where a constraint $P - T_P \geqslant 0$ does not exist or is not binding (the fiscal policy can adjust T_P).

With *competitive labor supply*, $(1 - t)w - a = 0$, that is $(1 - t)f_1 = a$. Comparison with equation 6 gives the optimal marginal rate in this case, $t = t_c$,

$$t_c = -\frac{f_{11}}{f_1}\frac{b + f_2}{1 - f_{12}}.$$

The condition without productivity effect of wages, that is $f_2 = f_{12} = 0$, is the one obtained above. The second multiplicative factor of the formula assembles the preference and productivity effects of the wage rate on the optimal tax. With the signs $f_1 > 0$, $b + f_2 > 0$, $f_{11} < 0$, $1 - f_{12} > 0$, we have $t_c > 0$. There must thus be a *marginal tax*. In consequence, the balance of the public budget requires that there be a *lump sum public expenditure or subsidy*. This optimal marginal rate *increases with b, f_2, and f_{12}, that is to say with the preference effects of wages and with the productivity effects of wages on the global production and on the marginal productivity of labor.*

With a *labor supply monopoly* (union) submitted to the free hiring constraint $f_1 - w = 0$, according to the results of Section 7 *the optimal tax assures the coincidence of the maxima, under this constraint, of $u(y, \ell, w)$—which* *may be in the form* $y + v(\ell, w)$*—in taking on the one hand* $y = f(\ell, w)$ *and on the other hand* $y = w\ell + P_w - T(w\ell, P_w)$ (P_w *being parametric). That implies*

$$\frac{(1-t)f_1 - a}{(1-t)\ell + b} = -\frac{f_{11}}{1-f_{12}} = \frac{f_1 - a}{f_2 + b} = \frac{-tf_1}{(1-t)\ell - f_2}.$$

These equalities give, for the optimal marginal rate $t = t_m$, in denoting $x = -(1-f_{12})f_1/f_{11}$ (thus $x > 0$),

$$t_m = \frac{\ell - f_2}{\ell + (1-f_{12})f_1/f_{11}} = \frac{\ell - f_2}{\ell - x}.$$

In the absence of a productivity effect of wages, $f_2 = f_{12} = 0$ and we find again the result of Section 7. Furthermore we remark that t_m does not depend explicitly on the wage preference effect b, which can be explained as indicated there.

The condition $t_m < 1$ says that ℓ and f_2 must be on the same side of x.

The numerator of t_m is, with sign changed, the marginal profit with respect to the wage rate, $f_2 - \ell$. We have $f_2 - \ell \lesseqgtr 0$ depending on whether the optimum is to the right or to the left of the efficiency choice of the firms E on the demand curve, that is to say whether $w \lesseqgtr \bar{w}$ and $\ell \lesseqgtr \bar{\ell}$. We have thus *a priori* four possible situations:

$f_2 < \ell < x$	$t_m < 0$	$w > \bar{w}$	$\ell < \bar{\ell}$
$x < \ell < f_2$	$t_m < 0$	$w < \bar{w}$	$\ell > \bar{\ell}$
$x < f_2 < \ell$	$t_m > 0$	$w > \bar{w}$	$\ell < \bar{\ell}$
$\ell < f_2 < x$	$t_m > 0$	$w < \bar{w}$	$\ell > \bar{\ell}$

The optimal fiscality implies a marginal subsidy in the first two cases and a marginal tax in the two others. The optimal wage, employment, and unemployment are higher or lower than those of the efficiency choice depending on the cases. The remarks of Section 1 suggest that the most plausible situation is where the efficiency point E is with larger ℓ and lower w than the optimum on the demand curve, that is the first and third cases. We then have $t_m < 0$ or $t_m > 0$, according to whether the value of x exceeds those of ℓ and f_2, or is inferior to them.

If the wage productivity is *labor-augmenting*, $f = \varphi[e(w) \cdot \ell]$ and there results

$$t_m = \frac{e}{1 + \varphi'/e\ell\varphi''}.$$

But we also have $f_{12} = e'\varphi' \cdot (1 + e\ell\varphi''/\varphi')$, and $f_{12} \lesseqgtr 0$ implies $-e\ell\varphi''/\varphi' \lesseqgtr 1$; thus, $-\varphi'/e\ell\varphi'' \lesseqgtr 1$ and $t_m \lesseqgtr 0$. *A priori* f_{12} can have any sign.[12]

The balanced budget condition then leads to the following consequences.

Proposition. The optimal fiscal policy in the presence of preference and productivity effects of wages can implement the first best optimum, in the general conditions indicated, with a labor market in competitive equilibrium or with a monopoly labor supply. In the case of competitive equilibrium, this policy includes public spending or lump sum transfer payments and a marginal tax on wage income. In the case of a labor supply monopoly, this policy does not depend directly upon the wage preference effect (this effect is taken in charge by the monopoly which this policy corrects), and with a labor-augmenting wage productivity this policy includes a marginal subsidy if $f_{12} > 0$ and public expenditures or lump sum transfer payments with a marginal tax on wage income in the opposite case.

(Here again, this subsidy can mean in fact a lesser rate on already existing taxes.)

13. The Domain of the Joint Explanation of Productivity, Wages, and Employment

In the three preceding sections, the wages figured in the utility and in the production functions in a sense side by side, rather independently of one another except for formal interaction. However, the phenomena that engender these influences are in reality closely intertwined. In particular, we should describe how wages influence productivity, and explain why the tax schedule on labor income was not also in the production function.

We denote by e the set of the *non-enforced labor characteristics*, i.e., the set of the characteristics of labor which influence production but are not specified or enforced by the wage contract. These characteristics describe, for example, effort, attention, voluntary training or information, will and good will, voluntary cooperation with other employees, zeal, initiative and voluntary innovation, fidelity which lowers turnover, various consequences of a conscientious approach to one's work or of an attachment to the firm leading to more or less psychic "internalization" of its objectives, etc. The production function is $F(\ell, e)$. A worker also has preferences on the characteristics e, so that the utility function is $U(y, \ell, w, e)$—with also the wage preferences. We assumed no income effect, i.e., ordinal U has a specification of the form $y + V(\ell, w, e)$. We denote

$$e(\ell, w) \equiv \arg\max_e U(y, \ell, w, e) = \arg\max_e V(\ell, w, e),$$

$$u(y, \ell, w) \equiv U[y, \ell, w, e(\ell, w)],$$

$$v(\ell, w) \equiv V[\ell, w, e(\ell, w)],$$

$$f(\ell, w) \equiv F[\ell, e(\ell, w)].$$

We remark that e, and therefore u, v, and f, do not depend on $y = w\ell + P_w + y_0 - T(w\ell, P_w)$, and therefore do not depend on the tax-subsidy schedule T and on P_w. That is due to the quasi-linearity assumption (no income effect). It also requires that e is not effectively limited by a constraint which depends on y—for example on consumption if y is consumed (a physiological effect of consumption on effort may be of this type). Then with both no income effect and no effective income-dependent constraint on the choice of e, $e(\ell, w)$ effectively depends on w, and therefore $f(\ell, w)$ effectively depends on w, only because w is in the function V, that is, directly in the function U (i.e., not only through y): *there is wage productivity only because there is wage preferences.*

The influence of w on e chosen by the workers often results from phenomena which have rich psycho-social or cultural meanings. This for instance appears in the psychological experiments noted in section 1.b. where the workers are motivated by senses of balance or of fairness or by self-esteem. As another example, return-gift behavior leads to greater productivity increase if a higher w is granted by the employer than if this raise is extracted from him. Yet a raise conquered by the employees may create among them a sentiment of satisfaction, of freedom, of control of one's situation, which may foster productivity.

In his ground-breaking study of 1982, Akerlof draws especially from a specific study by the celebrated "exchange sociologist" George Homans, and on key ideas of anthropology, the return-gift, and reciprocity. (Note that what he describes is not reciprocity with symmetrical roles, but a Stakelberg-like exploitation, by the firm, of the return-gift of effort by which the workers respond to a "gift" of a higher wage.[17]) But many other psycho-social phenomena intervene in the effect of wages on productivity. The few that we have noted in section 1.2 and in the present one show that these effects can go in both directions. Another study will consider systematically all these effects and obtain an idea as to their real global frequency and importance.

14. Concluding Remarks

14.1. Extensions of This Study

This study has several obvious extensions.

One is found in the microeconomic version, considering in particular each worker explicitly (or various categories of workers). Results similar to those obtained above are found. The new aspects come from the relations between the different tasks in the production function and —this is more novel—from the preferences of some bearing or depending on the wages of others, eventually through the intermediary of relative wages. As a result, wages can become collective concerns for the workers (the wage of each worker may influence negatively or positively or not at all the utility of another). This is the source of another inefficiency which the fiscal authorities (or a union capable of effecting or inducing transfer payments as we have noted) can deal with ("internalize"). This allows solutions with $b = 0$ or even $b < 0$ which would hardly be meaningful otherwise. For instance, if wages intervene in utility functions only through relative wages and if all wages vary proportionately, $b = 0$. Or, even, strong jealousy effects might give $b < 0$. Then two solutions without the free hiring constraint $w = f'$ become possible. One is the equivalent for labor of the "efficiency point," with ℓ and w which maximize $u(w\ell, \ell, w)$, thus at $w = a$ (the labor supply curve) and $\ell + b = 0$. The other one is the optimum optimorum with transfers, where $u[f(\ell, w), \ell, w]$ is maximum, that is, $f_1 = a \neq w$ and $b + f_2 = 0$ (or $f' = a \neq w$ and $b = 0$ if there is no productivity effect of wages); in practice, this would mean high wages recuperated by lump sum transfers refunded to the firms. With this "public good" aspect of wages, these solutions are no longer meaningless; they say that a wage is determined by equilibrium at the margin between its advantage in the eyes of the worker other than that of directly procuring purchasing power (and its productivity effect if there is one), and its "disadvantage" in the eyes of others. This describes a society where wages are determined essentially by norms, status, jealousies and envies, solidarities and oppositions, sentiments of justice and equity, and accepted habits and customs. These causes of wages, even when they are not the only ones and when labor productivity also intervenes, pose delicate ethical and political problems: should the government "respect" preferences as little ethical as jealousies or envies, or should it "launder" individual preferences that it endorses by neglecting some of their features, and, in this case, would the political process or the voters let it do it?

Furthermore, as the norms and all the sentiments and habits that underlie them are constructed by reference to the past, the above considerations have important intertemporal and dynamic implications. For example, the wage in the utility function noted in the text becomes its relation to a weighted average of past wages with the weight decreasing with time elapsed (or perhaps its comparison to a maximum of past wages). One interesting problem is that reality shows discontinuous behaviors from this point of view. Thus, after the deepening of the economic crisis in the early 1980s, the labor market structures have been profoundly and brutally modified in a number of countries (in 1982 in Italy and West Germany, with a certain parallel in 1983 in France, for example), by a process of which the best description seems to be a collapse of wage and employment norms.

Other extensions finally consist in the introduction of other norms intervening in the labor market, notably those relative to incomes and to labor, and in making further explicit the conditions of the goods market.

14.2. What Model of Models?

The analysis of the microeconomic foundations of macroeconomics is 20 years old. The era of maturity that opens should, in order to respond to needs, pass from the research of foundations to what one could call the dissolution of barriers, not only between "macro" and "micro" but also between "Keynesianisms" and "classicisms," between economic analyses on the one hand and psycho-social and meta-ethical analyses on the other, and consequently between the refinement in the theories of markets and its lack thereof in policy recommendations. The interesting point of this subject is that the most fruitful of these integrations are achieved each one thanks to the others.

The blurring of the macro-micro dichotomy was the very essence of the approach, and the one of the classic-Keynes dichotomy (which dates back to the origins of the question with Hicks, Lange, or Modigliani) should thrive with these "micro" developments. If the various rigidities are well explained from behaviors, the "equilibrium school," whose strong point is this methodological requirement, can raise no objection (in adding, however, that the equilibrium of supplies and demands must also be well explained and that man is more complex than these economists say). But what seems to be the more interesting is that classical and Keynesian realities can divide between themselves not only periods of economic life, or economic sectors, but even different aspects of the same phenomenon.

Thus, the preference effect of wages, which comes from the *supply* side, has nevertheless in a certain sense *five* important *Keynesian aspects*: because of this a fiscal policy can ameliorate the lot of everyone, the effects of comparisons of wages are considered by Keynes himself, and, when the workers together have some market power or when a public sector intervenes taking this effect into account, this effect induces at once a downward "rigidity" of wages, an excess of labor supply over labor demand given the wages, and a positive wage gap (that a sentence of Keynes identifies as "involuntary" unemployment).

In a general way, the analysis of the microeconomic foundations of macroeconomics should be extended to the determination of the optimal policy, notably for fiscal policy. This poses the problem of instruments and that of objectives. When prices and wages are explained in an endogenous way, that leads to studies of the type of the one just presented, with aspects of classical optimal taxation, which are naturally also introduced by the analyses of supply-side policies. As for the objectives, the criterion can no longer be one of "full employment," or the suppression of "involuntary unemployment" (and one could say the same for the other classical objectives of macroeconomic policy), but something more refined including directly Pareto-efficiency plus distributional objectives derived from the correct social ethic (the description of which is beyond our present scope[18]).

Finally, the consideration of the effects of the social roles of wages as norms, status, signs, or signals, on employment and on the good fiscal policy, is a particular case of a much more general need. Theoretical and applied economic analysis comes up against a series of major impasses from which one can escape only by consideration of psychic or social phenomena that it omits. Without wanting to expose these questions here, let us note for example that this is the case for questions like the explanations of price and wage rigidities, employment and unemployment, productivity and growth, what harm there is in inflation (and which could justify very costly stabilization policies), the social ethical criterion, the reason why individuals vote, choices under uncertainty, the concepts of equilibrium in game theory, without even counting the formation of preferences. What is indispensable to introduce is not only questions of information and cognitive capacities (about which economists think spontaneously), but also emotions, the "economy" of willpower, of psychic energy, of attention, of the divided and multiple self, ethics, norms, anomia, cognitive dissonance, status and sign, various social influences, etc. These psychic and social facts must be integrated into economic analysis in order to draw the pertinent consequences, and it should be done in particular in the modelization which remains one of the methods susceptible to be fruitful. The two chapters (2 and 19) of the *General Theory* that Keynes devotes to wage rigidities are still a good lesson: many remarks are striking at once by their realism and by the fact that they are not representable by standard models of "economic man." Would this be the manifestation of a general rule by which human choices have a rationality that is all the more bizarre (that is, complex) that they are more important, and that would apply not only to war, love, and politics but also to work and wages?

Acknowledgment

Translated from the French by Deirdre Domegan.

Notes

1. Various points in this study have benefited from the remarks of Mahomed Dore, Pierre Dehez, Felix Fitzroy, D. M. Nuti, Pierre Moesinger, Dominique Frécaut, and Pierre-André Chiappori.

2. Generally speaking, if the output is $f(\ell, w)$, the maximization of profit $f(\ell, w) - w\ell$ gives the two conditions $f_1 = w$ ("the wage is equal to the marginal productivity of labor") and $f_2 = \ell$ (*labor is equal to the marginal productivity of the wage*, which is more interesting). With the classical $f(\ell, w) = \varphi[e(w) \cdot \ell]$, these conditions become $f_1 = \varphi' e = w$, $f_2 = \varphi' e' \ell = \ell$, which implies $we' = e$ (maximum of e/w). In the problems with an output that is a constant q or a more general demand $D(w\ell, w) + x$ with relevant conditions, maximum profit gives the condition $f_1/w = f_2/\ell$—which again gives $we' = e$ in the case $f = \varphi(e\ell)$. As an example of what we said about $e(w)$, Akerlof's model (1982)—discussed below—does have a decreasing marginal productivity of wages, but it implies $e(0) < 0$ and $e(w) < 0$ for small w's! But as ℓ is the *time* spent working or the *number* of workers, we see that this "labor-augmenting" form of wage productivity is particular. Another form for instance could be "capital-augmenting" (for example, work with more careful timing may reduce the average level of inventories for a given output). If the production function is written $F[e(w) \cdot k, \ell]$ where k is the stock of capital at a unit cost of r, the unconstrained efficiency state where profit $F - rk - w\ell$ is maximum, or the minimization of cost $rk + w\ell$ under a given $F = q$, or profit maximization with a demand $F = D(w\ell, P) + x$, lead to the condition $e'w/e = w\ell/rk$, the ratio of labor and capital costs. This is compatible with a $e(0) \geqslant 0$ and $e'' < 0$, which implies $e' < e/w$, only if $w\ell < rk$, which is not really the case in modern economies for the economy as a whole (but which can be found in a particular industry). Stiglitz (1987), who uses the form $f = \varphi(e\ell)$, asserts he verified that the function $e(w)$ has the required shape in the case he considers, but that is not, for example, the case for a nutritional effect in a situation of "underdevelopment," which has no special reason to exhibit the initial increasing returns structure.

3. In the terms of a famous psychological theory, the "id" can push one to become employed in order to have an income to consume, whereas the "superego" refuses to accept so low a wage, or produces disagreeable sentiments of shame and uneasiness if one does. The "ego" achieves the synthesis between these two tendencies and the "reality principle" (outside constraints, which is in this case the labor demand).

4. George Akerlof proposes the most elaborate of economic studies aiming to explain wages that are higher than the monetary marginal disutility of labor by using concepts of "norm." But curiously enough, he does not present the most usual and obvious aspect, the *wage norm for workers*, which is our topic here. The reason is doubtlessly that he wishes to explain "*involuntary* unemployment," a question to which we will return. In (1980) Akerlof considers (1) a *wage norm for the employer* who wishes to pay fairly high wages to protect his local reputation (but would he not reach this objective or better it by not laying off workers—since the model retains equality of the wage to the marginal productivity of labor?). In (1982), in order to explain efficiency wages by a relation of reciprocity between the workers and the employer, Akerlof considers (2) an *effort norm for the workers*, (3) a *work norm* that is a norm of results per unit of work (related to effort), which is officialized and is a norm for the employer and probably also for the employees, and (4) a *reference wage* for the workers, influencing their effort norm (it increases with w/w_1 where w is the wage and w_1 the reference wage), and which is a weighted average of the wages of other firms and of unemployment benefits with the weights depending on the rate of unemployment and represents the average income of a worker if he leaves this firm. Furthermore, in these models, the wage is important to the workers only for the income that it brings them (the working time is fixed). (Let us note furthermore that these studies aim at determining the wages and do not touch upon fiscal policy, which will be our central objective.)

5. Concepts of choice theory can be used to represent more complex psychic and social phenomena, like, notably, multicriteria psychism (cf. for example the study "Psychoanalysis and Choice Theory" reprinted in Kolm 1987a, chapter VI), or reciprocity relations (cf. for example Kolm 1984a, part 4).

6. This is an application of the more general analysis of freedom in Kolm 1982, 1984.

7. They are distinguished from the prices in an "indirect utility function" by the fact that they violate Roy's identity.

8. Then there also can be a freedom preference for $\bar{\ell}$. But when $\ell = \bar{\ell}$ this preference bears on the same variable as the labor preference, and that can be described by only one variable, $\ell = \bar{\ell}$ in the utility function.

9. Remark that a higher income y also gives a higher freedom on the markets where it can be used, given the prices.

10. We even abstain here from introducing questions of the "voluntary" character of impulsive or compulsive acts, phenomena of the "weakness" or "strength" of

the will, or akrasia, or even the problem of free will. The differences between the preferences that guide behavior and those that judge the result would also be relevant for this discussion. Remarks in this spirit, on the "voluntary" character of unemployment, are presented by Hahn (1984) and Solow (1986), and this question is considered in a more elaborated manner by Kolm (1984c).

11. A number of consequences derived below from the presence of wage rates in utility and production functions hold more generally when there are prices in utility or production functions. Prices can be in utility or production functions for a number of reasons. Selling prices can have this situation for all the reasons that we have mentioned in the case of wages. Buyers often take prices as quality indicators (as does the future employer with the wage in a remark presented above), and prices thus influence their behavior by this channel. Conspicuous consumption (or its opposite discrete consumption) and in general status consumption also lead one to have direct preferences on prices (eventually on relative prices). The prices of a price index used to measure the real value of cash balances or of other nominal assets also enter into present preference or production functions, etc. The results obtained below which are meaningful for all these cases concern the working of competition, market equilibria, unconstrained solutions of this "efficiency wages" type, monopolies and bilateral monopolies, welfare consequences, consequences for "optimal taxation," etc. These issues were not considered by the previous studies of prices in utility functions, by Scitovsky (1945), Kalman (1968), Alcaly and Klevorick (1970), Allingham and Morishima (1973), and Pollak (1977). Note finally that this is but an aspect of a more general question studied by philosophers and psychologists, that of *preferences depending on the possibility set* (or on the *constraints*) studied for instance by Jon Elster (the title of his book *Sour Grapes* refers to one of the interpretations in this sense of La Fontaine's and others' fables), or of *preferences bearing on the possibility set* (in addition to bearing on what is chosen) to express a value of the freedom of choice in itself (Kolm 1982, 1984a).

12. Kolm 1988.

13. A "preference for inconspicuousness," which could lead to $b < 0$, does not seem to be able to predominate globally.

14. One could, for example, call this a "Marxist" structure, the threshold α being the subsistence wage for the young Marx and the workers' consumption norm for the older Marx. However, for $w > a$ where α is this threshold, Marx thinks that the labor supply increases with w for Malthusian reasons (without being explicit on the demographic time lengths and delays).

15. Cf. Kolm 1985, 1987b, c, d.

16. For example, in denoting $z = e\ell$, with $\varphi(z) = k_0 z^k$, $k_0 > 0$, $0 < k < 1$, we obtain $t = ((k-1)/k)e < 0$. With $\varphi(z) = k_0 \cdot [k_1^k - (z + k_1)^k]$, $k_0 > 0$, $k_1 > 0$, $k < 0$, we obtain $t = ez/(2z + k^2) > 0$. And with $\varphi(z) = k_0 \cdot [\text{Log}(1+z)]^k$, $k_0 > 0$, $0 < k < 1$, we obtain that t has the sign of $(k-1)z + [\text{Log}(1+z)]^{k-1}$, which is positive when z is sufficiently small and negative when z is sufficiently large.

17. See the analysis of these questions in Kolm 1984a, part 4.

18. See for instance Kolm 1985, 1987b, c, d.

References

Adams, J. S. 1965a. "Etudes expérimentales en matière d'inégalités de salaires, de productivité et de qualité du travail," *Synopsis* (Office belge pour l'accroissement de la productivité, Bruxelles), reproduced in *Psychologie sociale théorique et expérimentale,* ed. Faucheux, C., and Moscovici, S. Paris: Mouton, 1971.

Adams, J. S. 1965b. "Inequity in Social Exchange." In Bekowitz, L. (ed.), *Advances in Experimental Social Psychology,* 2, New York: Academic Press.

Adams, J. S., and Rosenbaum, W. E. 1964. "The Relationship of Worker Productivity to Cognitive Dissonance about Wage Inequities," *Journal of Abnormal and Social Psychology,* 69, 19–25.

Aglietta, M., and Brender, A. 1984. *Les métamorphoses de la Société salariale. La France en projet.* Paris: Calmann-Lévy.

Akerlof, G. A. 1980. "A Theory of Social Custom, of Which Unemployment May Be One Consequence." *Quarterly Journal of Economics* 94, June: 749–75.

Akerlof, G. 1982. "Labor Contracts as Partial Gift Exchange." *Quarterly Journal of Economics* 94, November: 543–569. *The Labor Market,* Cambridge University Press.

Alcaly, R. E., and Klevorick, A. K. 1970. "Judging Quality by Price, Snob Appeal and the New Consumer Theory." *Zeitschrift für Nationalökonomie* 30 (10): 53–64.

Allingham, M. G., and Morishima, M. 1973. "Veblen Effects and Portfolio Selection," in Morishima, M., ed., *Theory of Demand: Real and Monetary.* Oxford.

Amselek, P. 1980. "Norme et loi." *Archives de Philosophie du Droit* 25: 89–107.

Andrews, I. R. 1967. "Wage Inequity and Job Performance: An Experimental Study." *Journal of Applied Psychology* 51: 39–45.

Annable, J. E. 1977. "A Theory of Downward-Rigid Wages and Cyclical Unemployment." *Economic Inquiry* 15(9): 326–344.

Annable, J., Jr. 1984. *The Price of Industrial Labor.* Lexington Books.

Argyle, M. 1972. *The Social Psychology of Work.* Penguin.

Atias, C. 1984. "L'émergence des normes." *Cahiers du CREA* 3, May: 105–127.

Azariadis, C. 1975. "Implicit Contracts and Under-employment Equilibria." *Journal of Political Economy* 83: 1183–1202.

Baily, M. N. 1974. "Wages and Employment under Uncertain Demand." *Review of Economic Studies* 41: 37–50.

Baudrillard, J. 1972. *Pour une critique de l'économie politique du signe*. Paris: Gallimard.

Baxter, J. L. 1980. "A General Model of Wage Determination." *Bulletin of Economic Research* 32(9): 3–17.

Behrend, H. 1973. *Incomes Policy, Equity and Pay Increase Differentials*. Edinburgh: Scottish Academic Press.

Brown, J. A. C. 1954. *The Social Psychology of Industry*. Pelican.

Dunlop, J. T. 1957. "The Task of Contemporary Wage Theory." In Talyor, G. W., and Sisson, F. C. (eds.), *New Concepts in Wage Determination*. McGraw Hill.

Elster, J. *Sour Grapes*. Cambridge University Press.

Favereau, O. 1986. "La "Théorie Générale": de l'économie conventionnelle à l'économie des conventions." *Cahiers d'Economie Politique*, Université de Paris X-Nanterre, 12, 13, and 14 June.

Festinger, L. 1954. "A Theory of Social Comparison Processes." *Human Relations* 7: 117–140.

Field, A. J. 1984. "Microeconomics, Norms and Rationality." *Economic Development and Cultural Change*, 32(4): July, 682–711.

Fogarty, M. P. 1961. *The Just Wage*. Chapman and Hall.

Frank, R. H. 1984. "Are Workers Paid Their Marginal Product?" *American Economic Review* 74(4): 549–571.

Frank, R. H. 1985. *Choosing the Right Pond; Human Behavior and the Quest for Status*. Oxford University Press.

Galey, J. C., ed. 1985. *Différences, valeurs, hiérarchie*. Paris: éditions de la Maison des Sciences de l'homme.

Hahn, F. 1982. *Money and Inflation*. Basil Blackwell.

Hahn, F. 1984. Economic Theory and Keynes' Insights. Economic Theory Discussion Paper No. 72, University of Cambridge.

Hicks, J. 1932. *The Theory of Wages*. Macmillan.

Hicks, J. 1975. *The Crisis in Keynesian Economics*. Oxford.

Homans, G. 1962. *Sentiments and Activities*. Free Press of Glencoe.

Hyman, H. 1942. "The Psychology of Status." *Archives of Psychology* 29.

Jahoda, M. 1982. *Employment and Unemployment: A Social-Psychological Analysis*. Cambridge University Press.

Jaque, E. 1967. *Equitable Payment*. Penguin.

Kahneman, D., Knatsch, J., and Thaler, R. 1986. "Fairness as a Constraint on Profit-Seeking: Entitlements in the Market." *American Economic Review*, September.

Kaldor, N. 1985. *Economics without Equilibrium*. University College Cardiff Press.

Kalman, P. J. 1968. "Theory of Consumer Behavior When Prices Enter the Utility Function." *Econometrica* 36(2–10): 497–510.

Kelvin, P., and Jarrett, J. 1984. "*Unemployment: Its Social Psychological Effects*. Cambridge University Press.

Keynes, J. M. 1936. *The General Theory of Employment, Interest and Money*. Macmillan.

Kolm, S.-C. 1970. "La théorie de la courbe inflation-chômage." *Revue économique* 21(2).

Kolm, S.-C. 1971. "La taxation de la consommation ostentatoire." *Revue d'économie politique* 1.

Kolm, S.-C. 1982. *Le Bonheur-liberté*. Presses Universitaires de France.

Kolm, S.-C. 1984a. *La bonne économie (la Réciprocité générale)*. Presses Universitaires de France.

Kolm, S.-C. 1984b. *Sortir de la crise*. Hachette.

Kolm, S.-C. 1984c. *Le libéralisme moderne*. Presses Universitaires de France.

Kolm, S.-C. 1985. *Le Contrat social libéral*. Presses Universitaires de France.

Kolm, S.-C. 1986a. "Unemployment Resulting from Preferences on Wages and Prices." Toronto Conference for the 50th anniversary of Keynes' *General theory*, Proceedings: *Keynes and Public Policy after Eighty Years*, volume II, ed. Hamouda, O., and Smithin, N. Edward Elgar, 1988.

Kolm, S.-C. 1986b. L'Etat doit-il avoir des politiques de l'emploi, de stabilisation, macro-économique. Document de travail No. 48, CERAS.

Kolm, S.-C. 1986c. Chômage et inflation résultant des effets de norme et de statut des salaires et des prix. Document de travail No. 51, CERAS.

Kolm, S.-C. 1986d. Prix et normes. Document de travail No. 52, CERAS.

Kolm, S.-C. 1987a. *L'homme pluridimensionnel*. Albin Michel.

Kolm, S.-C. 1987b. Liberty-Based Public Economics; Its Foundations, Principle, Method, Application and Structural Results. Document de travail No. 60, CERAS.

Kolm, S.-C. 1987c. "The Freedom and Consensus Normative Theory of the State: The Liberal Social Contract." In *Individual Liberty and Democratic Decision-Making*, ed. Koslowski, P. Tübingen: J. C. B. Mohr (Paul Siebeck).

Kolm, S-C. 1987d. "Public Economics." In *New Palgrave Dictionary in Economics*. Macmillan.

Kolm, S.-C. 1988. Unemployment and Policies Resulting from the Norm, Status or Sign Effects of Wages. CERAS discussion paper No. 71.

Lawler, E. E. 1968. "Equity Theory as a Predictor of Productivity and Work Quality," *Psychological Bulletin*, 70, 596–610.

Leibenstein. "Bandwagon, Snob and Veblen Effects in the Theory of Consumers' Demand." *Quarterly Journal of Economics* 65(10): 183–207.

Lindbeck, A., and D. Snower. 1989. *The Insider-Outsider Theory of Employment and Unemployment*. MIT Press.

Lupton, B. 1983. *Wages and Salaries*, 2nd edition. Gower.

Malinvaud, E. 1983. *Essais sur la théorie du chômage*. Paris: Calmann-Lévy.

Malinvaud, E. 1984. *Mass Unemployment*. Basil Blackwell.

Malinvaud, E. 1986. "The Rise of Unemployment in France," *Economica* 210/S.

Marx, K. *Wages, Prices and Profits* (any edition).

Miyazaki, H. 1984. "Work Norms and Involuntary Unemployment." *Quarterly Journal of Economics* 99(2): 297–311.

Okun, A. M. 1981. *Prices and Quantities, A Macroeconomic Analysis*. Basil Blackwell.

Oswald, A. J. 1986. "Is Wage Rigidity Caused by 'Lay-offs by Seniority'?" In W. Beckerman, ed., *Wage Rigidity and Unemployment*. Johns Hopkins University Press.

Patchen, M. 1961. *The Choice of Wage Comparisons*. Prentice-Hall.

Perry, G. L. 1986. "Shifting Wage Norms and Their Implications." *American Economic Review* 76(2).

Pigou, A. C. 1933. *The Theory of Unemployment*.

Pigou, A. C. 1945. *Lapses from Full Employment*.

Piore, M. J. 1973. "Fragments of 'Sociological' Theory of Wages." *American Economic Review*, May: 377–384.

Piore, M. J. 1981. "Unemployment and Inflation: An Alternative View." In David C. Colander, ed., *Solutions to Unemployment*. Harcourt, Brace, Jovanovich.

Pollak, R. A. 1977. "Price Dependent Preferences." *American Economic Review* 67(10): 64–75.

Pritchard, R. D., Dunnette, M. D., and Jorgensen, D. O. 1972. "Effects of Perceptions of Equity and Inequity on Worker Performance and Satisfaction." *Journal of Applied Psychology* 56: 75–94.

Reynaud, B. 1986. "Règles et logique des relations salariales." *Economie et Statistique*, No. 192, October: 43–63.

Ribeaux, P., and Poppleton, S. E. 1978. *Psychology and Work.* Macmillan.

Richardson, R. 1971. *Fair Pay and Work.* Heineman.

Ross, A. M. 1957. "The External Wage Structure." In Taylor, G. H., and Pierson, F. (eds.), *New Concepts in Wage Determination.* McGraw-Hill.

Runciman, W. G. 1966. *Relative Deprivation and Social Justice.* Berkeley: University of California Press.

Sabourian, H. 1988. "Wage Norms and Involuntary Unemployment." *Economic Journal* 98 (Conference): 177–188.

Salais, R., and Thévenot, L. (eds.). 1986. *Le travail. Marchés, règles, conventions.* Paris: INSEE-Economica.

Schnapper, D. 1981. *L'épreuve du chômage.* Gallimard.

Schultze, C. L. 1985. "Microeconomic Efficiency and Nominal Wage Stickiness." *American Economic Review*, 75: 1–15.

Scitovsky, T. 1945. "Some Consequences of the Habit of Judging Quality by Price." *Review of Economic Studies* 12(10): 100–105.

Shaked, A., and Sutton, J. 1984. "Involuntary Unemployment as a Perfect Equilibrium in a Bargaining Model." *Econometrica* 52(6): 1351–1364.

Solow, R. 1979. "Another Possible Source of Wage Stickiness." *Journal of Macroeconomics* 5: 79–82.

Solow, R. 1980a. "On Theories of Unemployment." *American Economic Review* 70: 1–9.

Solow, R. 1980b. "Alternative Approaches to Macroeconomic Theory: A Partial View." *Canadian Journal of Economics* 12: 339–354.

Solow, R. 1986. "Unemployment: Getting the Question Right." *Economica*, No. 210/S.

Stiglitz, J. 1987. "The Causes and Consequences of the Dependence of Quality on Price." *Journal of Economic Literature* 25(1): 1–48.

Taylor, M. C. 1982. "Improved Conditions, Rising Expectations, and Dissatisfaction: A Test of the Past/Present Relative Deprivation Hypothesis." *Social Psychology Quarterly* 45: 24–33.

Trevithick, J. 1976. "Money Wage Inflexibility and the Keynesian Labor Supply Function." *Economic Journal* 86, June.

Ullmann-Margalit, E. 1977. *The Emergence of Norms.* Clarendon.

Veblen, T. 1989. *The Theory of the Leisure Class*. New York.

Vroom, V. H. 1964. *Work and Motivation*. Wiley.

Warr, P. 1983. "Work, Jobs and Unemployment." *Bulletin of the British Psychological Society* 36: 305–311.

White, H. 1981. *The Hidden Meaning of the Pay Conflict*. Macmillan.

Williams, P. 1981. *Fairness, Collective Bargaining and Incomes Policy*. Clarendon.

Wootton, B. 1955. *The Social Foundations of Wage Policy*. Allen & Unwin.

Yellen, J. 1984. "Efficiency Wages Models of Unemployment." *American Economic Review* 74(2): May, 200–205.

22 Wages, Investment, and Employment in a Semi-Open Economy

Jean-Pierre Laffargue

In a recent paper Malinvaud (1986) asked to what extent the stagnation of employment in France since 1973, and the concomitant increase in unemployment, had been due to an inappropriate level of the real wage rate. Two arguments were given, each supporting a different answer. On the one hand, a decrease of the cost of labor would be an incentive for firms to increase their productive capacities and to slow down the substitution of capital for labor. Both effects would benefit growth and employment. On the other hand, the reduction of the purchasing power of wage earners would result in a deficit in demand, and a stagnation of the economy. This last conclusion assumes that a redistribution of income, which deprives wage earners, will depress consumption. This paper will not make such an assumption. First because its consequences have been very much investigated. Second because its theoretical and empirical validity is far from convincing. A decrease of the wage rate will bring about an increase of private companies' profits or a decrease of the deficit of the public sector and of present and future tax liabilities. When these effects are taken into account the permanent income of households appears quite insensitive to the wage rate. Consequently this paper will give a much less balanced answer to Malinvaud's question. Here a decrease of the cost of labor and a fiscal policy that is consistent with this change will have welcome consequences on all economic targets whatever their time range.

Branson and Rotemberg (1980) gave a clever analysis which can be used as a good starting point for our investigation. Let us consider an economy with a unique commodity, i.e., where the purchasing power parity prevails, and with a fixed amount of capital in each country. Let us select one of these countries, small enough not to influence the world price level. We assume that the real wage rate ω which prevails in this country is exogenous, and that no rationing takes place on the goods market. The firms of this country determine their levels of output and employment in order to equalize their marginal productivity of labor to ω. If ω increases firms will adjust this productivity by reducing their workforce. Consequently unemployment will grow and business activity will become depressed. A rise in Government consumption will have no corrective effects on these evolutions, but it will increase absorption and the trade balance will deteriorate.

This explanation assumes that the real wage rate moves independently enough of the situation on the labor market so as to allow the disequilibrium of this market to last for many years. The sluggishness of the cost of labor in Europe has been verified by many empirical studies (e.g., Steinherr 1983; Artus 1983c). It will be one of the main assumptions of the model of this paper.

The increase of unemployment in Europe has been taking place for 20 years. But in their explanation Branson and Rotemberg assumed a fixed amount of capital. We have thought necessary to complete their model by adding an investment behavior consistent with the labor demand by firms.

Branson and Rotemberg also assumed that the firms of the country they considered could sell as much as they wanted: they were in the classical regime of fixed prices equilibria theory. However, most empirical studies conclude that over the last 12 years a majority of French firms have seen their sales constrained by an insufficient demand: they have been in the Keynesian regime of this theory. The simplest confirmation of this result is given by business surveys: the percentage of firms' managers, who said they could not produce more with their currently available stock of capital, was much higher from 1969 to 1974 than from 1976 to 1982 (Malinvaud 1983, pp. 203–204; Artus 1984a). A sophisticated analysis of the results of these surveys was made by Bouissou, Laffont, and Vuong (1984). They concluded that the proportion of firms with a demand-imposed constraint on their sales strongly increased in 1974–1975. Since that time it has always been higher than 50%, and often reached 60 or 70%. The econometrics of partial or general equilibrium models with sluggish prices reaches the same conclusions out of macroeconomic data. For instance, Lambert, Lubrano, and Sneessens (1984) found a proportion of firms in the Keynesian regime similar to those given above (see also Artus 1984b; Artus, Laroque, and Michel 1984; Artus and Avouy-Dovi (1984); Artus, Avouy-Dovi, and Laroque 1985). These last studies concluded that an increase in Government spending could reduce unemployment by up to 30% (of course this policy would have other unwelcome effects, on the balance of trade and prices for instance).

Artus (1983a,b, 1986) found interesting complementary results. He applied the econometrics of partial equilibrium models with sluggish prices to the market for exports. He concluded that these are not limited by an insufficient foreign demand, but by the supply which French firms consider to be profitable enough in relation to production costs and capacities. These firms, which were in the Keynesian regime in the 1970s, would have switched to the classical regime in the 1980s. This change would explain why French exports forecasts which are made by the Ministry of Finance, and which use exports functions where the most important variables mostly act on demand, have been systematically too optimistic since 1979. Two other results by Artus are worth mentioning. First French imports have always been determined by the domestic demand for foreign goods. Second the prices of exports and imports goods are not very sensitive to the disequilibrium that prevails on the markets for these goods.

We have tried to take into account all these empirical results by putting two sectors in our model (see, e.g., Korkman 1978; Neary 1980; Cuddington, Johansson, and Lofgren 1984, chapter 4; and the review by Henin and Marois 1985, pp. 15–24). The tradable goods sector faces international competition and an infinitely elastic demand at a price fixed by the rest of the world. The balance of trade depends upon the production of this sector and the domestic demand for tradable goods. This is consistent with Artus' empirical results. The nontradable goods sector is demand-constrained. This sector accounts for the high proportion of firms which were found to be in the Keynesian regime by the above empirical studies. The two different regimes can coexist because of some sluggishness of the relative price of tradable and nontradable goods. Of course this price could be modified by monetary and exchange policies. But this point will not be investigated further.

The equations of the model are given in the first section. The second section presents the balanced growth path and indicates how this path is modified by income and fiscal policies. The short-term consequences of these policies are investigated in Section 3. Section 4 considers the transitory dynamics. We conclude by summing up the results we have found and by proposing another interpretation of the model.

1. The Equations

The model considers a small country trading with the rest of the world. This country includes two sectors denoted 1 and 2, which, respectively, produce a tradable and a nontradable commodity. The price of the tradable goods is fixed by the world market for this commodity (the exchange rate is fixed). At this price any excess of domestic supply on domestic demand can be sold without limit to foreign countries. The production of nontradable goods cannot be exported, and the domestic demand for these goods can be supplied only by domestic firms.

We assume that the relative price of both commodities stays constant over time, and we normalize this price to 1. The real wage and interest rates, ω and r, are also kept constant, and are the same in both sectors. But we will investigate the consequences of an exogenous and permanent shift of ω; this change will be called income policy. These assumptions are extreme ways to account for the fact that prices are too slugglish to clear markets in the middle run. The economic interpretation of balanced growth paths, which will be considered later, must rest on this remark: of course these paths cannot represent permanent states of the economy.

Both sectors have the same production function. Scale returns are equal to 1, and the substitution elasticity between both factors σ is constant and less than 1. At any time the capital of each sector is predetermined and employment is perfectly flexible. The average cost of the installation of I_i new units of capital in sector i is equal to cI_i/K_i. c is a positive coefficient which represents the sensibility of the installation cost to the rate of investment. Firms take their investment and employment decisions by maximizing their discounted profit, possibly under a demand constraint. Finally the paper will ignore the depreciation of capital (thus $I_i = \dot{K}_i$) and technical progress.

1.1. The Investment and Demand of Labor by the Tradable Goods Sector

The firms in this sector face an unlimited demand. This case was investigated by Uzawa (1969) and Malgrange and Villa (1984). We will give only their results (succinct proof will be given in Appendix 1).

We denote output by Y_1 and employment by L_1. Capital intensity is defined by

$$k_1 = K_1/L_1. \tag{1}$$

The production function is $F(K_1, L_1)$. We introduce

$$f(k_1) = F(K_1, L_1)/L_1 = F(k_1, 1). \tag{2}$$

1. Firms determine employment by maximizing their current profit, i.e., by equalizing the marginal productivity of labor to the wage rate ω:

$$F'_L(K_1, L_1) = f(k_1) - k_1 f'(k_1) = \omega. \tag{3}$$

This equation implies that capital intensity is an increasing function of ω:

$$k_1 = k_1(\omega), \qquad \frac{dk_1}{d\omega} = -1/(k_1 f'') > 0. \tag{4}$$

2. Firms set the growth rate of their capital to a constant level a. a is selected for the marginal productivity of capital to be equal to the user's cost of this factor: $r(1 + ca) + ca(r - a)$. This expression includes the cost of interests for purchase and the installation of one unit of investment. It also accounts for the fact that the installation of one more unit of capital will increase the average cost of installation of all current investment but will decrease the same cost for future investment. This is formalized as follows [1]:

$$\dot{K}_1/K_1 = a, \tag{5a}$$

$$F'_k(K_1, L_1) = f'[k_1(\omega)] = r + ca(2r - a), \tag{5b}$$

$$\frac{da}{d\omega} = \frac{1}{2ck_1(r - a)} < 0. \tag{5c}$$

Equation 5c shows that the lower the wage rate the higher a: when ω is weak the productivity of capital is strong and this balances the higher average installation cost which results from a faster accumulation. This paper will assume a to be positive or zero, i.e., that the tradable goods sector does not contract permanently. This requires that ω and r are not too high. The opposite situation was investigated by Malinvaud (1982), who called it classical depression.

In this sector output and employment also grow at rate a. The initial values of these variables can be computed from equations 1 and 2. The initial value of capital is predetermined:

$$L_1 = \frac{K_1}{k_1(\omega)}, \frac{dL_1}{d\omega} = -\frac{\sigma L_1 f}{\omega k_1 f'} < 0, \tag{1'}$$

$$Y_1 = \frac{K_1 f[k_1(\omega)]}{k_1(\omega)}, \frac{dY_1}{d\omega} = -\frac{\sigma L_1 f}{k_1 f'} < 0. \tag{2'}$$

A decrease of the real wage rate ω raises the growth rate a of the sector. However, as its capital intensity is positively related to ω, employment and output will immediately jump: more manpower will be allocated to the capital available at time 0, which will increase production.

1.2. The Investment and Demand of Labor by the Nontradable Goods Sector

At any time, the firms of this sector face a demand D_2 for their goods. They will serve this demand by hiring the necessary amount of labor:

$$F(K_2, L_2) = D_2. \tag{6}$$

Firms will find it worth their while to meet the whole demand if their marginal productivity of labor stays higher than the wage rate:

$$F'_L(K_2, L_2) \geqslant \omega. \tag{7}$$

We can deduce, from this and equation 3,

$$K_2/D_2 \geqslant K_1/Y_1 = k_1(\omega)/f[k_1(\omega)]. \tag{8}$$

The demand of nontradable goods is too weak for the amount of capital that is available in the sector. Thus, firms hire less labor and use a more intensive capital technique than those that would maximize their current profit if they were not demand constrained.

To determine their level of investment firms must foresee future demand. The economy is pulled by the tradable goods sector that grows at the constant rate a. We will assume that the expected demand for the goods of the other sector grows at this same rate. To simplify, the initial value of this demand will be taken equal to current sales. The optimization program which firms must solve was investigated by Malgrange and Villa (1984). We will only give their conclusions (a short proof will be given in Appendix 2).

1. First firms choose their desired capital intensity which minimizes their production cost. For this capital intensity the ratio of marginal productivities of capital to labor is equal to the ratio of factor costs: $[r + ca(2r - a)]/\omega$. In the tradable goods sector each marginal productivity is always equal to the cost of its factor. Thus, the desired capital intensity of the nontradable goods sector is equal to the current one of the other sector: $k_1(\omega)$.

2. Second firms determine their desired amount of capital consistent with a level of output just equal to expected demand. Thus, the foreseen growth rate of this capital is a, and its current value is

$$K_2^* = D_2 k_1(\omega)/f[k_1(\omega)]. \tag{9}$$

Relation 8 implies

$$K_2 \geqslant K_2^*. \tag{10}$$

Equation 10 means that the available amount of capital is larger than the desired one.

3. Finally firms adjust available to desired capital according to the dynamic process:

$$\frac{\dot{K}_2}{K_2} = \lambda[\omega, a(\omega)] \operatorname{Log}(K_2^*/K_2) + a(\omega) \qquad \frac{\partial\lambda}{\partial\omega} < 0, \quad \frac{\partial\lambda}{\partial a} > 0. \tag{11}$$

1.3. The Other Equations of the Model

These equations have been taken as simple as possible. Household's consumption is proportional to domestic product:

$$C = \gamma(Y_1 + Y_2), \qquad 0 < \gamma < 1. \tag{12}$$

Government consumption grows at the long-run rate of the economy a:

$$G = G_0 e^{at}. \tag{13}$$

A permanent shift of G_0, starting at time 0, will be called fiscal policy. Domestic demand D is equal to the sum of both consumptions and investment:

$$D = C + G + \dot{K}_1 + \dot{K}_2. \tag{14}$$

D is allocated between goods 1 and 2 in the proportions $1 - m$ and m:

$$D_1 = (1 - m)D, \; D_2 = mD. \tag{15}$$

Finally, labor supply N is always high enough for the economy to stay in an unemployment situation:

$$L_1 + L_2 < N. \tag{16}$$

1.4. The Balance of Trade

The surplus of the balance can be written

$$B = Y_1 - D_1 = Y_1 - (1 - m)D. \tag{17}$$

It is equal to the excess of production on domestic demand of tradable goods.[2] This demand is equal to the proportion $1 - m$, of total domestic demand D. As the output of nontradable goods Y_2 is just equal to the demand for it mD, the surplus of the balance of trade can be rewritten:

$$B = Y_1 - (1/m - 1)\, Y_2 = [Y_1/Y_2 - (1-m)/m]\, Y_2. \tag{18}$$

This balance is in equilibrium when the allocation of production between sectors is the same as the allocation of domestic demand between goods (this last, $m/(1 - m)$ is fixed). If the country produces *relatively* more tradable goods than it uses, its trade balance will be in surplus. It will be in deficit in the opposite situation.

2. The Middle Run

This term will denote the balanced growth path of the model. On this path all the economic variables grow at the same rate a, as the capital of the tradable goods sector. We saw that when factor costs decrease, i.e., when profitability rises in Malinvaud's terminology, then a increases. The variables of this sector will represent the initial values of the middle-run path. The determination of these variables for the tradable goods sector has already been investigated in section 1.1.

2.1. The Nontradable Goods Sector

In the middle run capital intensity has reached its desired value, and is the same as in the other sector: k_1. Section 1.1 showed that the marginal productivity of labor at k_1 is equal to the wage rate. Thus, the notional and effective supplies of nontradable goods have become equal.[3] The disequilibrium of the market has vanished in spite of the fixity of the relative price of the two goods. The last assumption should look more reasonable now because of this result. Let us put

$$p(\omega) = \dot{K}_2 / Y_2 + \gamma = a(\omega)\, k_1(\omega)/f[k_1(\omega)] + \gamma,$$

$$\frac{\partial p}{\partial \omega} = \{ -1/[2c(r-a)] + a\sigma/f' \}/f, \tag{19}$$

and

$$A(\omega, G_0) = G_0 + \gamma Y_1(\omega) + a(\omega) K_1,$$

$$\frac{\partial A}{\partial \omega} = -L_1 \{ \gamma\sigma f/(f' k_1) + 1/[2c(r-a)] \} < 0. \tag{20}$$

After some elimination of variables we get the expressions of output and employment in the nontradable goods sector:

$$Y_2 = MA, \text{ with } M = m/(1 - mp), \tag{21}$$

$$L_2 = Y_2/f[k_1(\omega)]. \tag{22}$$

$mA(\omega, G_0)$ represents the autonomous demand for commodity 2. $A(\omega, G_0)$ is the total autonomous demand and has three components:

1. Government consumption G_0.
2. The part of household's consumption that is related to the output of the

tradable goods sector. This consumption increases when the real wage rate ω decreases.

3. The investment by the tradable goods sector. This investment rises when the growth rate of this sector lessens, thus when ω decreases.

$mp(\omega)$ represents the propensity to spend on commodity 2, and $p(\omega)$ is the total propensity to spend. It is the sum of two components:

1. The propensity to invest ($\dot{K}_2/Y_2 = \dot{K}_1/Y_1$). If the wage rate ω decreases, two opposite effects take place: (a) The growth rate of the economy, thus of its capital ($\dot{K}_2/K_2 = \dot{K}_1/K_1$) increases. (b) Production becomes more labor intensive, thus the ratio of capital to output ($K_2/Y_2 = K_1/Y_1$) decreases. However, the first effect is stronger than the second and the propensity to invest rises.[4]
2. The propensity to consume γ which has been exogenously fixed.

The regularity of the results requires the propensity to spend on nontradable goods, mp, be be less than one. This condition can be written $m(aK_1/Y_1 + \gamma) < 1$. It implies the positivity of the multiplier M and is satisfied for any reasonable value of parameters.

A decrease of the wage rate ω raises autonomous demand and the multiplier. Thus, the output of the nontradable goods sector increases. Employment rises too, first because production is higher and second because it is more labor intensive.

The medium-run effects of fiscal policy are given by

$$\frac{\partial Y_2}{\partial G_0} = M \tag{23}$$

and

$$\frac{\partial L_2}{\partial G_0} = \frac{M}{f[k_1(\omega)]}. \tag{24}$$

2.2. The Trade Balance

Equation 18 and the previous results give

$$B = Y_1(\omega) - (1/m - 1)Y_2(\omega, G_0 = B(\omega, G_0)). \tag{25}$$

When Government consumption increases, the output of tradable goods stays unchanged and the output of the other commodity rises. Thus, the trade balance deteriorates. When the cost of labor ω increases the output of both sectors increases, and the direction of change of the balance of trade is uncertain. If this balance was initially in equilibrium we could show

$$\frac{\partial B}{\partial \omega} = \{1/[2c(r-a)] - (1-\gamma)\sigma f/(k_1 f')\} L_1/(1-mp). \tag{26}$$

This relation can be written

$$\frac{\partial B}{\partial \omega} = \left[-\frac{\partial \dot{K}_1}{\partial \omega} + (1-\gamma)\frac{\partial Y_1}{\partial \omega}\right] \Big/ (1-mp). \tag{27}$$

If m was zero, i.e., if only the tradable goods sector existed, a decrease of the wage rate would have two effects on the balance of trade, the first positive and the second negative: (a) The excess of output on consumption would increase by $(1-\gamma)\ \partial Y_1/\partial\omega$. (b) Investment, which is a component of demand, would rise by $\partial \dot{K}_1/\partial\omega$. The positive effect would be the stronger if (a) the substitution elasticity σ was sufficiently high: then the employment and output per unit of capital would increase; (b) the propensity to consume γ was weak enough; and (c) the average cost of capital installation was sufficiently sensitive to the rate of accumulation in order to slow down the increase of this rate (c high). Equation 27 shows that this interpretation is still valid if both sectors coexist ($m \neq 0$).

A mix of income and fiscal policies can keep the balance of trade unchanged and improve the situation in both sectors. A decrease of the real wage rate will raise output and employment; then if the trade balance improves, these effects can be strengthened in the nontradable goods sector by fiscal expansion[5]; if not the excessive increase of the output of the last sector in relation to the other will be corrected by a decrease of Government consumption.

3. The Short Run

3.1. The Nontradable Goods Sector

The immediate effects of a permanent change of the real wage rate or of Government consumption on the output or the employment of this sector are quite different in the short run and in the long run. Now the available capital is predetermined and higher than its desired amount. It is easy to show that

$$dY_2 = N dG_0 + N\left\{A'_\omega + K_2\left[a'_\omega + \lambda'_\omega\left(\mathrm{Log}\frac{f_2}{k_2} - \mathrm{Log}\frac{f_1}{k_1}\right) + \lambda\frac{\sigma}{k_1 f'_1}\right]\right\} d\omega, \tag{28}$$

with $N = m/(1 - mq)$ and $q = \gamma + \lambda K_2/Y_2$, and

$$dL_2 = \frac{dY_2}{F'_L(K_2, L_2)}. \tag{29}$$

mq represents the marginal propensity of sector 2 to spend on the commodity it produces. q is the total marginal propensity to spend of this sector: when its output increases by dY_2, its consumption rises by γdY_2, and the amount of desired capital K_2^* by $(k_1/f_1)\,dY_2$; then equation (11) shows that investment increases by:

$$\lambda K_2\, dK_2^*/K_2^* = \lambda K_2\, dY_2/Y_2.$$

The regularity of the results requires mq to be less than one. This condition will be satisfied if the available amount of capital adjusts slowly enough to its desired value (i.e., if λ is low) or if the relative weight of the nontradable goods sector m is weak enough.[6] Then the short-run multiplier N is positive.

A decrease of the real wage rate by $d\omega < 0$ will modify total demand and consequently the output of nontradable goods. This last change will in turn react on total demand. The direct effect of income policy, which does not take into account the alteration in the output of nontradable goods, is represented by the term within brackets in equation 28. The global consequence of this policy is N times its direct effect, which can be split into four components:

1. The demand by the tradable goods sector increases by $A'_\omega\, d\omega > 0$, as we saw in the previous section.
2. The long-run accumulation rate a increases, as we saw in Section 1, and investment by the nontradable goods sector rises by $a'_\omega\, K_2\, d\omega > 0$.
3. The available capital in this sector is higher than its desired value and will adjust at rate λ. This implies a disinvestment, which becomes faster when ω decreases, because λ rises in these circumstances (term $\lambda'_\omega K_2\,[\mathrm{Log}(f_2/k_2) - \mathrm{Log}(f_1/k_1)]\,d\omega < 0$).
4. Capital intensity and the desired amount of capital are inversely related to ω. This strengthens the previous disinvestment (term: $[\lambda K_2 \sigma/(k_1 f'_1)]\,d\omega < 0$).

Components 1 and 2 increase total demand and components 3 and 4 have the opposite consequence. Thus, the direct effects of a reduction of the cost of labor are uncertain in the short run: the output and employment of the nontradable goods sector may increase or decrease. The immediate consequences of fiscal policy are given by

$$\frac{\partial Y_2}{\partial G_0} = N \tag{30}$$

and

$$\frac{\partial L_2}{\partial G_0} = \frac{N}{F'_L(K_2, L_2)}. \tag{31}$$

The middle-run and short-run propensities to spend are, respectively, $p = ak_1/f_1 + \gamma$ and $q = \lambda K_2/Y_2 + \gamma$ (equations 19 and 28). As $K_2/Y_2 > k_1/f_1$ (inequality 8), and because empirical studies find the adjustment parameter λ to be larger than the growth rate a, we have $q > p$. The multiplier, which measures the effect of an increase of Government consumption on the output of the nontradable goods sector, is higher in the short run than in the middle run.

3.2. The Trade Balance

A decrease of the wage rate ω immediately raises the output of the tradable goods. But the effect on the output of the other commodity is uncertain. So we do not know how the trade balance B will be modified. However, if this balance was initially in equilibrium, and if capital intensities of both sectors do not differ by too much, it is easy to show that the derivative of B relative to ω is N/M times larger in the short run than the middle run (given by Section 2.6). So this balance changes in the same direction at both ranges.

If Government consumption increases, Y_2 rises and the trade balance deteriorates to a larger extent than in the middle run. A mix of income and fiscal policies can keep the balance of trade unchanged and improve the policy mix situation in both sectors. The only difference with the middle run is a smaller change in Government consumption. The decrease of labor cost may possibly have an expansionary effect on sector 1 and contract sector 2. Then the trade balance improves and some room is left for an expansionary fiscal policy, which will prevent sector 2 from going into recession. This result agrees with the recommendations of Malinvaud (1982) and Sachs (1982), which were to correct the transitory depressive effect of a rigorous income policy by an expansionary fiscal or monetary policy.

4. The Dynamics of the Nontradable Goods Sector

The previous sections investigated the immediate and final effects of a permanent change of economic policy. Now we must analyze the transitory path that the economy follows between the short and the middle run. This path was already described in Section 1.1 for the variables of the tradable goods sector. We still have to look at the variables of the other sector. We start by dividing them by their trend e^{at} and we write the equations of the model in terms of these new "reduced" variables:

$$K'_2 = K_2/e^{at}, \qquad D'_2 = D_2/e^{at}, \qquad L'_2 = L_2/e^{at}. \tag{32}$$

Now the model has a steady state that is identical to the initial values of the balanced growth path of Section 2. Let us assume the economy to be in the neighborhood of this state. If we compute a linear approximation of the equations we get, after some elimination of variables,

$$\Delta\dot{K}'_2 = -\varphi\Delta K'_2 \text{ with } \varphi = \lambda(1 - mp)/(1 - mq), \qquad p < q < 1/m. \tag{33}$$

Δ represents the difference between the current value of a reduced variable and its steady state. p and q are the total marginal propensities to spend by the nontradable goods sector, respectively, in the short run and the middle run. Equation 33 determines stable dynamics with a rate of convergence equal to $-\varphi$.

Inequality 8 must be satisfied for the nontradable goods sector to be in the Keynesian regime. When this condition is expressed with reduced variables it becomes

$$\Delta\dot{K}'_2 \geqslant [k_1/f(k_1)]\Delta D'_2. \tag{34}$$

After some elimination of variables we get

$$\frac{f(k_1)}{k_1}\frac{1 - mp}{1 - mq}\Delta K'_2 \geqslant 0, \text{ or } \Delta K'_2 \geqslant 0. \tag{35}$$

This relation means that the sector initially has an excess amount of capital, larger than the value taken by this variable on the middle-run path at the same time.

In the case of investment the relation between original and reduced variables is

$$\dot{K}_2 = e^{at}(\dot{K}'_2 + aK'_2). \tag{36}$$

From equation 36 and previous conditions we deduce

$$\dot{K}_2 = e^{at}[(-\varphi + a)(K'_2(0) - \hat{K}'_2)e^{\varphi t} + a\hat{K}'_2)], \qquad 0 < a < \varphi \tag{37}$$

where ˆ denotes the steady state. It may easily be noticed that investment is positive at any time if, and only if, it is positive at time 0. This last condition is equivalent to

$$(K'_2(0) - \hat{K}'_2)/K'_2(0) \langle a/\varphi. \tag{38}$$

It is satisfied if $K'_2(0)/\hat{K}'_2 \langle (\varphi - a)$, i.e., if the capital available at time 0 is not too high. This result can easily be understood. We simultaneously have an investment of growth and a disinvestment of adjustment. The first will be larger than the second if this one is weak enough, i.e., if the excess of initial capital is small enough.

Conclusion

This article has developed a model of a country with two productive sectors. The first faces the competition of the rest of the world which takes the form of a given price and an unlimited demand. The second does not face such competition, but suffers from a domestic demand that is too weak in comparison to the available capital and the cost of labor. The trade balance is in equilibrium when the structures by commodities of production and demand are the same (the second structure is exogenously given). The conclusions are the juxtaposition of the results reached in two extreme situations. The first focuses on the substitution between capital and labor. The second centers around the dependence of the accumulation rate of the first sector upon its profitability.

1. Let us assume capital to be fixed in both sectors (this will be the case if c, the sensitivity of the installation cost to the accumulation rate, is infinite). A decrease of the real wage rate will induce firms of the tradable goods sector to hire more labor and to raise their output. This will result in a higher distributed income, which will increase consumption and the output of nontradable commodities. But as long as the propensity to consume is less than one, the first sector will inflate more than the second and the trade balance will improve. Then it is possible to strengthen the better situation of employment and output in the nontradable goods sector by a fiscal expansion.

2. We assume now the two factors to be complementary ($\sigma = 0$, see figure 1). Then the capital intensity of both sectors is fixed, and employment is proportional to output. We also assume that before time 0 outputs Y_1 and Y_2 grew at the same rate and that the trade balance was in

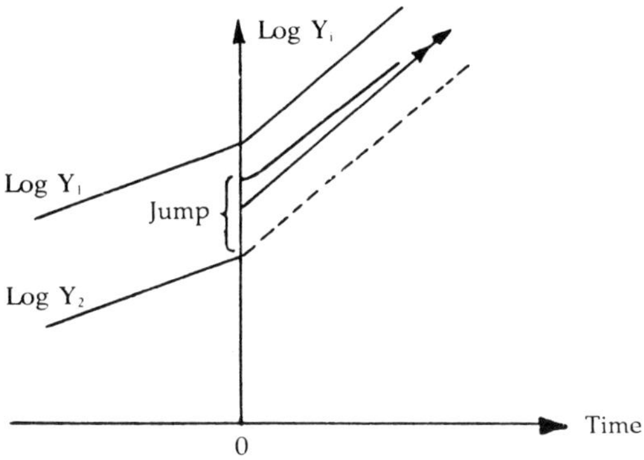

Figure 1.

equilibrium. At this time the cost of labor permanently decreases by a given amount, thus the profitability of capital rises. Consequently, the growth rate of Y_1 and the asymptotic growth rate of Y_2 increase. But this change induces a higher investment, hence an immediate increase of demand and a positive jump of the output Y_2 of nontradable goods. The share of these goods in the total domestic product increases and the trade balance deteriorates. A decrease of Government consumption will correct this disequilibrium and remove the discontinuity of the Y_2 path (dotted line in figure 1).

A model that may look very different *a priori* would also consider two sectors. The first would produce an importable commodity. The domestic demand for it would be met by domestic and foreign firms at the world price. The second sector would make exportable goods the price of which would be fixed by domestic firms and would be rigid. These firms would face an insufficient demand by nationals and foreigners. Artus (1986) identified this situation in France before 1978. Now, as Cuddington, Johansson, and Lofgren (1984, p. 129) noticed, if the foreign demand for exports was zero and if we renamed the two goods tradable and nontradable, we would get exactly the model of this article. If the foreign demand was independent of endogenous domestic variables, i.e., if it was exogenous, we would only get a small generalization of our model. Thus, this one can account for an economic situation that is very different from the one we wanted to investigate.

This paper inspired an econometric study on French data by Artus, Avouyi-Dovi, and Laffargue (1987). In this research the two sectors were manufacturing and the rest of the economy, respectively. It clearly appeared that since the mid-1970s the first sector had suffered from too weak productive capacities in comparison to demand; the second sector had been constrained by an insufficient demand. These results agree with the assumptions of this paper. However the disequilibrium of the nonmanufacturing sector was always weak and a too ambitious fiscal policy could have switched the regime. Moreover the foreign trade in manufacturing commodities appeared not very sensitive to prices, which goes against the assumption of this paper of an infinite elasticity of the demand of tradable goods. The reason for the sluggishness of these prices must still be found: why would firms not increase their prices if excess of demand weakly depended on them? This question is currently being investigated.

Appendix 1

Firms maximize the present value of their cash flows:

$$\max_{L_1 \dot{K}_1} \int_o^{+\infty} [F(K_1, L_1) - \omega L_1 - \dot{K}_1 (1 + c\dot{K}_1/K_1)] e^{-rt} dt$$

with $K_1(0)$ given.

Euler's conditions are

$$f(k_1) - f'(k_1) k_1 = \omega,$$

$$2\dot{a} + a^2 - 2ra + [f'(k_1) - r]/c = 0, \qquad a = \dot{K}/K_1.$$

The transversality condition is

$$\lim_{t \to \infty} e^{-rt} K_1 (1 + 2ca) = 0.$$

It implies that a immediately adjusts to its smaller steady-state value (which is unstable for the differential equation).

Appendix 2

Firms minimize the present value of their future costs, under their demand constraint. First they determine employment L_2 by $D_2(0) e^{at} = F(K_2, L_2)$. Then they compute investment by

$$\text{Min} \int_0^{+\infty} [\omega L_2 + \dot{K}_2 (1 + c\dot{K}_2/K_2)] e^{-rt} dt, \quad K_2(0) \text{ given.}$$

Let us put $a_2 = \dot{K}_2/K_2$ and $u = \log K_2 - a$.

Euler's condition gives

$$2\dot{a}_2 + a_2^2 - 2ra_2 + [f'(k_2) - r]/c$$
$$= f'(k_2)\{1 - \omega/[f(k_2) - f'(k_2)k_2]\}/c.$$

In the steady state we have $k_2 = k_1$, $u = \bar{u} = \log[D_2(0)k_1/f(k_1)]$.

We compute a linear approximation in the neighborhood of this state:

$$\ddot{u} - (r - a)\dot{u} - [f(k_1)/(2c\sigma\omega)](u - \bar{u}) = 0.$$

The transversality condition implies that only the negative root of the characteristic equation must be retained:

$$\lambda = [r - a - \sqrt{(r - a)^2 + 2f(k_1)/(c\sigma\omega)}]/2.$$

Then $\dot{K}_2/K_2 = a + \lambda \log[K_2 f(k_1)/(k_1 D_2(0)e^{at})]$.

Acknowledgments

This research has benefited from a grant by the "Commissariat Général du Plan." A preliminary version was presented at the workshops of this institution, the "Direction de la Prévision" and the "Séminaire d'Economie Monétaire Internationale de Paris." We are grateful for the helpful remarks and suggestions that were made at these meetings. Our most special thanks are for Artus and Avouyi-Dovi and an anonymous referee.

Notes

1. The transversality condition of the program of the firms implies that the accumulation rate of capital is less than the interest rate: $a < r$. Equation 5b, which is a second degree equation in a, has real roots only if $f'(k_1) < r(1 + cr)$. This requires r and ω to be sufficiently high. Then the sum of these roots is equal to $2r$. Only the smallest satisfies the transversality condition.

2. This article assumes that the installation cost of capital takes the form of a destruction of tradable goods. This cost should appear with the minus sign in the definition of the surplus of the trade balance. We have prefered to omit it from equation 17 in order not to make our development too cumbersome by the introduction of mechanisms that are neither important nor interesting.

3. This result rests upon the facts that both sectors face the same factor costs and have the same production function, which is homogeneous of degree 1.

4. We have assumed that $\sigma < 1$. Equation 5b implies that $f' > r + 2ca(r - a)$. Then $a\sigma/f' < 1/[r/a + 2c(r - a)] < 1/[2c(r - a)]$.

5. Dreze and Modigliani (1981) built a very different model for Belgium, with numerical values given to parameters. Their conclusion was that a decrease of real wage would improve the trade balance, which would leave some room for fiscal expansion. However, the saturation of the productive capacities and the weak substitutability of labor to capital in the short run imply that the increase of employment would be very slow.

6. The regularity condition would also be satisfied if consumption would adjust to domestic products slowly, and not instantaneously as here.

References

Artus, P. 1983a. Les exportations: approche par le déséquilibre. ENSAE and Unité de Recherche INSEE Document de travail 8302.

Artus, P. 1983b. La courbe J dans trois grands pays industriels: la France, l'Allemagne et le Japon. ENSAE and Unité de Recherche INSEE Document de travail 8304.

Artus, P. 1983c. "Formation des prix et des salaires dans cinq grands pays industrialisés." *Annales de l'INSEE* 49: 5–52.

Artus, P. 1984a. "Capacité de production, demande de facteurs et incertitude sur la demande." *Annales de l'INSEE* 53: 3–29.

Artus, P. 1984b. "Analyse du marché des biens dans le secteur industriel." *Annales de l'INSEE* 55–56: 77–107.

Artus, P. 1986. "Comment fonctionne le marché des exportations?" *Annales d'Economie et de Statistique* 2: 3–36.

Artus, P., and Avouyi-Dovi, S. 1984. "Une estimation comparative de modéles avec rationnement quantitatif pour la France et les Etats-Unis." *Economie Appliquée* 37(3–4): 489–522.

Artus, P., Avouyi-Dovi, S., and Laffargue, J.-P. 1987. "Un modèle économétrique de déséquilibre à deux secteurs et son apport à l'analyse des politiques économiques." *Observations et diagnostics économiques. Revue de l'OFCE* 21: 211–236.

Artus, P., Avouyi-Dovi, S., and Laroque, G. 1985. "Estimation d'une maquette macroéconomique trimestrielle avec rationnements quantitatifs." *Annales de l'INSEE* 57: 3–25.

Artus, P., Laroque, G., and Michel, G. 1984. "Estimation of a Quarterly Macroeconomic Model with Quantity Rationing." *Econometrica* 52(6): 1387–1414.

Bouissou, M.-B., Laffont, J.-J., and Vuong, Q. H. 1984. "Econométrie du déséquilibre sur données microéconomiques." *Annales de l'INSEE* 55–56: 109–151.

Branson, W. H., and Rotemberg, J. J. 1980. "International Adjustment with Wage Rigidity." *European Economic Review* 13(3): 309–341 (with comments by J. Sachs and R. Portes).

Cuddington, J. T., Johansson, P.-O., and Lofgren, K.-G. 1984. *Disequilibrium in Open Economies*. Basil Blackwell.

Dreze, J.-H., and Modigliani, F. 1981. "The Trade-off between Real Wages and Employment in an Open Economy (Belgium)." *European Economic Review* 15(1): 1–40.

Henin, P.-Y., and Marois, W. 1985. "Sur les déséquilibres d'une économie ouverte: une revue des recherches récentes." In Henin, P.-Y., Marois, W., and Michel, P. (eds.),*Déséquilibres en économie ouverte*. Economica.

Korman, S. 1978. "The Devaluation Cycle." *Oxford Economic Papers* 30: 357–366.

Lambert, J.-P., Lubrano, M., and Snessens, H. R. 1984. "Emploi et chômage en France de 1955 à 1982: un modèle macroéconomique annuel avec rationnement." *Annales de l'INSEE* 55–56: 39–75.

Malgrange, P., and Villa, P. 1984. "Comportement d'investissement avec coûts d'adjustements et contraintes quantitatives." *Annales de l'INSEE* 53: 31–61.

Malinvaud, E. 1982. "Wages and Unemployment." *Economic Journal* 92: 1–12.

Malinvaud, E. 1983a. "*Essais sur la théorie du chômage*. Paris: Calman-Lévy.

Malinvaud, E. 1983b. Profitability and Investment Facing Uncertain Demand. ENSAE and Unité de Recherche INSEE Document de travail 8303.

Malinvaud, E. 1986. "Jusqu'où la rigeur salariale devrait-elle aller? Une exploration théorique de la question." *Revue Economique* 37: 181–205.

Neary, J. P. 1980. "Non-traded Goods and the Balance of Trade in a Neo-Keynesian Temporary Equilibrium." *Quarterly Journal of Economics* 95: 403–429.

Sachs, J. D. 1983. "Real Wages and Unemployment in the OECD Countries." *Brookings Papers on Economic Activity* 1: 255–304 (with a comment by R. J. Gordon).

Steinherr, A. 1983. Income Distribution and Employment in the European Communities. 1960–1982. Economic Papers, Commission of the European Communities, No. 23.

Uzawa, H. 1969. "Time Preference and the Penrose Effect in a Two Class Model of Economic Growth." *Journal of Political Economy* 77: 628–654.

23 The Impact of a Policy of Investment Subsidies on Unemployment

Philippe Michel

1. Introduction

In the Western world, corporate taxation and investment subsidies are common practice. Since the seminal work of Modigliani and Miller (1958) and of Hall and Jorgenson (1967), many economic studies have been devoted to this subject (see for example King's book 1977; Poterba and Summers 1983). Relaxing the assumption of perfect price flexibility leads one to an analysis of quantity adjustments in a disequilibrium framework (Barro and Grossman 1971; Benassy 1975; Dreze 1975; Malinvaud 1977). Following Malinvaud (1980), many authors have studied the dynamics of capital formation in this context (d'Autume 1982; Blanchard and Sachs 1982; Fourgeaud and Michel 1982; Henin and Michel 1982; Michel 1982; Picard 1982. Moreover, the study of economic policy and social welfare pricing in a disequilibrium economy have also been examined (Bernard 1982; Dreze 1985; Marchand, Minz, and Pestieau 1983; Picard 1983; Fourgeaud, Lenclud, and Picard 1985. Following these two approaches (i.e., those of capital formation and policy analysis in disequilibrium) we examine the effects of investment subsidies in an economy with unemployment.

The difficulty of studying dynamics in disequilibrium makes it possible to do so only with simplifying assumptions. Both the formulation of the model and the type of disequilibrium we consider in this paper are straightforward. We focus on the case of *classical unemployment* with real wage rigidity. In order to study the *decentralized* economy in this context, we consider investment subsidies that sustain a second best growth path.

The *centralized* model is simply a modified version of the Ramsey one-sector optimal growth model. The full employment assumption is replaced with a fixed lower bound on the marginal productivity of labor. When this constraint is binding, full employment can be reached only with a larger capital stock. The solution is a second best growth path. This is not an equilibrium path since the social benefit of employment resulting from the increased capital stock will not be taken into account by profit-maximizing firms.

In order to sustain the second best growth path as an equilibrium in a decentralized economy, government intervention is necessary. Intertemporal equilibrium with perfect foresight is studied in a model with one representative consumer and one representative firm. Government intervention is limited to lump sum taxes on consumer income and to payments of investment subsidies to firms. The subsidies, which exactly cover the difference between public and private valuations of capital, lead to an equilibrium that coincides with the second best growth path. The difference between these two valuations of capital is equal to the difference between the average productivity and the marginal productivity of capital.

2. Second Best Growth with a Labor Productivity Constraint

A constraint on the marginal productivity of labor is introduced in the Ramsey (1928) optimal growth model and a second best growth path results.

The one-sector optimal growth model can be written

$$\text{Maximize} \int_0^\infty e^{-\delta t} U(c(t))\, dt \tag{1}$$

subject to

$$\begin{aligned} &c(t) + i(t) \leqslant F(k(t), n(t)), \\ &c(t) \geqslant 0, \qquad i(t) \geqslant 0, \qquad 0 \leqslant n(t) \leqslant 1, \\ &\dot{k}(t) = i(t), \qquad k(0) = k_0. \end{aligned} \tag{2}$$

All variables are expressed in reduced form, per unit of labor supply: consumption $c(t)$, investment $i(t)$, capital stock $k(t)$, and employment $n(t)$. The production function F is concave and increasing, with constant return to scale and decreasing returns to each factor, capital and labor.

In order to simplify notations, capital depreciation is not explicit, but is implicitly substracted in the production function. Thus, throughout the study, average and marginal productivities of capital will be *net* of depreciation.

Now assume that the central planner controls investment but not the employment level. Wage rigidity is represented by a fixed lower bound w

on the marginal productivity of labor:

$$F'_n(k(t), n(t)) \geqslant w. \tag{3}$$

2.1. An Equivalent Form of the Constraint on the Marginal Productivity of Labor

Condition 3 is equivalent to a labor demand constraint:

$$n(t) \leqslant n^d(k(t)), \qquad \text{where } F'_n(k, n^d(k)) = w.$$

Let $\bar{k}$ be the minimum capital stock required for full employment: $n^d(\bar{k}) = 1$, or $F'_n(\bar{k}, 1) = w$. The property that F is homogeneous of degree 1 implies that F'_n is homogeneous of degree 0 and

$$F'_n(k/n^d(k), 1) = w = F'_n(\bar{k}, 1).$$

Thus, $n^d(k) = k/\bar{k}$, and constraint 3 can be replaced by the equivalent constraint

$$F(k(t), n(t)) \leqslant F(k(t), n^d(k(t))) = k(t)\, F(\bar{k}, 1)/\bar{k}, \tag{3'}$$

which imposes an upper bound on the average productivity of capital $F(k, n)/k$. This upper bound is equal to the average productivity $F(\bar{k}, 1)/\bar{k}$ of the full employment capital stock $\bar{k}$.

This equivalent form of constraint 3 is easy to understand. The assumptions of constant returns to scale and a given marginal productivity of labor imply both a constant labor-capital ratio and a constant production-capital ratio.

2.2. Optimality Conditions

Two constraints limit production in the second best growth problem (1, 2, 3′)—the full employment limitation and the upper bound on the average productivity of capital:

$$\begin{aligned} c + i &\leqslant F(k, 1), \\ c + i &\leqslant kF(\bar{k}, 1)/\bar{k}. \end{aligned} \tag{4}$$

Optimal choices of consumption and investment maximize the Hamiltonian

$$H = U(c) + qi + \alpha[F(k, 1) - c - i] + \beta[kF\,\bar{k}, 1)/(\bar{k} - c - i].$$

Thus, an interior optimal solution ($c > 0, i > 0$) satisfies

$$U'(c) = \alpha + \beta = q. \tag{5}$$

The marginal utility of consumption is equal to both the total value of production, $\alpha + \beta$, and the marginal social value of capital q. The evolution equation of q is

$$\dot{q} = \delta q - \partial H/\partial k = \delta q - \alpha F'_k(k, 1) - \beta F(\bar{k}, 1)/\bar{k}. \tag{6}$$

The multipliers α and β are nonnegative and satisfy

$$\alpha[F(k, 1) - c - i] = 0 \text{ and } \beta[kF(\bar{k}, 1)/\bar{k} - c - i] = 0. \tag{7}$$

2.3. Short-Term Disequilibrium

Since the multipliers α and β are not simultaneously zero (see relation 5), the relations in 7 imply

$$c + i = \min\{F(k, 1), kF(\bar{k}, 1)/\bar{k}\} = F(k, n).$$

The optimal level of employment is

$$n = \min\{1, k/\bar{k}\}.$$

When $k < \bar{k}$, there is unemployment ($n = k/\bar{k} < 1$), and when $k \geqslant \bar{k}$, there is full employment ($n = 1$). Along an unemployment trajectory, the average productivity of capital is constant: $F(k, n)/k = F(\bar{k}, 1)/\bar{k}$.

2.4. Stationary Equilibrium

The stationary equilibrium $(\hat{k}, \hat{n})$ satisfies the following properties:

$$\begin{aligned} &\delta(\alpha + \beta) = \alpha F'_k(\hat{k}, 1) + \beta F(\bar{k}, 1)/\bar{k}, \\ &\hat{n} = \min\{1, \hat{k}/\bar{k}\}, \\ &\alpha(1 - \hat{n}) = 0, \\ &\beta(\bar{k} - \hat{k}) = 0. \end{aligned} \tag{8}$$

Since α and β are not simultaneously zero, there are three possibilities.

- With $\alpha > 0$ and $\beta = 0$, the stationary equilibrium is given by

$$\hat{n} = 1 \text{ and } F'_k(\hat{k}, 1) = \delta.$$

This is the *unconstrained* Ramsey stationary equilibrium at which the *margi-*

nal productivity of capital is equal to the time rate of preference δ. This stationary equilibrium holds iff $\bar{k} \leqslant \hat{k}$, i.e., iff $F'_k(\bar{k}, 1) \geqslant \delta$.

• With $\alpha = 0$ and $\beta > 0$, a stationary equilibrium with *unemployment* is obtained at which the *average* productivity of capital is equal to the time rate of preference: $F(\hat{k}, \hat{n})/\hat{k} = F(\bar{k}, 1)/\bar{k} = \delta$. In this case, for any initial stock $k_0 < \bar{k}$, the stationary trajectory, $\hat{k} = k_0$ and $\hat{n} = k_0/\bar{k} = n_0$, is optimal since it satisfies the sufficient conditions for optimality (Arrow and Kurz 1970).

• In the third case, $\alpha > 0$ and $\beta > 0$, the stationary equilibrium is a *constrained full employment* equilibrium: $\hat{k} = \bar{k}$ and $\hat{n} = 1$. This stationary equilibrium corresponds to the case where the time rate of preference appears *between* the marginal productivity and the *average* productivity of capital:

$$F'_k(\bar{k}, 1) < \delta < F(\bar{k}, 1)/\bar{k}.$$

Remark. Only when $\delta \leqslant F(\bar{k}, 1)/\bar{k}$, a stationary equilibrium (with positive capital stock) has been obtained. When the average productivity of capital $F(\bar{k}, 1)/\bar{k}$ is smaller than δ, then the optimal values of k and n converge to zero. This corresponds to the case of *increasing unemployment*.

2.5. Interpretation: Two Different Factor Price Frontiers

In a decentralized economy, the factor price frontier (F.P.F.) is defined by the equality of each price, δ for capital and w for labor, with their respective marginal productivities:

$$F'_k(k, 1) = \delta \text{ and } F'_n(k, 1) = w. \tag{9}$$

When these two factor prices are sticky, the dynamics of the economy crucially depends on the position of the factor prices with respect to the F.P.F. Above the F.P.F., i.e., where prices are too high, the capital stock diminishes and converges to zero leading to increasing unemployment. Below the F.P.F., the usual neoclassical capital formation prevails with full employment (see Laussel 1980; Michel 1982; Henin and Michel 1982). We will refer to the F.P.F. defined by equation 9 as the *marginal* F.P.F. to distinguish it from the following one.

In our study of second best growth, there is another F.P.F. which helps to separate alternative stationary equilibria. This F.P.F. is obtained by substituting the marginal productivity of capital by its average productivity:

$$F(k, 1)/k = \delta \qquad \text{and} \qquad F'_n(k, 1) = w. \tag{10}$$

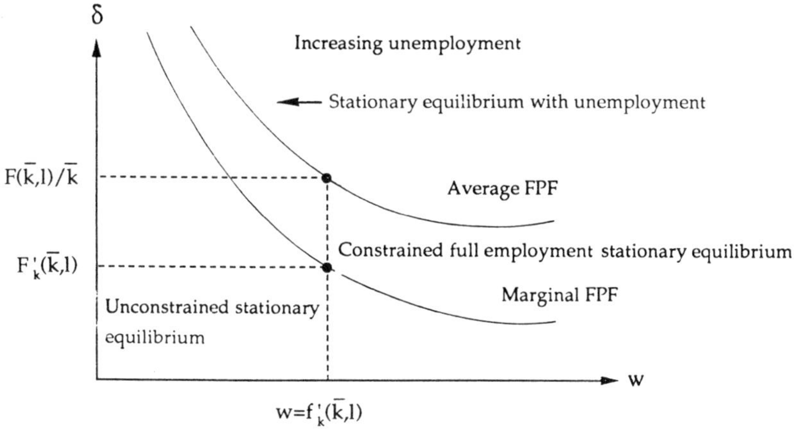

Figure 1.
Types of stationary equilibria.

We will call equation 10 the *average* F.P.F. Between the two F.P.F.s, the stationary equilibrium is a constrained full employment equilibrium (see figure 1). Below the marginal F.P.F., unconstrained full employment stationary equilibria appear. Above the average F.P.F., there is increasing unemployment.

The most interesting case occurs when factor prices are excessive but not too high, i.e., somewhere between the two F.P.F.s. In this case, the optimal centralized investment decision reverses the decentralized tendancy of the economy (toward increasing unemployment) and leads the economy to a constrained full employment stationary equilibrium.

This occurs as a result of the difference between private and public valuations of capital when there is some unemployment of labor. In this case, the public valuation of capital is based on the average productivity of capital rather than on its marginal productivity. This property is demonstrated below.

2.6. Second Best Dynamics

From relation 6, we have the following expression for the user cost of capital (as calculated by the central planner):

$$\delta - \dot{q}/q = (\alpha/q)\, F_k' (k, 1) + (\beta/q)\, F(\bar{k}, 1)/\bar{k}. \tag{11}$$

Here, the user cost of capital consists of a combination of both the marginal and average productivities of capital.

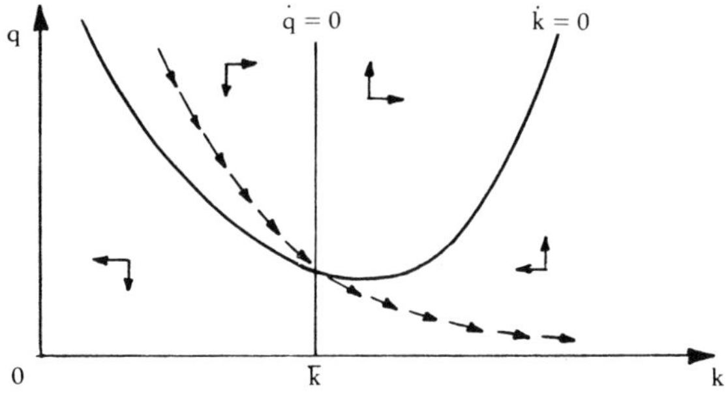

Figure 2.
Dynamics in the case of a constrained full employment stationary equilibrium.

When unemployment exists, i.e., for $k < \bar{k}$, then $\alpha = 0$ and $\beta = q$. Thus, the user cost of capital is equal to its *average* productivity (which is constant): $F(k, n)/k = F(\bar{k}, 1)/\bar{k}$. When there is excess capacity, i.e., when $k > \bar{k}$, then $\alpha = q$ and $\beta = 0$, and thus the user cost of capital is equal to its *marginal* productivity.

At the constrained full employment stationary equilibrium $\bar{k}$, the user cost of capital takes an *intermediate* value between the marginal and average productivities of capital. In calculating this intermediate value, the central planner determines exactly that portion of the average productivity that is necessary to maintain full employment.

Optimal dynamics is represented in figure 2 for the case of a constrained full employment stationary equilibrium.

The difference between private and public valuations of capital is clear. From the central planner's point of view, when there is unemployment, an increase in capital is accompanied by a proportionate increase in labor and thus the global product increases in proportion to the *average* productivity of capital. From the firms perspective, profits increase only in proportion to the *marginal* productivity of capital.

The second best growth path was obtained under the assumption that the central planner could not control wage costs but did control investment. Now we will look at the possibility of sustaining this second best growth path in a decentralized economy with the aid of investment subsidies.

3. Sustaining Second Best Growth in a Decentralized Economy

In a simple dynamic model with two representative agents, one producer and one consumer, the perfect foresight intertemporal equilibrium coincides with the centralized optimal growth path (Abel and Blanchard 1983; d'Autume and Michel 1987).

This property, the result of the Pareto optimality of intertemporal competitive equilibrium, does not apply when the economy is in disequilibrium. Thus, government intervention will be required in order to sustain second best growth in a decentralized economy. We limit the study to the standard simple model with one good and one real asset. The government collects lump sum taxes from consumers in order to finance investment subsidies to firms.

The *representative consumer* holds all his savings in the form of a real asset, x. His short-term budget constraint is

$$\dot{x} = rx + \pi + wn - c - \theta \tag{12}$$

where r is the real interest rate, π represents profits, wn is wage income, c is consumption, and θ represents lump sum taxes.

The representative consumer maximizes his intertemporal utility (the objective function 1 subject to his intertemporal budget constraint. Optimal consumption satisfies

$$U'(c) = \alpha e^{\delta t - R(t)}, \qquad \text{where } R(t) = \int_0^t r(s)\,ds.$$

The constant α is obtained through the equality of discounted sums of intertemporal income and consumption, or, equivalently, from the transversality condition (d'Autume and Michel 1987):

$$\lim_{t \to \infty} e^{-R} x = 0.$$

Thus, the following conditions, together with equation 12, characterize the consumer's optimal decisions:

$$\frac{d}{dt} \operatorname{Log} U'(c) = \delta - r \qquad \text{and} \qquad \lim_{t \to \infty} e^{-R} x = 0. \tag{13}$$

The *representative producer* maximizes the discounted sum of his net receipts

$$\int_0^\infty e^{-R} \pi dt, \qquad \text{where } \pi = F(k, n) - wn - ai \tag{14}$$

subject to the constraints $\dot{k} = i$ and $n \leqslant 1$ (i.e., the investment condition and the labor supply constraint). The real cost of investment, a, is equal to the difference between the price of the good, 1, and the subsidy rate, σ:

$$a = 1 - \sigma. \tag{15}$$

Maximizing the Hamiltonian

$$H = F(k, n) - wn - ai + pi$$

yields $p = a$ and $n = \min\{1, k/\bar{k}\}$. The evolution equation of p, the shadow price of capital, is

$$\dot{p} = rp - F'_k(k, n).$$

Thus, the optimal capital stock[1] is determined by the equality of the marginal productivity of capital and the user cost of capital (net of subsidies): $F'_k = ra - \dot{a}$. The following conditions characterize the producer's optimal decisions:

$$n = \min\{1, k/\bar{k}\} \text{ and } F'_k(k, n) = ra - \dot{a}. \tag{16}$$

In order to simplify the presentation, we assume that the government budget is always balanced. Thus, lump-sum taxes are equal to investment subsidies:

$$\theta = \sigma i = (1 - a)i.$$

Instantaneous equilibrium conditions imply

$$\pi = F(k, n) - wn - ai,\ F(k, n) = c + i, \text{ and } x = 0. \tag{17}$$

The perfect foresight intertemporal equilibrium is characterized by conditions 13, 16, and 17. In this equilibrium the rate of investment subsidies is exogenous. The interest rate is endogenous and adjusts in order to equalize savings and investment at each point in time. The instantaneous equilibrium conditions, which imply $x = 0$, guarantee that the intertemporal budget constraint facing the consumer is satisfied.

3.1. Optimal Investment Subsidies

Consider the second best growth path $(\tilde{k}, \tilde{n})$ analyzed in Section 2. Investment subsidies supporting this second best growth must induce a marginal utility of consumption exactly equal to the marginal value of capital q of the central planner (equation 5). As a consequence, the equilibrium interest rate in the decentralized economy must satisfy $\delta - r = \dot{q}/q$ (by equation 13) and thus the real cost of investment for the firm must satisfy (by equation 16)

$$\dot{a} = (\delta - \dot{q}/q)\,a - F'_k(\tilde{k}, \tilde{n}). \tag{18}$$

The solution q of equation 6 satisfies $\dot{q}/q < \delta$; since the coefficient of a in 18 is positive, equation 18 admits a *unique* bounded solution, which is

$$\tilde{a}(t) = \int_t^\infty \left[\exp - \int_t^s (\delta - \dot{q}/q)\, du\right] F'_k(\tilde{k}, \tilde{n})\, ds. \tag{19}$$

Thus, there exists only one possible subsidy policy supporting the second best growth path. It is easy to verify that the intertemporal equilibrium conditions 13, 16, and 17 are satisfied with this subsidy policy, $\tilde{\sigma}(t) = 1 - \tilde{a}(t)$. This equilibrium is obtained with the second best growth path variables and $\tilde{x} = 0$, $\tilde{\theta} = (1 - \tilde{a})\tilde{i}$, and $\tilde{r} = \delta - \dot{q}/q$. Thus, the *optimal investment subsidies given by equation 19 support the second best growth path as an intertemporal equilibrium in the decentralized economy.*

At the stationary equilibrium, the optimal rate of subsidies

$$\hat{\sigma} = 1 - \hat{a} = [\delta - F'_k(\hat{k}, \hat{n})]/\delta$$

will cover the gap between the rate of time preference and the marginal productivity of capital.

Remark. In our study, we have excluded the possibility of labor subsidies. Such subsidies would lead the economy to the first best growth path. However, it may be interesting to contrast the actual transfers required for sustaining the two different policies—labor subsidies versus investment subsidies. In the long run, investment subsidies are low since they apply only to replacement investment; but labor subsidies would not be low since they are required permanently to cover the gap between the full employment marginal productivity of labor and the cost of labor. In a study based on Belgium data, simulations appeared to support government intervention in the form of investment subsidies over wage subsidies (Erlich, Ginsburgh, and Michel 1988).

3.2. Uniqueness of the Intertemporal Equilibrium

The economic policy of optimal investment subsidies will guarantee the second best growth only if the perfect foresight intertemporal equilibrium is *unique*. As is well known, the uniqueness of rational expectation equilibria is difficult to study and the results are not obvious (see, for example, Calvo 1978; Azariadis 1981). For the model considered here, it is possible to show that there may be other equilibrium growth paths with excessive capital formation when optimal subsidies are high. But if the rate of investment subsidies stays below some boundary, then the intertemporal equilibrium is *unique.*[2]

Conclusion

This study introduced an interesting property. If there is some labor unemployment, then the central planner must base his valuation of capital not on the *marginal* productivity of capital but on its *average* productivity.

Moreover, central control of investment decisions will lead the economy to a second best growth path with full employment in the case where labor costs are excessive (but not too high).

In a decentralized economy, this second best growth path can be sustained as an intertemporal equilibrium with appropriate investment subsidies. The uniqueness of the equilibrium is obtained when the subsidies are not too large.

Acknowledgments

I am grateful to Jacques Dreze, François Melese, and Pierre Picard for their comments on a preceding version of this paper. The comments of two referees were also helpful.

Notes

1. Inertia of capital formation is represented with an assumption of capital adjustment costs (Eisner and Strotz 1963; Lucas 1967). To simplify the study, we assume that these costs are negligible.

2. The proofs of these properties are rather long and technical. This material is available upon request.

References

Abel, A. B., and O. J. Blanchard. 1983. "An Intertemporal Model of Saving and Investment." *Econometrica* 51(3): 675–692.

Arrow, K. J., and M. Kurz. 1970. *Public Investment. The Rate of Return and Optimal Fiscal Policy*. Johns Hopkins University Press.

d'Autume, A. 1982. "Un modèle de croissance en déséquilibre." In *Croissance et accumulation en déséquilibre*, ed. Henin and Michel. Economica.

d'Autume, A., and P. Michel. 1987. "Transversality Conditions, Budget Constraints and the Determinary of a Perfect Foresight Equilibrium in a Monetary Growth Model." *European Economic Review* 31: 1343–1367.

Azariadis, C. 1981. "Self-fulfilling Prophecies." *Journal of Economic Theory* 25(3): 380–396.

Barro, R. J., and H. I. Grossman. 1971. "A General Disequilibrium Model of Income and Employment." *American Economic Review* 61(1): 82–93.

Benassy, J. P. 1975. "Neo-Keynesian Disequilibrium Theory in a Monetary Economy." *Review of Economic Studies* 42: 503–523.

Bernard, A. 1982. Contrainte extérieure, aléas macroéconomiques et prix fictifs pour le calcul économique. Cahiers du Séminaire d'Econométrie, CNRS, no. 24.

Blanchard, O. J., and J. Sachs. 1982. "Anticipations, Recessions and Policy: An Intertemporal Disequilibrium Model. "*Annales de l'INSEE* 47–48: 117–144.

Calvo, G. A. 1978. "On the Indeterminacy of Interest Rates and Wages with Perfect Foresight. "*Journal of Economic Theory* 19: 321–337.

Chirinko, R. S., and R. Eisner. 1983. "Tax Policy in Major U.S. Macroeconomic Econometric Models." *Journal of Public Economics* 20: 139–166.

Dreze, J. H. 1975. "Existence of an Equilibrium under Price Rigidity and Quantity Rationing." *International Economic Review* 16: 301–320.

Dreze, J. H. 1985. "Second-best Analysis with Markets in Disequilibrium: Public Sector Pricing in a Keynesian Regime." *European Economic Review* 29: 263–301.

Eisner, R., and R. H. Strotz. 1963. "Determinants of Business Investment." In Commission on Money and Credit, *Impacts of Monetary Policy*. Prentice-Hall.

Erlich, S., V. Ginsburgh, and P. Michel. 1988. "Faut-il subventionner l'investissement ou l'emploi en Belgique? Une approche d'équilibre général." In *Gestion de l'économie et de l'entreprise. L'approche quantitative*. Brussels: De Boeck.

Fourgeaud, C., and P. Michel. 1982. "Une analyse dynamique de déséquilibre." In *Croissance et Accumulation en Déséquilibre*. Economica.

Fourgeaud, C., B. Lenclud, and P. Picard. 1985. "Calcul économique et déséquilibres en économie ouverte." In *Deséquilibres en économie ouverte*, Hénin, P. Y., Marois, W. and Michel, Ph., eds. Economica.

Hall, R. E., and D. W. Jorgensen. 1987. "Tax Policy and Investment Behaviour." *American Economic Review* 53: 247–259.

Hayashi, F. 1982. "Tobin's Marginal q and Average q: A Neoclassical Interpretation." *Econometrica* 50(1): 213–224.

Henin, P. Y., and P. Michel. 1982. "Harrodian and Neoclassical Paths in a Constrained Growth Model." *Economic Letters* 10(3–4): 237–242.

King, M. A. 1977. *Public Policy and the Corporation*. Chapman and Hall.

Laussel, D. 1980. "Sentiers de Croissance, Cycles et Dépression." *Revue d'Economie Politique* 90: 564–588.

Lucas, R. E. 1967. "Adjustment Costs and the Theory of Supply." *Journal of Political Economy* 75: 321–334.

Malinvaud, E. 1977. *The Theory of Unemployment Reconsidered.* Basil Blackwell.

Malinvaud, E. 1980. *Profitability and Unemployment.* Cambridge University Press.

Marchand, M., J. Minz, and P. Pestieau. 1983. Public Production and Shadow Pricing in a Model of Disequilibrium in Labour and Capital Markets. *CORE* (D. P.) No. 83-15.

Michel, P. 1982. "Trois facteurs de la crise dans un modèle de croissance contrainte." *Revue Economique* 33(5): 807–838.

Modigliani, F., and M. H. Miller. 1958. "Cost of Capital, Corporation Finance and the Theory of Investment." *American Economic Review* 48: 261–297.

Picard, P. 1982. "Inflation, croissance et déséquilibre." In *Croissance et Accumulation en Déséquilibre,* Henin and Michel, eds. Economica.

Picard, P. 1983. Prix fictifs et déséquilibres en économie ouverte. *Cahiers du Séminaire d'Econométrie,* CNRS, no. 25.

Poterba, J. M., and L. H. Summers. 1983. "Dividend Taxes, Corporate Investment, and 'q'." *Journal of Public Economics* 22: 135–167.

Ramsey, F. 1928. "A Mathematical Theory of Savings." *Economic Journal* 38: 543–559.

24

Investment, Profitability, and Classical Unemployment

Pierre-Alain Muet and
Henri Sterdyniak

The theory of fixed-price equilibriums was initially and chiefly developed in the context of short-term analysis (Barro and Grossman 1971; Benassy 1976; Malinvaud 1977). The theory shows classical unemployment to be linked either to excessive real wages or to insufficient capital stock. However, as real wages and capital stock are treated as exogenous, it is impossible to analyze either the persistence of the regime or the extent to which it can be influenced by economic policy. As it happens, the interpretation of classical unemployment and the recommendations for its solution will depend on whether the capital inadequacy is due simply to poor demand-level forecasting by firms, to a very strong demand growth that cannot be immediately met by supply because of adjustment costs, or, on the contrary, to an inadequate profitability that prevents firms from setting up the capital stock required to meet a perfectly well-forecast demand.

Two mechanisms play a crucial role in the persistence or disappearance of classical unemployment in the medium term: price and wage setting and capital accumulation. The classical-unemployment regime tends to disappear when prices and wages are upwardly flexible but downwardly sticky, or when wages are only partially indexed on prices (Benassy 1984; Dehez and Fitoussi 1987). If the price-wage dynamics are taken into account, the change in real wages will depend on disequilibriums in the goods and labor markets (see especially Honkapohja 1979; Malinvaud 1980; Michel and Picard 1982). This results in a broader regime typology, since a role is given not only to the constraint on production, but also to the constraints on supply and demand in the labor and goods markets. Classical unemployment can persist when the income demands of agents and firms are too high and wages perfectly indexed. This poses an economic-policy dilemma: boosting demand aggravates goods-market rationing and inflation in the short run, but, by causing real wages to fall, helps to increase notional supply, hence output in the long run. By contrast, a demand-restrictive policy can prevent firms from rebuilding their profits.

The endogenization of the capital stock, by means of a multiregime investment function, also complicates the disequilibrium typology, since investment is made dependent on constraints expected in the future (see, for example, Neary and Stiglitz 1983). If one rejects the pattern of neo-classical-growth models in which investment is determined by savings (as in Ito 1980) in favor of an investment function that depends on expected demand and on profitability, one obtains hybrid situations where demand, through investment, influences productive capacity and therefore actual output, even in the regime where the latter is constrained by supply. We propose here to develop simple models that will allow a discussion of disequilibrium typology in disequilibrium-growth models featuring slow wage adjustments and an investment behavior of firms whereby profitability (defined as the difference between the profit rate and the interest rate) determines an optimal rate of productive-capacity utilization.

The first part of this paper examines the influence of profitability on investment, a factor for which two explanations have been put forward. The first, developed by Malinvaud (1980), rests on demand uncertainty, which leads firms to install a productive capacity such that the *ex ante* profit rate multiplied by the probability that demand will exceed installed capacity is equal to the cost of capital. The relation between productive capacities and demand is therefore an increasing function of profitability, defined as the relation between the *ex ante* profit rate and the interest rate. The second explanation, suggested by Picard (1982), is based on the existence of a large number of firms, a situation that leads the firms to create excess capacities so long as the rate of profit realized *ex post* by each firm exceeds the cost of capital. By using a quantity-adjustment process comparable to a Cournot-Nash equilibrium, we will show that when the profit rate exceeds the interest rate, when the number of firms is large, and when the demand (or labor) obtainable by each firm is proportional to its productive capacity, the aggregate excess capacity is proportional to profitability as in the demand-uncertainty hypothesis. A synthesis of the two approaches shows that the output level and the frequency of disequilibriums depend on the number of firms and on whether the uncertainty is of a macro- or micro-economic nature.

The second part studies the dynamics of a disequilibrium-growth model in which investment depends on profitability, but prices and wages are exogenous.

The third part discusses the endogenization of prices and wages. Because of the complexities of the dynamics involved, our study is limited to long-term regimes assuming an aggregate demand controlled by the government. The price-wage dynamics determine real wages; these influence capital accumulation, which has a feedback on price and wage setting. We first examine the case of a fixed-coefficient production function. We then consider the case of substitutable factors, taking simultaneously into account the effects of profitability and relative factor cost in the determination of productive capacity and techniques.

1. Investment and Profitability

In this part, we look at two factors that cause profitability to influence investment in a model where production techniques are sticky in the short term:

- the existence of a large number of firms, and
- demand uncertainty.

In both cases the optimal productive capacity is such that the effective profit rate, that is, the *ex ante* profit rate multiplied by the productive-capacity utilization rate, is equal to the cost of capital. The inclusion of demand uncertainty supposes a distinction between the case of a single firm and that of a large number of firms and a definition of the type of uncertainty. In order to avoid needless complications, we shall adopt as does Malinvaud (1987) a static formulation of the putty-clay model. When expectations do not include regime shifts and when they reflect steady changes in the variables, the model can indeed always be converted to the static formulation provided the user cost of capital is suitably defined (see, for example, Avouyi-Dovi and Muet 1987, Appendix). Let us consider a putty-clay production function with constant returns to scale and sum up the choice of production techniques by a relation between the amount of labor per output unit (L) and the amount of capital per output unit (v):

$$L = L(v) \qquad \textit{ex ante} \text{ production function.} \tag{1}$$

$L(v)$ is a decreasing function whose derivative $L'(v)$ is the marginal rate of substitution. With a Cobb-Douglas function, we get, for example,

$$Q = N^a K^{1-a} \qquad L(v) = (v)^{-(1-a)/a}.$$

If the production function has fixed coefficients (clay-clay model), L and v are constants. In this particular case we can simplify the model even further by choosing the labor and output units so that L equals 1 (one unit of labor is required to produce one unit of good). The relation between actual production and employment is, in the putty-clay or clay-clay models, linear:

$$N = L(v) \cdot Q \tag{2}$$

and the productive capacity is a function of the equipment volume:

$$\bar{Q} = \frac{K}{v}. \tag{3}$$

1.1. Investment and Profitability in the Absence of Uncertainty

When returns to scale are constant and no demand uncertainty exists, profitability influences the determination of investment only through the aggregation of individual behavior. This is explained as follows. If there is only one firm, it will determine its optimal capital K or optimal productive capacity $\bar{Q}$ according to the output it expects to sell if it is demand-constrained (D) or to produce with the available labor force ($\bar{N}$) if it is not demand-constrained. So long as the return on the installed equipment exceeds the interest rate, it is in the firm's interest to adjust its capital to one of these values.

1.1.1. Case of a Single Firm

Let ω be real wages, r the interest rate, and δ the capital replacement rate. The optimal productive capacity is obtained with the usual program that maximizes the real return net of the cost of capital under demand and full-employment constraints:

$$\begin{aligned} &\text{Max}[Q - \omega N - (r + \delta)\, vQ, \\ &Q \leqslant \bar{Q} \quad \text{and} \quad L(v)\, Q \leqslant N \quad \text{(production function)}, \\ &Q \leqslant D \quad \text{(demand constraint)}, \\ &N \leqslant \bar{N} \quad \text{(full-employment constraint)}. \end{aligned} \tag{4}$$

Let λ_q and λ_n be the Lagrangian multipliers linked to the demand and full-employment constraints, respectively. Allowing for the fact that, at the optimum, the production-function constraints are saturated, the first-order conditions linked to the constraints are written as

$$1 + \frac{L(v)}{L'(v)}(r + \delta) - v(r + \delta) = \lambda_q$$

and

$$-\omega - \frac{(r+\delta)}{L'(v)} = \lambda_n.$$

When the firm is demand-constrained ($\lambda_q > 0, \lambda_n = 0$), we get

$$Q = \bar{Q} = D \qquad \text{and} \qquad N = L(v)\,Q < \bar{N},$$

and the first-order conditions express the fact that the marginal rate of substitution equals the ratio of the cost of capital to real wages and that the profit rate exceeds the cost of capital:

$$-L'(v) = \frac{(r+\delta)}{\omega} \quad \text{and} \quad \pi_0 = \frac{1-\omega L(v)}{v} > (r+\delta).$$

When the firm is constrained by the labor supply ($\lambda_q = 0, \lambda_n > 0$) we have

$$Q = \bar{Q} = \bar{N}/L(v) < D,$$

and the first-order conditions express the fact that the marginal productivity of capital equals the cost of capital and is lower than the profit rate:

$$\frac{-\,L'(v)}{L(v) - vL'(v)} = r + \delta \quad \text{and} \quad \pi_0 = \frac{1-\omega L(v)}{v} > (r+\delta).$$

Profitability here is a prerequisite for investment (investment is not positive unless $\pi_0 \geqslant r + \delta$) but does not affect investment volume directly. This is no longer the case when the firm is faced with competitors in the market.

1.1.2. *Case in which Many Firms Exist*

We suppose that there exist a sufficiently large number of firms p, all having the same production function. Each firm (denoted by the index i) determines its capital to be installed K_i and its production techniques (summed up by the capital coefficient v_i) by maximizing its profit net of the cost of capital and by taking other firms' decisions (installed capacities $\bar{Q}_j$) as given. Let $\bar{Q}_i$ be the capacity installed by the firm i and Q_i actual output. The profit net of the cost of capital is therefore

$$\Pi_i = Q_i - \omega N_i - (r+\delta)\,v_i\bar{Q}_i. \tag{5}$$

We assume that demand D_i (in the case of excess supply in the goods market) or the quantity of labor available to firm i (in the case of excess demand in the labor market) is proportional to the firm's size, measured by the productive capacity or the potential employment connected with that capacity. Optimal output Q_i, employment N_i, productive capacity $\bar{Q}_i$, and capital coefficient v_i are determined by the following program:

$$\text{Max}\,\{Q_i - \omega N_i - (r+\delta)\, v_i \bar{Q}_i\},$$

$$Q_i \leqslant \bar{Q}_i \quad \text{(multiplier } \mu),$$

$$L(v_i)\, Q_i \leqslant N_i \quad \text{(multiplier } \lambda),$$

$$Q_i \leqslant D \frac{\bar{Q}_i}{\bar{Q}_i + \sum_{j \neq i} \bar{Q}_j} \quad \text{(multiplier } \lambda_q), \tag{6}$$

$$N_i \leqslant \bar{N} \frac{L(v_i)\, \bar{Q}_i}{L(v_i)\, \bar{Q}_i + \sum_{j \neq i} L(v_j)\, \bar{Q}_j} \quad \text{(multiplier } \lambda_n),$$

with $\bar{Q}_j$ and v_j given ($i \neq j$).

Deriving the Lagrangian with respect to Q_i, $\bar{Q}_i$, N_i, and v_i, writing employment associated with full capacity utilization as $\bar{\bar{N}}$, and assuming the number of firms p tends toward infinity ($\bar{Q}_i/\bar{Q}$ and N_i/N tend toward zero), we obtain the following four first-order conditions:

$$L'_{Qi} = 1 - L(v_i)\,\lambda - \mu - \lambda_q = 0,$$

$$L'_{Ni} = -\,\omega + \lambda - \lambda_n = 0,$$

$$L'_{vi} = -\bar{Q}_i(r+\delta) - \lambda L'(v_i)\, Q_i + \lambda_n L'(v_i) \frac{\bar{N}}{\bar{\bar{N}}} \bar{Q}_i = 0,$$

$$L'_{\bar{Q}i} = -\, v_i(r+\delta) + \mu + \lambda_q \frac{D}{\bar{Q}} + \lambda_n L(v_i) \frac{\bar{N}}{\bar{\bar{N}}} = 0$$

with $\bar{\bar{N}} = \sum_j L(v_j)\, \bar{Q}_j$.

When the firms are *demand-constrained* ($\lambda_q > 0, \lambda_n = 0$) or *constrained by the available labor supply* ($\lambda_q = 0, \lambda_n > 0$), the full productive-capacity utilization constraint cannot be binding ($\mu = 0$ except for a special value of ω and $r + \delta$), and the first-order conditions lead to the same equations (7 and 8) in both cases.

The productive-capacity utilization rate is equal to the ratio of the interest rate to the *ex ante* profit rate:

$$\frac{Q}{\bar{Q}} = \frac{r+\delta}{\dfrac{1-\omega L(v)}{v}} \qquad \text{with } Q = D \text{ or } Q = \frac{\bar{N}}{L(v)} \tag{7}$$

and the marginal rate of substitution multiplied by the productive-capacity utilization rate is equal to the relative capital-labor cost:

$$-\frac{Q}{\bar{Q}}L'(v) = \frac{r+\delta}{\omega}. \tag{8}$$

The excess productive capacity is therefore all the greater as profitability (the ratio of the *ex ante* profit to the interest rate) is higher. Equation 7 may be written as an equality between the interest rate and the installed equipment's effective rate of return (*ex post* profit rate π, equal to the *ex ante* rate π_0 corrected for the capacity-utilization rate):

$$\pi = \frac{Q[1-\omega L(v)]}{\bar{Q}v} = \frac{Q}{\bar{Q}}\pi_0 = r + \delta. \tag{7'}$$

Allowing for equation 7, we can also write equation 8 as the equality between the marginal rate of substitution and the ratio of the *ex ante* profit rate to the wage rate ω:

$$-\mathrm{L}'(\mathrm{v}) = \frac{[1-\omega\mathrm{L}(\mathrm{v})]/\mathrm{v}}{\omega}. \tag{8'}$$

The production technique (summed up by the coefficient v) therefore depends solely on the cost of labor and not on the cost of capital. In either case, investment is not positive unless the *ex ante* profit rate π_0 exceeds the interest rate ($r + \delta$). When it is smaller, the available productive capacities are excessive (classical unemployment) and gross investment is zero. We shall now examine how this analysis is modified when one assumes, as Malinvaud (1980, 1987) does, that the influence of profit on the investment decision stems from demand uncertainty.

1.2. Demand Uncertainty

When demand D for the firm's output is random, we can show, using the previous model (see Malinvaud 1987, p. 9), that the firms must invest until the cost of capital ($\mathrm{r} + \delta$) equals the *ex ante* profit rate multiplied by the probability that installed capacity will be effectively utilized:

$$\mathrm{Prob}(D \geqslant \bar{Q}) = \frac{r+\delta}{\pi_0} \tag{9}$$

and until the marginal rate of substitution multiplied by the mean productive-capacity utilization rate equals the relative capital-labor cost.

The capital stock and the equilibrium productive capacity depend on demand, the profit rate, and the interest rate. However, to turn this connection as Malinvaud (1980) does into a linear relationship between investment and profitability (defined as the difference between the profit rate and the interest rate) entails a certain loss of micro/macroeconomic consistency. To draw the full implications of this analysis and to link the investment function to regime occurrence, we must investigate the causes, micro- or macroeconomic, of demand uncertainty and distinguish, as before, between the case of a single firm and that of a multitude of firms.

The inclusion of demand uncertainty leads to long-term situations that are intermediate between the different regimes of the fixed-price equilibriums theory. However, when the probability distribution is bounded, the possibility of pure regimes remains. To illustrate the resulting accumulation regimes, we shall introduce an especially simple probability distribution by assuming that the demand for the firm's output has a mean D and a uniform distribution density in the interval $[D(1 - \varepsilon), D(1 + \varepsilon)]$. We shall also use a complementary-factor production function with $L = 1$. As this freezes production techniques, condition 9 suffices to determine optimal productive capacity.

Let us first consider a *macroeconomic uncertainty*. The government controls the average level of demand D but not its changes, whose magnitude is measured by ε.

1.2.1. *Single Firm, Macroeconomic Uncertainty*

Let $P(x)$ be the cumulative function of the probability distribution of demand (probability that demand will be smaller than or equal to x). The mathematical expectation of production (Q) is therefore equal to

$$Q = E(x, \bar{Q}, \bar{N}) = \int_0^{\mathrm{Min}[\bar{Q},\bar{N}]} xP'(x)\,dx + \mathrm{Min}[\bar{Q}, \bar{N}](1 - P(\mathrm{Min}[\bar{Q}, \bar{N}]).$$

Maximizing the mean of profit net of the cost of capital

$$\mathrm{Max}\{\pi_0 E(x, \bar{Q}, \bar{N}) - (r + \delta)\bar{Q}\} \tag{10}$$

gives us an optimal productive capacity determined by the marginal condition 9 if the capacity is smaller than full employment:

$$1 - P(\bar{Q}) = \frac{r + \delta}{\pi_0}$$

or otherwise gives us a productive capacity equal to $\bar{N}$.

The chosen probability distribution yields three regimes, which depend on the mean value of demand D, full-employment output N, and the optimal productive capacity determined by condition 9.

a. When the firm is not constrained in the labor market, that is, when the optimal capacity is smaller than full-employment output, the effective capacity is equal to that optimal capacity, which is written

$$\bar{Q} = D\left(1 + \varepsilon\left(1 - \frac{2(r + \delta)}{\pi_0}\right)\right) \qquad \text{if } r + \delta < \pi_0. \tag{11}$$

In each period, the output level is equal to the minimum of demand and productive capacity. Its mean overtime is

$$Q = D\left[1 - \varepsilon\left(\frac{r + \delta}{\pi_0}\right)^2\right]. \tag{12}$$

Classical unemployment prevails with a frequency of $(r + \delta)/\pi_0$; Keynesian employment with a frequency of $1 - [(r + \delta)/\pi_0]$. Profitability therefore determines the time frequency of each regime.

b. If optimal capacity exceeds full-employment output, the firm limits its capacity to full-employment output. We then have

$$\bar{Q} = \bar{N} \tag{13}$$

and

$$Q = D - \frac{1}{4\varepsilon D}(D(1 + \varepsilon) - \bar{N})^2. \tag{14}$$

Classical unemployment prevails with a frequency of $(1/2\varepsilon D)$ $(\bar{N} - D + \varepsilon D)$; Keynesian employment with a frequency of $(1/2\varepsilon D)$ $(D + \varepsilon D - \bar{N})$.

c. If $D(1 - \varepsilon) > \bar{N}$, full-employment always prevails: $Q = \bar{Q} = \bar{N}$.

Figures 1a and 1b show how productive capacity and output vary in terms of D. The comparison between the two figures shows that for a given demand, higher profitability leads to higher productive capacities, greater output, and fewer unsatisfied demands for goods. However, this holds true only if demand is weak with respect to available labor.

1.2.2. *Infinity of Firms, Macroeconomic Uncertainty*

Aggregate demand is a random variable with the same characteristics as in the previous section. We assume that

- there are a great number of firms;
- actual output is distributed in proportion to each firm's installed capacity;

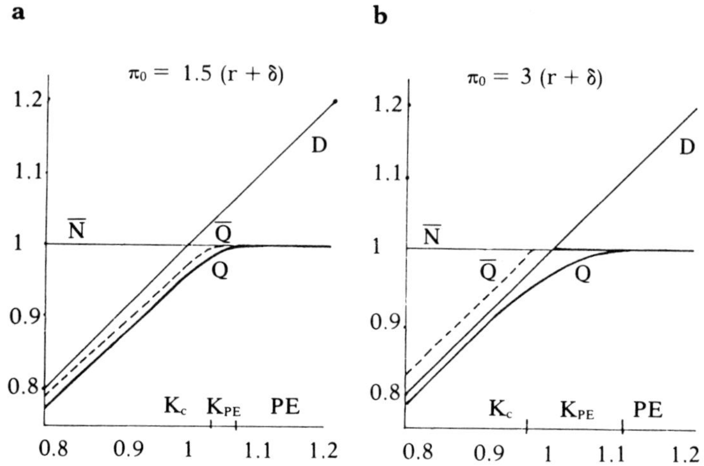

Figure 1.
Regimes in the single-firm case. (a) Low profitability; (b) high profitability.

• firms have a rational expectation of future demand and of the situation prevailing at the macroscopic level.

The mean of aggregate actual output therefore has the same expression as before ($E(x, \bar{Q}, \bar{N})$ and the productive capacity installed by firm i is calculated from the program

$$\mathrm{Max}\left\{\pi_0 E(x, \bar{Q}, \bar{N}) \frac{\bar{Q}_i}{\bar{Q}} - (r + \delta)\, \bar{Q}_i\right\} \qquad \text{with } \sum_i \bar{Q}_i = \bar{Q}. \tag{15}$$

The first-order conditions are written

$$\frac{\partial L}{\partial \bar{Q}_i} = \pi_0 \frac{Q}{\bar{Q}} - (r + \delta) - \lambda = 0 \qquad \text{with } Q = E(x, \bar{Q}, \bar{N}),$$

$$\frac{\partial L}{\partial \bar{Q}} = \pi_0 \frac{\bar{Q}_i}{\bar{Q}}\left[1 - P(\bar{Q}) - \frac{Q}{\bar{Q}}\right] + \lambda = 0 \qquad \text{if } \bar{Q} < \bar{N},$$

$$\frac{\partial L}{\partial \bar{Q}} = -\,\pi_0 \frac{\bar{Q}_i}{\bar{Q}} \frac{Q}{\bar{Q}} + \lambda = 0 \qquad \text{if } \bar{Q} > \bar{N}.$$

When the number of firms tends toward infinity, $\bar{Q}_i/\bar{Q}$ tends toward zero; λ therefore tends toward zero and the productive capacity is determined by the equality between the *ex post* profit rate and the interest rate:

$$\bar{Q} = Q \cdot \frac{\pi_0}{r + \delta} \qquad \text{with } r + \delta < \pi_0 \text{ and } Q = E(x, \bar{Q}, \bar{N}).$$

With the chosen probability distribution, the uncertainty is not significant unless $D(1 - \varepsilon) < \bar{N}$ and optimal capacities do not exceed $D(1 + \varepsilon)$. Three regimes appear:

a. If $\pi_0 > (r + \delta)\ (1 + \varepsilon)$, firms always invest adequately. Depending on the demand level, we therefore have Keynesian unemployment if $D(1 - \varepsilon) < \bar{N}$, full employment if $D(1 + \varepsilon) > \bar{N}$, and a hybrid regime if $D(1 - \varepsilon) < \bar{N} < D(1 + \varepsilon)$ with $Q = D - (1/4\varepsilon D)\ (D(1 + \varepsilon) - \bar{N})^2$.

b. If $r + \delta < \pi_0 < (r + \delta)\ (1 + \varepsilon)$, firms do not invest enough to satisfy demand consistently. The pure Keynesian regime is replaced by two hybrid regimes. Productive capacity $\bar{Q}$ and mean production Q are determined by

$$\bar{Q} = Q \frac{\pi_0}{r + \delta}$$

and

$$Q = D - \frac{1}{4\varepsilon D}(D(1 + \varepsilon) - \mathrm{Min}(\bar{Q}, N))^2.$$

For low levels of demand, we have a hybrid Keynesian/classical regime; for higher levels, a hybrid Keynesian/full-employment regime; then, full employment. This is illustrated in figure 2a, where $\varepsilon = 10\%$ and $\pi_0 = 1.05(r + \delta)$. So long as $D \leqslant 0.961$, the regime is sometimes Keynesian, sometimes classical. The occurrence of classical unemployment here is linked both to the low level of demand and to low profitability: for a given profitability, the rise in demand allows an increase in output without increasing unsatisfied demands for goods. When $D \geqslant 0.961$, productive capacity exceeds full employment, and the economy sometimes experiences either the Keynesian regime or full employment: the profitability effect ceases. Lastly, if $D \geqslant 1.10$, full employment prevails continuously, at the cost of strong unsatisfied demands.

1.2.3. *Microeconomic Uncertainty*

We now assume that aggregate demand D is perfectly known but that the demand D_i for each firm's individual output is random and proportional on average to the firm's installed productive capacity. If we sum up the uncertainty by a random zero-mean variable u, the demand for the firm's output is

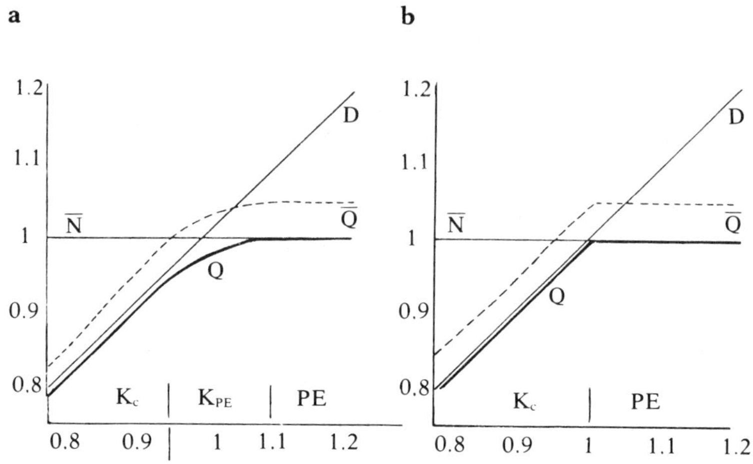

Figure 2.
Infinity of firms, low profitability $(r + \delta) < \pi_0 < (1 + \epsilon)(r + \delta)$. (a) Macroeconomic uncertainty; (b) microeconomic uncertainty.

$$D_i = \frac{\bar{Q}_i}{\bar{\bar{Q}}} D(1 + u_i) \quad \text{with } E(u_i) = 0; \quad \sum_{i=1}^{p} \frac{\bar{Q}_i}{\bar{\bar{Q}}} u_i = 0. \tag{16}$$

We also assume that firms entertain a perfect expectation of the macroeconomic situation. Accordingly, we must distinguish between full employment and underemployment.

a. When full employment prevails, actual output Q is equal to $\bar{N}$ and demand uncertainty does not affect the determination of firms' installed productive capacity. As in the case when uncertainty is absent, this capacity follows from the equality between the capacity utilization rate and the interest rate/profit rate ratio:

$$\bar{Q} = Q\frac{\pi_0}{r + \delta} \quad (\text{with } r + \delta < \pi_0).$$

b. When installed productive capacity is smaller than full-employment output, each firm's output may be limited either by demand or by installed capacity:

$$Q_i = \text{Min}\left[\frac{\bar{Q}_i}{\bar{\bar{Q}}} D(1 + u_i), \bar{Q}_i\right] = \frac{\bar{Q}_i}{\bar{\bar{Q}}} \text{Min}[D(1 + u_i), \bar{Q}].$$

To solve the model, we shall assume an infinity of firms. This will allow us to assume both that the probability distributions (u_i) are independent and that the mathematical expectation of the sum of Q_i outputs coincides with total output Q. If we assign to each individual firm the same probability distribution (u) possessing a cumulative function $P(u)$, the Q_i mathematical expectation is written

$$E(Q_i) = \frac{\bar{Q}_i}{\bar{\bar{Q}}} Q \qquad \text{with}$$

$$Q = D \int_0^{(\bar{Q}-D)/D} (1+u)\,P'(u)\,du + \bar{Q}\left[1 - P\left(\frac{\bar{Q}-D}{D}\right)\right].$$

The optimal productive capacity, that is, the one that maximizes the mean of profit net of the cost of capital, is therefore once again determined by the condition

$$\bar{Q} = Q\frac{\pi_0}{r+\delta} \qquad (\text{with } r + \delta < \pi_0).$$

As an example, we shall assume as before a uniform-probability density over the interval $[1-\varepsilon, 1+\varepsilon]$. With this distribution, we must distinguish between two cases, depending on whether the installed capacities enable demand to be consistently satisfied or not:

a. If $\pi_0 > (1+\varepsilon)(r+\delta)$, firms always invest sufficiently and actual output is $Q = \mathrm{Min}(D, \bar{N})$.

b. If $r + \delta < \pi_0 < (1+\varepsilon)(r+\delta)$, firms do not invest enough to satisfy all the demand peaks. We then have

$$Q = D - \frac{1}{4\varepsilon D}(D(1+\varepsilon) - \bar{Q})^2 \qquad \text{if } Q \leqslant \bar{N}.$$

Unlike the case in which the uncertainty is macroeconomic, the Keynesian/full-employment regime does not occur, since firms have a sure knowledge of the full-employment macroeconomic situation (see Figure 2b). The output level is therefore higher, when underemployment prevails, than with macroeconomic uncertainty.

To sum up, in a demand-uncertainty model, the occurrence of classical unemployment is equally linked to inadequate demand and insufficient profitability. Whatever the nature of the uncertainty, unemployment is always partly Keynesian.

2. Capital Accumulation

In this part, we look at what happens when capital accumulation enters into a disequilibrium-growth model in which investment depends on profitability and prices and wages are sticky.

2.1. The Model

We shall confine ourselves here to the simplest model with profitability: an infinity of firms, with no uncertainty. Since we assume prices to be sticky, there is no capital/labor substitution. Accordingly, we can use a complementary-factor production function ($L(v) = 1$). The labor supply measured in effective units, that is, increased by labor-productivity growth (Harrod-neutral technical progress), expands at a constant rate n. At each instant, actual output is equal to demand, productive capacity, or full-employment output, whichever is smallest:

$$Q_t = \text{Min}\left\{D_t, \bar{N}_t, \frac{K_t}{v}\right\} \qquad \text{with } \bar{N}_t = N_0 e^{nt}. \tag{1}$$

Demand has three components: consumption C_t, investment I_t, and the autonomous component A_t growing at the rate g.

To study the short- to medium-term dynamics, we must specify the relationship between investment and desired productive capacity. Investment depends on three factors: the expected change in output, the desired capital/output ratio, and the productive-capacity utilization rate (written θ). We assume that autonomous demand has a long-term growth rate (g) lower or equal to the natural rate n. Output therefore also grows at the rate g and firms will adjust their productive capacity to allow for the observed disequilibriums between this capacity and the output corresponding to demand or full employment (η is a time constant embodying the response lag of the investment to the disequilibriums):

$$I_t = \frac{dK}{dt} + \delta K_t = (g + \delta) K_t + \eta \left[\frac{v}{\theta}\text{Min}(D_t, \bar{N}_t) - K_t\right] \tag{2}$$

with

$$\theta = \frac{r + \delta}{\pi_0} < 1.$$

When the profit rate is lower than the interest rate, gross investment is zero ($I_t = 0$ if $\pi_0 \leqslant r + \delta$). We further assume that investment is never rationed.

When consumption C_t is not constrained, it consists of a share c of output. Aggregate demand D is therefore determined by the standard multiplier

$$D_t = \frac{I_t + A_t}{s} \qquad \text{with } A_t = A_0 e^{gt} \text{ and } s = 1 - c. \tag{3}$$

We can solve the model conveniently by rewriting it with reduced variables, that is, by dividing Q, K, and D by the labor supply. We then get, using obvious notations,

$$q_t = \text{Min}\left\{d_t, 1, \frac{k_t}{v}\right\},$$

$$\frac{dk_t}{dt} = (g - n)\, k_t + \eta \left[\frac{v}{\theta}\text{Min}\,(d_t, 1) - k_t\right],$$

$$d_t = \frac{1}{s}\left[\frac{dk_t}{dt} + (n + \delta)\, k_t + a_t\right].$$

2.2. Balanced Growth with Full Employment

To obtain a balanced-growth solution with full employment, the "guaranteed" and "natural" growth rates must be equal ($g = n$) and the profit rate must equal the interest rate so as to allow full capital utilization ($\theta = 1$). Next, the values of autonomous demand and capital per head must match both full employment and full productive-capacity utilization:

$$1 = \frac{(n + \delta)\, k_t + a_t}{s} = \frac{k_t}{v}.$$

When these conditions are not met, the three standard disequilibrium situations occur: classical unemployment, Keynesian unemployment, and overemployment (or repressed inflation).

2.3. Keynesian Unemployment (CK)

Output is limited by demand and there is excess supply in the labor market:

$$\text{(CK)} \quad q_t = d_t < \text{Min}\left\{1, \frac{k_t}{v}\right\}.$$

The system's evolution results from the equations

$$\text{(1 CK)}\quad q_t = \frac{1}{s}\left[\frac{dk_t}{dt} + (\mathrm{n} + \delta)\,k_t + a_t\right]$$

and

$$\text{(2 CK)}\quad \frac{dk_t}{dt} = (g - n)\,k_t + \eta\left[\frac{v}{\theta}q_t - k_t\right].$$

At each instant, output per head is expressed in terms of capital and autonomous demand per head multiplied by the usual multiplier:

$$q_t = \frac{(g + \delta - \eta)\,k_t + a_t}{s - \eta(v/\theta)}.$$

Apart from the *CK* inequalities, the existence of a Keynesian situation and, as we shall see, the stability of this situation requires the standard condition of a finite multiplier and therefore of a sufficiently slow adjustment of investment ($\eta < sv/\theta$). We naturally find the usual properties of the "multiplier-accelerator": the multiplier effect of an increase in autonomous demand is augmented by the investment's sensitivity to demand (term with $-\eta v/\theta$) but the increase in capital dampens the effect in the long run, at least when the investment is not too slow to adjust to disequilibriums ($g + \delta < \eta < sv/\theta$). An increase in profitability through a higher profit rate or lower interest rate increases desired capital and therefore investment and, through the multiplier effect, output. The values of autonomous demand a_t and capital k_t that lead to Keynesian unemployment are defined by the inequalities

$$d_t < 1 \Rightarrow a_t < (s - \eta(v/\theta)) + [\eta - (g + \delta)]\,k_t$$

and

$$d_t < \frac{k_t}{v} \Rightarrow a_t < \left[\frac{s}{v} - (g + \delta) + \eta(1 - 1/\theta)\right]k_t.$$

2.4. Classical Unemployment with Investment Governed by Demand (CU1)

Output is limited by capital and there is an excess supply in the labor market. However, because of the form of the investment function, we must distinguish between two regimes according to whether the changes in investment are governed by demand or by the labor supply. In the first type of classical unemployment, demand is smaller than full-employment output and higher than the productive capacity:

(CC1) $\frac{k_t}{v} < d_t < 1.$

Production and capital are in this case determined by the equations

(2 CC1) $\frac{dk_t}{dt} = (g - n)\, k_t + \eta \left[\frac{v}{\theta} \cdot d_t - k_t \right],$

(1 CC1) $q_t = \frac{k_t}{v},$

(3) $d_t = \frac{1}{s} \left[\frac{dk_t}{dt} + (n + \delta)\, k_t + a_t \right].$

The differential equation that determines changes in capital is the same as in the Keynesian regime, and the economy eventually shifts into Keynesian unemployment. This classical-unemployment situation is therefore transitory and, although output is limited by capital, an increase in autonomous demand boosts investment and, later, capital and output. Similarly, an improvement in profitability increases capital and output. The values of a_t and k_t that lead to an instantaneous regime of the classical type with demand-governed investment (CU1) are defined by the inequalities

(CC1) $k_t \left[\frac{s}{v} - (g + \delta) + \eta(1 - 1/\theta) \right]$

$< a_t < [s - \eta v/\theta]\, q + [\eta - (g + \delta)]\, k_t.$

2.5. Classical Unemployment with Investment Governed by the Labor Supply (CU2)

This situation, like the previous one, is transitory: as we shall see, economic change leads to either overemployment or Keynesian unemployment, sometimes with an intermediate phase of type-1 classical unemployment.

The change in the system is described by the following two equations:

(1 CC2) $q_t = \frac{k_t}{v},$

(2 CC2) $\frac{dk_t}{dt} = (g - n)\, k_t + \eta \left[\frac{v}{\theta} - k_t \right]$

and the regime's existences conditions are

(CC2) $k_t < v \qquad a_t > (s - \eta(v/\theta)) + [\eta - (g + \delta)]\,k_t.$

2.6. Overemployment of Repressed-Inflation Regime (RI)

This regime occurs when a_t and k_t are such that

(IC) $k_t > v \qquad a_t > (s - \eta(v/\theta)) + [\eta - (g + \delta)]\,k_t.$

Changes in the system are determined by

(1 IC) $q_t = 1$

and

(2 IC) $\dfrac{dk_t}{dt} = (g - n)\,k_t + \eta\left[\dfrac{v}{\theta} - k_t\right].$

2.7. The Regimes and Economic Change

Figure 3 depicts the regimes in a diagram of capital/autonomous demand per head (k_t, a_t). The separators are the following straight lines:

$$a_t = (s - \eta(v/\theta)) + [\eta - (g + \delta)]\,k_t \tag{4}$$

(classical unemployment 1,2 and Keynesian unemployment/overemployment)

$$a_t = \left[\frac{s}{v} - (g + \delta) + \eta(1 - 1/\theta)\right]k_t \tag{5}$$

(classical unemployment 1/Keynesian unemployment)

$$k_t = v \tag{6}$$

(classical unemployment 2/overemployment).

The long-term solutions (when $\theta < 1$ and $g = n$) are located on the straight lines

$$a_t = \left[\frac{s\theta}{v} - (g + \delta)\right]k_t, \tag{7}$$

$$k_t = \frac{v}{\theta}. \tag{8}$$

The slope of equation 7 is smaller than that of equation 5 when θ is smaller than 1 (profit rate exceeds interest rate) and when the stability

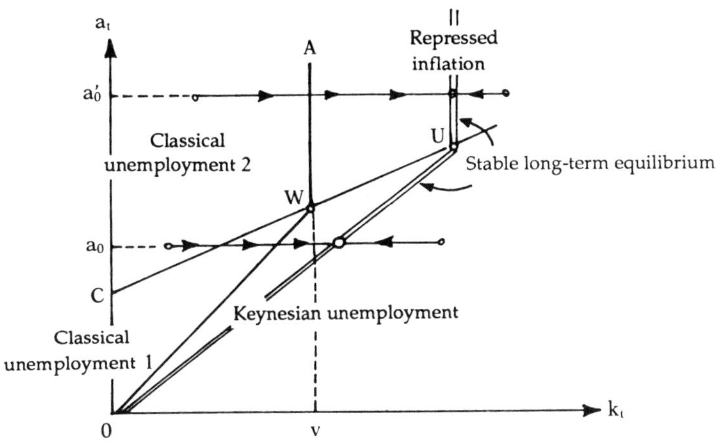

Figure 3.
The four instantaneous regimes and the long-term solutions ($g = n, \theta < 1$).

condition holds ($\eta < s\theta/v$). The long-term solutions are therefore always in the Keynesian or overemployment regions.

The stability of the solutions is immediate. In the case of overemployment, it follows directly from the accumulation relation (2RI). In the case of Keynesian unemployment, with k^* denoting the long-term solution, the differential equation describing k's movement can be written in the customary form:

$$\frac{dk_t}{dt} = -\frac{s - (n + \delta)}{(s - \eta(v/\theta))}(k_t - k^*) \tag{9}$$

that provides stability when investment adjustment is sufficiently slow ($\eta < s\theta/v$).

The system's dynamics are simple when g equals n, for in this case the autonomous demand per head is constant ($a_t = a_0$) and the representative point (k_t, a_t) shifts along a horizontal line toward the stable long-term equilibrium. Several changes of regime can then occur:

a. The slope of the CW line (equation 5) separating the two classical-unemployment regimes can be positive or negative, depending on the value of η in the interval $[0, (s\theta/v)]$. The shift from classical unemployment to overemployment or Keynesian unemployment can therefore be effected by crossing the other regions, as shown in figure 3.

b. When g is lower than n, a_t decreases at the rate $(g - n)$ and the economy, asymptotic to the line OU (figure 4), eventually moves toward Keynesian unemployment. Indeed, the long-term asymptotic regime

(q_t^*, k_t^*) is

$$q_t^* = \frac{a_0 e^{-(n-g)t}}{s - (g + \delta)\frac{v}{\theta}} = k_t^* \frac{\theta}{v}. \tag{10}$$

c. When the *profit rate equals the interest rate,* the long-term productive-capacity utilization rate is equal to 1 and the stable long-term situations coincide with the regime frontiers (full employment with excess demand WA ≡ UA′ or underemployment with goods-market equilibrium OW ≡ OU).

d. Finally, *if the profit rate is lower than the interest rate,* gross investment is zero. Capital diminishes at the rate δ and capital per head at the rate $(n + \delta)$. Demand, proportional to autonomous demand, grows at the rate g. It therefore eventually moves into excess and the economy sinks into classical unemployment, whatever the initial situation (figure 5).

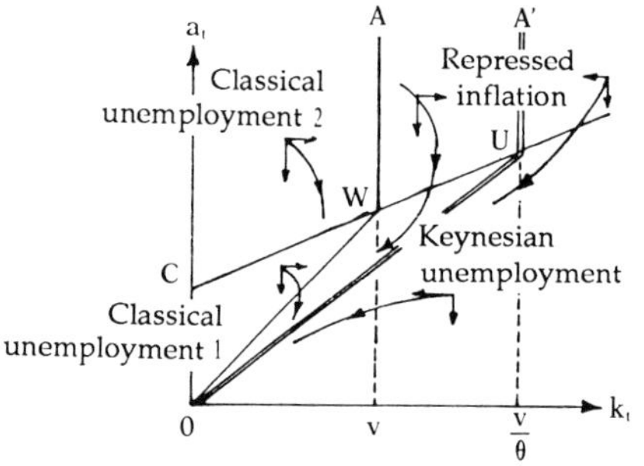

Figure 4.
Regime changes when $g < n$: profit rate higher than interest rate.

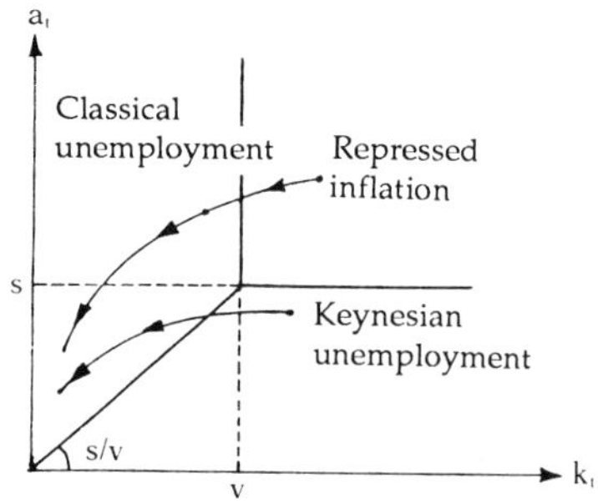

Figure 5.
Regime changes when $g < n$: profit rate lower than interest rate.

In this model with sticky prices and wages there is no limit to the collapse of output and capital in a situation of Keynesian unemployment (if $g < n$) and when the *ex ante* profit rate is lower than the interest rate. To obtain a more realistic model, we must discard the price-stickiness hypothesis.

3. Price-Wage Dynamics and Productive Capacity

We have so far studied the determination and dynamics of optimal capital with fixed prices and wages. We shall now analyze the laws of wage and price changes with exogenous productive capacity, and then combine the two approaches. There are several ways to describe price-wage dynamics. We shall focus on a particular formulation (Section 3.1), but also look at two other possibilities (Sections 3.2 and 3.3). Our study is limited to the long-term equilibriums obtained with stabilized inflation rate, real wage, and capacity utilization rate. Since we concentrate on the way in which supply adjusts to demand and not on demand determinants, we shall assume that the government controls the real interest rate and, via fiscal policy, sets the level of aggregate demand.

3.1. With the Dynamics N

The first formulation is based on a *perfect symmetry* between prices and wages. These are sensitive to two disequilibria, corresponding to the market situation and distribution conflicts, respectively. Wages (prices) increase when the labor demand exceeds supply (when the commodity demand exceeds supply) or when the wage is below the wage desired by workers (the mark-up margin smaller than the desired mark-up margin). With a fixed-coefficient production function, and an output/labor ratio of 1, we have

$$Q = \mathrm{Min}(\bar{Q}, D, \bar{N}) \qquad \text{and} \qquad Q^{\circ} = \mathrm{Min}(\bar{N}, \bar{Q}) \qquad N^{\mathrm{d}} = \mathrm{Min}(D, \bar{Q}).$$

Hence, normal wages will be written

$$\dot{w} = \lambda(N^{\mathrm{d}} - \bar{N}) + \alpha(\omega_{\mathrm{s}} + p - w)$$

with ω_{s} the real wage desired by workers. This must not be interpreted as due solely to the workers' determination, but as the wage level implicitly resulting from wage bargaining.

Prices will be written

$$\dot{p} = \mu(D - Q^{\circ}) + \beta(w + m - p);$$

p, w, and ω are the logarithms of price and of nominal and real wage rates; m the firms' desired mark-up margin ($\text{Log}(1 + m) \simeq m$); and $\dot{p}$ and $\dot{w}$ the growth rates of p and w.

This formulation assumes a fixed lag in the indexing of wages on prices and in the response of prices to costs (this is what Debonneuil and Sterdyniak 1984 call the N model). As a result, the relation between inflation and market disequilibriums is structural. This double-disequilibrium model, which is symmetrical in respect of wages and prices, is applied by Pitchford and Turnovsky (1975) and Modigliani and Padoa-Schioppa (1978). The link with the disequilibrium theory is derived from Michel and Picard (1982).

3.1.1. *Exogenous Productive Capacity*

Stable equilibrium will prevail when real wages are fixed ($\dot{w} = \dot{p}$), that is, in a situation of quasiequilibrium as defined by Hansen (1951).

We then get

$$\omega = \frac{1}{\alpha + \beta}(\alpha\omega_s - \beta m + \lambda(N^d - \bar{N}) - \mu(D - Q^o))$$

$$= \omega_e + \lambda'(N^d - \bar{N}) - \mu'(D - Q^o)$$

with ω_e the required wage rate and

$$\dot{p} = \frac{1}{\alpha + \beta}(\alpha\beta(\omega_s + m) + \beta\lambda(N^d - \bar{N}) + \alpha\mu(D - Q^o))$$

$$= \dot{p}_e + \lambda''(N^d - \bar{N}) + \mu''(D - Q^o)$$

with $\dot{p}_e$ the required inflation rate.

Real wages correspond to an equilibrium between the demands of workers and firms. This equilibrium is shifted by tensions in the labor and goods markets. Real wages rise when goods-market tensions ease and labor-market tensions intensify. The inflation rate is a growing function of the demands of workers and firms as well as of market tensions. When we take account of the impact of market tensions on the price-wage dynamics, we must allow not for three but for five regimes, since a regime is defined not only by the constraint on production but also by those that affect price and wage movements. This is illustrated in table 1. The equilibrium inflation rate is lower than the required rate in the two Keynesian unemployment situations and higher in the full-employment situations. In general, real wages can be lower or higher than the required wage except in classical unemployment, where it is always lower. In the special case where $\alpha = \beta$

Table 1.
The Five Regimes with Endogenous Prices and Wages

		Difference with required values		Resolution when $\alpha = \beta; \lambda = \mu$	
Regime	Conditions	Real wage	Inflation	Real wage	Inflation
Keynesian/classical K_{CU}	$Q = D < \bar{Q} < \bar{N}$	Undetermined	$\dot{p} < \dot{p}_e$	$\omega_e + \lambda'(Q - \bar{N})$	$\dot{p}_e + \lambda''(2D - \bar{Q} - \bar{N})$
Keynesian/full-employment K_{FE}	$Q = D < \bar{N} < \bar{Q}$	Undetermined	$\dot{p} < \dot{p}_e$	ω_e	$\dot{p}_e + 2\lambda''(D - \bar{N})$
Classical CU	$Q = \bar{Q} < \mathrm{Min}(D, \bar{N})$	$\omega < \omega_e$	Undetermined	$\omega_e + \lambda'(2\bar{Q} - \bar{N} - D)$	$\dot{p}_e + \lambda''(D - \bar{N})$
Full-employment/Keynesian FE_K	$Q = \bar{N} < D < \bar{Q}$	Undetermined	$\dot{p} > \dot{p}_e$	ω_e	$\dot{p}_e + 2\lambda''(D - \bar{N})$
Full-employment/classical FE_{CU}	$Q = \bar{N} < \bar{Q} < D$	Undetermined	$\dot{p} > \dot{p}_e$	$\omega_e + \lambda'(\bar{Q} - D)$	$\dot{p}_e + \lambda''(\bar{Q} + D - 2\bar{N})$

and $\lambda = \mu$, that is, where tensions play equally high in both markets, the wage is also lower than the required wage in the Keynesian/classical and full-employment/classical regimes. The values of $\dot{p}$ and ω corresponding to this particular case (used later on) are listed in the last two columns of the table.

3.1.2. *Endogenous Productive Capacity*

As in Section 2, we return to the simplest determination of productive capacity incorporating profitability: the model with a large number of firms, without uncertainty, and with complementary factors. The productive capacity is therefore

$$\bar{Q} = \frac{1 - \omega}{v(r + \delta)} Q \qquad \text{if } \omega \leqslant 1 - v(r + \delta).$$

There are two disequilibrium typologies depending on the values of ω_e and r.

a. When the *ex ante* wage rate and the interest rate are low ($\omega_e < 1 - v(r + \delta)$) the productive capacity exceeds output, and the capital constraint does not apply. When demand is weak, we have a Keynesian/classical regime (figure 6): because of the weakness of demand, productive capacities are smaller than full-employment capacities. In this regime, downward pressures are stronger in the labor market than in the goods market, hence $\omega < \omega_e$. When demand rises, $\bar{Q}$ overtakes $\bar{N}$ (Keynesian/full-employment regime) and the real wage is not influenced by the level of demand, whose effect is symmetrical on both markets. Full employment corresponds to $D > \bar{N}$. We have a full-employment/Keynesian regime ($\bar{Q} > D$) where the real wage is determined by the same equation as in the preceding regime; then a full-employment/classical regime when $\bar{Q} < D$, where a rise in demand causes a fall in the real wage, as it affects the goods market but not the labor market.

b. When the *ex ante* wage rate and the interest rate are high ($\omega_e > 1 - v(r + \delta)$), pressures in the labor and goods markets must be strong enough to drive the real wage below $1 - v(r + \delta)$. We then have a discontinuity between a Keynesian/classical regime with weak demand and a full-employment/classical regime with strong demand (figure 7).

At low demand levels, the regime is Keynesian and output keeps up with demand, but this will last only so long as

$$D \leqslant \bar{N} - \frac{1}{\lambda}(1 - \omega_e - v(r + \delta)).$$

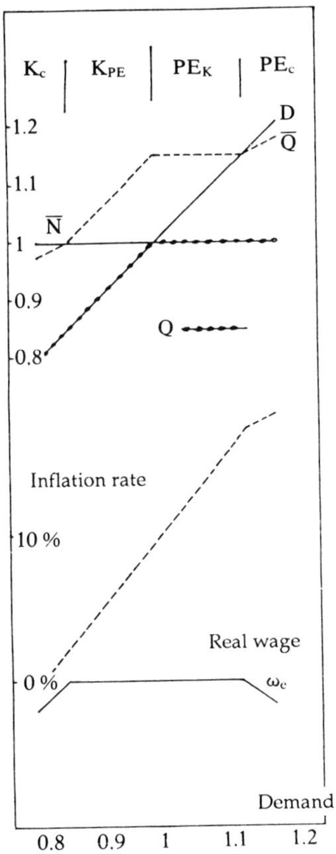

Figure 6.
Typology of regime with a low required wage. $\alpha = \beta = 0.5$, $\lambda = \mu = 0.5$, $v = 2$, $\delta = 6\%$, $\omega_e = 0.75$, and $r = 4\%$.

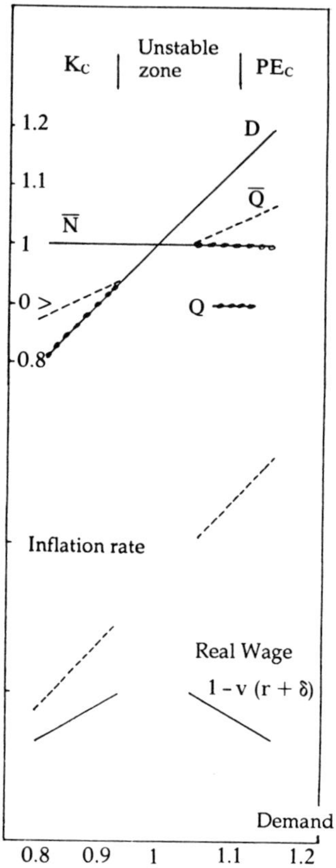

Figure 7.
Typology of regime with a high required wage. $\alpha = \beta = 0.5$, $\lambda = \mu = 0.5$, $v = 2$, $\delta = 6\%$, $\omega_e = 0.75$, and $r = 8\%$.

At higher demand levels, the real wage is too high and the regime is not stable. Let us assume for simplicity's sake that $D = \bar{N}$. If $\bar{Q} = D$, the real wage value is ω_e, firms have no incentive to invest since the profit rate is lower than the interest rate, productive capacity falls, and we therefore get classical unemployment. When the real wage has fallen sufficiently, firms resume their investments and create new productive capacities, but this drives up the real wage and investment becomes unprofitable once more, and so on. Investment decisions and the determination of real wages are incompatible.

At very high demand levels, the disequilibrium in the goods market allows the real wage to be driven below $(1 - v(r + \delta))$. The resulting full-employment/classical regime is marked by strong tensions in the goods market and therefore by high inflation.

At a given required wage, the government, if it controls the real interest rate, can set the productive-capacity utilization rate at the level it desires; it can also effect a trade-off between the unemployment rate and the inflation rate by adjusting demand. On the other hand, if the government cannot bring down the real interest rate from an excessive level, its only alternatives are high unemployment or a full-employment situation with very high inflation. We now look at two other possible formulations of price-wage dynamics (see Debonneuil and Sterdyniak 1984), which produce very different results.

3.2. The N^a Dynamics

In this formulation, workers and firms are capable of adjusting their wages and prices according to expected inflation. For wages, this gives

$$\dot{w} = \dot{p}^{\mathrm{a}} + \lambda(N^{\mathrm{d}} - \bar{N}) + \alpha(\omega_{\mathrm{s}} + p - w).$$

Here, there is no stable relationship between the inflation rate and market disequilibriums. The inflation rate is historically determined by the past history of disequilibriums. When inflation and real wages are stable, we have

$$\omega = \omega_{\mathrm{s}} + \frac{\lambda}{\alpha}(N^{\mathrm{d}} - \bar{N}) = m - \frac{\mu}{\beta}(D - Q^{\mathrm{o}}).$$

3.2.1. *Given Productive Capacity*

When productive capacity is given, only one level of demand allows the stable situation to be reached. If we limit ourselves to the case where producer demands are excessive ($\omega_s + m > 0$) and where tensions have a similar effect on both markets ($\mu = \lambda$ and $\beta = \alpha$), we are led to distinguish between two cases:

If $\bar{N} < \bar{Q}$, the only solution is a Keynesian regime where

$$Q = D = \bar{N} - \frac{\omega_s + m}{2\lambda/\alpha}.$$

The regime is Keynesian merely in appearance, as demand determines output in the short run but the only long-term demand level that will stabilize inflation is determined by the supply conditions (the full-employment level and agents' demands).

If $\bar{Q} < \bar{N}$, two stable regimes are possible:

a. A Keynesian regime with

$$Q = D = \frac{\bar{N} + \bar{Q}}{2} - \frac{\omega_s + m}{2\lambda/\alpha} \qquad \text{if } \bar{Q} > \bar{N} - \frac{\omega_s + m}{\lambda/\alpha}.$$

Here again, despite the Keynesian situation, stable long-term demand is determined by supply conditions, is an increasing function of productive capacities and is a decreasing function of producer demands.

b. A classical regime with

$$Q = \bar{Q} \qquad D = \bar{N} - \frac{\omega_s + m}{\lambda/\alpha} \qquad \text{if } \bar{Q} < \bar{N} - \frac{\omega_s + m}{\lambda/\alpha}.$$

To stabilize the real wage, demand must lie between productive capacities and the full-employment level. This requires, at equilibrium, an excess demand in the goods market.

3.2.2. *Endogenous Productive Capacity*

Once again, we shall restrict ourselves to the case in which agents' demands are excessive. The only stable regime here is the Keynesian one. Only one level of demand allows a stable long-term equilibrium. If the interest rate is low, we have a Keynesian/full-employment regime characterized by $D < \bar{N} < \bar{Q}$; if the interest rate is high, we have a Keynesian/classical regime characterized by $D < \bar{Q} < \bar{N}$. To obtain a stable long-term equilibrium, we must have $\omega > 1 - v(r + \delta)$; this requires $m > v(r + \delta)$. The Keynesian/classical regime is characterized by

$$Q = D = \frac{\bar{N} + \bar{Q}}{2} - \frac{\omega_s + m}{2\lambda/\alpha},$$

$$\bar{Q} = \frac{1 - \omega}{v(r + \delta)} Q,$$

and

$$\omega = \frac{\omega_s - m}{2} + \frac{\bar{Q} - \bar{N}}{2\lambda/\alpha}.$$

For example, for $\omega_s = 0.8$, $m = 0.4$, $v(r + \delta) = 0.3$, $\bar{N} = 1$, the equilibrium corresponds to

$$Q = D = 0.875; \quad \bar{Q} = 0.95; \quad \omega = 0.675.$$

This is a Keynesian unemployment, which cannot be cured by boosting demand but by reducing the demands of capitalists and, more important, of workers. Because of their differentiated impact on real wages and therefore on productive capacities, a cut in workers' demands will effectively have a greater impact on output than a cut in capitalists' demands.

3.3. With a Phillips Curve

The earlier formulations assumed perfect symmetry between price and wage formation. Such symmetry does not correspond to the standard specification of the Phillips curve, in which unemployment drives down not the wage level but the wage growth rate. One must accordingly break the wage-price symmetry. Firms have a structural desired mark-up margin, but the real wage is determined historically. Wage bargaining depends on past wage levels.

If the wage equation is written $\dot{w} = \dot{p} + \lambda(N^d - \bar{N}) + a$ with $a > 0$ the long-run demand level cannot differ in a balanced-growth situation from $N_n = \bar{N} - (a/\lambda)$, which is the employment corresponding to the natural unemployment rate.

The price equation single-handedly determines the real wage level, which is an increasing function of inflation and of disequilibriums in the goods market alone:

$$\omega = \mu + \frac{\dot{p}}{\beta} + \frac{\mu}{\beta}(Q^o - D) \qquad \text{with } Q^o = \text{Min}(\bar{Q}, \bar{N}).$$

3.3.1. *Exogenous Productive Capacity*

If the productive-capacity level is exogenous, the only long-term possibilities are the two Keynesian regimes or the classical-unemployment regime;

the full-employment regime disappears. In this scheme, the economy initially experiences an excessive real wage and strong inflation, but a transitional unemployment period is needed to drive down both the inflation rate and the real wage.

3.3.2. Endogenous Productive Capacity

If the productive capacity is endogenous, the only remaining alternatives in the long run are the Keynesian/full-employment regime ($\bar{Q} > \bar{N}$) if the inflation level is low and the real wage correspondingly low, and the Keynesian/classical regime ($\bar{N} > \bar{Q}$) if inflation is higher. These stable long-term equilibriums correspond to

$$\omega \geqslant 1 - v(r + \delta) \Rightarrow \dot{p} \leqslant \beta(1 + m - v(r + \delta)).$$

Inflation cannot lastingly exceed a certain level, or else the real wage is too high compared with capital-accumulation requirements. If demand stays pegged at the level corresponding to the natural-unemployment rate, but inflation exceeds the borderline value, then firms will not invest. The regime shifts into transitory classical unemployment until the real wage and the inflation rate have fallen sufficiently. A low real interest rate allows a higher inflation rate and a lower profit rate.

4. Profitability and Capital Labor Substitution

4.1. Putty-Clay Hypothesis

We now assume the production function to be putty-clay. As a result, profitability acts through two channels: the capital/labor ratio and the output/productive capacity ratio. We return to the model in Section 1.1.2 in the special case of a Cobb-Douglas production function: $Q = AN^a K^{1-a}$. The capacity utilization rate is

$$\frac{Q}{\bar{Q}} = \theta = \frac{r + \delta}{1 - a}\left(\frac{\omega}{a}\right)^{a/(1-a)}\left(\frac{1}{A}\right)^{1/(1-a)}$$

Capital is

$$K = (1 - a)\frac{\theta}{r + \delta}\bar{Q} = \frac{1 - a}{r + \delta}Q.$$

Full-capacity employment is

$$N_{\mathrm{m}} = \frac{a}{\omega}\bar{Q}$$

and effective employment is

$$N = \frac{a}{\omega} Q.$$

Full-employment output is

$$Q_{\mathrm{m}} = \frac{\omega}{a} \bar{N}.$$

The dissymmetry between capital and labor stems from the fact that, *ex post*, employment adjusts to the demand level (if $Q < \bar{Q}$), but capital does not. For a given interest rate, real wage, and demand, there is no solution if $\theta > 1$: the profit rate is lower than the interest rate and firms will not invest.

If $\theta \leqslant 1$, two regimes are possible:

- If $D < Q_{\mathrm{m}}$, demand limits output:

$$Q = D, N = \frac{a}{\omega} D.$$

- If $D > Q_{\mathrm{m}}$, it is the available labor force that limits output:

$$N = \bar{N}, Q = \frac{\omega}{a} \bar{N}.$$

If $\theta = 1$, the economy is, additionally, on the classical-regime frontier. For a given real wage, this equality seems rather unlikely. However, we shall see that for an endogenous real wage the case becomes much more likely.

4.2. A Special Case

The real-wage determination mechanism described in Section 3 is written, with the model N and in the special case where $\mu' = \lambda'$:

$$\omega = \omega_{\mathrm{e}} + \lambda'[(N^{\mathrm{d}} - \bar{N}) - (D - Q^{\mathrm{o}})]$$

with

$$N^{\mathrm{d}} = \frac{a}{\omega} \mathrm{Min}(\bar{Q}, D), \qquad Q^{\mathrm{o}} = \mathrm{Min}(\bar{Q}, Q_{\mathrm{m}}), \qquad \text{and } Q_{\mathrm{m}} = \frac{\omega}{a} \bar{N}.$$

For a given interest rate, ω_{r} will be the real wage corresponding to $\theta = 1$. It is important to distinguish whether the required wage ω_{e} is lower or higher than ω_{r}.

4.3. Relatively Low Required Wage

If the required wage is relatively low ($\omega_e < \omega_r$), one of four regimes can prevail. If demand is very low, unemployment is Keynesian: the potential supply of goods is determined by the productive capacities and output by demand. Figure 8 and table 2 describe the movement of output, employment, productive capacity, the real wage, and the inflation rate when demand rises (the numerical values chosen are $a = 0.7$, $r + \delta = 15\%$, $\omega_r = 0.7$, and $\omega_e = 0.68$). The real wage is lower than ω_e and therefore, *a fortiori*, than ω_r so $\theta < 1$.

When demand rises, so does output. When demand is sufficiently strong, the potential supply of goods is limited by full employment. In such a Keynesian regime, the real wage settles at ω_e since the goods-market and labor-market disequilibriums match.

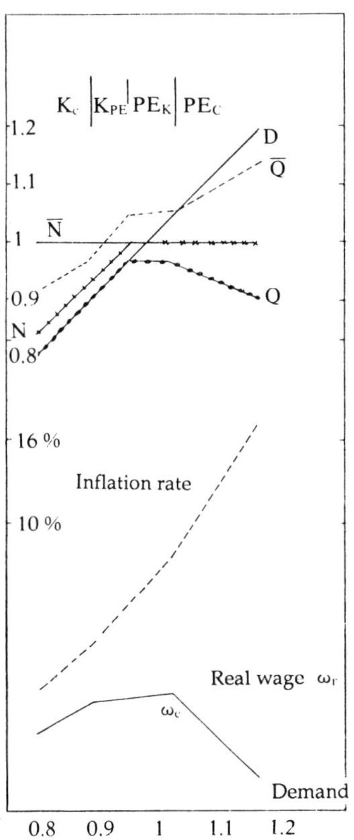

Figure 8.
Changes in output, employment, and inflation: $\omega_e < \omega_r$.

Table 2.
Regimes When the Required Salary is Low

	D borderline values	Labor-market disequilibrium	Goods-market disequilibrium	Impact on real wages	Impact on inflation
Keynesian regime 1		$D - Q_m$	$D - \bar{Q}$	$\bar{Q} - Q_m$	$2D - \bar{Q} - Q_m$
	$\theta \omega_e \frac{\bar{N}}{a}$				
Keynesian regime 2		$D - Q_m$	$D - Q_m$	0	$2(D - Q_m)$
	$\omega_e \frac{\bar{N}}{a}$				
Full employment 1		$D - Q_m$	$D - Q_m$	0	$2(D - Q_m)$
	$\frac{\omega_e}{\theta} \frac{\bar{N}}{a}$				
Full employment 2		$\bar{Q} - Q_m$	$D - Q_m$	$\bar{Q} - D$	$\bar{Q} + D - 2Q_m$

This regime is reached when $D \geqslant \theta\omega_e(\bar{N}/a)$. The inflationary impact of higher demand is stronger here than in the preceding regime, for Q_m does not grow with D (whereas $\bar{Q}$ followed D).

When $D \geqslant \omega_e(\bar{N}/a)$, the economy shifts into a repressed-inflation regime. The real wage stays at ω_e. Output corresponds to full employment for a real wage of ω_e.

Finally, when $D \geqslant (\omega_e/\theta)(\bar{N}/a)$, demand overtakes productives capacities. The repressed-inflation regime still holds but higher demand now causes a fall in real wages and therefore in output, owing to capital/labor substitution. The inflationary effect of higher demand is intensified even further.

The classical-unemployment regime never occurs when $\omega_e < \omega_r$.

4.4. High Required Wage

If the required wage is high ($\omega_e > \omega_r$), one of three regimes may be obtained. When demand is weak, the Keynesian regime prevails. High unemployment makes it possible to drive the real wage below ω_r (and therefore θ below 1).

This regime prevails so long as

$$\theta < 1 \Rightarrow \omega = \omega_e + \lambda'\left(\frac{\omega D}{a} - \bar{N}\right) \leqslant \omega_r \Rightarrow D = \frac{\omega_r}{a}\bar{N} - \frac{\omega_e - \omega_r}{\lambda'}.$$

Beyond that point, the regime shifts to classical unemployment (figure 9, table 3). Output is limited by productive capacity, which, however, rises in step with demand. In fact, output settles at a level where market disequilibriums drive the real wage back to ω_r. We then have $\theta = 1$ and

$$\omega = \omega_r = \omega_e + \lambda'\left(2Q - \frac{\omega_r}{a}\bar{N} - D\right) \Rightarrow Q = \frac{1}{2}\left(D + \frac{\omega_r}{a}\bar{N}\right) + \frac{\omega_r - \omega_e}{2\lambda'}.$$

Although this is a classical regime, output rises with but not as much as demand, for the greater pressures in the goods market must offset those in the labor market. Finally, when

$$Q > N \Rightarrow D \geqslant \frac{\omega_r}{a}\bar{N} + \frac{\omega_e - \omega_r}{\lambda'},$$

the economy moves into full employment. From then on, a rise in demand causes a fall in the real wage and, therefore, through capital/labor substitution, a fall in output.

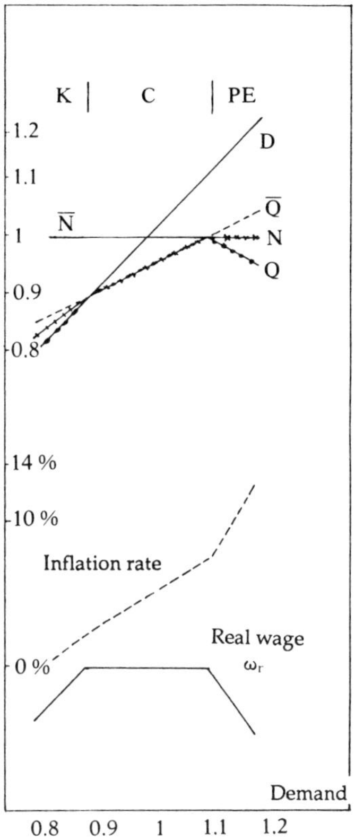

Figure 9.
Changes in output, employment, and inflation: $\omega_e > \omega_r$.

The inflation rate is an increasing function of demand. The impact of demand growth on the inflation rate diminishes slightly when the regime shifts from Keynesian to classical, then rises sharply with the shift from classical to repressed-inflation.

Figure 10, plotted for a given required-wage rate ($\omega_e = 0.75$), shows the equilibrium typology as a function of the real interest rate and of demand. Classical unemployment corresponds to high interest-rate values, Keynesian unemployment to low demand levels, and repressed inflation to high demand levels.

For a given required wage, can we define an optimal demand-management policy? If we confine ourselves to full-employment situations, the optima are located on the frontier of the K/CU or FE/CU regions. If the real wage is too high relative to the golden-rule interest rate ($r_0 = n + \delta$) an assumption we shall now make the product available for consumption

Table 3.
Regimes When the Required Wage is High

	D borderline values	Labor-market disequilibrium	Goods-market disequilibrium	Impact on real wages	Impact on inflation
Keynesian regime		$D - Q_m$	$D - \bar{Q}$	$\bar{Q} - Q_m$	$2D - Q_m - \bar{Q}$
	$\frac{\omega_r}{a}\bar{N} - \frac{\omega_e - \omega_r}{\lambda'}$				
Classical regime		$\bar{Q} - Q_m$	$D - \bar{Q}$	$2\bar{Q} - D - Q_m$	$D - Q_m$
	$\frac{\omega_r \bar{N}}{a} + \frac{\omega_e - \omega_r}{\lambda'}$				
Full employment		$\bar{Q} - Q_m$	$D - Q_m$	$Q - D$	$\bar{Q} + D - 2Q_m$

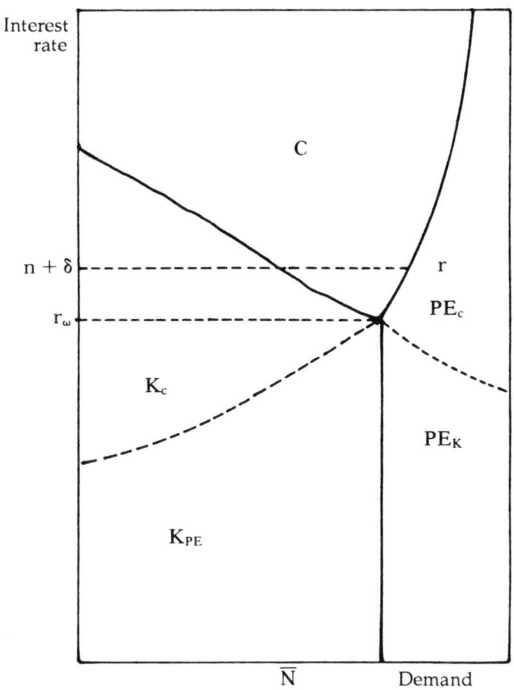

Figure 10.
Disequilibrium typology in a model with substitution capital/labor.

$(Q - (n + \delta)K)$ increases when the interest rate increases along the FE frontier so long as $r < r_0$; similarly, it decreases when r increases in excess of r_0. The inflation rate rises when r increases along the FE/CU frontier. Let r_ω be the interest rate corresponding to $\theta = 1$ for $\omega = \omega_e$. The full-employment optima are on the FE/CU frontier between r_ω and r_0: along this frontier, the inflation rate increases in step with the interest rate, but the available product rises. This means that the interest rate can be deliberately kept very low so as to put pressure on the goods market and therefore to drive the inflation rate down. On the other hand, when the interest rate is equal to $n + \delta$, the level of demand allows a trade-off between output, available product, and employment on the one hand and inflation and unsatisfied demand on the other.

References

Avouyi-Dovi, S., and Muet, P.-A. 1987. "L'effet des incitations fiscales sur l'investissement." *Observations et Diagnostics Economiques*, January: 149–174.

Barro, R., and Grossman, H. 1971. "A General Disequilibrium Model of Income and Employment." *American Economic Review*, March: 82–93.

Benassy, J.-P. 1976. "Théorie du déséquilibre et fondements microéconomiques de la macroéconomie." *Revue Economique*, September: 755–804.

Benassy, J.-P. 1984. "A Non-Walrasian Model of Employment with Partial Price Flexibility and Indexation." In Feiwel, G., ed., *Trends in Contemporary Macroeconomics and Distribution*. Macmillan.

Debonneuil, M., and Sterdyniak, H. 1984. "La boucle prix-salaires dans l'inflation." *Revue Economique*, March: 267–311.

Dehez, P., and Fitoussi, J.-P. 1987. "Stagflation et indexation des salaires." In Fitoussi, J.-P., and Muet, P.-A., eds., *Macrodynamique et déséquilibres*. Economica.

Hansen, B. 1951. *A Study in the Theory of Inflation*. Allen & Unwin.

Honkapohja, S. 1979. "On the Dynamics of Disequilibrium in a Macro-Model with Flexible Wages and Prices." In Aoki, M., and Marzollo, A., eds., *New Trends in Dynamic System Theory and Economics*. Academic.

Ito, T. 1980. "Disequilibrium Growth Theory." *Journal of Economic Theory*, December: 380–409.

Malinvaud, E. 1977. *The Theory of Unemployment Reconsidered*. Basil Blackwell.

Malinvaud, E. 1980. *Profitability and Unemployment*. Cambridge University Press.

Malinvaud, E. 1986. "Jusqu'où la rigueur salariale devrait-elle aller?" *Revue Economique*, March: 181–206.

Malinvaud, E. 1987. "Capital productif, incertitude et profitabilité." *Annales d'Economie et de Statistique*, January–March: 1–36.

Michel, P., and Picard, P. 1982. "Ajustements inflationnistes et déséquilibres." In Henin, P.- Y., and Michel, P., eds., *Croissance et accumulation en déséquilibre*. Economica.

Modigliani, F., and Padoa-Schioppa, T. 1978. "*The Management of an Open Economy with '100% plus' Wage Indexation*." Essays in International Finance, Princeton University, December.

Neary, J., and Stiglitz, J. 1983. "Toward a Reconstruction of Keynesian Economics: Expectations and Constrained Equilibria." *Quarterly Journal of Economics*, Supplement: 199–228.

Picard, P. 1982. "Inflation, croissance et déséquilibre." In Henin, P.-Y., and Michel, P., eds., *Croissance et accumulation en déséquilibre*. Economica.

Pitchford, J., and Turnovsky, S. G. 1975. "Income Distribution and Taxes in an Inflationary Context," *Economica*, August: 272–282.